ROMMEL'S WAR IN AFRICA

ROMMEL'S WAR IN AFRICA

By

WOLF HECKMANN

Foreword by

GENERAL SIR JOHN HACKETT

KONECKY&KONECKY

Konecky & Konecky
156 Fifth Avenue
New York, N.Y. 10010

Translated from the third corrected German edition
of *Rommels Krieg in Afrika*.
Copyright © 1976 by Gustav Lubbe Verlag
This translation copyright © 1981 by Doubleday
& Company, Inc. and Granada Publishing
Foreword copyright © 1981 by General Sir John Hackett

This edition published by arrangement with Doubleday,
a division of Bantam Doubleday Dell Publishing Group, Inc.

ISBN: 1-56852-041-7

Printed in the United States of America

Contents

Preface to the English-language Edition

The campaign in North Africa contributed far more to the outcome of the Second World War than appears at first sight.

In the short term, the struggle in the desert served quite obvious objectives. Hitler sent help to the Italians in Libya because he was afraid that they would leave the Axis alliance in the event of their defeat in North Africa. Later, Britain was forced to move out into the desert because her base in Egypt and even the Arab oil fields appeared to be at risk. And in the end, the Allies secured North Africa to provide themselves with a springboard for their attack on southern Europe. Set beside the immense movements of history these battle objectives pale into insignificance, important though they may have seemed at the time. The Italians only stayed the course for a relatively short while; Britain's Egyptian base was never seriously in jeopardy, and the Arab oil not at all, as I hope to demonstrate in this book; for the British, the attack on the Italians was an emergency solution, at least in part intended to reassure their Soviet allies pending the real battle for "Fortress Europe" in Normandy.

In the course of the great events of war there are certainly many ramifications of cause and effect; peripheral events do influence those at the center. Thus the eventual elimination of the Italians and the consequent further reduction of the German defense capability of course influenced the outcome of the campaign and the operations that were to follow; just as Hitler's inclination ruthlessly to go on investing men

and resources in obvious failures like North Africa affected the Allies'
prospects in Central Europe.

But far more significant was the fact that the war in Africa was a decisive dress rehearsal for the Allies which influenced the future of the
fighting in Europe to an extent it is hardly possible to estimate.

First the British and then the Americans learned a painful lesson in
modern warfare between El Alamein and Bizerta—a lesson which
qualified them to defeat Nazi Germany. Evidence of the sad, blood-
soaked wrong-turning the British had taken in armored tactics and in
the design and use of tanks and anti-tank weapons has emerged from
dusty old volumes of archives and from the testimony of veterans of
the fighting.

This wrong-turning influenced the course of events during the first
part of the African campaign more than any other factor—more, even,
than the astonishing figure of Rommel. At this stage, the German
Wehrmacht appeared nothing short of unbeatable. Embarrassing for
those responsible and therefore seldom mentioned (at least by them),
this wrong-turning was a main reason why Erwin Rommel became possibly the most overrated commander of an army in world history. Certainly, he had unusual qualities, from personal courage and toughness
to a gift for inspiring utterly spent troops to perform unbelievable feats.
But that was not the whole Rommel.

It has not been easy to assemble a picture of this many-sided man
which, after decades of glorification, would satisfy my wish for fidelity
to the truth. The Germans from his entourage who survived were for
the most part professional officers who since the war have been more
and more inclined to keep the Rommel image immaculate. And among
the victors there has been a sizable chorus, led by Churchill and Montgomery, which sang the praises of "Rommel the genius"—among other
things to enhance their own importance. Only patient work among the
archives and a search for documents scattered all over the world have
shed light little by little into a darkness paradoxically made all the
more obscure by the floodlights of glory trained on the Rommel image.
When I have been able to produce one such scrap of indisputable
truth, I have occasionally called on a witness to speak. Some of these,
who were professional officers, asked for discretion out of regard for
their ex-servicemen's unions.

But in the end it became clear beyond dispute that Hitler's favorite
general resembled his Führer in his thirst for glory and his addiction to
illusions—for all his positive traits and despite being forced to commit
suicide as a suspected opponent of Hitler. I hope to make it clear in
this book how out of keeping his high-flying dreams were with his ac-

tual resources; and also that he was always in a position to shift to his subordinates the responsibility for fiascos of his own making.

Once his opponents in the field had corrected their course, once they had learned their lessons from him and had got hold of some even halfway comparable tanks and anti-tank weapons, Rommel's performance was not spectacular. When toward the end of 1942 he—just like the German Wehrmacht in Europe—had overstepped Clausewitz's so-called "culmination point"; when none of his exotic objectives on the Nile, in the Persian Gulf, or even beyond the Caucasus seemed attainable anymore, the war in Africa was no longer *his* war. And although his old fire would occasionally still flicker into life in Tunisia and later in Europe, it was really not his war anymore. Rommel wanted glory and victory. Even at the cost of his life; or of a few thousand soldiers' lives.

This book, intended for German readers in the first place, was not written out of a purely destructive delight in laying low an idolized and much-admired historical figure. True, the superhuman Rommel image is here cut down to human scale. But the point is precisely that it is *human*. In the inhuman system he served to his very last hour (and especially in his last hour) he remained a man, with all his faults and weaknesses, and one who bore the imprint of a time which, long before Hitler, had been far from representing one of the more glorious pages of Christian/Western civilization. Legends may have been edifying on the Children's Hour, with the heroes in shining armor on this side and the stupid villains on that, with the Goodies here and the Baddies there. Historiography should not aim to edify but to set out what really happened.

It seems to me worth stating that the war in Africa was decided by gun ranges and armor-piercing effectiveness, by thicknesses of armor, and by tactics rather than by a single hero figure, because I should like to see more *understanding* and less *emotion* in making historical judgments.

The worst disasters in history have been motivated by emotion. The most revolting torrents of blood have been shed by "idealist" followers of an idol, regardless of common sense. A sixteen-year-old German at the war's end (who in the years to come was to recognize just what, as a young fool, he had fought for with lethal weapons) perhaps sees this particularly clearly.

Now, as an aging man, I should like once more to be ready to fight for one thing: to uphold the system which we have been able to take over at least in the Western part of our defeated country—the system which hinges on understanding and is based on doubt about rulers.

Doubt is the child of understanding. It is a basic component of democracy. It can at first be a handicap in a showdown with a system fueled by emotion. Is that perhaps another lesson to be drawn from the blood-soaked wrong-turning that characterized democracy's struggle with totalitarianism in Africa? The world being what it is, one must—despite all doubt—be ready to defend the right to doubt. That's how it seems to me.

Wolf Heckmann
Munich, May 1979

Foreword

By General Sir John Hackett, GCB, CBE, DSO, MC

Wolf Heckmann's book *Rommel's War in Africa,* to which I am pleased to be able to contribute this Foreword, develops two closely related but separable themes. There is first of all the war itself—the fighting along the Mediterranean coast of North Africa, largely in desert country, during the first three and a half years of the Second World War, with Italians and then Germans on the one side and troops of the British Commonwealth (though with considerable American additions toward the end) upon the other. It was a war in which the British, and the Americans too, made expensive mistakes and through them learned the war-fighting method, involving the effective combination of tanks, guns, infantry, and air power, which was later to prove so successful in Europe.

The second theme of this book is Rommel himself—the person he was, the way in which he made war, his profound and powerful influence on the course of the campaign, the importance and the impact of his strengths and weaknesses and of his relations with others, above all with Hitler and the High Command in the German Reich. These two areas of interest overlap, all the more so because of the high degree of personalization which Rommel's own part in these events engendered, both on the German side and on the British side as well. They are not, however, coterminous. There was more to this war than Rommel and, though his personal influence on both sides of the battle was very great, the two themes can be looked at separately, at least to begin with. I propose to do this, starting with the war.

The fighting in the coastal strip, two thousand miles long and rarely more than a couple of hundred miles deep, between the Nile Valley and Morocco, much of it (and most of it where the action lay) virtually empty desert, was in many ways unique. Of urban settlement there was very little. What there was consisted mostly of small seaside townships, few and far between. The population was sparse, poor, and seminomadic. There was not much that could get damaged in the fighting and not many people, besides the soldiers themselves, to get hurt in it. This was essential warfare, without the hardship and misery suffered by unhappy people plunged into war by pure mischance, and without the heartrending destruction of beautiful and ancient things which can never be replaced. If anything can be called a clean war, the war in the Western Desert can fairly claim to have been just that. It was also an open war, in which mobility was everything, and a war, at least early on, of small numbers on either side, in which on our own side (until the Eighth Army came into being and then grew fashionable) nearly everybody seemed to know nearly everybody else. It was a war of wide spaces in which you could easily get lost and often did. I remember once counting up more than forty contiguous map squares in which there was nothing printed at all. But the desert climate was healthy and bracing and the occasional unwelcome event —a dust storm, heavy rain, a *khamsin*—could not prevent the young men living in it from feeling physically fit and well. It was a war fought fiercely, but between fighting men who got to know and to respect and even to like each other. It was, in Rommel's own phrase, *Krieg ohne Hass*—war without hate.

It was, in fact, a war which many on our side, particularly in those early days, quite frankly found enjoyable. Fear was your frequent companion. You saw your friends killed or horribly hurt. You got hurt yourself, but this was all happening in a situation which to most young men has a great attraction. There was no choice but to operate to a limited objective and forget everything else. There was this patrol you were on; then there was going to be another big battle; and after that another; and then sometime the whole campaign in Africa would be over (won by us, of course) and after that, in the remote future, the war would somehow come to an end. It was not only possible to dismiss everything that was not immediately before you; it was your positive duty to do so. Tiresome responsibilities at home or somewhere else, in the present or the future, outside the compelling interests of the squadron (or whatever it was) in the here and now—all those worries could be dismissed, and a load shed. There was lightness of heart. It was all interesting, too, and exciting, and the company was very good. In a war the logical man finds his way, if he can, to the sharp end and the company he finds there is unequaled. This campaign, particularly in its earlier stages, was also an exercise in extensive warfare, offering ample opportunities to practice almost the first principle of war, which is of course always to soldier as far away from the next higher headquarters as you can. There was a zest and gusto about it all which is most faithfully reflected in this book. What I am saying is certainly not just the product of selective reminiscence in aging men. Of course the better, funnier bits are more readily remembered than what was grim and somber. But I recall, for example, observing in early 1942 that there was clearly no justice in this world. There you were in the desert, living a healthy, active life, playing with fascinating things among delightful people, with a bad fright about, say, every second Thursday but never overworked and having on the whole a splendid time. Then you went back to Cairo for a few days leave and would meet some old friend, who was a staff officer in Gray Pillars (our name for the building which housed GHQ Middle East) working all day and night, pale from overstrain—and it was *he* who bought *you* a bottle of champagne! When a scheme was introduced called Python, under which people were sent back to Britain if they had been abroad for a certain time (much shorter, in fact, than most of the older hands had been abroad already), many officers had to exercise considerable guile and ingenuity to avoid being sent away from where the war was to where it wasn't. Most of us really *liked* being there.

The sharper the end, of course, the simpler it all was. You could *see* Jerry. You knew where he was and what he was doing. You did not have to rely on what you were told, which farther back was always inadequate and usually exaggerated. With a rearguard armored squadron during the great withdrawal of the summer of 1942 (which, as we all know now and this book amply shows, need never have happened if British command in the field had been a little less incompetent), I can remember once telling myself with some satisfaction, as I watched the enemy's armored cars through my binoculars, that I must be the last British officer out of captivity this side of the Pillars of Hercules—no doubt quite wrongly because, though I did not know it at the time, the Long Range Desert Group was operating somewhere out there deep in the void. But such a situation, if sometimes a trifle hazardous, had the merit of simplicity. You knew exactly what was happening and what was likely to happen next, and you could make a pretty good guess at how soon that would be. As my squadron withdrew, we often passed through locations of higher HQs, which had been hastily abandoned, probably on a misleading report of imminent encirclement. We, on the other hand, were withdrawing no faster than the speed of the enemy's advance demanded and so had plenty of time to collect up some of the good things often left behind in a hasty departure. We called this part of our war the "withdrawal along the Fortnum & Mason line" and had never had it so good, even though there was something of a battle pretty well every day. I recall the difficulty I once had in deciding whether it was worth shedding two large tubs of marmalade to make room on my own little tank for the half case of gin that could not possibly be left behind for Jerry.

There are still very many old members about the place who will remember all this and will be captivated by Wolf Heckmann's re-creation of it. He has moved pretty freely around Britain, turning up stones, as it were, and finding under them strange creatures, each with stories of his own particular desert war. I shall be very far from alone in finding friends on nearly every page where he writes about us, and what he has to tell has a real ring of authenticity. It is also generous.

In a German military hospital at Mersa Matruh, during the Axis withdrawal after Alamein, a thousand casualties who cannot be moved are soon to become prisoners. A grim foreboding hangs over these men, silently wondering what will happen. All of a sudden, Englishmen were walking through the ward, friendly and solicitous. The worst cases were immediately flown out to Cairo and Alexandria. . . . There is no bitterness here, no rancor. Instead, there is real understanding of what makes men at the sharp end tick. What was new to me, in this book, was to be shown a picture of what it was like at the sharp end on the other side. This account is beyond all doubt authentic. If the author gets it right about our side, how can he fail to get it right about his own? The way he tells his story is attractive, too. He takes real characters (dozens are mentioned by name from our own people and I found I knew every one—he gets *them* right, too) and follows some of the experiences of each. He also does this for members of the Afrika Korps. They turn up again and again and this lends a continuity to Heckmann's story which grips the reader.

This is a book by a man who hates war, who writes with compassion, good sense and humor, and quite without malice. He is grieved by the possibility that this could ever happen again and saddened by the thought that Britons and Germans had ever been trying to kill each other.

I come now to Rommel. There is no doubt about the depth of the impression this man made, as a person, on the war in Africa. It was felt at many different levels. Churchill said in the House of Commons in November 1941, "We have a very daring and skillful opponent against us, and, may I say across the havoc of war, a great general."

He was later to say in Cairo (according to General Sir Ian Jacobs' diary), striding up and down late at night, "Rommel, Rommel, Rommel, Rommel! What else matters but beating him?"

When Montgomery arrived in the Middle East, he regarded Rommel as a personal antagonist and kept his enemy's picture on the wall of the caravan in which he lived.

Monty said to David Stirling (of the SAS) and me, in a little private altercation which also has its place in history (though it need not concern us here): "My mandate is to destroy Rommel and I intend"—tapping the open map upon the table at El Alamein—"to destroy him here." It was not, it will be noted, the "enemy," or "the Axis Forces," or "the Afrika Korps." It was "Rommel."

This personification went very far down—to the level, in fact, of the people about whom this admirable book is written. In the armored regiment of which my own squadron was part—and no doubt in others, too—they called him "Harry."

"I wouldn't go too far that way, sir," said a sergeant to me, when I had returned to the regiment after a wound and a spell of light duty elsewhere, during which the Germans had really begun to make their presence in the desert felt. "I wouldn't go out there; Harry might get you." There were, it is true, German patrols about, and one of these might pick us up. That was what was meant by "Harry"; it was "Harry" Rommel that the sergeant had in mind.

As a commander in mobile warfare, Rommel was outstanding. He would take tremendous risks—risks often quite unjustified either by the tactical situation or—still more—by the supply position. He must have given his staff officers nightmares.

After every major war, during which reputations of one sort or another have been made, there is a reassessment of the principal characters. The really great—the Wellingtons, the Marlboroughs—stay where they were. These are the people in the first division of the league. Others, whose reputations have been high during the war—perhaps higher than they deserve—sometimes come down rather lower than is strictly fair. In the end, having come down from an undeserved high point to an undeserved low point, they level out at about where they really belong.

Rommel's reputation at the end of the Second World War was very high. I was myself one of those who admired him greatly. I rejoiced in the opportunity given me as postwar commander of the 7th Armored Division (what we used to call, in the early days in the desert, quite simply "the Armored Division" because there was no other—and some might maintain that this is still true) to meet Frau Rommel more than once and enjoyed the society of this good, simple, intelligent woman who absolutely declined to be a hero's widow. I also met more than once that admirable public servant, her son, Manfred. In my enthusiasm to find out more about the makeup of this remarkable man, I managed to procure, as BGS (Intelligence) in Vienna in 1946, a copy of *Infanterie greift an* (*The Infantry Is Attacking*) and was enthralled by it. I was much influenced thereafter by the possibilities of flexibility offered by a regiment of three battalions, operating as one whole, in which the companies could be swiftly shifted from one part of the battle to another to build up strength where it was needed. Speaking from memory, I rather think that Rommel himself, as a captain in command of a company in the First World War, once found himself commanding a force of no less than eight companies when others had been brought in to exploit an advantage created by his own. I do not think we have ever made enough use in the British Army of the regiment as an operational entity.

Wolf Heckmann is, it must be immediately acknowledged, highly critical of Rommel. He does not like his dependence upon the Führer for support where the High Command would not have endorsed it. Halder, the German Army's Chief of Staff, thought that Rommel was unbalanced and inspired too much by personal ambition. He (and others, including Keitel) openly proclaimed their opinion that Rommel was insane—"this soldier" in Halder's description of him had "gone quite mad." It is worth recording that the detractors of that brilliant, wayward young British general, James Wolfe, gave their opinion to King George II that he, too, was mad. The King replied that he only wished Wolfe would bite some of his other generals. Rommel may have been egotistical, vain, self-seeking, often unfair and sometimes no great respecter of truth, someone in whose complex makeup the most wholly admirable single feature was his deep devotion to his wife. His planning, if you could call it that, may have driven his supply staff to despair. There was clearly little sense in his abandonment of the battle still unresolved in Libya to take an armored force in a swift dash toward the Delta, only possible if he were to be able to pick up fuel in great abundance from supply dumps captured on the way. It is not easy to defend his conduct of operations in North Africa, pressing on at the farthest extent of a tenuous supply line, when it was clearly evident that the fuel and ammunition most urgently required could not be got to him across the Mediterranean at the rate of loss then being inflicted by the British. On the other hand, though he had many enemies, he could inspire troops to follow him to a degree few have equaled. He was bold, imaginative, and brave, with a tactical sense at times approaching genius. His method of command was forceful, direct, and personal. If he wanted something done, he was there to get it done and he was harsh on those he thought had failed him. There was no better commander of armored troops in a fluid battle, on either side in any theater of the war and no one was more willingly followed by troops. They understood him as thoroughly as he understood them. He led, as all good leaders to, from the inside.

We are told how a large group of British prisoners on one occasion made a sudden rush to the edge of their place of confinement, which caused anxiety to their captors but which was animated only by a desire to get a closer look at the man they had for so long been fighting, as he passed by. This story tells us a great deal.

It is possible that Heckmann rates him a little on the low side. It is also possible that reconsideration later on will bring Rommel back to where he really belongs. Where that might be is something we shall have to wait to see. It may well be rather higher than the point at which Wolf Heckmann leaves him.

I can think of many people who will read this book with enormous pleasure for its authentic evocation of what war in the desert was like. I can also imagine that very many more, who were not there but would like to know about it, will find here a thoughtful and reliable guide into the experiences of those who fought each other on the lowest level at the sharpest end, in that unique manifestation, the war in the Western Desert, the war without hate.

BOOK ONE

An Impetuous Person

Prologue: An Eerie Encounter

A show without an audience

When Lieutenant General Rommel came to North Africa, in February 1941, and immediately fell frantically to work, he was like an actor giving a spellbinding performance to an empty auditorium: he had his first scanty units parade past the Governor's Palace in Tripoli several times over, to create the illusion that he had a formidable fighting force. With his irresistible mixture of charm and bullying, he drove his Italian workmen to build in record time two hundred wooden dummy tanks onto some old car chassis.

But the enemy, whom he was trying to impress and discourage from advancing any farther, had virtually ceased to exist. East of Tripolitania's borders there was more or less a military vacuum. The battle-tested British troops, who in the past months had swept the numerically far superior Italians out of Cyrenaica, had been replaced by units which were inexperienced and pitifully equipped. And nobody cared a rap about Rommel, let alone about his tank army straight out of the carpenter's shop and the conjuror's box of tricks.

Seldom, if ever, in the age of the airplane and modern communications have hostile forces faced each other in such ignorance. Each side had a false idea of the other: Rommel was expecting hard-hitting assault divisions, when what were actually there were depleted, barely trained units.

And where shipload after shipload of mustard-keen and superbly trained and armed Germans were being disembarked, the British thought there was little more than the confused remnants of the Italian army in Libya, its heavy weapons strewn over the desert between Sidi Barrani and El Agheila.

It is fairly clear that Rommel soon realized his mistake. But being a man who knew how to combine courage and ambition with a well-developed feeling for theatrical effect, the last thing he was likely to do was to inform his superiors of the enemy's weakness.

In any case, military disasters are as a rule likeliest to happen to the man who underrates the enemy's strength.

There was a variety of reasons for the ignorance of the British: Before the Second World War, it was the job of the French to maintain a network of agents in North Africa and to gather intelligence in Italian Libya. In the vague hope of perhaps being able to avoid war with Italy, following the capitulation of France, the British Government forbade anything that might have annoyed the touchy Mussolini.

Thus it came about that there was not a single British agent in Tripoli to report on Rommel's multiple march-pasts. So the show was a flop as far as the producer was concerned, but that was, in fact, the best thing that could have happened to him.

Neither was there any aerial reconnaissance. The few aircraft left behind in the desert—two squadrons of Hurricane fighters and a few twin-engined Blenheim bombers—were fighting for bare survival. So Rommel's wooden tanks creaked around in the desert without anyone to see them.

Nevertheless, ground reconnaissance units did report the arrival of German troops on the African front. But, farther in the rear, everyone thought they had been seeing ghosts, particularly since other intelligence reports suggested there were no Germans in Africa.

First casualty: A bedroll

Corporal Harry Short gave his driver a gentle kick—the best way to give orders in the little Marmon-Harrington armored car. There was no intercom; and the tiny 95 hp engine screamed at high revs in rough country.

The driver brought the car obediently to a halt. The corporal looked uncertainly westward, where behind the hills a trail of dust was rising —and it was coming nearer.

Short took his car behind a hillock in such a way that he was just able to keep an eye on some knolls to the west. As far as he knew, the

Italians remaining after the last fighting ten days ago had run all the way to Tripoli. So what might this be coming toward him?

He gave a start and ducked a little, although the clear morning sun was behind his back, when the weird thing hove into distant view: an eight-wheeled armored reconnaissance vehicle, with an awesome gun. Like a caterpillar in great haste, the elongated vehicle crawled to the top of the hill opposite. There was a soft rumbling of a powerful engine; from under a frame aerial, hefty men wearing peak caps were looking eastward, only to drive off in reverse as quickly as they had come.

It was an impressive sight, suggesting power and perfection; and it filled Short with apprehension.

Those must have been Germans. He recognized them, not only by their peak caps but also by the heavy reconnaissance cars, with drivers both back and front, which could therefore be driven in reverse as fast and as safely as forward. Moreover, the whole performance, silent and decisive, had made as un-Italian an impression as possible. When he was sure his own dust cloud would no longer attract the enemy, Harry Short continued his patrol: along the border track between Cyrenaica and Tripolitania, from Fort El Agheila to the Marada Oasis, 110 kilometers inland.

He was in the King's Dragoon Guards, an ex-cavalry unit, which had good reason to feel well and truly lost on the border between Cyrenaica and Tripolitania. No sooner had the Dragoons relieved the 11th Hussars as reconnaissance troops than the entire battle-tested 7th Armored Division began to melt away from all around them. Worn-out tanks and trucks were limping down the long road to the Nile Delta; men parched by the desert sun were saying good-bye with that twinkle in the eye characteristic of those who, after a long, dry campaign, can see the bars of Cairo before them like a mirage.

It was only two years since the Dragoons, KDG for short (and also known as the "King's Dancing Girls"), had exchanged their leggy horses—for all the world like thoroughbred dancing girls—for their armored cars. Now here they were, careening around in the angular Marmon-Harringtons: barely 8–12 mm of armor, one machine gun, a one-shot popgun of 0.55 (14 mm) caliber called a Boys Rifle as its heaviest armament. The manufacturer claimed it had armor-piercing capability, which may even have been true if by an armored vehicle one meant a tin can like the Marmon-Harrington.

They were as inexperienced as they were fearless. There was nothing for it but to accept the changing times with humor. This must have contributed to the fact that the KDG contained a markedly larger percentage of nonconformist "originals" than is usual among the military.

There was, for instance, Lieutenant E. T. (Bill) Williams. This brilliant officer—he was to become Montgomery's Chief of Intelligence—with his round scholar's spectacles and his stooping shoulders, somewhat like an overgrown schoolboy's, did not look much like a warrior. And when the regiment arrived in the desert, he flatly refused to take any notice of some vitally important trifles. To take one example: A considerable amount of trouble could be avoided if, at the outset of the evening's briefing of troop commanders, one noted the bearing of one's own vehicle with a pocket compass. This was because these briefings began by the squadron commander's car as the last light faded, and ended in pitch darkness; and because, owing to the constant nuisance of air attacks, the armored cars were left widely dispersed in the desert.

But Lieutenant Williams often dispensed with this tiresome chore and, equally, often lost his way back to his car and then wandered about the squadron's area in the icy desert night, shivering with cold, until dawn. This habit of his had won him a certain notoriety even in his subaltern days, until eventually the regiment's word for getting lost was to "do a Bill Williams."

Since it was this same Bill Williams whose troops exchanged the first shots in anger with the Afrika Korps, the encountered had a decidedly ludicrous side to it. It was on 20 February 1941, at about 1500 hours, on the coast road near El Agheila, that three British scout cars came across three of the giant eight-wheelers, as well as a motorcycle combination and a truck armed with a machine gun. Both sides fired somewhat hastily and inaccurately; no serious damage was done, apart from some scratches inflicted by Lance Corporal Allen's Boys Rifle on the paintwork of one of the German vehicles. Lieutenant Williams craftily tried to outflank the enemy in the hilly terrain south of the road and to attack him in the rear. Unfortunately, his troops got stuck in the sand.

By the time they had dug themselves out, the light was failing. Orders came on the radio to rejoin the squadron. Bravely but unwisely, the lieutenant decided to make one more sweep by himself along the road.

All was quiet. When he saw another armored car standing near the guard hut at the frontier, Williams was not surprised: the squadron had informed him that Lieutenant Weaver had been ordered up to support him. But the other car was standing diagonally across the narrow road, blocking it.

"Sound your horn," Williams roared at his driver, Trooper Butler. Responding to the signal, the other car made way and moved toward them. It was only a few meters away when Williams spotted the eight wheels, the German army cross, and the turret with its gun. Both drivers stepped on their accelerators; both turrets spat fire. Seconds later, as they tore past each other, there was a cushioned jolt. It was not until they were back with the squadron that Williams discovered the enemy had torn off his bedroll and a large tent tarpaulin, which were lashed outside, as he had raced past. But not even these valuables were lost; that same night, Harry Short drove up to the scene of the drama, found them lying in the middle of the road, and brought them triumphantly back to their rightful owner.

This "phony war" did not last long; four days later, even the staff at the rear had to admit that the Germans were here. Moreover, *Gross-deutsche Rundfunk,* the Greater German Radio, carried a report on the skirmish at Fort El Agheila.

At that time, the border fort was no-man's-land; since the KDG had no infantry support, it was far too exposed a place for them to hold overnight. At first light, the Marmon-Harringtons would carefully creep up to it and, avoiding the wrecked and stinking interior of the fort, occupy the surrounding hills as observation posts.

By way of a "gunner" they usually had Lieutenant Tracey Rowley, an Australian who had charge of a pair of 4 cm Bofors automatic cannon, mounted on a lorry in a rough-and-ready manner. Because of their leisurely but emphatic firing sequence, these guns were known to the British as Pom-Poms. Rowley was fond of talking about his time as a seventeen-year-old mercenary with Chiang Kai-shek; and his total indifference both to danger and military regulations was impressive to behold.

Thus he had turned a pair of army trousers into shorts by a few energetic snips of the scissors. The frayed ends dangled around his thighs, in the style regarded as chic by teenagers thirty years later. Whenever there was an air attack, he would sit on one of the mudguards of his "Pom-Pom truck" without batting an eyelid in the hail of bullets.

At dawn on 24 February, they were once again rolling toward the fort: Lieutenant Williams's troop in the lead, Corporal Short behind, and the Australian bringing up the rear.

The surprise burst of fire from the fort came like a bolt from the blue: It was the typical whipcrack of high-velocity guns. Machine-gun bullets whistled past and the lead scout car, commanded by Lance Corporal Allen, jolted to a halt. Harry Short immediately drove his car off the road to the left. To his amazement, the next second the "Pom-Pom truck" hurtled past him at top speed making for the fort, Lieutenant Rowley, with his windblown hair and his frayed shorts, sitting on the mudguard.

He had overtaken Allen's car and was a good way ahead when a machine-gun burst sliced through the cab and killed the driver. A second later, the eight-wheeled reconnaissance cars and motorcycle com-

binations came roaring down the hill. Short watched from a safe distance as the Germans took Rowley, Allen, and his driver, White,
prisoner and disappeared westward, towing the wrecked Marmon-Harrington.

Much later, he came across Rowley again in an Italian prisoner-of-
war camp. "What on earth did you think you were doing, driving at the
fort like that?" he asked him. "I thought we were winning," Rowley
said morosely.

The coalition of late starters

Three days after the El Agheila skirmish, the Cabinet met in London
with Churchill in the chair. The Prime Minister, true to his habit of
pursuing a target once he had it in his sights, dictated into the minutes:
"It would be a mistake to draw pessimistic conclusions from the fact
that British and German armored vehicles have clashed in Libya. The
German forces were driven back; there is no indication that they are
preparing for any significant actions, let alone an attack across the
Libyan desert. It is not known how many of these German mechanized
units have been brought to Libya."

A serious threat to Libya might have interfered with Churchill's
other plans. He therefore refused to accept the facts.

Barely five weeks later, Churchill was to marshall material evidence
to prove that his Commander in Chief, Middle East, had failed to notice that he was in danger of being outflanked in the Western Desert.
Excessive fairness is one weakness Churchill never suffered from; his
qualities lay in other, more or less opposite, directions. When, on 10
May 1940, immediately after the German attack on the Netherlands,
Belgium, and France, he was summoned to head the Cabinet, it was
not because of his nobility of mind. It was because in her hour of need,
Britain needed a fighter untroubled by doubts. She could hardly have
found a better one.

All the more so since Churchill concentrated his indefatigable energy
on the principal enemy, Germany, and since he was ready to ally himself with anyone to come through the struggle.

Soon after he took power, he wooed the Italian dictator Benito
Mussolini, whom he loathed, with a solemn peace appeal in which he
declared he had "never been an enemy of Italy's greatness."

But this attempt to secure Britain's position in the Mediterranean
came too late. France had collapsed and the Duce thought he knew on
whose side his dream of an Italian *Imperium* was likelier to become a
reality.

For a long time he had hesitated, despising his fellow dictator north of the Alps. After a first meeting in Venice on 14 July 1934, when according to Signora Rachele Mussolini, the Führer stood about awkwardly "in a raincoat several sizes too big for him, not knowing what to do with his hands," the Duce also had roared with laughter at the following description by a French journalist: "A little plumber, who seemed to be carrying a chamber pot about with him: It was his hat."

Mussolini still thought himself to be the senior Fascist dictator and felt that there was something provincial and gauche in the extreme violence of the national socialists, held as they were in the grip of their race mania. In Italy, Fascism, for all its martial roar, was mellowed by the wink-and-nod of Mediterranean urbanity. But it was precisely this contrast, which at first made him feel so superior, that was to become the trauma of his final years. For Mussolini inexorably drifted into the role of the junior partner, who watched with astonishment and envy with what determination the "little plumber" was able to motivate his masses. He was, of course, in no way inferior to Hitler when it came to lust for conquest, for they were both the products of the history of their peoples—peoples which, after centuries of division and lethargy, were now, as late starters in the imperialist race, developing the greed of the have-nots. To that extent, the Berlin-Rome Axis, even after its extension to Tokyo, was not just a coalition of the wicked against the Western democracies—although, especially in view of the Nazis' deeds, it was to become one—but also a comradeship-in-arms of the latecomers and underdogs.

The age of colonial conquest and oppression was to conclude and, to some extent, to defeat itself by producing some of its worst monsters yet: frightful and grotesquely exaggerated caricatures of the colonizers. They were unthinkable without their Western/Christian forerunners, from Cortès to Kitchener; but they were a relapse all the same, and relapses are, as a rule, worse than the original disease.

Unable to understand that a freely elected government in a working democracy could not have dealings with an anachronism of his sort, disregarding countless broken treaties and crimes, Hitler was to the end of his days unable to understand why Britain had not been prepared to enter into a sort of Germanic complicity with him. Had he not explicitly said that in setting up his colonial empire he wanted only to enslave the Slav *Untermenschen* (subhumans) and leave the British empire alone, unmolested?

Hitler afraid of the British

The ex-NCO Mussolini, who in the First World War had broken with his socialist friends and, acting from nationalist convictions, had

fought against the German-Austrian Army, dreamed of a rebirth of the
Imperium Romanum. Nevertheless, he had a realistic enough estimation of his own strength in relation to the other Great Powers involved
in the Mediterranean—Britain and France—to fear a European war.
Instead, to round off Italy's possessions in East Africa, he attacked un-
derdeveloped Ethiopia in 1936 and could bask in the glory of the victorious conqueror—even though smashing the armies of the Negus,
with their medieval equipment, was no great feat of heroism.

Under Britain's leadership, the League of Nations decreed paper
sanctions; from Mussolini's colleague Hitler there was friendly applause. Joint intervention on the side of the insurgent Falangists in the
Spanish Civil War brought a further *rapprochement,* sealed with the
"Berlin-Rome Axis." When he visited Berlin in 1937, the man who
met Mussolini was no longer his awkward guest of the Venice days; a
triumphant Hitler, amid exulting demonstrations and the rumble of
military march-pasts, taught him respect and, for the first time, fear.

As soon as he returned home, the Duce introduced the *passo
Romano,* an imitation of the German goose step, into the Italian army.
Hitler took Austria, forced Britain and France to make humiliating
concessions in the Munich crisis, then immediately threw the Munich
Agreement at their feet, going on to smash Czechoslovakia. There was
no doubt about it: in such a world, all you had to do was grab.

Mussolini ordered the occupation of Albania, a bridgehead on the
opposite shore of the Adriatic. In the "Pact of Steel" of 22 May 1939,
an out-and-out war alliance, Germany and Italy forged their unity, although, after the Pact was signed, the constantly vacillating Duce sent
Hitler a letter full of explanations, in which he made reservations and
informed him that his army would not be ready for war before 1943.

Berlin would not hear of it and silenced even that splendid witness,
Enno von Rintelen, military attaché at the German embassy in Rome,
who had sent in a report on the pathetic state of the Italians' armaments. He was admonished by the Reich Foreign Minister, Ribbentrop, to show a "more positive attitude" and a memorandum by the
"Foreign Armies" Department inspired by him was pulped.

Hitler whipped up the Polish crisis; but when news reached him of a
British-Polish alliance and of yet another refusal by the Duce to go
ahead, he once more hung back from his firmly planned attack on his
eastern neighbor. However, a few days later the die was cast, and
Mussolini promised to continue his war preparations as a deterrent to
the Allies, while secretly informing the British and French ambassadors
that he would not attack. The governments of those two countries declared war on Germany.

Poland collapsed; the impulsive Mussolini, whose few firm convictions included a fierce anti-Communism, was furious beyond measure with Hitler for plotting with Stalin. Documentary films seen by Mussolini, showing the perfect functioning of the German war machine, however, further increased his fears.

When dictators, especially those of this caliber, make history, events often take a farcical course: Mussolini was immensely flattered because, in his victory speech in Danzig, Hitler had mentioned him twice. And he had a great idea with which he would straighten out his world image and explain away the cordial relations between his victorious ally and the Soviet Union: Bolshevism, he explained beamingly to his son-in-law, Count Ciano, was in reality not Bolshevism at all, but a Slav variety of his own Fascism. In his memoirs, Ciano says he had trouble preventing Mussolini from publicizing this stunning discovery in a great press campaign.

Whenever the Duce took off on one of his soaring flights of imagination, the leaden realities would drag him down by the boots. Whenever he came across a German, he would brag mightily about Italy's imminent belligerent status; but no one knew whether the "millions of bayonets" he boasted about had any rifles attached to them.

He wanted to maintain a stance consistent with that of his allies, so he stopped the delivery of aircraft engines to France and of other war material to Britain, including a type of training aircraft for which contracts had been signed. Too bad that the chronic currency shortage of his country, so poor in raw materials, now became more acute and thus further held back his feeble rearmament efforts. And that the British, who dominated the Mediterranean from Gibraltar via Malta and Cyprus to Suez, stopped ships carrying urgently needed coal to Italy.

He would make them pay for it dearly, the Duce roared to his intimates. It was in this atmosphere, and under the influence of the reports from the German western front, where Hitler's armored spearheads were driving forward with devastating effect, that Mussolini received the peace appeal of the new British Prime Minister, Winston Churchill. His reply was cold: He recalled that after the attack on Ethiopia, Britain had organized sanctions against Italy when the latter was "about to secure for herself a small place in the sun. . . . I would also remind you of the state of effective servitude in which Italy at present finds herself in the Mediterranean. If your government declared war on Germany to defend the honor of your signature, then you will understand that the same feeling of honor and respect for the obligations undertaken in the Italian-German treaty will guide Italian policies now and in the future, in the face of all contingencies."

The Italian forces could not do anything significant by the time the Duce declared war on Britain and on an already collapsing France, on

10 June. Not until eight days later did they cross the French frontier, by which time Marshal Pétain had sued Hitler for an armistice. The distribution of booty, for the sake of which Mussolini had wanted "at least one thousand dead" by way of an entrance fee, failed to materialize.

Hitler was still hoping for an accommodation with Britain. Excessively harsh terms for France would merely strengthen the resolution of the British to continue the struggle. When the Führer, in his triumphant speech in the Reichstag on 19 July, made "an appeal to common sense in Britain too," Mussolini was afraid that Churchill might give in. "That would give him a great deal of pain, because he wants war, now more than ever," wrote Ciano in his diary.

"He need not have fretted himself," commented a grim Churchill later; "he was not to be denied all the war he wanted."

Even after Churchill's icy rejection of his peace feelers, Hitler did not alter his attitude to France. The southeastern third of the country remained unoccupied and, in Vichy, a Cabinet under Marshal Pétain ruled with relative independence. Apart from minor territorial concessions on the common frontier in the south, there was nothing for Mussolini: no talk of Corsica, no thoughts of Tunisia, France's North African possession next door to Italian Tripolitania. The reasons for this are clear: Hitler still had to beware lest the considerable potential of the French colonies slip through the Vichy regime's fingers and add to British strength; moreover, the disadvantages of any war fought by a coalition, and particularly of one so amateurishly prepared, were evident. So the Berlin-Rome Axis vacillated; each wanted something else without admitting it to the other. The two dictators strutted arm in arm from one theater of war to the next until things became too much for them. In the months that followed, the points were set, the outcome programmed.

For Hitler, there had never been any doubt. In his book *Mein Kampf,* he told all the world that the German *Lebensraum* (living space), which had to be won, lay in the east. Immediately after the Polish campaign, an interesting directive was issued: "Our interests require the following: Provision must be made for the fact that the area has a military importance for us as a forward *glacis* and that it may be used for deployment. For this reason, railways, roads, and communications must be kept in good order and used for our purposes."

A few months later, Hitler ordered his Chief Wehrmacht Adjutant, Colonel Rudolf Schmundt, to reconnoiter East Prussia for a suitable place for a *Führerhauptquartier* (Führer's headquarters). The place was near Rastenburg and was to become known to the world as the *Wolfschanze* (Wolf's Lair).

For Hitler, the struggle against the Western Powers was a burdensome necessity, to secure his rear for his great colonial plans in the east. It would therefore have been logical to conquer Britain first. But it was only halfheartedly that he gave instructions to draw up plans for Operation Sealion, the cross-Channel strike. It is fairly certain that he never seriously contemplated such an attack. Hitler was afraid of the British, and he evidently had a deep-rooted horror of amphibious operations. For him, the sea was sinister.

So he hovered for days on the brink of panic and hysteria as, during the invasion of Norway, British naval forces shot up German destroyers while a British expeditionary corps made a landing. Hitler wrote off Norway and ordered General Dietl to withdraw. The operation succeeded only because the OKW held the order back. One of Hitler's statements at this time explains his fear of the British: "I know the British soldier from the First World War. Once he settles in somewhere, we'll never get him out," he said to his aides.[1]

This fear also determined his activities in the months following the defeat of France. Hitler, otherwise so resolute, studied the most varied plans restlessly and helplessly, hoping to injure Britain in some way without having to engage in an open struggle for the island. In vain did he seek to impel Spain and what was left of France to become active belligerents. All were bound to see that the interests of these two Mediterranean littoral states inevitably clashed with each other and with those of his ally Mussolini, and that the German dictator was from the outset determined to cheat all three of them. Nothing, therefore, came of it. However, his next step—to involve even the ultimate enemy, the Soviet Union, in an alliance against Britain—was only seemingly inconsistent with his eastern plans. For him, the British remained by far the most dangerous enemy; the foul villainy of conquering or at least forcing them to fall in line with the assistance of the colossus in the east, and then to strike at his ally, would have been quite in his style.

For, steadfastly, the goal remained the east, in order to apply "the eternal natural law of the strong," which "gives Germany the right before the tribunal of history to subjugate these peoples of inferior race, to rule them and to put them to useful work." Which was why Hitler was, if anything, rather relieved at the failure of his attempt to put together a gigantic continental coalition against Britain. The unwillingness of the other partners took the decision out of his hands:

[1] In the autumn of 1914, the Bavarian List infantry regiment, in which Hitler served, suffered very heavy casualties near the Belgian town of Ypres in an attempt to break through to the Channel. It was Hitler's first taste of action. The defenders were British.

very well—he would annihilate the Soviet Union first; the sequence
was, after all, immaterial; the lesser races would be polished off in a
few months.

Graziani: the reluctant offensive

But before this miscalculation became apparent, the conqueror's Italian junior partner messed things up. Mussolini had been watching with
growing fury how history was being made without him. The war had
brought Italy nothing—on the contrary. In her "mare nostrum," she
was in fact held fast as if in a bag. The exits—the straits of Gibraltar
and the Suez Canal—were firmly in British hands, as was the heavily
armed rocky island of Malta, which lay across the route to Italy's
North African colony of Libya. Ethiopia and the neighboring Italian
Somaliland were virtually cut off and could be reached only by air via
the Sudan.

In the Balkans, which in the Duce's view were clearly his sphere of
interest, frontiers had begun to move without Italy getting any of the
benefit; and what was worse, Germany was developing more and more
into the dominant power.

Already during the western campaign (the timing could hardly have
been a coincidence), Stalin had started by making his ally pay up:
Romania must give up Bessarabia, ceded by Russia under pressure
after the First World War. After briefly hesitating, Hitler agreed.

Bulgaria and Hungary likewise had territorial demands on Romania.
Nobody bothered anymore to consult France and Britain which, together with Turkey, had guaranteed Romania's frontiers by treaty. Turkey declared herself neutral. The German Reich played the kindly
uncle at Romania's expense. The signature of the Italian Foreign
Minister, Count Ciano, beside Ribbentrop's under the Vienna Award,
which made new dispositions on these frontier questions, had the air of
a trifling gesture of consideration to a poor relation.

Mussolini's pride was deeply injured. Had it not been precisely their
disappointment at Italy's meager share of the booty in the First World
War that had motivated the Fascists to band together under the *fascio*
(the bundle of rods)? This time, he swore to himself and his confidants,
he would help himself.

Why, after all, did he have the bridgehead of Albania across the
water? From there, one could attack either Greece or Yugoslavia. . . .

True, warnings kept emanating from Berlin: Hitler wanted the
Balkans kept quiet. Any activity by his Axis partner could furnish Britain with an opportunity to establish herself in Greece or Yugoslavia
and to threaten the Ploesti oilfields in Romania, which were vital to

Germany. The Duce should concentrate his efforts against Britain—perhaps he could attack the small garrison in Egypt from Libya. The idea had in any case occurred to Mussolini already, but his Commander in Chief in Libya, Marshal Graziani, had proved unbelievably refractory. On paper, the chances did not look bad: After the defeat of France he was relieved of the obligation to guard Libya's western border against French Tunisia and had 215,000 men under arms facing 36,000 British. But the marshal appeared to have an extremely realistic estimation of the fighting prowess of his men. He kept postponing the start of the offensive he had been ordered to launch.

Finally Mussolini ordered the attack to start on 13 September 1940. Otherwise, Graziani was fired. "Never has a military operation been carried out so much against the wishes of its commander," wrote Ciano in his diary.

Reluctantly, Graziani set his troops in motion. The weak British units withdrew, fighting skillfully. The Italians managed to advance a bare 90 kilometers to Sidi Barrani. There, their impetus faltered; Graziani's orders were first of all to build a water conduit along the conquered coastal strip. Meanwhile, British convoys with weapons and reinforcements were steaming around the Cape and up toward Suez. The warrior Prime Minister, Churchill, had been gnashing his teeth because his Admiralty had insisted on using this long but safe route instead of the short but perilous passage through the Mediterranean. Now it was clear that there was plenty of time. Among the troops now being safely landed in Egypt was an important unit: the 7th Royal Tank Regiment, which in the French campaign had given Rommel's 7th Panzer Division a tough time at Arras in a counterattack. Its improved Matilda Mark-II infantry support tanks had 80 mm of frontal armoring. There was no Italian weapon in all North Africa which could penetrate armor as thick as that.

Meanwhile, the Duce was having fresh troubles in the Balkans. General Ion Antonescu had established himself as dictator in turbulent Romania. He renewed an old proposal to Hitler that he should send a military mission to Romania to help train her forces. The Führer grasped the opportunity to station not only German soldiers there but also strong anti-aircraft and Luftwaffe units to protect the Ploesti oil-wells.

Nobody invited the Duce to take part. He was furious: his partner in the "Pact of Steel" had kept this chess move a secret from him, while apparently Count Ciano, who was only too ready to throw sand into the German-Italian machinery, was allowed to take a hand in the game: Ribbentrop had told him at an early stage about the arrangement with Romania.

In the end, Italy was allowed to send a few air force officers to Bucharest. Once again, the gesture looked like charity. According to Ciano's diary, Mussolini said: "They behave as if we did not exist at all. But now I'll repay them in their own coin."

Little by little, the Italian garrison in Albania had been brought up to a strength of 125,000. At the same time, Italy stepped up the war of nerves it had been waging against Greece for some time.

The ruler of that country, General and Premier Ioannis Metaxas, would have made a good third member of the Hitler-Mussolini partnership. He had been ruling as dictator since 1936, had his political opponents sent into exile, locked up, or killed, sympathized with Nazi Germany, and had copied both the Gestapo and the Hitler Youth. But when the Greek Ambassador to Berlin tried to complain about Mussolini's brutal bullying, he was at first not even allowed to see Ribbentrop, and then fobbed off with the remark that his government should apply to Rome.

There were ample grounds for the complaint. After an extensive press campaign, incidents proliferated on the Albanian-Greek border. Finally the destroyer *Helle*, which was lying dressed overall at Trinos for a religious festival, was torpedoed and sunk by an officially unidentified, but unmistakably Italian, submarine.

Metaxas refrained from any reaction. When fragments of the *Helle* torpedo were found and were proved to be of Italian provenance, the censored Greek press was not even allowed to report the fact. The war-hungry Duce was not on any account to be provided with a pretext for an attack. But by mid-October 1940, he had at last decided to attack, without any pretext and without the consent of his ally.

On 15 October a conference took place at the Palazzo Venezia to discuss Operation Greece. Marshal Pietro Badoglio, the Chief of General Staff, advised strongly against: the forces in Albania were inadequate. But Count Ciano; Visconti-Prasca, the Commander in Chief, Albania; and the governor of Albania, Jacomini, were firmly of the opinion that no serious resistance was to be expected from the Greeks. On the contrary, Ciano, who had caused hefty sums of slush money to be distributed in the Greek capital, had been assured "by certain leaders in Athens" that the Greeks were waiting eagerly to "greet the Italian liberators."

In the end, Mussolini ordered Epirus to be occupied up to the Bay of Arta, with its port of Preveza, and forbade any information to be given to his German allies. When the alert Enno von Rintelen, meanwhile appointed "German General at Italian Army Headquarters," heard that there were troop concentrations on the Albanian-Greek border and asked Badoglio for information, the latter replied that precautionary moves were being taken to ensure an immediate intervention in case of a possible landing by the British in Greece.

The Duce behaved like a cunning village mayor providing himself with a sort of alibi: On 19 October he wrote a letter to Hitler, saying that he could not tolerate the Greeks' everlasting provocations. He let the letter rest on his desk until 23 October and then sent it to Berlin by messenger, knowing full well that Hitler would by then be on the Spanish border, trying to entice Franco into his continental coalition.

Hitler and Mussolini met in Florence on 28 October. Not until he was on the way there did Hitler discover that at dawn Italian troops had crossed the Greek frontier. While waiting for his ally, Mussolini ran in a state of great agitation up and down the platform at Florence station, asking every few minutes whether there were any reports yet of a spectacular victory. There were none, so all he could greet Hitler with were the words: "Führer, we are on the march!"

Hitler had thought about the Duce's letter in the train and had come to the conclusion that his partner would surely not be such an ass as to attack just when the autumn rains were likely to start in the Greek mountains and winter was just around the corner. He was not to know that what Mussolini had in mind was not a long campaign but nothing less than instant victory. However, the Greeks did not play the game. Although inferior in numbers, and pathetically ill-equipped, they knew their mountains and they fought with the fury of the innocent victim of attack. By 22 November the last Italian soldier had been driven from Greek soil. Thousands died in the icy cold of the Pindhos mountains. Not much later, Greek spearheads penetrated 50 kilometers into Albania. Mussolini was in a pensive mood; every now and then ideas of historic significance came to him. He now informed his son-in-law that the afforestation of the entire Apennine range must go ahead because that would make Italy's climate harsher and thus the character of its people harder.

A tank named Matilda

Churchill's preoccupations were more immediate. On 8 November he heard from his Commander in Chief, Middle East, Sir Archibald Wavell, about a plan which on his own admission made him "purr like ten tomcats." The general, who with the arrival of the "Matilda regiment" now had a splendid offensive weapon at his command, had had enough of waiting in the Western Desert until Graziani at long last found it convenient to resume his advance from Sidi Baranni. His plan was to move his troops up to the sluggish enemy unseen, in night marches, and strike a surprise blow.

Churchill and his War Cabinet were only too delighted to agree: Here at last was chance of a bet at attractive odds.

While preparations for this were in train, Admiral Cunningham, Commander of the British Mediterranean Fleet, on 11 November sent the aircraft carrier *Illustrious* halfway from Malta to Taranto, where the Italian fleet lay at anchor. Twenty Swordfish torpedo bombers took off under cover of darkness. Two hours later, half the Italian warships had been put out of action for months. Only two aircraft failed to return to the *Illustrious*. It was with pleasure that Churchill observed that on the same day an Italian bomber squadron, escorted by some sixty fighters, took part in a German air raid on Britain at Mussolini's express wish. The battle-tested British fighter pilots engaged them and shot down eight bombers and five fighters. Said Churchill: "That was their first and last intervention in our domestic affairs."

Meanwhile, an army of 25,000 men was practicing for the attack in the Egyptian desert. The chain of fortifications south of Sidi Baranni, where Graziani's army was dug in, was rebuilt in precise detail on the basis of aerial photography. The fifty Matilda crews of the Royal Tank Regiment in particular practiced breaking into the enemy lines and coordination with the infantry, and especially with the 4th Indian Division. At dawn on 9 December 1940 they pounced, having crept up to within sight of the unsuspecting Italians, tanks, artillery, and all. The rumble of engines and tracks was cleverly drowned by low-level air attacks.

The Matilda[2] proved to be an awesome tool. The 24-ton monster, conceived only for infantry support and with its two 87 hp engines actually rather underpowered, advancing in leisurely but apparently unstoppable fashion, had a devastating effect on the Italians. Their brave gunners, some of them still equipped with wooden-wheeled guns from the First World War, kept on firing their shells at the juggernauts until they were within a few meters' range, only to see them bounce off and disappear into the sky as small glowing dots of light.

The tanks broke into the Italian positions, crushing guns and crews or mowing the men down with their machine guns. The Italian armor —even the most powerful tank model, the Carro Armato M-13, being far too poorly armored and carrying guns firing low-velocity shells which barely even scratched the Matildas—was quite helpless. One British tank commander was yelling angrily at his gunner because the

---

[2] The tank obtained its nickname, Matilda, which became official, from its predecessor, the Mark I, the silhouette of which, particularly because of its cowled water-cooled turret-mounted machine gun, looked like Matilda the Duck of the then popular comic series. The small and narrow-tracked vehicle moreover waddled like a duck.

man had fired several times at a Carro Armato without any apparent result. Only when they were right on top of it did they both realize that the wretched thing had been riddled with holes like a cardboard box. Against such an adversary, the two-pounder gun (40 mm caliber with the respectable muzzle velocity of 853 m/sec) was quite adequate. . . .

On the morning of the second day, a delighted Churchill received the report that it was impossible to count the prisoners, but that there were about "20 acres of officers and 100 acres of other ranks." In fact the prisoners numbered 38,000—three divisions had ceased to exist and the booty included 237 guns and 73 tanks.

Of the fifty Matildas, only one had to be written off as a total loss: The crew had set fire to their vehicle when, right in an enemy position, the tracks were shot away. In one tank, the four-man crew had been killed when the driver opened the visor of his viewing port and an artillery shell went clean through at that very moment. In no case had the armor been pierced; on one Matilda, thirty-eight dents caused by hits were counted, yet it was still fully operational.

1. Hitler Orders Operation Sunflower

The bold Swabian[1]

What had been conceived as a limited operation became Britain's first great triumph of the Second World War: Although General Wavell had had to withdraw one infantry division to send to East Africa,[2] the tiny Western Desert Force had chased the Italians clean out of Cyrenaica. The Matildas rattled into the fortifications of Sidi Omar, Bardia, Tobruk and Mechili, until the Italians outran them. On 6 February, the British took Benghazi. A few days later, they were standing outside El Agheila on the border of Tripolitania. They had taken 130,000 prisoners, annihilated 10 divisions, and destroyed or captured 850 guns and 450 tanks. The British lost less than 600 men. But after their 800-kilometer race, the troops were exhausted and their weapons and equipment, especially the few tanks which had survived the rough terrain, were in poor condition.

Prime Minister Churchill kept bombarding Wavell with orders. A grave threat to the British position in the Mediterranean appeared: Hitler had changed his attitude, which had been that "the Alps divide the theaters of war" and that south of them all war operations were a

[1] Translator's note: German folklore classes Swabians as cowards.

[2] There, Italian troops under the Duke of Aosta had conquered British Somaliland in August 1940, only to lose it in early 1941, together with Italian Somaliland and part of Ethiopia. They were forced to surrender on 19 April 1941.

matter for his ally. But at the same time his *Ostland* (eastern) mania prevented him from doing more than the necessary minimum. All action was designed to save Mussolini's face and more or less to secure the southern flank, with particular emphasis on guarding the Romanian oilfields. More than ever he was convinced that he could dispense with fighting Britain in earnest; he merely had to annihilate the Soviet Union, thus destroying the last British hope of a "continental dagger," and the island kingdom would yield or collapse.

This calculation put paid also to the plan of Admiral Raeder, which Hitler had fancied for a while; the plan was to give Germany's Italian ally massive support, with the aim of driving the British out of North Africa and then, by taking Malta, Cyprus, and Gibraltar, out of the whole Mediterranean; the Italian fleet would then be able to join in the blockade of the British Isles to starve them out.

Hitler was unwilling to get embroiled south of the Alps and, despite Raeder's plan, tried to keep the commitment as small as possible.

Toward the end of 1940, when the Italians suffered their first reverses in Greece and North Africa, he had the 10th Air Corps moved to Italy, but told Rommel that he would not allow a single man or a single *pfennig* to be sent to North Africa.

Out of pique with Mussolini, Hitler thought the best thing would be to let his ally stew in his own juice. But the British had taken Crete; Ploesti was within range of their bombers.

On 11 January, in his Directive No. 22, he ordered preparations to be made to give active support to the Italians in Albania and Libya: "The situation in the Mediterranean makes it necessary to provide German assistance, on strategic, political, and psychological grounds. Tripolitania must be held."

On 19 January he met Mussolini, who accepted a "blocking force" for North Africa but refused a proferred mountain division for Albania. Three days later Tobruk fell.

It became obvious that a "blocking force" would not do.

Militarily, the loss of North Africa would be quite bearable, Hitler told his commanders in chief early in February. But he was afraid that the atmosphere might deteriorate in the camp of his Axis ally to the point where the alliance might be severed. At the same time, he had great hopes of a "quick success in North Africa": Might it not be feasible to deprive the British of their base there and thus reach a peaceful solution in the Balkans?

He would therefore send to Africa not a "blocking" but an attacking force. And the commander would be Lieutenant General Erwin Rommel.

The dictator, spoiled by military success, was confidently sending his soldiers to North Africa to fight the British, whom he was usually so afraid of, although his forces had to be supplied across the Mediterranean which, for the time being at least, was dominated by the enemy. Colonel General Franz Halder, Chief of the Army General Staff, had written in his diary in late October 1940—before the disastrous defeat of the Italians—that one German division in Libya could certainly throw the British back over the Nile and give the Luftwaffe the opportunity to "make life impossible for the British in the Eastern Mediterranean." At around this time, while the political leadership was vacillating, his staff was indefatigably working out one new plan after another. The idea of a thrust from Romania through Bulgaria and Turkey to Syria, to join the Italians at the Suez Canal via Palestine, had already been considered. On one occasion, Halder made a distinctly reproachful entry to the effect that the army was expected to be ready for anything, "without any clear orders coming forth." Below the surface, tensions were positively crackling in the Wehrmacht leadership; it was everyone against everyone else, and the head of the Luftwaffe, Göring, against them all; Halder, guardian of the Holy Grail of ancient General Staff virtue, opposed the OKW, Hitler's creature—at times (in whispers) called "Corporal Hitler's Military Bureau." General Wilhelm Keitel, head of the OKW, was to earn himself the ugly nickname *"Lakeitel,"* or "lackey." At the Army High Command (OKH) headquarters, the head of that organization, General von Brauchitsch, tried to stay more or less out of it.

Meanwhile, diligent general staffs were putting the final polish on their plans; the code names of various projects on which Hitler was keeping the members of the staffs busy blossomed with colorful labels: Felix—the seizure of Gibraltar; Marita—attack on Greece; Attila—occupation of the remainder of France; and, once again, Sealion—the invasion of Britain, which would soon turn into Shark, a dummy "imminent invasion" exercise to conceal the cancellation of the real one; and Barbarossa, the surprise attack on the Soviet Union.

This, then, was the situation when Rommel rushed headlong to Libya. Reluctantly, Hitler diverted a small part of his Barbarossa force; not only to help his reeling ally in Africa, but also in the vague hope that his pet general would somehow make enough of a stir to neutralize the Balkan problem for the time being. From now on, nothing must be allowed to interfere with Barbarossa.

That this did not prove possible, that the southern theaters of war eventually demanded a substantial effort at the expense of the Ostland adventure, may have decided the outcome of the war. At the very least, it dramatically influenced its course. Moreover, the fact that Rommel created more of a stir than had been expected of him and his small force also played a part. Down the long boot of Italy, across a perilous sea, and across hundreds of kilometers of barren country ran the over-stretched lines of communication, at the far end of which the turbulent general clamored loudly for more—more fuel, ammunition, weapons, equipment, and troops.

The code name for the commitment of German troops in Africa was Sunflower. Unconsciously, someone had hit upon the perfect symbol: a huge and showy flower at the end of a long and rather fragile stem.

The lights come on in Tripoli

In mid-February, Tripoli was still swarming with exhausted and de-moralized Italian soldiers out of the desert, telling fearful tales about the might and perfection of the British war machine. In one respect they had infected the whole town: Terrified of air raids, everyone started shouting if anyone switched on even the smallest light after dark. But when on the night of 15 February the lights went on in the port of Tripoli, both the Arab and Italian inhabitants of the town came running from their houses: What was happening that night was so mon-strous, and at the same time so matter-of-fact, that they all forgot their fears. Huge floodlights bathed ships and wharves alike in bright light; and well-fed, self-assured, clean-shaven Germans unloaded their ex-pensive and solid-looking paraphernalia of war with uncanny speed and precision, without having to raise their voices even once. The Ital-ian army doctor Tobino, today head of the psychiatric clinic in the town of Lucca, jotted down an account of the event:

> We had been awaiting the British fatalistically—almost gladly. At least the whole business would be over. But the Germans came in-stead. . . . Until then, our troops had always disembarked amid great chaos, their faces grim.
>
> It took us at least three days to disembark one division. Then every-thing would get mixed up, so that it took at least ten days to find it all again and to reorganize the troops.
>
> But the Germans were parading about the streets in white gloves by next morning. The men who had fled from Cyrenaica, and the war-weary people of Tripoli, just stood there and stared. Most of those who shortly beforehand had been saying how good and generous the British were, and how they were our friends, again started talking big.

The white gloves were an exaggeration, but they would have matched the mood of the troops. For the young soldiers, of Recon-naissance Unit No. 3, many of them Berliners, who were the first ar-rivals, had some fun on parade. By order of their commanders, they revved up the engines of their armored reconnaissance cars and BMW motorcycle combinations after first passing the review stand and, tearing around a few back streets, joined the tail end of the parade again to double the effectiveness of the show.

The twenty-four-year old Warrant Officer Claus Wernicke crouched on his heavy BMW and did his best to keep a dead-pan expression on his face, although he had the definite impression that he had been recognized and greeted with extra applause the second time around. Like most of his comrades in the unit and throughout the German army, he had a feeling of boundless superiority.

They had gone through the Polish and French campaigns; could anyone still doubt the words of the much-sung song: "For today Germany is ours, tomorrow it will be the whole world"?

They had been issued weird uniforms on board ship: green, with puttees, evidently ancient stock. If questioned on the journey, they were to say they were volunteers who wanted to join the Italians. (In the case of later arrivals, this masquerade was dispensed with.)

On the ship between Naples and Tripoli, they were sitting in a somewhat explosive environment. There were boxes of ammunition everywhere, and cans of fuel were lashed to every bulkhead. But it never occurred to anyone to worry; instead, there were roars of laughter at the stories of their comrades who had managed to pay a visit to some willing and very reasonably priced ladies and were now cursing the time they had wasted on those puttees—both before and after.

Hitler himself, no less, had laid down the rules for their behavior in his Directive No. 22e.

A "military and political duty of the highest order" had been laid upon them: to give psychological as well as other assistance to their allies, who were inadequately equipped as a result of the "limited productivity of Italy's war economy." "You must therefore be free of any wounding superiority, regardless of all your justified and proud awareness of your own worth, and of what you have accomplished. . . ."

At the quayside in Tripoli stood an officer, no longer young, but erect and wiry, wearing the Knight's Cross and the *Pour le Mérite,* with a riveting look which gripped you while being at the same time somehow turned inward. This was not merely the mark of an unusual personality; it also resulted from the fact that he never wore spectacles in public, although he was nearsighted in one eye and farsighted in the other. This was Lieutenant General Erwin Rommel, then fifty years old.

The bold Swabian had a lot to thank Hitler for. Although his extraordinary bravery and tactical skill had earned him the *Pour le*

Mérite in the First World War, his career in the 100,000-strong army of the Republic had been somewhat sluggish.

He remained a captain for fifteen years; this much-decorated son of a professor had no chance at all of joining the select circle of the General Staff—of those wearing the "intelligence stripe."[3]

Not until 1933 was he promoted to major, and it was then that he had his first fleeting contacts with Hitler. However, it was hardly thanks to this that from then on, in the headlong expansion of the Wehrmacht, Rommel shared in the general acceleration of promotion: In 1935 he became a lieutenant colonel and instructor at the Potsdam Military Academy. And the highest Party echelons had plans for him, although he had never been an NSDAP (Nazi Party) member. He was to become military instructor to the SA (Nazi storm troops) and later to the Hitler Youth. In 1937 he published his manual on tactics, *Infantarie greift an*, read by an enthusiastic Hitler. During the next year Rommel was made full colonel and commandant of the Wiener Neustadt Military Academy. But before that, at Hitler's wish, he had commanded the Führer Escort Battalion during the march into the Sudetenland. He performed the same duty in the attack on Poland.

He was now close enough to the Supreme Warlord to express a wish: He would like to command a Panzer division. He was given the 7th—a favor not usually shown an infantryman.

But Hitler had not been mistaken in his judgment. In the French campaign, Rommel's unit became known as the "ghost division," which broke through relentlessly and then went racing through the enemy's hinterland. Its commander thought nothing of giving a hand with bridge-building under enemy fire, standing up to his chest in water. But he did not justify Hitler's later remark that he was "an unbelievably hard man" by brilliant military feats alone: When a prisoner of war, a "fanatical"-looking French officer, refused to get into a particular vehicle, there was, according to Rommel's dispatches, no alternative but to gun him down there and then.

The capitulation of France inspired Rommel to publish a book on the victorious campaign of the 7th Panzer Division, in which he did not bother to hide his light under a bushel. This somewhat American view of the value of "public relations" made his name known but got him into trouble with the more conservative elements in the Wehrmacht: Halder hindered publication by denying permission for some photographs to be included in the book.[4] Moreover, the commander of the

[3] Translator's note: A red stripe down the side of the trouser legs denoted a General Staff member.

[4] The busy general noted indignantly in his war diary after a discussion with Staff Major Dingler of the Army Publishing Department on 20 August: "Many

15th Panzer Regiment, 5th Panzer Division, protested in a rage that his part in some actions, for which Rommel's unit was given all the credit, had also been worth mentioning, especially since he had earned the Knight's Cross for them at the time. This was Colonel Johannes Streich. A few months later, Streich, by then commander of the 5th Light Division, was relieved of his command in the desert and sent home by his commanding general, Rommel.

At any rate, there was plenty of reason for grumbling in the Wehrmacht when the newly fledged Lieutenant General Erwin Rommel became Supreme Commander, Africa. As far as Halder was concerned, he was already in trouble, and the "OKW Party," Keitel and Jodl, always treated with distrust this kind of vertical takeoff as a result of the Führer's favors. Hitler, however, was quite undisturbed and continued to show good will by giving Rommel his Chief Wehrmacht Adjutant, Rudolf Schmundt, to take to Africa with him for the initial phase.

The two of them had evidently discussed the injustice Rommel had experienced in his literary work. For, immediately after returning and reporting to Hitler, Schmundt wrote to Africa on 19 February, addressing himself to the "Highly-esteemed dear Herr General": "You may rest assured that it has been settled with the Führer that there will be no more distortions of historical merit."

The two officers undertook reconnaissance flights together and inspected the shattered units of Germany's allies, without being aware of the weakness of the enemy.

The weakness of the Italians, on the other hand, was self-evident. So Schmundt returned to Germany with a lengthy shopping list.

That was another thing that did not exactly endear Rommel to his superiors in the OKW and the OKH, who felt he was going over their heads. Schmundt wrote:

> On Sunday I went to the Berghof [Hitler's home], where the Führer was most impatient for news. . . . His entire attention is concentrated on the Libyan theater of war; and he is now uneasy about the next fortnight. All my requests have been given priority as far as possible, on the Führer's authority.
>
> 1. The Reichsmarschall [Göring] has personally and with immediate effect allotted you, Herr General, a reconnaissance squadron consisting of two Heinkel-111s, several Junkers-52s, and six Storchs.
>
> 2. The army is speeding up consignments of anti-tank weapons and mines.
>
> . . .

---

photos of the 7th Panzer Div. I refuse to sign." And again on 20 December 1940: "Propaganda maps depicting the 'victorious campaign' of individual divisions are contrary to regulations governing the reporting of this war."

5. Signal units, and the No. 1 Panzer Unit, are being moved up by General von Rintelen.

6. Orders have been given substantially to reinforce the 10th Flying Corps.

The 15th Panzer Division is being sent out now, and the Führer himself is seeing to it that it is suitably equipped. Supplies will moreover be speeded up as much as possible. . . .

The next, concluding paragraph of the letter shows that Hitler had one of his rare moments of humor (with a massive admixture of poison) when he thought up a name for the force that was to fight at the side of the Italians: "The Führer wants to give the Corps a name as soon as it is down there. How would you fancy Deutsches Afrika Korps, by analogy with the Alpen Korps of the First World War?"[5]

In his letter replying to the Wehrmacht adjutant, and in his first situation reports for the OKH, Rommel was still worried that the British might at any moment resume their advance to the west. He also dramatized things reporting several times that the enemy was getting ready to resume his attack in the area of Agedabia.

But on 9 March he reported to the OKH that it would be both desirable and possible for him to go over to the attack before the start of the hot summer weather in June and July: "The first objective of an attack would be the reconquest of Cyrenaica; the second, northern Egypt and the Suez Canal." At this time, however, he still made it a condition that the 15th Panzer Division would have to arrive first. On the basic point that an attack should be made as soon as possible there was no difference of opinion between Rommel and his superiors, at this or at any other time.

Halder had on 28 February minuted the result of a discussion with Brauchitsch thus: "Exchange of views on operation in Libya. We must beware of trying to meddle too much in it." He also noted after the briefing of, now Major General, Johannes Streich: "Accent on offensive and on the urgency of the task."

Quite reasonably, he gave thought to the question of how supplies could be kept up across such inhospitable country. Result: Provided one stuck to Cyrenaica, the thing was possible if the smaller ports this side of Tobruk, especially Benghazi, could be taken. Pressing on to Egypt seemed to him clearly out of the question.

[5] Even when giving Rommel his assignment, Hitler is said to have had his eye not only on his military qualities, but also on the fact that he had been decorated for gallantry in the Alpen Korps fighting against the Italians. Earlier, Mussolini had sent to Berlin as Military Attaché an officer who had negotiated with the German Reich after the First World War as a member of one of the delegations of the victors. This had infuriated Hitler beyond measure.

To be sure, even the cool-headed Halder clearly believed that the Soviet Union would easily be disposed of by the autumn. His notes for a report to Hitler on 17 March include the following: "Attack on Egypt: 1st Panzer Corps to be rested once it becomes available from Barbarossa (prepared)."[6]

"We had a great day. . . ."

Three days later Rommel arrived in Berlin to report. Although the minds of the top brass were now set on the eastern adventure, he was granted astonishingly large parts of another "shopping list"—no doubt thanks to his "direct line" to the Supreme Warlord. A "secret command paper," signed by Brauchitsch personally the next day, shows clear signs of agreement with Rommel's own 9 March assessment of the situation.

Brauchitsch wrote: After the arrival of the 15th Panzer Division, the Agedabia area must be taken for use as a jumping-off point for further operations. He continued: "Whether it is possible to continue the offensive operation envisaged by the Afrika Korps in the general direction of Tobruk, or whether the arrival of reinforcements envisaged for a later date must be awaited, will depend on the outcome of the fighting for Agedabia, and especially on whether it will be possible to beat the British armored corps decisively around Agedabia."

This was more or less what Rommel had suggested, and this is what was decided. Only there was no such thing as "a British armored corps around Agedabia." Instead, the strongest force available to the British consisted of a few worn-out, thin-skinned, and poorly armed Cruiser tanks.[7] And the man who found this fact out for Rommel was his close friend, Streich.

The hard Rommel, an obsessive worker, had one touching habit: Every day he would write at least a few lines to his wife. In the deci-

---

[6] Even later in 1941, when Rommel was standing on the Egyptian frontier and demanded reinforcements, supplies, and transport, the OKH's communications were still along the same lines: "Once Barbarossa is over in the autumn, anything is possible. . . ."

[7] The 7th Royal Tank Regiment, with its sturdy Matildas, had long since been fighting in East Africa. German quarters took some time to take notice of this tank type. Halder's diary, 4 March 1941: "Great excitement on the Mountain [Hitler's home, the Berghof] caused by arrival of pictures of British tanks with 80 mm armor. . . ." This, despite the fact that at least one of the Matildas had been captured in France and saw service with a German unit, bearing German military markings, fitted with an anti-tank gun and fondly christened "Oswald" by its crew.

sive days after his return from Berlin, his letters are full of hidden allu-
sions:

25 March: Safely back here. In Rome I was received by the Duce.
Now I am glad to be back at the front. . . .

26 March: . . . I have to hold the troops back, or they would
charge. . . . Our Italian colleagues go around with long faces because
the British are getting cocky. . . .

27 March: . . . As a result of our latest operations, we have
"harvested" an airfield with lots of gasoline and a generator of 6–10
kw/h capacity.

28 March: There is a storm, and the sea, as the Italians say, is
"*furioso.*"

29 March: Today, I am going back to Tripoli. . . . I hope to be back
this evening. Just in case, I'll take my washing things along as matters
could turn out otherwise than planned. (Evening) back. Conferences
ended very satisfactorily.

1 April: As you probably know from the Wehrmacht communiqué,
we had a great day yesterday. . . .

2 April: These are eventful days for us. But we are making progress.

3 April: Since 31 March we have been attacking with remarkable
success. The staff people in Tripoli, Rome, and possibly Berlin will be
astonished. I have dared to proceed against earlier orders and directives,
because I saw an opportunity. In the end they will give their approval
and I am sure that anyone would have done the same in my place. The
first objective—planned for the end of May—has been reached. The
British are on the run. . . . Our losses are unusually light. It has so far
been quite impossible to take stock of the material we have captured.
As you may imagine, I cannot sleep for joy. . . .

4 April: Yesterday was a great and successful day. I received a message from the Führer, congratulating me on my unexpected success and
giving me directives for the continuation of operations which are fully
in accordance with my own views. . . .

5 April: Let us hope that the great game we are playing will prosper. . . .

The "monster" catches Corporal Short

"Please God, take these bloody planes away and I'll promise to be a
good boy always." Although a whole string of Me-110 fighter-bombers

was screaming down spewing fire, Corporal Short of the King's Dragoon Guards couldn't help grinning when he heard this frantic cry. The sergeant who had uttered it was normally a bit of a daredevil, afraid of nothing. But like everyone between El Agheila and Benghazi, he had had just about all the Luftwaffe he could take in these closing days of February.

The coastal road was generally known as "bomb alley"; vehicles without armor were allowed to use it in daylight only by special permission. Not that anyone in his senses bothered to try. In January, when the 10th Flying Corps, transferred by Hitler to the Mediterranean, had become active, there had been disquieting news: The aircraft carrier *Illustrious,* whose torpedo bombers had so decisively defeated the Italian fleet at Taranto, had been in turn badly damaged by Stuka dive bombers, attacking with foolhardy audacity. They had also sunk the cruiser *Southampton.* Conventional He-111 bombers were mining the Suez Canal; and the KDG's armored cars were being pursued by Ju-87s and Me-110s until, in the coverless desert, they felt like "cherries on a cake."

On 27 February, three days after the clash at Fort El Agheila, Major Lindsay's C-Squadron was being particularly heavily strafed. Reinforced with two 25-pounder guns,[8] two little two-pounder anti-tank guns, two Pom-Poms, and some Australian infantrymen, reconnaissance car crews had set up an ambush near the frontier: Should the Germans again feel tempted to visit Fort El Agheila, the KDG could be ready for them with something of bigger caliber than the pitiful Boys Rifles of the Marmon-Harringtons. Australian engineers had even mined the road; until then, offers to provide mine defenses had been turned down on the grounds that purely defensive weapons were bad for the men's morale. But instead of the German reconnaissance cars, it was the planes that came. First a Henschel-126 reconnaissance aircraft came buzzing about their heads—a particularly noisome type, whose pilots had earned grudging admiration by the way they would lurk between dunes to evade the Pom-Poms and would suddenly come swooping over the ridges, even having the cheek to chuck hand grenades at the British armored cars.

"Now we'll get the Me-110s down on our necks," said Corporal Short gloomily.

Over in the turret in his vehicle, Major "Mick" Lindsay was checking his anti-aircraft machine gun, nursing a somewhat sore back. A few days earlier, an attacking fighter-bomber had hit the interior lining of

[8] Field howitzers of 3.45″ approx.=88 mm caliber, often used in action over open sights, against tanks as well. For this reason known in the Afrika Korps by the respectful name of *"Ratsch-Bum"* ("Crash-Bang").

the squadron commander's turret while he was firing his machine gun. The projectile had ricocheted around and lodged itself in the muscles of his shoulder. Immediately afterward, Short heard over the radio the voice of his commander, saying: "Christ, they've got *me!*" A member of the crew with some first-aid knowledge had extracted the bullet with an oily pair of pliers. Lindsay absolutely refused to show the hole to a doctor.

This time, in the ambush position on the border, things became serious. Twelve Me-110s came in from the sea. Forty minutes later three armored cars and two trucks had been destroyed and ten men, including Lindsay's deputy, Captain Delmege, had been badly wounded. The indestructible major stood, pale and furious, amid a heap of spent shell cases. As usual, the machine-gun fire from the cars had had no effect whatever on the attackers. On the other hand, most of the wounded had been firing machine guns.

A second attack, by a smaller formation of aircraft, destroyed another car, and the commander of the regiment said over the radio: "Looks like the Germans don't want you there."

The ambush was abandoned, since no one would fall into it anyway. However, Harry Short and his lieutenant, Howard, fell into a German trap. At first light on 2 March they were again driving toward El Agheila. The sand dunes were still casting long blue shadows and in one of them something moved.

Short and Howard sent their three cars over to the left to provide cover on the flank and crept up the next hill to have a closer look. Hardly had they reached the top when they came under withering fire —automatic weapons and, in between, that whipcrack sound. . . . They were the first to hear the voice of a gun everyone would soon get to know in the African theater of war: the 88 mm anti-aircraft gun.

The two cars on the hill scurried away from one another and hastily sought cover behind some camel-thorn bushes. Short could see from the corner of his eye that two of the great eight-wheeler reconnaissance cars were facing the three little Marmon-Harringtons. Shortly afterward, there was a rattling and roaring sound alongside—and an immense tire came to a halt by his head. He decided to stand up very slowly. He now saw at close quarters the weird thing which had crossed his path a mere fortnight ago and a bare couple of miles farther south. The hefty-looking men in peaked caps were smiling at him in a friendly manner. His gloomy premonitions had been justified.

While Short and his lieutenant were being taken to the rear, photographed by journalists, and entertained by an amiable elderly gentleman wearing a general's insignia (Streich), Major Lindsay would gladly have torn from limb to limb the hapless lance corporal who had ordered the three cars to retreat. After a wild chase they had succeeded in getting safely back to their squadron. But on calmer reflection, he had to admit that it was better to have left the two commanders in the lurch than to have allowed the Germans, with their superior weapons, to destroy three expensive vehicles.

Confusion and flight

In addition to the eight-wheeled monsters, from mid-March onward the crews of the scout cars occasionally also spotted medium tanks on the German side. Faced with their devastating-looking gun barrels, they could only dash for cover behind the nearest dune. The air was thick with German aircraft, and the infuriating Henschel reconnaissance planes seemed to sniff out every last slit trench. Occasionally, a few British Hurricane fighters would turn up, but could score only when they managed to catch some of the cumbersome Ju-87 Stukas on their own. Much more often they succumbed to the heavily armed Me-110s. About a dozen times, the KDG had to tow onto the road some riddled machine and its cursing pilot who had crash-landed. Air Force mechanics, working all night, would patch the machines up on the road.

At regimental headquarters the Stukas chased the commander, Colonel McQuorquodale, off his thunderbox; and his fellow countryman, Lindsay, laughed so much he forgot to throw himself flat.

A further visit to regimental headquarters resulted in mixed feelings; Brigadier Rimington, commander of the 3rd Armored Brigade, brought the happy news that the KDG's reports about the presence of German light units was now believed at staff headquarters. From Corporal Short's first encounter to Lieutenant Williams's Battle of the Bedroll and long afterward, grinning chairborne warriors had been assuring each other that the Dragoons, new to the business, had evidently mistaken some scared Italian rearguards for the formidable Germans.

The brigadier now reported that a limited German advance was to be expected early in April. When it came, the Dragoons were to retreat, maintaining contact with the enemy. As a reconnaissance unit, it was in any case not the KDG's job to repel any attacks; but this talk of withdrawal was very disappointing. Two months ago they were still discussing whether they would advance to Tripoli immediately, or a little later. Would they have to run away from the Germans forever?

On the morning of 24 March Lieutenant Williams was once more leading his patrol. Fort El Agheila was again occupied by the Germans and this time they were making it clear that they intended to stay.

Under a hail of fire, Williams withdrew his small unit, reinforced by infantrymen with anti-tank guns, into the dunes south of the road.

There, however, he immediately ran into a heavy armored reconnaissance car. His little anti-tank gun fired. The heavy automatic weapons of the eight-wheeler barked back, killing one gunner and gravely injuring another. There was nothing for it but to turn tail. Meanwhile, Lieutenant Whetherly had worked his way up to the road from the south. "Enemy tanks and trucks, with infantry, on the airfield and on the road. Italian flag over fort," he reported on his radio.

One group of Panzers rumbled on toward the frontier. The one in front ran onto a mine meant for Major Lindsay's ambush. Before it withdrew, Whetherly could see two lifeless bodies being hoisted out of the vehicle—the first dead of the Afrika Korps.[9]

It was also Lieutenant Whetherly who gave the first report of the start of Rommel's offensive. Early in the morning on 31 March, he saw tanks with the German military cross far to the south, in the area of Giofer, driving eastward. Soon afterward, Lieutenant Budden also reported German tanks approaching between El Agheila and the salt marshes of Marsa el Brega. All day long the scouts, with their thin-skinned cars, stayed just beyond the range of the German tanks' guns. Their precise reports were included with a commendation in the war diary of the 2nd Armored Division, at the orders of its commander.

But in the evening the order came to retreat almost 50 kilometers behind Marsa el Brega. Curious . . . The map showed that the Marsa el Brega gap, between rugged country and salt marshes across which one could not drive, was the best defense position. Would there then be no attempt at all to stop the Germans?

In the days to come, the crews of the scout cars began to get a steadily growing feeling of unreality. More and more orders to retreat, which had to be performed amid a motorcade of vehicles streaming toward the rear; hardly any contact with the enemy; on the other hand plenty of rumors and chaos, bordering on panic, on the roads and tracks leading north and east. Occasionally they would lose radio contact with the division altogether; then they would get confusing and contradictory orders.

Major Lindsay and his C-Squadron, who had been guarding the entrance to the Wadi Faregh far to the south, which was negotiable by vehicles, first heard of the general retreat as night was falling. In pitch darkness they traveled over rugged terrain.

"I'll go ahead; and I shall navigate by the stars," the major announced. His men were astonished: The amazing Mick could even do astronavigation! He did not confide to anyone that he knew only one star: the polestar. They were, after all, going north. So they went rum-

---

[9] A German soldier had earlier shot a comrade dead by mistake in the dark.

bling on through the night, the tall major in front, feeling for rocks with his feet; in the leading vehicle a driver who could see in the dark like a cat. Eventually they saw a fire blazing under the polestar, made for it, and found they were burning tanks.

They were standing on the coastal road, which was empty of people as far as the eye could see. Nowhere on the red-hot steel hulks was a hole to be seen.

"They were never shot up," one man said. "These are the 5th Royal Tank Regiment's broken-down old Cruisers. One of them packs up every few miles. They must have set fire to them as being beyond repair."

"We must press on," said the major.

The original cliff coastline climbs steeply out of the coastal plain, which was once the bottom of the sea. It can be negotiated by vehicles only in a few places, and in those places vast traffic jams had developed. Most untypically, the Luftwaffe left this easy prey unmolested. The Dragoons soon realized that the Messerschmitts and Junkers had other quite specific targets on the far side of the climb: over and over again they came across burnt-out and blown-up oil-tanker lorries. Between Msus and Maraua there was an enormous grayish-black mushroom of smoke: Stukas had set a large fuel dump on fire there; an entire convoy of eighteen oil tankers had gone up with it.

It looked as if all organization, the entire command structure, had collapsed. One after another the orders to retreat came in, sometimes over the intermittently audible radio, sometimes through liaison officers, then through accidental encounters in the mêlée on the road north and east. But only rarely did any orders arrive to perform the normal functions of a reconnaissance unit: to stay in touch with the enemy, out of range, and to report what he is doing.

When they did set eyes on columns of Germans in the open country south of the hills, they usually consisted of a few reconnaissance cars and lorries, perhaps with some artillery and anti-tank guns. Seeing them, you could not help wondering: "Why are we running away from that lot?"

To replace the wounded Captain Delmege, a new deputy squadron commander had reached Major Lindsay: Captain Tony Llewellyn-Palmer. He fitted perfectly into this weird but fearless crew: his car contained, as a supernumerary crew member, a hen, a pretty little thing, which he had procured so as to wring its neck on a suitable occasion. But the bird had begun to lay eggs, thus saving herself from the pot.

On one occasion, a German column caught up with them. This time it had a few tanks with it. Captain Llewellyn-Palmer's armored car was still standing with its hatch open in the pancake-flat desert, although the Germans were almost within range.

"Let's get out of here," Lindsay called over, "or they'll get us." "Can't go yet," said his deputy. "I'm waiting for my chicken." They could hear the roar of the Panzers' engines and the rattling of their tracks when, as if recognizing the danger, the hen appeared, half-running and half-flying, and cackling excitedly, from behind some bushes. With undiminished speed, she disappeared into the scout car, the hatches crashed shut, and the wild chase was resumed.

Eventually, Captain Llewellyn-Palmer did wring his hen's neck, for when they came to rest after this retreat, no one could long stand the sight of a chicken, without his mouth watering in remembrance of almost-forgotten delights.

They just managed to slip into the fortress of Tobruk before Rommel's forces "closed the bag."

2. Rommel Tears Up the Textbook

Where have the tanks gone?

Rommel had returned to Africa with the intention of conducting a limited attack. The ease with which Streich's small party had occupied Fort El Agheila could only reinforce his resolution.

In the end even the CGS, Halder had said, in the course of the 20 March discussion, that with the forces then available they might consider "taking control of the approaches to Agedabia."[1] Meanwhile 8,000 men of the 5th Light Division had landed in Tripoli, including the 5th Panzer Regiment, which was equipped mostly with the powerful Panzers III and IV, both far superior to the Cruiser. The Italian Ariete armored division was also under Rommel's command. This division had not been involved in the Graziani debacle.

But the attack was to go no farther than the "approaches to Agedabia." When Rommel's Chief of Staff, Lieutenant Colonel von dem Borne, said in the course of a discussion with "Air Commander Africa" that they could advance farther provided it was possible to break through the Marsa el Brega gap, he curtly turned him down, saying that such a course would be contrary to OKH orders. And when

[1] The exact words in his diary. The next day's directive by Brauchitsch recommended waiting for the 15th Panzer Division. Equally contrary to this directive was Halder's view that no attack "on the Tobruk line" would be possible before autumn. Thus in the much-vaunted OKH, the left hand did not know what the right hand was doing.

General Streich led his troops in the first set-piece attack on fortified British positions, his commander gave him a pretty free hand, in remarkable and noticeable contrast to the far-reaching way in which Rommel later interfered in the conduct of the battle.

The operation was not at first running very satisfactorily. All the British had available behind the infantry positions between the sea and the salt pans was a regiment of 25-pounders; but their fire was unpleasantly accurate. Two Panzer attacks were thrown back. Although the high-explosive shells were ineffective against the German armor, direct hits were enough to tear the tracks off the bogeys and to give the crews a nasty shaking. On top of which, the Panzers kept getting stuck on a sandy ridge.

Not even Stuka attacks silenced the gunners; and in Streich's command post, where people had to keep throwing themselves flat on the sand because of hits from the indefatigable 25-pounders, the binoculars were forever scanning the undulating horizon: A counterattack by tanks just now would have been the last straw. Luckily there was nothing more formidable to be seen than a few two-man armored vehicles armed with machine guns, which in the French campaign had failed to present a threat even to scout cars.[2]

This gave Streich a chance to use infantry to solve the first crisis of the Afrika Korps in the classic land of tank battles. When darkness fell, he sent a machine-gun battalion north of the road close to the shore into the British right flank. Today one can venture the opinion that this advance was one of the most fateful of the African campaign. The attack of the well-trained foot soldiers, who made skillful use of the cover provided by the dunes, made obsolete the old-fashioned British book of rules, which was based on the assumption of an orderly, tidy battlefield, with neatly separated lines, on which one had especially to beware of being outflanked, let alone encircled.

The British commander did what Wellington, too, would have done. He withdrew. As for Johannes Streich, he would not have learned his lesson from fighting against the British on the Channel coast had he not immediately, and without special orders from his commanding general, followed up with his entire division.[3] The only bottleneck in the whole of Cyrenaica, where there are only 13 kilometers available for maneuvering between the sea and the impassable salt pans, had been

[2] During maneuvers immediately before the outbreak of war, the angry crews had chalked on the side of these "Bren carriers": "Not for combat use. Only mild steel."

[3] What was available could of course hardly be described as "an entire division." It consisted essentially of the Panzer regiment, the reconnaissance unit, two machine-gun battalions, and twelve pieces of artillery.

opened up. "Hauser," he told his Chief of Staff, "we are continuing the advance on Agedabia." For him, as a Panzerman, it was a textbook reaction.

Rommel, who at first showed some surprise and did not approve of Streich's action until he'd had a long look at the map, by now could not have cared less about any textbook. On the morning of 2 April, before the first units had reached Agedabia, two important items of intelligence reached him:

(1) Although smallish infantry units, supported by artillery, had given battle on two further occasions, reconnaissance aircraft reported columns of vehicles moving eastward throughout Cyrenaica.

(2) The very first tank battle had shown that the British Cruiser tanks, with their two-pounder guns, could do the Panzer III hardly any damage, even at a range of 1,000 meters, whereas the Panzer's 50 mm tank gun, for instance, went straight through their 23 mm frontal armor.

He therefore threw to the winds the wisdom of the textbooks, according to which a wise commander is best advised not to divide his forces in pursuing an enemy who, although he is giving ground, is not beaten. Rommel not only divided his forces, he split them into three. When he saw his chance, he became a restless and ruthless thruster, who did not ask of his men anymore than he asked of himself—which was to be superhuman.

Major General Kirchheim, who was touring Libya for the OKH, suddenly found himself commandeered by Rommel and sent northward and eastward along the coast road with elements of the Italian Brescia Division. Streich, as it happened, had under him only a mixed combat group consisting of elements of his division, which Rommel was driving right across the desert toward Fort Mechili, a place where ancient Bedouin tracks meet. When the Italian General Gariboldi, to whom the Afrika Korps was still tactically subordinate, full of worries about flanks and other sacred cows, wanted to put the brakes on, Rommel settled the matter with the remark that he had no intention of missing good opportunities.

He was doing it all wrong—and therefore right—this outsider in the "international union of generals." The established practice is that before the start of any operation that will have a range of some hundreds of kilometers, the wise logistician will calculate to a hair what supplies are to be transported where, when, and in how many lorries; and, moreover, that he will draw up numerous alternative programs to provide for various contingencies. The man who decides on such an undertaking overnight is bound to come a cropper in the hostile desert—unless his name is Rommel.

This meant that when the fuel of Streich's Panzers ran out, before the very eyes of the outraged divisional staff, everything not essential for shooting or running was thrown off the supply trucks. It also meant that the men slept rough on ground sheets in the desert. Moreover, he had the Ju-52 fuel (supplied by the fat Reichsmarschall through the mediation of the Führer's adjutant, Schmundt) flown straight to the front and had the good luck to have only two of the tanker aircraft shot up on the ground in the first critical phase.

It is also part of the established practice that one finds out the opponent's order of battle and works out his reactions in advance, and that every separate unit receives written orders accordingly. Among the few papers that did emanate from Rommel were scraps thrown from a Fieseler Storch short-takeoff reconnaissance aircraft, with demands to get on with it or he would come down there himself. For he flew his own reconnaissance and directed his hastily thrown-together combat groups according to developments. It was therefore inevitable that his commands should occasionally cancel each other out.

One of the small columns traveling without armor, which had been observed by the KDG's vehicles, had the longest journey: It consisted of Lieutenant Colonel Ponath's 8th Machine Gun Battalion and was pushing diagonally across the Cyrenaica Bulge to Derna, to regain the coastal road there and to deny it to the retreating British units. It was a 450-kilometer drive through mostly trackless desert, by inexperienced men equipped with vehicles that would not have been described as cross-country ones even for use in European woods and meadows.[4]

This kind of journey can be done only by people who believe that nothing can go wrong. Not even an early encounter with the British, which had gone in favor of the other side, could change this attitude in any way. On 23 March, Lieutenant Weaver of the KDG C-Squadron had surprised three reconnaissance cars and an anti-tank gun near Giofer just when they were hopelessly bogged down. Although the British set three trucks on fire and could be driven off only by aircraft hastily summoned by radio, the recollection of the skirmish that remained was a good-natured appreciation of the pluck with which the British kept coming on in their vintage vehicles. The only man upset was the cook, Leo, because they had shot his lovely new field kitchen full of holes.

Thirsty, exhausted, continually having to dig out their vehicles when they became stuck in the sand, and from time to time spurred on by the ubiquitous Rommel, the Machine Gun Battalion struggled through to

---

[4] Someone had decided that heavy vehicles in the desert must have double tires on the rear axle. They sank extra deep into the sand and were destroyed with monotonous regularity by stones wedged between them.

Derna, some of them actually getting there in three days. They took some four hundred prisoners on the way and caught the two most important British generals. But at the airfield in Derna they again came upon their dashing adversaries, the KDG. At this time, the column of British vehicles crawling westward snaked 25 kilometers back to Giovanni Berta. From there the coastal road winds toward Tobruk in hairpin bends rising up into the mountains again—very inconvenient for a hasty retreat. . . .

Rommel had not been able to keep together even his armored force. Although the push through the desert toward Mechili and Tobruk was the most important one, he had to send a somewhat heavier formation along the coastal road ahead of Major General Kirchheim and his lightly armed infantry toward Benghazi. So he reinforced the 3rd Reconnaissance Unit with some artillery out of the total of twelve German guns available and with one company of Panzers from the 5th Regiment.

Weeping for Greater Germany

Joachim Saenger, radio operator in the company commander's Panzer III, was thinking as the others were: This dead-flat plain ahead is the place for a halt. On the horizon to the north, the mountains rise to Benina, Benghazi's airfield, which they had to take.

"What the hell . . ." said the company commander.

Hardly had the armored column come to a halt on the flat surface than one vehicle after another sank right up to the drive wheels, making a strange grating noise. A dry salt-lake bed, over the crust of which the wind had blown a deceptive layer of sand, is no place to park a twenty-ton tank. But who knows that when he is newly out of Europe? Cursing and sweating, they managed to free the less badly stricken vehicles and used them to tow out a few of the others, but a part of the company remained hopelessly bogged down and had to wait for tractors. From the mountains came the noise of fighting. It was clear that the infantry had attacked on their own. The surviving Panzers went clattering toward a trench. It was, at the age of twenty-two, Saenger's first taste of battle. Only much later did he realize that the sharp rattling he could occasionally hear had been caused by the shells from the British tanks' popguns bouncing harmlessly off his tank.

But then there was a shattering crash, the Panzer went a little way up in the air and came to a halt with a jolt.

The entire crew, with the exception of Lieutenant Sandrock, was inexperienced. They looked at each other white-faced and felt half dead already. Had they been hit by an anti-tank gun? The lieutenant yelled

at Saenger to stop the others; there was a minefield here. He managed
to send out his report in a reasonably firm voice, but the other Panzers
drove on unconcerned. Then there were two more loud bangs and two
broken chains hung limply. And then a third explosion.

Warrant Officer Lämmerhirt had jumped from his Panzer straight
onto a mine. All they found of him was his cap. The lieutenant gave
Saenger a furious look—but he carefully examined the ground before
he jumped from the Panzer to take over an undamaged one. Later, it
was discovered that the radio frequencies had been shifted on the way
from Germany. Test transmissions to tune the sets had been forbidden
prior to going into action. That was why the others had not heard the
mine warning.

It was hours before they were again on the move, exhausted after
mending the tracks under the burning sun. The sounds of fighting from
the mountains had ceased. The stragglers set course for Mechili. The
mountains were left behind on the left, and they were making for the
desert.

They were driving downwind so that each vehicle was running in its
own dust cloud. They closed the hatches and donned gas masks; but
the dust penetrated everywhere and the blistering heat drove everyone,
including the driver, onto the deck behind the turret armor. Saenger
tore the gas mask off his face; he felt he was suffocating. He cried with
exhaustion and helplessness and was very ashamed of himself. But then
he noticed tear stains on the dust-covered faces of the others. And so
they drove behind their regiment to Mechili, weeping for Greater Germany.

Drama at Mechili

Throughout the desert south of the mountains, everything bearing
German markings was making for the desert fort.

North of the mountains the situation had become reasonably clear;
Benghazi had been taken. The British, in the course of their disengagement, had set fire to a few more supply depots.

On a road strewn with wrecks stood a Panzer III, another straggler
from the 5th Regiment. From the turret the twenty-year-old gunner
Werner Fenck yelled "Hohenecker!" His comrade, Hohenecker, had
somewhat irresponsibly gone off around a corner, perhaps to have a
pee.

But the call had remarkable results, because it was repeated from a
neighboring house in a foreign accent, at first tentatively and then more
and more loudly in unison, until happy and excited Arabs were danc-

ing around the Panzer with hands held high, all shouting "Hohenecker!"

They had evidently taken the word to signify peaceful intentions and the call ran around the town like wildfire.

But Hohenecker himself turned up, looking somewhat sheepish: The commander of a scout car, too, was looking dubiously down at some Arabs grinning at him and roaring: "Hohenecker!"

Around Mechili the situation would also have struck people as rather funny—had they been prepared to overlook the fact that a few thousand people there were trying to kill each other.

Rommel's unorthodox methods of procuring fuel had sufficed to keep only the wheeled vehicles of Streich's combat group more or less mobile. The fuel-guzzling Panzers kept running dry. So it came about that Streich eventually reached the Mechili area with a small force, the heaviest armament of which consisted of a couple of little 20 mm self-propelled twin cannon.

Meanwhile, aerial reconnaissance yielded the information that an enemy force numbering some thousands, and accompanied by many vehicles, was assembled at the desert fort. Late in the afternoon on 6 April, the tireless Rommel landed his Storch near Streich. He sent the divisional commander off to find Lieutenant Colonel von Schwerin's group, which was also approaching without armor. He himself tried to round up the artillery of the Italian Ariete Division, which was supposed to be somewhere to the west.

Since his own search remained fruitless, all he could do to Streich, who also returned empty-handed, was to give him a black look. To complete the job, he flew off again westward to give a mighty prod to the Panzer commander, Colonel Olbrich, who had got stuck with the bulk of his regiment—partly because they were out of fuel and partly because the terrain was not negotiable by vehicles.

Next day, Schwerin turned up, having "done a small recce." In addition, there was even a reinforced battalion of Bersaglieri, one Ariete battery of artillery, and to top it all—sweet music to Streich's ears—there was the rattle and squeak of Panzer tracks: It was Panzer Major Bolbrinker with the remainder of the 1st Detachment, 5th Regiment. And a very odd-looking lot they were: Seven little Panzer IIs flocked around a mighty Panzer IV like chickens around a mother hen. The big Panzer, black as hell and without any camouflage paint (no time for that in Tripoli), loomed all the larger over them.

In command of the monster was Lieutenant Albrecht Zorn; it was the only one in his company to come unscathed through the tank track-destroying stone desert south of the mountain. The sun sank, and on the gentle hills around Mechili sat this scratch force facing the fort,

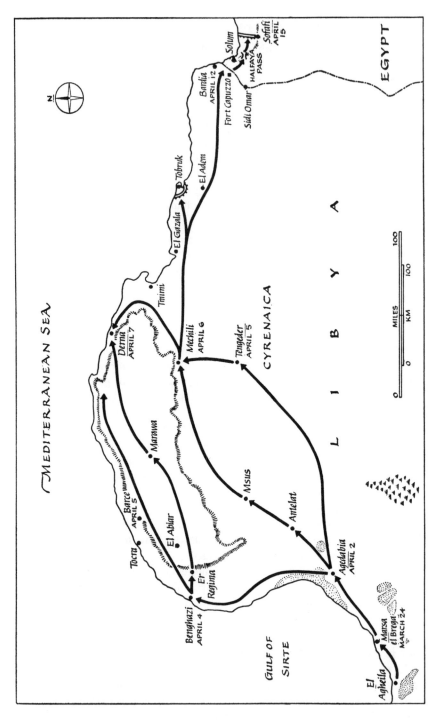

Blitz through Cyrenaica: April 1941

with its towers rising over a defensive wall. The restless commander jumped from his Storch: "Tomorrow we attack, Streich!"

Even before the engines of Zorn's Panzer and of the "chickens" around it had warmed up on the morning of 8 April, the defenders had also woken from their torpor: At first light, they formed their vehicles into a column. Major Bolbrinker did not bother with them, but, as arranged, directed his attack at the fort.

Zorn's monster thundered on a zigzag course among the infantry positions; his radio operator amused himself by firing his machine gun and, from time to time, throwing egg grenades out of the open turret hatch. Small-arms fire rattled on the flanks. There was a lengthy holdup somewhere; meanwhile, one could see all sorts of vehicles racing around in the fort itself.

As the Panzers at long last got going again, they saw at right angles to the direction of their advance a *wadi* turned into an anti-tank ditch with blocks. Behind the ditch stood one of the little anti-tank guns, the shells of which bounced off the mighty bows of Zorn's tank. He stopped to fire a high-explosive shell toward it and immediately gave his order to the driver: "Over we go!"

In the excitement of the moment, the driver made a small mistake: he forgot that with the modern transmission of the Panzer IV the lower gear had to be preselected before being engaged. So, as the machine crept over the wadi, it stood for maddening seconds with its floor plate sticking up at an angle, instead of tilting immediately over the edge with all the power of low gear and resuming its progress. He felt dazed as the direct hit crashed through the thin floor plate, smashing his left leg. The turret hatch has fallen on my head, he thought woozily. He got out somehow and slid over the stern. To cap it all, he burned his back on the hot exhaust.

Only then did he notice that his leg was dangling about in his trouser leg without any feeling. Some Panzer IIs drove past him at speed, pausing to fire across the wadi. To one side, he saw Indian infantrymen climb out of their foxholes and run away.

The commander of the vehicle maintenance unit, who had been watching the battle through a telescope, alerted a field surgeon and thus saved Zorn from bleeding to death. The rest of the crew were all dead.

Cyrenaica is "denuded"

On the night of 9 April all hell broke loose in Mersa Matruh. The little huddle of white houses—once a fashionable coastal resort for the well-to-do of Cairo, given extra glamour by the fact that Antony and

Cleopatra had bathed there in their day—was buzzing with rumors about the might and speed of the German advance.

Covered in dust, tall Bedford trucks were rolling in from the west. Each driver, unshaven and hollow-eyed, looked as if for a long time he had taken his foot off the accelerator only to refill the tank.

Lieutenant Tim Llewellyn-Palmer of the 7th Hussars, younger brother of the chicken-owning KDG captain, looked around with a shrug. He had come from the Delta with an advance guard of his regiment's B-Squadron. They were supposed to cover the Libyan border with a hastily assembled force of Mark VI "light" tanks—two machine guns, maximum armor thickness of 15 mm but an 88 hp motor capable of 56 kmph. It promised to be an unpleasant, wearisome, and dry job. Palmer made for the bar of the Hotel Hillier with a purposeful air.

On the dusty airfield, mechanics were loading huge crates onto lorries.

"Hello, Tim! Great to see you," said a little man in shorts, covered in dust from his shoes to his sparse hair; only his freshly polished monocle glinted in his finely chiseled face. It was General Sir Archibald P. Wavell, Commander in Chief, Middle East.

"Be a good lad, Tim. Run along and get me a plane. Mine's just crashed in the desert." The C-in-C seemed to find this funny. In any event, Tim found a Flying Officer who promised to rustle up an aircraft reserved for VIPs. It would take some time.

The young lieutenant went back to Wavell, who was not only his Commander in Chief but also a fatherly friend to the Palmer brothers.[5]

"I've just come from Tobruk," the general said. "Everything seems okay there. A squadron of Matildas is on its way to the fortress. We'll hold the place."

To Palmer it seemed that this was the first sensible word he had heard about the situation in the past week. The fifty-eight-year-old general seemed neither tired nor nervous. He was already noted for his "staying power" in difficult situations.

"Sorry I can't stay here," Wavell continued coolly, "but I'm off to Greece in a hurry. Things aren't going too well there either. Pity we had to start that business, when the Germans were already on their way to Africa."

The general seemed to be thinking back a few weeks. At that time, after the Italians had been driven from Cyrenaica, he had stood at the

---

[5] Four Llewellyn-Palmers were officers: Julian, Wavell's ADC, lost his life in a Stuka attack near Sollum. Peter was killed in 1942 in the Allied landing in Madagascar. Tony was until recently the Regimental Colonel of the Dragoons; and Tim, a retired colonel, died in 1978 in Wiltshire, where he had a country property.

summit of his career. His Prime Minister in London seemed to think him capable of anything. It should have been a warning to him.

In fact, the mischief had begun earlier—the Italians were still sitting in Tobruk when Churchill signaled Wavell on 10 January 1941: "Nothing must hamper the capture of Tobruk; but thereafter all operations in Libya are subordinated to aiding Greece. . . . We expect and require prompt and active compliance with our decisions, for which we bear full responsibility."

At this time, agents had reported steadily growing German troop concentrations in Romania. Churchill had been convinced that Hitler would send them through Bulgaria to Greece, to come to the aid of his Italian allies, who were being pressed hard in Albania. In that eventuality the Prime Minister had been absolutely determined to help Britain's ally, Greece.

Wavell, on the other hand, had supposed—at that time almost entirely correctly—that the threatening deployment belonged more to the sphere of psychological warfare, especially since he was loath to forgo the opportunity to put the Italians off Egypt once and for all.

Churchill and the chiefs of staff had reluctantly agreed to continue the chase, but hardly had Benghazi been taken and El Agheila reached, when a fresh cable arrived: Churchill wrote glumly that he would have been quite content with making a safe flank for Egypt at Tobruk. But since things had gone this far, "you should . . . make yourself secure in Benghazi and concentrate all available forces in the Delta in preparation for a movement to Europe."

Yet the Prime Minister was aware that with his limited forces Wavell could not throw back an energetic German thrust in Greece. His reasons for—in his own words—"transferring to Greece the fighting portion of the army which has defended Egypt" were political.

In the Balkans, Romania, Hungary, and Bulgaria now stood unequivocally in the Axis camp, and only Yugoslavia and Turkey remained to be recruited as possible allies, or at least to be persuaded not to join the enemy coalition. But if Britain left Greece in the lurch, even this hope would be gone. A successful resistance, on the other hand, "might even pull in both Turks and Yugoslavs," Churchill wrote. (With political hindsight he was certainly right, as events were to show; even more right than he himself could have guessed at the time, despite the fact that Turkey would not let herself be "pulled in." With military hindsight, Britain's forces in the Middle and Near East were utterly overstretched, especially since Wavell had not only to hold the desert flank at El Agheila and fight against superior Italian forces in East Africa and Eritrea, but he had also been instructed to occupy Rhodes—an Italian possession since 1924—"as soon as possible" for use as an air base.)

Churchill's later contention that he had known nothing about the weakening of the desert flank, and had issued no orders that would have brought it about, was very far from the truth and grossly unfair to Wavell, who was in any case doing his willing and uncomplaining best to satisfy his headstrong political master. The Foreign Secretary, Eden, whom Churchill had sent to the Mediterranean with the Chief of the Imperial General Staff to expedite his plans for Greece, reported quite unambiguously to London on 20 February: "General Wavell proposes the following military dispositions: Cyrenaica will be garrisoned by one of the less trained and equipped Australian divisions; the Indian Motor Brigade, at present under training; and one armored brigade group which is all that remains of the 7th Armored Division.[6] You will remember that this division was never at full strength."

This was noted in London without comment, since it also tallied with the instructions once more confirmed by the chiefs of staff: to hold the desert flank with the "minimum possible forces."

The first British army units landed in Greece on 7 March. London had urged that the shipments should be speeded up in every possible way. The transports and warships of the British Mediterranean Fleet were plying busily backward and forward. Ironically, the principal obstacle to the departure of the troops from Egypt was the Germans, who kept mining the Suez Canal.

The code breakers of "Ultra"

Wavell, who at the end of a comprehensive report to London as recently as 2 March had come to the conclusion that no major attack from Tripolitania was to be expected before late summer, became anxious later in March. What disturbed him was information coming from the most secret source of the Second World War; so secret that only in the mid-seventies were reports about it allowed to leak out.[7]

These reports, after an interval of more than thirty years, are changing the history of the war, throwing light onto some dark areas and sweeping away some well-established myths. One such myth is the "Italian betrayal," eagerly trotted out in almost every account of the war in Africa.

The higher and very highest staff echelons of the German Wehr-

---

[6] Actually the 2nd Armored Division, just out from Britain. The 7th, as indicated, had been ordered back to the Delta after the winter campaign.

[7] *The Ultra Secret,* by Group Captain Frederick Winterbotham, one of Britain's most important intelligence officers. See also Anthony Cave Brown: *Die unsichtbare Front (Bodyguard of Lies,* London, 1976), an excellent and comprehensive account of the work of the intelligence services on both sides.

macht used a machine named Enigma to encode radio messages. The apparatus contained a number of cylinders, which could be turned in relation to each other and contained all the letters of the alphabet. Before a message "in clear" was fed in, the drums were turned according to a predetermined key. Provided the recipient of a radio signal knew how the cylinders were set at the transmitting end, his appropriately programmed Enigma receiver would turn the *macédoine* of letters into a clear text, and at lightning speed. Governed by the program, the drums would simply turn back to the original positions.

The principle was no great secret: A German firm, which had bought the patent from a Dutchman through intermediaries, had offered Enigma in the 1920s to the embassies of the industrialized countries in Berlin. That the Wehrmacht had taken this system over was soon discovered by the Polish, French, and British secret services. The Poles and French had even managed to get hold of an original Enigma machine in the thirties. But that alone did them no good. The fact that the cylinders could be turned against one another at random meant that there was a virtually limitless number of possible combinations. Even the manufacturer of the first primitive Enigma model, which was offered for sale for encoding industrial secrets, could credibly claim that you would have to calculate day and night for forty-two thousand years before you had gone through all the possible combinations and made sense of the hodgepodge.

When, on one occasion, the Western allies were briefly able to tap a secret service source for the key in use at that moment, it did not get them much farther forward: The source dried up, a few small cylinders were given a turn one way and others the other way, and the worldwide network of aerials the British secret service had set up once again received nothing but an incomprehensible jumble of letters and numbers.

And then the predecessors of computers—the tools which have rightly been called the wonders of our century—took a hand in the story.

Although Britain had before the war neglected its armaments in the worst possible way (and had even treated a very early pioneer of jet engines[8] abominably), she had nevertheless made several investments in the technology of the future, such as radio navigation, radar, atomic energy, and the beginnings of computer technology. And while in Germany the first inventor of a computer landed in an asylum in the thirties, British scientists succeeded in developing a machine which could

[8] Although Frank Whittle was knighted after the Second World War, he had earlier been hampered in putting his idea into practice to such an extent that his book in places reads like a parody; see *Jet: the Story of a Pioneer*, London, 1953.

actually perform the rapid series of calculations necessary to ungarble the scramblings of the Enigma transmitting machine.

It was christened the "Bomb" and was installed at a secret establishment at Bletchley Park. The code-breaking operation as a whole had the cover name Ultra. When in 1940 the "Bomb" was for the first time fed with reports encoded by Enigma, it was still far from fully developed. At first it would "find" the chosen combination only occasionally and fortuitously. Scientists burrowed in the maze of wires inside the huge copper box. Slowly, their results improved. In the years following the summer of 1942, hardly a single important signal escaped Ultra. But the code crackers also supplied some vital information as early as the Battle of Britain and during the sinking of the German battleship *Bismarck*.

It was naturally vital for the British to keep the existence of Ultra a secret. Among the very few who were in the secret was Sir Archibald Wavell in Cairo. And in his case it was soon apparent that a code half-cracked, in combination with an unusual and capricious opponent, could be a considerable handicap.

Group Captain Winterbotham, head of the operation, remembers exactly how Churchill himself had personally questioned him as to when German troops would be arriving in Africa. He was able to hand him the text of the radio signals in which the OKH had briefed Rommel: The 5th Light Division would arrive in April, and the 15th Panzer Division in May.

This information, which was immediately communicated to Wavell, must have substantially contributed to the denuding of the desert flank, with its unfortunate consequences. It must also have contributed to the disbelief with which the KDG's reports about the presence of German troops were received.

Presumably, the "Bomb" had decoded some earlier messages, but not the later ones.[9] To which must be added the unpredictability of Rommel: thanks to his "direct line" to Hitler via the latter's personal ADC, Schmundt, he managed to have his transport arrangements speeded up without the need for radio signals. And then there was his habit of acting without consulting his superiors. . . . No wonder Wavell had been caught on the wrong foot. Only after his optimistic situation report of 2 March (into which Churchill, despite his own knowledge of the reasons for it, later took care to rub his nose) did Wavell find out through Ultra that Germans must after all be presumed present in Tripolitania. On 20 March he advised London that he was worried about the possibility of an attack, since the dead-flat country

[9] For instance, it was at one time planned to send a German division first to Albania and only then to ship the Afrika Korps to Africa.

south of Benghazi offered no suitable blocking positions. Churchill, the man responsible for the bloodletting on the desert flank, six days later pretended innocence in his reply: "I presume you are only waiting for the tortoise to stick his head out far enough before chopping it off. . . ."

Wavell's answer on 27 March, three days after the occupation of El Agheila, strongly suggests that the Commander in Chief was inadequately informed, despite the fact that the KDG's detailed reports from the border are on record:

> No evidence yet that there are many Germans at El Agheila;[10] probably mainly Italians with small stiffening of Germans. . . .
> Have to admit to having taken considerable risk in Cyrenaica after capture of Benghazi in order to provide maximum support to Greece. . . .
> 7th Armored Division returned to Cairo and, since it has no reserve tanks, must await repairs, which will take time. . . . My main difficulty is transport.

At this time, Wavell had sent 59,000 men and 8,000 vehicles to Greece.

The lack of transport in Cyrenaica soon assumed catastrophic proportions. The Luftwaffe had completely wrecked the harbor at Benghazi so that no more supplies could be unloaded there.

Only in Tobruk, 320 kilometers away by road, was material being put ashore. And the organization was in general so poor that two expensive trucks, sent out with a long list of spares wanted, returned days later with one speedometer cable.

Things were no better when it came to communications equipment. The units leaving for Greece naturally had priority for radio equipment. There were not even enough field telephones in Cyrenaica. Staff officers had to rely more and more on the Benghazi civilian telephone network built by the Italians. Every unit would send out "salvage parties" whose job was supposed to be to recover radio equipment out of wrecked Italian tanks. But in most cases not a squeak was to be got out of any Italian set.

The backbone of the British armored force was made up of Carro Armato M-13s captured in working condition or capable of being repaired. By the time the German attack began, the crews of these tin cans had hardly had time to familiarize themselves with them; what they did have time to discover was that after ten to twelve minutes' run-

---

[10] The intelligence service had not been able to provide much more about their GOC, Rommel, than that he had shown himself to be "an impetuous person" in France.

ning, their engines hopelessly overheated. There were in any case only thirty of them; and most of these Italian tanks simply ground to a halt in the first stages of the retreat.

The 2nd Armored Division arrived in the Western Desert in a somewhat depleted state: Wavell had immediately diverted one regiment to Greece. The remainder of the division's somewhat worn-out vehicles had to cover the journey from the railhead at Mersa Matruh to the Agedabia area on their own tracks and wheels. The Cruiser Mark-II-A13 tanks simply collapsed on the way. Hardly wonders of mechanical reliability in any case, they were by now so worn out that all any technical officer could say was: "It's not worth putting new engines in—the transmissions, drive shafts, and tracks are done for anyway." By the end of March not one of the thirty tanks was mobile, let alone fit for action.

Wavell later said that he did not know the state this "fresh" division was in; at least not when he ordered back to the Delta the 7th Armored Division, which after eight months of uninterrupted action was certainly entitled to a rest and refit. The Cruisers of the 7th, too, had to trundle the 650 kilometers of road back to Mersa Matruh on their own tracks. It was without doubt an enormous waste. Churchill later held Wavell responsible for this, but he ignored the fundamental problem: If you want effective military performance by mechanized forces in this kind of country, you have got to provide them with mobile maintenance units—like those the Afrika Korps had. Wavell would in any case have been out of his mind had he transferred his inadequate and immobile repair capacity to the remote desert exclusively with the 7th Division in mind, without any regard for his other theaters of war.

A particular shortcoming was that the commanders in the field did not make enough fuss, soon enough and loud enough. On the other hand, they hardly had any opportunity. For Lieutenant General Philip Neame—a highly decorated soldier and a VC, but without desert experience, who moreover did not take over the Cyrenaica command until the end of February—found that he had neither an adequate staff nor even the barest communications facilities. And Major General Gambier-Parry, Commander of the 2nd Armored Division, was freshly out of England.

One general, however, did make some fuss, but his voice did not (at first) count for much. He was Major General L. J. Morshead, Commander of the 9th Australian Infantry Division. By the end of February, only one brigade of his Diggers had arrived, with pitifully few anti-tank weapons and machine guns. In addition, he wrote to Wavell in Cairo, the area provided "no more obstacles than a billiard table" and was therefore not the best place for nonmotorized infantry.

The Australian's energies, however, were soon diverted into a vehement quarrel with Neame. The point at issue was the peculiar interpretation the rough diamonds from the South Seas gave to discipline. This was hard enough to bear anyway for an officer of His Britannic Majesty, but was nevertheless tolerated with a grin by everyone who had seen the Australians in action (as had also been the case in the First World War). But Neame was evidently not one of these, for as late as 31 March, when the German attack was already in progress, he took the time to send Morshead a long letter: "I must bring to your attention that there have been further instances of Australian drunkenness in Benghazi. An inebriated Australian soldier even came into my own HQ. . . . Words fail me to express my disgust. . . . Your division will not become a useful instrument of war until you improve discipline. . . ." And so on for several pages.

Morshead therefore wrote back as good as he got, to the effect that he would not put up with this anti-Australian attitude. In his diary he noted: "Take the case of the Australian soldier who walked into the officers' mess, Barce. He was with two British soldiers. Whatever happened to them?" But such problems gave way to more serious ones.

After the breakthrough by the Germans toward Agedabia, Neame acted in accordance with a written directive by Wavell, issued on 26 March, when the imbalance of the forces of the desert flank began to dawn on him. Neame, Wavell had written, should be particularly careful to keep his forces intact and should not regard any particular piece of ground as vital. "Even should the enemy reoccupy Benghazi, it would be of minimal military significance, despite the propaganda and prestige value; and we should on no account risk defeat just to hold Benghazi."

Neame thereupon held Gambier-Parry on a tight rein: He was not to employ his tanks in any counterattack without explicit authorization. In view of the highly inadequate communications available, this was hardly wise and may well have been responsible for the infantry being left without armored support at the decisive moment in the Marsa el Brega gap. The Cruisers and M-13s accordingly did little more than follow confused orders to retreat, and suffered mechanical breakdowns on the way.

The 6th Royal Tank Regiment (the one with the Italian tanks), for instance, received orders on 4 April to join up with its support group[11] but could establish neither its whereabouts nor radio frequency. Two days later, while the sole surviving squadron was observing the mandatory break to allow its boiling engines to cool down, it came under—

---

[11] The infantry and artillery components of an armored division.

fortunately rather inaccurate—fire from an easterly direction. This "greeting" came from the 5th Royal Tank Regiment, which had received orders to treat all vehicles to its west as hostile.

Wavell, to whom the general confusion was no secret, flew to Barce to see Neame. He brought with him General O'Connor, who had experience of the desert. O'Connor was a diminutive and peppery Irishman. The idea was to hand the Cyrenaica command over to O'Connor; but the latter thought it would be better if he acted only as adviser to Neame. The problem was to organize the type of retreat Wavell had had in mind in his 26 March orders: not to run away pell-mell, but to maintain contact with the enemy and to do him as much damage as possible. But this intention had come to nothing—and not merely because of the catastrophic state of communications. Once the reins slip from your hands in a rearward movement, they are difficult to seize again. The opinion had spread through the British units that the Germans were simply unstoppable.

However, it also became evident that the Australians' total lack of respect was not directed only at His Majesty's corps of officers. An enemy with a roar like thunder tended to make them rather stubborn too.

The few serious engagements in these early days of April included the battle for the slopes east of Benghazi where Lieutenant Sandrock's Panzer company had its unpleasant experience with the salt lakes and the mines.

Three companies of General Morshead's 9th Division, reinforced by four pieces of artillery, held these positions for a day against the reinforced 3rd Reconnaissance Unit of Lieutenant Colonel Freiherr von Wechmar.

Morshead's group, which was considered badly trained,[12] made up for its lack of equipment by courage. When the artillery packed up, the heaviest piece remaining was a small captured Italian mortar, served by its crew, under Sergeant McLaughlin, in a somewhat unorthodox manner: The thing was pretty useless for a start and recoiled so mightily each time it was fired that one Aussie, as strong as an ox, would hold the barrel down and another would lie on the ground plate. To put the Germans, who were so used to winning, off their stroke, the Australians even mounted a counterattack, firing from the hip like cowboys. The 3rd Reconnaissance Unit's war diary speaks of bitter hand-to-hand fighting.

The bulk of the three companies was able to disengage themselves from the enemy under cover of darkness and to withdraw into the

[12] See Eden's telegram, p. 48.

mountains to the east. There the British found a column of trucks driven by Cypriots, with which they drove through the burning town of Barce, taking up positions on the slopes beyond it. An isolated unit of twenty-five men missed the rendezvous but nevertheless fought its way through on foot as far as Gazala. The roads and paths in between were in German hands. The unit broke up. Only one man came through: On the night of 10 May, the twenty-two-year-old Private P. H. Jenkins staggered half unconscious into one of the outposts of the fortress of Tobruk.

On the evening of 6 April confusion reigned supreme in Cyrenaica. Neame, O'Connor, and Morshead met in Maraua. Communications with Gambier-Parry's 2nd Armored Division had broken down. Positive news was available only from the tough Australians east of Barce, who had shot up some units feeling their way farther forward. Aerial reconnaissance had meanwhile shown unambiguously that the Germans were so mad as to advance across the desert south of the mountains in several columns. Would it still be possible to establish a defense line from Gazala to Mechili?

Morshead drove ahead and passed Derna shortly before the spearhead of the 8th Machine Gun Battalion under Lieutenant Colonel Ponath got there. Neame and O'Connor wanted to avoid Derna and go direct to Tmimi. But in the darkness their driver took the wrong track. The two generals, having dozed off with exhaustion, woke up to find that someone had held their car up and had the cheek to shine a torch into it. Before O'Connor, who had just about had enough anyway, could utter a damn-and-blast, he recognized the foreign-looking tropical headgear. They had been taken prisoner.

Only a stone's throw away was Derna airfield and immediately behind it the road, which turns southward from the town at this point and again climbs the steep flank of the escarpment. There, a broad river of vehicles was that night still streaming along the steep road, built here as elsewhere to a superb standard by the Italians. They were making for Tmimi-Tobruk; and of course no one had any way of knowing that quite close at hand a group of exhausted Germans, half dead with thirst, was holding captive the two most important generals this side of the Nile.

The few units which were still moving in good order included the King's Dragoon Guards, with their Marmon-Harringtons which, under their unprepossessing exteriors, must evidently have had hearts of gold, for they kept going, come hell or high water.

Most of the reconnaissance-car men had just reached the peak when Ponath's little outfit attempted to advance across the airfield toward the road. Hastily, Regimental HQ organized a "defense party," joined by some gunners who happened to be passing with their 25-pounders and anti-tank guns. It immediately became evident that the enemy was very weak. Only Lieutenant Whetherly, reconnoitering southward, had to clear off in a hurry when he ran into some well-aimed fire from a 37 mm anti-tank gun. However, he got away without a scratch.

Meanwhile, the bulk of Ponath's combat group had arrived on the other side of the airfield. Any British vehicle, like that of the two generals, that turned up along the desert track was "bagged" by the Germans and directed into the "prisoners' gorge." The bag included a complete field hospital in which German and British medical staffs looked jointly after the wounded of both sides.

In the afternoon, the 5th Royal Tank Regiment, now down to seven Cruisers, was trying to climb from Derna up to the summit of the pass. The going was too tough for three of the Cruisers; they had to be blown up. The remaining four were destroyed later, in the course of an attempted counterattack on the Ponath group. Meanwhile the last stragglers had passed Derna. Sappers blew up supplies and a stretch of the pass road. The KDG too had passed through. The order now was: Everybody into Tobruk!

The decision had been made in Cairo. In the presence of the Foreign Secretary, Eden, and of the Chief of the Imperial General Staff, Sir John Dill, Wavell had taken counsel with Admiral Cunningham, Commander of the Navy's Middle East Fleet, and with the RAF commander, Longmore: Can we at least hold Tobruk?

Cunningham's contribution was decisive. He thought that despite other commitments he could supply the fortress from the sea.

Wavell stopped all ship movements to Greece. An entire Australian infantry division was ready to sail.

The next morning he woke to the news that Neame and O'Connor were presumed captured. Wavell himself flew to Tobruk to confer with Morshead, whose Diggers were already clearing out sand-clogged anti-tank ditches, mending barbed-wire obstacles, and laying mines. Wavell behaved coolly, although the knowledge that he had made a grave mistake, even if under pressure of his supreme commander, must have weighed heavily on him at this time.

However, after a short discussion with Morshead, he saw a glimmer of hope.

Morshead, as was the general rule in the Australian army, was a true "citizen general,"[13] head of a department in a Sydney shipping firm.

---

[13] As a rule professional officers did only the staff work; field commanders were supposed to be recruited only from among civilians promoted on merit. It was therefore taken for granted among Australians that they had, as it were, an "antimilitarist army."

With his swarthy southern complexion and his slight figure, Leslie Morshead in no way fitted the general picture of a giant from the Australian outback; but he was nevertheless a much-decorated veteran of the First World War, who had commanded a battalion in France when only twenty-five. His quiet decisiveness had won him the respect of the collection of individualists he was leading who, for some reason, called him "Ming the Merciless."

One brigade of the 9th Division had been in Tobruk for some weeks and the rest were coming back from the west, in good order, even if they were doing so in the most amazing vehicles. One group of the 20th Infantry Brigade—the one which, according to Neame, would "never be a useful instrument of war"—had, after heavy fighting in the course of the retreat, improvised for itself a trailer outfit consisting of one sound truck and a shell-holed Italian ten-tonner which had lost its sides and which accommodated all of them. The Diggers were hanging on to it, clinging to each other, clutching their rifles, and giving the impression of being amazed and annoyed. They referred to the retreat in the jargon of the racecourse as the "Benghazi–Tobruk Handicap."

It looked as though Tobruk had been taken over by a very reliable but somewhat unusual force. And more healthy units were arriving on the road from Derna: the Dragoons with their reconnaissance cars, several batteries of the trusty 25-pounders. From the Delta, a brigade of the 7th Australian Division—the one Wavell had stopped from embarking for Greece—was under way. In addition, there were all the AA artillery, field artillery, Matildas and Cruisers that could be scraped together in the depots and workshops.

A crash-landing in the desert

There was a sandstorm blowing when Wavell's two-engined Lockheed Lodestar taxied out for takeoff on the sandy airfield at Tobruk. The first thing that happened was that one of the brakes started binding; the general had to get out.

At last they could start but after a few minutes' flight, the oil pressure in one of the two engines fell to zero. The pilot landed in the desert. A Hurricane came to a halt next to them: Flight Lieutenant Storrar had spotted the C-in-C's machine on the ground. He gave a hand with cleaning out the filter. The Lodestar took off again, but this time Storrar's machine would not start. He had to walk back to Tobruk.

The Lodestar, however, flew barely a quarter of an hour before the oil pressure fell again.

The sun had sunk behind the horizon with true African speed. The pilot tried to continue on one engine; but it, too, was beginning to overheat. When the oil-temperature needle was well into the red, the pilot set about making a landing, which would have succeeded splendidly had not the ubiquitous sand caused one of the brakes to bind again. The machine skidded; the port wing and tail were torn off. With notable sang-froid, Wavell suggested they should first of all brew up some tea. However, when car headlights appeared in the distance, he withdrew into the desert as a precaution and burned his secret papers. But it was only a British desert patrol, which took him to Sollum. There, Wavell rang his HQ in Cairo, where his staff officers had given up all hope, since the machine was six hours overdue.

Late at night Wavell reached the airfield at Mersa Matruh. As he was bidding Tim Llewellyn-Palmer good-bye, he said with a smile: "Make sure you get to the frontier before the Germans."

Evidently he did not yet know that on the previous day a last heavy blow had been dealt his desert army at Mechili.

Mechili: the other side

Captain Charles Armitage of the Royal Horse Artillery (RHA)[14] was enjoying his leave in Cairo.

Since the campaign against the Italians, the young officer had a reputation as an outstanding tactician and the only thing that could harm his career was unfriendly treatment by the enemy.

The campaign had begun like this: Armitage's unit had been exactly a fortnight in the desert when it all began. As a rule the Italian positions would be attacked on the same well-tried system: While the Matildas made a frontal break-in with the infantry, the fast but thin-skinned Cruisers of the 7th Armored Division would make a left hook through the desert to cut off the enemy's retreat.

Armitage and his half battery of four guns were attached to the 8th Hussars. In their first attack, they were supposed to reach the coastal road to Sollum in the neighborhood of Buq Buq.

The Hussars kept up a cracking pace in the rough country. Armitage, who was with the vanguard, noted to his chagrin that his guns, towed by four-wheeled tractors, were being left farther and farther behind.

When the Italian positions on the far side of the road came into view, the commander of the tank said to him: "Okay, old boy, give 'em

---

[14] Despite their modern transport, the RHA were still so called to distinguish them from the Field Artillery, which was generally used for infantry support, while the RHA worked with armored units. The difference soon vanished and the RHA, following the example of the field artillery, had its strength raised from 16 to 24 guns for the regiment.

hell with your guns! We're going in now." He did not show the least inclination to wait for the guns. Armitage, who had been assessing the
Italian artillery positions through his field glasses, knew that his thinly
armored wards, unlike the Matildas, would get into bad trouble if they
attacked without artillery preparation.

In the end, the Hussars gave him five minutes. Over the radio, Armitage established that his No. 1 Troop was nine kilometers behind them.
With a range of hardly more than 10 kilometers, the thing could just
about be done. So he called for a salvo, just to see where the things
landed. Alas! There was nothing to be seen. Meanwhile, the Italians
were also firing, so there was just as little to hear as to see amid the
noise of battle. A second salvo, fired at maximum elevation, produced
no result either. "We can't be shooting that short," thought Armitage
despondently and ordered: "Down 400!"

The shell landed right in the middle of the enemy emplacements. Armitage got his gunners to fire away for all they were worth, and in the
end it looked like a splendidly planned affair: When the Hussars raced
through the Italians' battery positions, the survivors had their noses in
the sand. Not one Cruiser was lost. Some thousands of prisoners were
taken. The commander of the Hussars reported over the radio that he
had "reached the second B in Buq Buq"—a remark that so amused
Churchill that he put it in his memoirs. Armitage naturally saw no
reason to spread around the finer details of his achievement as a
gunner, and from then on he was known as a monstrously clever chap.

Working with the Hussars, they arrived at Agedabia. The 7th Armored Division was pulled back; the gunners had to remain up front.
Leave was being granted generously. What could happen anyway? The
regimental commander drove to Cairo. Captain Armitage followed by
thumbing a lift, for the shortage of transport was already becoming noticeable.

The black monster

When news of the German advance reached Cairo in April, Armitage ran his CO to earth at Shepheard's Hotel just as he was getting
ready to leave. They collected a few of their men and rustled up a
truck for them. They drove off to the west, the CO's staff car leading
the way. Beyond Tobruk they came upon crowds of people streaming
to the rear; someone told them that their regiment was on its way to
Mechili.

They therefore turned left. The desert track to the south was empty.
There was a sandstorm. Once, the driving clouds of sand parted and,
like a creature from another world, a small, long-legged aircraft bear-

ing a swastika on its tail fin flew across the road at a right angle 30 meters ahead of them. Under the high wings they could distinctly see two men in the cockpit. They threw themselves on the seats and grabbed their rifles, but the cloud of sand again closed like a curtain between them and the aircraft. Today one can be certain that what they saw was the GOC of the German Afrika Korps in his Fieseler Storch.

In the Mechili area there was a swarm of vehicles and men. The colonel went to see General Gambier-Parry, who had no idea what his 2nd Armored Division, or what was left of it, was actually doing.

The supply columns were in Mechili, but he did not know where to send them. The general suggested that the gunners should stay with him until there was some more precise information. That was on the afternoon of 6 April. When they looked around next morning, the appearance of the gently undulating desert had changed greatly for the worse: Everywhere, but concentrated more particularly around the tracks leading to the south and east, enemy vehicles stood, scattered in loose groups.

As the day went by, the impression grew that the other side did not know what they were supposed to be doing either. Their numbers did not seem all that great, whereas in Mechili there was the whole of the 3rd Indian Motor Brigade—only lightly armed and hardly trained at all, but after all comprising more than two thousand men. The rest of the picture was rather bleak: a couple of pieces of artillery, masses of vehicles scattered all over the place, and a single Cruiser Mark-II-A13 tank, belonging to Gambier-Parry's Divisional HQ. In fact, this solitary vehicle was by the evening of 7 April the only tank of the entire 2nd Armored Division, the last four having been destroyed by the 8th Machine Gun Battalion over at Derna.

It was an eerie, unreal sort of a day: The two hostile camps seemed to be staring at each other as if hypnotized. Occasionally, sounds of battle would come from somewhere in fits and starts; sometimes a machine gun would fire from the other side, the spent bullets hitting the sand harmlessly.

In the evening, the little aircraft could be seen circling again, eventually flying off to the west. Nobody suspected that it contained the enemy GOC, in a distinctly gloomy mood, who was trying to move some heavy weapons up from his units that were floundering about somewhere in the rough country.

Gambier-Parry, too, was waiting for reinforcements. He had managed to establish intermittent contact with HQ Cyrenaica, to discover that nothing was known about his 3rd Brigade (the two regiments, with their Cruisers and the Italian M-13s). Just as the light was fading, the little aircraft landed again over on the other side.

There was a noise of engines roaring and tracks rattling. Gambier-Parry decided to break out the following morning.

The gunners had also heard the noise of the Panzers. They saw six armored vehicles and a frightening, vast, pitch-black thing with a short, fat barrel that made a most demoralizing impression on them.[15]

The morning of 8 April dawned. Right from the start, everything went wrong. The solitary Cruiser did not turn up at the agreed rendezvous. A squadron of the 3rd Motor Brigade went roaring away on its own, found itself in the middle of a battery of the Italian Ariete division, and charged the terrified gunners with bayonets. There was quite a massacre, but still the column, although standing ready, did not move.

The infantry disengaged. Unfortunately, the Italian gunners reorganized rapidly after the assault and when the Cruiser came rumbling along, they promptly shot it up. Its entire crew was killed. The column, which consisted almost entirely of "soft" vehicles, now moved off. As it happened, it was making for the HQ of General Streich, who himself seized a rifle. The twin-barreled 20 mm cannon had a more devastating effect: The column swung away.

At the same time, the Germans bore down on the anti-tank emplacement behind the fortified wadi. The Australian Rayner was in command of one of the little two-pounder guns. He saw the great black tank coming straight at him. They fired away, but the shells bounced off without making any impression. As the Panzer tried clumsily to surmount the obstacle, Rayner roared: "Give him one more up the arse!" In the next second, shells from the other Panzers hit the little gun, heavily wounded Rayner in the legs, and killed the rest of the crew—they would never know that they had put the black monster out of action with a direct hit through the floor plate.

The great column stood about in disorder. Shells were exploding between the unprotected trucks and killed or wounded the infantrymen in them. No one followed the law of desert warfare: Even the most pointless movement is better than standing still. Gambier-Parry decided to surrender. But Colonel Williams of the artillery would not hear of giving up.

Captain Armitage saw his boss approaching with a most gloomy expression on his face. He jumped into the car and growled: "Let's get the hell out of here!"

---

[15] Charles Armitage, now a retired brigadier, who farms in Wiltshire, considered right up to the time of his conversation with the author that it was a typically Rommel-style psychological trick not to have Lieutenant Zorn's Panzer IV painted in camouflage colors but to leave it pitch black to make it look more frightening.

Meanwhile, a little column had gathered around them: In addition to the colonel's staff car, there were three trucks with soldiers from their unit. "We'll sneak off toward Benghazi," said the colonel. Benghazi lay to the northwest, where the enemy did not seem much in evidence.

The little column shot away, accelerator pedals on the floor. No one tried to stop them, and after half an hour they paused to look around. Not a soul as far as the eye could see. Nevertheless, their column had been augmented by one vehicle: a three-quarter-tonner, driven by a dark man in glasses, had simply tagged along. He was an Indian doctor from the 3rd Motor Brigade. The back of his truck was piled high with gasoline cans—a welcome guest. "What would I do in captivity?" the doctor asked. "The Germans have the best doctors anyway."

Only a few kilometers farther north lay the rugged spurs of the mountains, furrowed by the wadis which had bitten deep into them— the imprint of the winter's tempestuous rains. At this time of the year, they were full of greenery and brushwood. "We'll go to ground there," said the colonel.

They urged their vehicles as far up one of the wadis as possible and camouflaged them with branches they collected from the brush. There was even a spacious cave, which had evidently served the Bedouin as a shelter for their sheep. At any rate, that's how it smelled. Not that it stopped the colonel from lying down to sleep in it. Armitage was too wrought up for that; to keep busy, he wandered about and inspected the soldiers and vehicles.

Half an hour after sunset they moved off. Armitage warned the drivers not to make any unnecessary noise, and not to rev their engines. He himself took the wheel of the staff car.

They kept to a southerly course, into the desert. Their plan was not to turn east until they had covered a good deal of ground and were safe from enemy vehicles, and then to make for the wire fence between Libya and Egypt. That would be the best aid to navigation in the roadless desert.

There was no moon; the stars were bright. A few of them stood remarkably low on the horizon. But before Armitage could recognize them as the side lights of approaching vehicles, they had virtually run into the Germans.

The British stepped on their accelerators and raced back in a great arc, all lights extinguished. Half a kilometer farther away, they braked and got their weapons ready. But the German column drove by them at speed—evidently they were just as frightened.

Once again, the British set course for the south. Minutes later they had to run for it again, when they met another German column, which luckily wanted to have nothing to do with them either. "Traffic like

Piccadilly Circus," remarked the colonel. The idea that they might turn about was again rejected. Since the place was in any case alive with Germans, it really didn't matter which way they went.

After a bottle of whiskey had been handed around, the future no longer looked quite so bleak. They drove on for another half hour; nothing happened. Suddenly they became aware that they were driving through a German camp. Vehicles stood scattered about; the rugged outlines of heavy trucks could be made out everywhere.

Armitage accelerated, kept to a southerly course and concentrated on not hitting any of the monsters. Not one shot was fired. Were the Germans as frightened as they were? Today one can conclude that they were simply utterly exhausted.

By sunrise, the little column of gunners was a good 25 kilometers south of Mechili and traveling east.

They were frying up a decent breakfast when they heard an engine. It was that long-legged thing with the swastika again.

They ran cursing for their weapons; but the pilot turned away. Not much comfort in that for them: He was bound to have radioed a report. They therefore drove on eastward, as fast as springs and axles could bear.

In the noonday heat they rested, scantily camouflaged by a few camel-thorn bushes. In the afternoon they finally reached the border fence.

At a distance, they saw that some earthworks had been thrown up; a defense position, evidently. That was all they could make out in the heat haze. When you thought about it calmly, one was bound to come to the conclusion that not even those crazy Germans could have come this far. They, therefore, approached. They were still some 500 meters away when white flags suddenly appeared over the spot: They were Egyptians,[16] well-equipped with heavy machine guns and anti-tank guns, but firmly determined not to tangle with any savage infidels—and especially not with any Germans.

Near Sollum, Colonel Williams and his party at last found some British troops. There they heard that Tobruk had been cut off by the Germans and that their regiment was inside the fortress. Days later they boarded a ship in Alexandria, bound for Tobruk. It was not, as they had hoped, a destroyer, but a broken-down old freighter without any shelter from the sun. Says Armitage: "I'm always sick, even when the sea is calm; but on this trip I was too frightened to throw up."

They arrived in Tobruk unmolested, although the ships ahead and astern of them were sunk. At last, on 16 April, they reached their regiment again.

[16] King Farouk's quasi-independent Egypt kept its army during the war; it was never involved in any fighting.

In captivity

The entire 3rd Motor Brigade, General Gambier-Parry, together with his Divisional HQ and many stragglers, were captured in Mechili—two thousand men altogether. However, in addition to the gunners, many other groups had shown that it was possible to break through the weak ring of the German-Italian forces. Most of them ended up in Tobruk. A huge pitch-black cloud hung over Mechili; Gambier-Parry had ordered the fuel dump to be set alight.

The oily plume of smoke showed the way for the German units, both large and small, which were still struggling through the desert—or worse, through a countryside strewn with huge rocks and cleft by wadis and mountain spurs. They included elements of the 2nd Reconnaissance Unit, the 5th Panzer Regiment, and supply convoys which had laboriously repaired their stranded broken-down vehicles. "Let us hope that the great game will succeed. . . ." It was only three days since Rommel had written those words.

It seems that he himself had briefly shuddered at the risk he had taken. His force, far too small anyway, was broken up, and it lacked not just ammunition but almost everything. His trail was marked by vehicles which had broken down or run dry; every isolated group was easy prey for a counterthrust by energetic and concentrated enemy forces.

The British had not yet been decisively beaten; it had not been possible—in the jargon of this blood-soaked trade—to annihilate their "live resources." Rommel had two trumps in this "great game" and he could assess only one of them accurately: the incredible willingness of his men, who obeyed him blindly in a strange and hostile environment, to fight and to make sacrifices. But this would do the trick only if it was played together with the second trump: the British inferiority in weapons, the collapse of their command structure helped by inadequate aerial reconnaissance, the shortage of modern communications equipment and—one may add—the absence of a commanding personality with qualities even remotely equal to Rommel's.

And look who was now transferring his Corps Field HQ to his mini-aircraft! Had there been a generals' trade union, it would have had to expel Rommel.

No rest for the Germans

Rommel did not allow himself or his men any rest after the surprise success of Mechili. Only a moment did he spare to rejoice at the booty which, despite the burning fuel dump, was substantial and highly welcome: particularly the desert-going vehicles of the Indian Motor Brigade, which were now bringing the prisoners to Benghazi into Italian custody (in accordance with an agreement between the German and Italian governments). Immediately afterward, they went straight into service as part of the Afrika Korps' decimated vehicle fleet.

One item of booty was to become a sort of trademark for Rommel in the years to come: the pair of dust goggles, which were to remain immovably fixed to the peak of his cap.

As his ADC has reported in a book,[17] Rommel came upon the goggles when he took possession, for his own and his staff's use, of two enormous, lightly armored vans, fitted with radio and office equipment. Even a general could sometimes take some booty, Rommel remarked, and fixed the goggles on his cap between the eagle carrying the swastika and the peak.

It was still possible to describe the losses on the German side as light, in view of the ground won and the enormous amount of booty. That was of course no consolation to the families of those who lay under a heap of stones in the desert, neatly marked with a cross in the burial officer's "interment plan"—for there must be order, even in death.

No consolation either for those who were taken to the rear in agony with smashed limbs or mangled organs; such as Lieutenant Zorn, who knew he must henceforth limp through life without his left leg. A good old "Auntie" Ju-52—a Lufthansa civilian machine—brought him to Italy, flown right down at sea level by Captain Müller.

Fate now and then plays macabre jokes in time of war: Zorn had already been taken away from Mechili after an emergency operation when his sergeant major also arrived there with parts of his fourth company.

Near the wrecked Panzer, the sergeant found a leg, complete with a boot which bore the name "Lt Zorn." The man naturally thought his company commander had died in the Panzer IV. In due course, therefore, Zorn's mother in Naumburg/Saale received a box, marked by the

---

[17] Heinz Werner Schmidt: *With Rommel in the Desert*. Although it contains some inaccuracies (such as: "We caught the British commander, General Gambier-Parry, in his tent"), this refreshingly written book provides unchallengeable information drawn from personal experience. Thus Schmidt reports that on 7 April Rommel's Chief of Staff, von dem Borne, and his "G1 Ops," Ehlert, had no idea where Rommel was or what his intentions were. They had eventually sent Schmidt out in a Storch to order all columns: "Advance straight to Tobruk, bypassing Mechili." The pilot, however, was forced to land in a sandstorm and Schmidt did not reach the 5th Light Division's Divisional HQ until the morning of 8 April, immediately before the attack on Mechili.

field post office as "property of Lieutenant Albrecht Zorn, killed in action." The error was soon cleared up. Today Albrecht Zorn, L1.D., a wiry man in his late fifties, is a senior official in the Federal Justice Ministry.

The infantry too, both German and Italian, collected some booty at Mechili. The Italians, not much pampered in life, were agog at the treasures: tins of apricots and ham and—for the lucky visitors to the store of the officers' mess—gin and whiskey. At this stage, the taking of booty had not yet been regulated with the German thoroughness that was to characterize it later.

Warrant Officer Claus Wernicke, covered in sweat, arriving straight from the desert where he had more carried than ridden his heavy BMW, was the first to dive into the clothing stores. Here there were stacks of the comfortable, ample, well-ventilated shirts and underwear worn by the desert-wise British. Wernicke carefully converted his measurements from centimeters to inches and helped himself liberally.

On its way to Mechili, one unit had a typical *ghibli* experience. Just as the sandstorm started, they had spotted an enemy battery of four guns, encircled it, and duly took three of the crews prisoner. But then the storm reached its peak and in the swirling masses of sand and dust, they could no longer find the fourth gun, which had been clearly visible just a moment ago. The commander of the unit was glad to have at least the full complement of his own people together again.

Sergeant Major Wilhelm Wendt, 1st Company, 5th Panzer Regiment, who was standing in for a troop commander invalided out by a land mine at El Agheila, first of all procured himself some plain water at Mechili.

The tough thirty-year-old from the Altmark—at his age he counted as an "elderly gentleman" in the Afrika Korps—had carefully eked out the meager water ration allowed for desert travel; but during the last lap of the journey he had noticed the desperate expression and chapped lips of his driver, who was so desiccated that he could hardly even croak. He handed the poor fellow his flask and watched with well-concealed chagrin while its entire contents disappeared at one gulp. In the hours that were to follow, Wendt thrashed desperately around in the rear of the Panzer, gasping like a fish out of water, dry down to the tips of his toes.

At this time, radio operator Joachim Saenger's crew were reduced to walking; to cap it all, the engine of their Panzer gave up the ghost in the stone desert south of the mountains.

Hardly any of the Panzers, which had been unloaded in Tripoli in tiptop condition, could still be described as fit for action. The inadequately filtered engines had long since swallowed too much sand and dust, worn pistons were knocking worryingly, and tracks and bogey wheels were in a dreadful state. As the much-reduced flock once again moved off, driven toward Tobruk by the unrelenting Rommel, a further defect began to show itself, which was likely to be particularly embarrassing during the renewed fighting that lay ahead: The omnipresent sand had reached the turning gear of the turrets, which were squeaking and grinding. Some were already completely jammed; others would turn only a part of their traverse. The anxious "Papa" Streich reported to Rommel that during the next respite he would have the turrets taken off and cleaned out; and at first he even obtained approval for this. But then came a countermanding order: No rest, no cleaning. Everything that could still crawl forward was to make for Tobruk, via Tmimi, without delay.

"A new Cannae is being prepared," Rommel had written in his diary. He was convinced that he would be able to repeat, at Tobruk, Hannibal's classic battle of encirclement and that the steadily growing number of enemy troops there would give him his greatest triumph yet.

He thought he knew what the Australians and British, who were now streaming toward Tobruk, wanted in the tiny port, squatting there at the foot of two huge steps of a staircase: They undoubtedly wanted to escape by sea. Had they not so far always run away, in France as in Africa? And was not a suspiciously large number of ships making for Tobruk out of Alexandria and the Nile Delta? They must be on their way to fetch the beaten horde. The only question was whether they would succeed in pulling off another Dunkirk here.

He would spoil their little game.

3. Quarrel Among Generals

"Ming the Merciless" rules in Tobruk

Rommel did not know as yet that the ships were not coming for an evacuation; they were, on the contrary, bringing reinforcements into the fortress. And he could not know what "Ming the Merciless"—General Morshead, commander of Tobruk—was saying to his assembled commanders that same day: "We'll have no Dunkirk here. If we get out of here, it will be down a road we have cleared for ourselves in battle. But there will be no surrender and no retreat."

The general knew his Diggers. He made quite sure that two points were made quite clear to them and to the British units: The sea behind them was not an avenue for retreat, but a supply route for bringing up munitions and supplies, and Tobruk was not simply a fortress under siege; it was to be a thorn in the enemy's side.

The men, who, in any case, had had enough of running away without having made contact with the enemy, now had a task and an objective before them. A ghibli—which the British called by the Arabic name khamsin—raged for two days: 9 and 10 April. The seething sand did not hinder their redoubled efforts to make the defenses ready. Naked men in gas masks, their skins covered in a mixture of sweat and reddish dust, swung their spades and pickaxes like phantoms in a swirling cloud.

In laying out the fortifications, the Italians had made clever use of the steep sides of the wadis cut deeply into the stony ground by the water rushing to the sea after downpours from the escarpment. To the south, these natural obstacles were connected with each other only by an anti-tank perimeter trench. All along the wadis and the trench ran a double line of concrete emplacements, deeply embedded, skillfully blending with the terrain and, in the prevailing heat haze of Africa, virtually invisible.

A good scheme, but the eternally drifting sand had silted almost everything up; the barbed-wire obstacles had been torn and the extensive minefields either cleared or defused. All this could be made good. What was more serious was the shortage of weapons with which to furnish the fine concrete emplacements in the manner their builders had intended: generally with an anti-tank gun flanked by machine guns.

The Australians, who had not been trained until they were in the desert, had been given as few of these costly weapons as possible. Puny as the two-pounder anti-tank gun—by now generally referred to as the "pea shooter" or "popgun"—was against the medium Panzers, it would have been advantageous to have a few more than the sixteen pieces available. Things did not look too cheerful when it came to tanks, either: 25 Cruisers, 4 Matildas, 15 of the light Mark VIs armed only with machine guns, and of course the Dragoons' 30 Marmon-Harringtons, which were, however, beginning to fall apart.

Artillery, on the other hand, was one relatively bright spot: In addition to a regiment of light (18-pounder) and medium (60-pounder) guns, four regiments, or altogether 72, of the 25-pounders were either available or on their way by sea.

Some 25,000 men, just half of them Australian infantry, were getting ready to defend the place. General Morshead moved seven of his thirteen infantry battalions to the first line, each with a reserve company to back it up. One company thus had around one and a half kilometers of front line to hold—not a particularly strong manning level. Morshead told his commanders that breaches of the line were to be expected: "In which case, you'll just have to chuck 'em out again."

Since, in the absence of anti-tank guns, the infantry could do nothing against the tanks, they were to allow themselves to be bypassed, and only attack the accompanying infantry. Any available tank formations, but more particularly the gunners with their 25-pounders firing over open sights, would then engage the Panzers.

It was a plan that relied to a frightening extent on untrained infantry keeping cool heads in face of an enemy who had meanwhile acquired a reputation of being virtually invincible. It was to be the indefatigable 8th Machine Gun Battalion at whose expense Morshead's confidence in his "undisciplined Diggers was to prove fully justified.

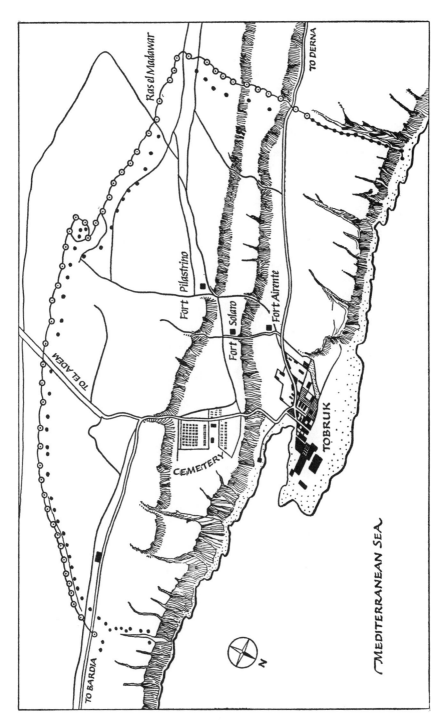

Two steps down to the desert fortress of Tobruk

Lieutenant Colonel Ponath and his men had no time to recover after their journey through the desert and the difficult days at Derna. Rommel immediately sent them off to Tobruk. For two days, Australian rearguards fought vigorous delaying actions with them along the coastal road. Meanwhile, Ponath's men again came up against their old enemies, the KDG, who were doing reconnaissance work and directing artillery fire—and whose "extraordinarily audacious" bearing was noted in the history of the battalion.[1]

It was already becoming clear that Rommel's hopes of penetrating into Tobruk at about the same time as the enemy arrived there would not be fulfilled. But the general, overtired and driven on by ambition, would not heed the warning signs. Nor could he have, for that matter: Fate had set a trap for him into which he stumbled blindly. Superficially, the situation was strikingly reminiscent of his greatest military triumph until then, barely a year earlier at St. Valéry, a small port on the western bank of the Somme estuary, where at the beginning of June 1940 German troops had bottled up the British 51st Division. There were more than 8,000 crack troops there from the Highlands of Scotland, as well as 4,000 Frenchmen. British ships were coming in to evacuate them, but artillery from Rommel's 7th Panzer Division reached the heights west of the harbor in time to prevent embarkation. St. Valéry had to surrender. The 12,000 prisoners included four generals.

A general's journey into death

"Kirchheim, I want you to go ahead to Tobruk. Look for an artillery position from where we can shell the harbor." With this order, Rommel sent the "commandeered" OKH general forward.

The dream of St. Valéry . . . Yet this order made clear the difference between the Tobruk and the well-planned French campaign: Here there were no satisfactory maps from which one could have ascertained that any effective shelling of the harbor, at least with the weapons available, would have been possible only from the edge of the sheer *jebel,* far inside the fortifications.[2]

---

[1] *Nur ein Bataillon* . . . , by Heinz-Dietrich Aberger, Adalbert van Thaysen, and Kurt Ziemer. On the night of 9 April, Major Lindsay's C-Squadron of the KDG was, with the Australians, en route for the "prisoners' gorge," run by the German 8th Machine Gun Battalion near Derna, which had become well known in Tobruk. On the way, however, they realized the hopelessness of their rescue attempt and turned back.

[2] Most published German work stresses that the "treacherous" or at least uncooperative Italians—a favorite sneer—did not provide proper maps of their fortified positions until after the first disastrous attacks. However, it is evident

Major General Kirchheim was wounded on the coast road by bullets from a strafing aircraft. While he was still being bandaged, Major General von Prittwitz und Gaffron, commander of the 15th Panzer Division, came by. He had traveled ahead of the first of his men, who were being disembarked in Tripoli, and had immediately been given a similar reconnaissance mission by Rommel. Kirchheim reported after the war in a clearly reproachful tone that Rommel had told him and Prittwitz that the coastal road was secure up to Kilometer 13. Thus the divisional commander drove to his death quite confidently.

The 8th Machine Gun Battalion was held up at Kilometer 17. The coastal road here crossed a deep wadi. The bridge had been blown up, and from the far side of the precipice came small arms, anti-tank, and artillery fire. All one could do was to stick one's nose deep in the sand. When a car flying a commander's pennant turned up from the rear, the men waved it down energetically and yelled "Halt." But the open car drove on and was immediately pierced by an anti-tank shell. Prittwitz and his driver were both dead.

The men on the far side of the wadi were Australian infantry who the previous winter had collected from the mass of captured Italian weapons a 47 mm anti-tank gun and a few 75 and 105 mm field guns. Later that afternoon they saw the Germans go back and disappear southward with their transport. Expecting the enemy to try again before long, from another direction, they withdrew six kilometers to their final defense position. The battle for Tobruk began the next day. It was Good Friday, 11 April 1941.

"The British are evacuating. . . ."

Meanwhile German troops had reached the Tobruk area in pretty full strength. Calm reflection would have led to the conclusion that their numbers were not even sufficient to build a reasonably viable siege ring around the 45-kilometer Tobruk perimeter. Their poorly motorized Italian allies had sent some minor infantry units along the coast road and these had arrived in the area west of the fortress. Meanwhile the Ariete armored division was still struggling through the desert with its awful M-13s. From Tripoli, three companies of motorcycle troops, the vanguard of the 15th Panzer Division, were approaching.

Once again, Rommel divided his weak forces into three: He sent the 2nd Machine Gun Battalion, with some AA guns and artillery, to the east flank of Tobruk, to block the coast road there. The 3rd Recon-

---

that in view of the chaotic advance, which depended on moment-to-moment decisions, it would have needed a clairvoyant at the right map section to send the right maps up at the right moment.

naissance Unit, reinforced by the motorcycle combinations, pushed farther eastward: for the idea was to push on to Suez after the "New
Cannae" of Tobruk.

What remained for an attack were those vehicles of the 5th Panzer
Regiment which had remained intact or had been repaired; some small
sapper and light Panzer units; eight pieces of artillery (virtually without any ammunition); a few light and heavy AA guns and—the only
infantry unit, this—the mercilessly chivvied 8th Machine Gun Battalion. The dream of St. Valéry . . . On that occasion too, this battalion,
attached to the 7th Panzer Division, had been under Rommel's command.

Together with the order to attack, the battalion received intelligence
that, according to aerial reconnaissance, the British were evacuating the
fortress. They would therefore have to get to grips with them quickly.

In addition, "dust procedure" had been ordered: As long as the advance was with vehicles, they would be driving well strung out; the
Panzer Regiment would do the same, so as to stir up an immense cloud,
as if produced by large units.

However, the men on the other side could consequently form an
early idea of the direction of the advance. They were the 20th
Australian Infantry Brigade, whose conduct had so upset General
Neame. After the artillery spotters of the KDG, in their Marmon-Harringtons, had reported back the range, the first shells of the Australians
hit the approaching troops when they were still in their vehicles. The
German infantry could take only a few more rushes northeastward—
the direction of their attack. The stony ground intensified the effectiveness of the shrapnel. It was impossible to dig any proper foxholes;
they scraped shallow depressions with entrenching tools, side arms, and
bare hands. Medical orderlies dragged to the rear bloody, screaming
bundles, which but a moment ago had been keen and vigorous men.

The Panzers turned about, towing behind them a few vehicles with
broken tracks. The infantrymen remained pinned on the ground for, in
addition to the artillery, they had also come under small-arms fire.

Night saved the stricken force—for the time being.

A fresh attack was ordered for the following day, again without artillery. The Panzers came at eleven in the morning and, followed by British artillery shell hits, raced through the positions of their own infantry.
As the latter's war diary remarked, not without a note of reproach:
"We are forced . . . to take cover from our own Panzers to avoid
being run down."

What is more, the wild Panzer chase did not last long: The regiment
came up against the anti-tank trench and turned back. "We can't get
through," shouted one officer as they roared by.

The situation of the previous day was repeated, but worse, since the infantry now lay closer to the enemy positions.

They had been in action almost continuously for a fortnight, were lying under the burning sun, tormented by thirst and plagued by an army of billions of flies, sketchily protected by the heaps of stones they had scraped together, small-arms fire whizzing by them at the slightest movement. No break in the firing, even if a man simply must have a shit. . . . The stench, the fear of death, and the screaming of the wounded.

Order: 8th Machine Gun Battalion will hold the position it has reached. Another night, with the chance to establish the position a bit better, to get hold of some of the water and food which had been brought up for them. Another sunrise and the torture continues. Rommel had not yet dreamed his dream of St. Valéry to the full.

> The GOC, German forces in Libya, calls on the British to lay down their arms. Individual soldiers signaling with a white handkerchief will not be fired on. Strong German forces have surrounded Tobruk. There is no point in trying to escape. Remember Mechili. Our bombers and Stukas lie in wait for your ships in the harbor.

Leaflets with this text in English were released over Tobruk by the thousand. The Diggers had a good laugh at the German assumption that they still had white handkerchiefs. But more remarkable is Rommel's rock-hard conviction, which shines forth from these sentences, that the one thing on the enemy's mind was flight, by land or by sea. According to General Streich, he finished that Easter Sunday with a violent altercation with Rommel. He and his G1 Ops, Major Hauser, had said that further attacks had no chance of success.

In his personal notes, Rommel noted "unjustified pessimism on the part of the 5th Light." According to Streich, the point at issue was the interpretation of air reconnaissance: He maintains he immediately surmised that reinforcements were being brought up, whereas Rommel stubbornly insisted on his view that the British were "demolishing and evacuating the fortress."

The first tank-landing craft

What was really happening on that Easter Sunday down there in the port of Tobruk represented a piece of the history of war: For the first time, tanks were being landed from special tank-landing craft—ugly things with rectangular bows, which folded down and thus formed a ramp over which one tank after another could drive onto dry land under its own power.

They were to open their great jaws off Sicily, at Salerno and Anzio, and in the end on the Normandy beaches, and disgorge their steel cargoes—symbols of the power of imagination of a man who even in Britain's darkest hour never doubted that his country would withstand every blow and would in the end go over to the attack again: Winston Churchill.

As early as the summer of 1940, when France lay defeated and the whole world was wondering when it would be Britain's turn, that old lion of genius had given orders for ships like these to be built.[3] When Rommel's offensive began, the first eighteen of them lay moored in the Suez Canal Company's harbor at Port Tawfiq. They were to be used in the planned conquest of the Dodecanese (the "Twelve Islands" in the Aegean).

Once Admiral Cunningham undertook to keep Tobruk supplied, he allowed these craft, code-named "A-lighters," to be released. The first convoy of five landing craft, an anti-aircraft sloop and a converted trawler/submarine chaser arrived at the harbor mouth of Tobruk at dawn on Easter Sunday. An air raid was just beginning and, by the light of the flashes from the gun muzzles and of the exploding bombs, the crews saw the wreck-strewn harbor and the white houses pockmarked by shrapnel—and as a precautionary measure, the whole convoy sailed out to the open sea again.

Astonishingly, they were not spotted, survived a further air raid in the harbor, during which two freighters were sunk, and were able to discharge their precious cargoes: heavy Matildas, 25-pounders, ammunition, and food. As night fell, they sailed away again. Their exhausts which, clumsily, were mounted immediately behind the bridge, transmitted the noise of the two 650 hp engines into everyone's ears and drowned the buzzing of the German reconnaissance aircraft flying high over Tobruk, the reports of which seemed to confirm Rommel's verdict, maintained through thick and thin: They are withdrawing. . . .

The Machine Gun Battalion had spent another bloody day in front of the Australians' positions. If anything, the artillery and infantry fire had intensified; it was clear that the other side had concentrated its reserves. They seemed to have plenty of ammunition and to spare over there, since they were using artillery to shoot at individual men. This was what happened to Ponath, who had been ordered back to the division in the afternoon. When he returned, completely exhausted after twice running for his life through enemy fire, he began with a stony

[3] The "Mulberry" artificial harbors, which contributed decisively to the success of the Normandy invasion, had been Churchill's idea, laid down years earlier in a directive: "They *must* float up and down with the tide. The anchor problem must be mastered. . . . Don't argue the matter. . . ."

face to dictate to his adjutant: "The OC has ordered another attack on Tobruk. . . ."

Says Streich: "In view of my attitude, Rommel personally took over the conduct of the operation which, after having been prepared by him in every particular, began shortly before nightfall."

Rommel let the battalion commander know that the attack, ordered to take place at 1800 hours, would be preceded not only by light and heavy anti-aircraft guns but also by "a concentrated artillery strike" at the enemy's infantry positions. Although Rommel wrote in his memoirs about support by "massed German and Italian artillery," in actual fact not one shot was fired on the Axis side.[4]

As to the AA . . . "Expendable"—the terminology of war is apt: the 88 mm guns, as big as barn doors, moved into position as ordered on the dead-flat, stony terrain immediately behind the infantry. It was a miracle that they managed to fire off a few volleys before their crews were massacred or had fled.

Even more hopeless was the fate of the light battery with its 20 mm guns. Orders were to drive up to the anti-tank trench and to attack the infantry positions. Out of the entire battery only one lieutenant and six men came back.

Over the tank ditch

The infantry attack gained hardly any ground either. And indeed how could it, without support from any other arm of the forces and against an enemy who had been ready for days? The situation was so bad that the battalion commander did not even manage to inform all his companies of the coming attack: One runner after another was shot dead.

Once again the sun fell like a stone behind the horizon. In the darkness, Ponath himself, accompanied by some of his men and a group of sappers, felt his way forward to the anti-tank ditch. Every sound, every accidental chink seemed to carry for many kilometers in the still and starry night; but they managed to make a narrow passage negotiable for vehicles and to clear it of mines and barbed wire.

A reconnaissance group set out and over a distance of several hundred meters found no trace of the enemy. Nobody realized that the advance, which was to be in a northeasterly direction, happened to have hit precisely the gap between the double row of strongpoints arranged in an "open hatch" position. Ponath followed his battalion. He had,

---

[4] Johannes Streich thinks he remembers that the Italian artillery did not turn up until that night and that the German artillery was meanwhile without any ammunition.

after all, reason to believe that he had achieved a secure "bridgehead" across the anti-tank ditch—and reported back accordingly.

As Streich recalls it, Rommel said he had now demonstrated how to do it, and that the thing was possible. At any rate, according to Lieutenant Heinz Werner Schmidt, he transferred the further responsibility for the operation back to Streich, saying, with meaningful emphasis: "I expect this attack to be conducted under your personal leadership and with the utmost determination." In his book, first published in 1951, Schmidt, otherwise an uncritical admirer of Rommel, found his treatment of Streich "remorseless."

Out in the desert, again as cold as ice, it was made clear to the men of the Machine Gun Battalion in a singularly ruthless way that by no means could their bridgehead be considered secure.

Ponath's infantrymen had begun immediately to dig themselves in after a makeshift fashion. The moon had meanwhile risen and was behind them. The enemy could not be far away. All the eerier was the stillness; the scraping and clattering of spades seemed to be making an awful noise.

Suddenly there was a shout from far right: a few swift movements in the pale moonlight. Two shadows slipped away: In the dust lay a dying man, transfixed by a bayonet.

On the other, western, side of the bridgehead, in Strongpoint No. 33, Sydneysider Lieutenant Mackell and his men had observed the Germans digging. The lieutenant decided to make a circuit around the enemy with a raiding party and attack him in the flank. The maneuver worked, and the Australians stormed the digging Germans from barely 50 meters, bayonets fixed, throwing hand grenades and shooting from the hip. At the same time the men in the strongpoint fired away with everything they had.

The slightly built Lieutenant Mackell was struggling with a German, when he saw another one leap at him, pistol at the ready.

"Jack!" yelled Mackell.

Corporal Jack Edmonston, from a sheep station in New South Wales, came to his aid with the bayonet, although he himself had bullet wounds in the stomach and neck. The corporal, bleeding profusely, struck down both the Germans. Mackell picked up his rifle and together both of them threw themselves into the fight again, yelling hoarsely. Mackell broke his bayonet in the chest of one man and knocked down another with the butt of his rifle. When no enemy was to be seen standing, Jack Edmonston collapsed, and died the same night. He was posthumously awarded the Victoria Cross. The Australians broke out of their positions a few more times with such raiding parties, on one occasion singing their defiant vagabond song "Waltzing

Matilda,"[5] which had acquired fresh meaning in North Africa thanks to the heavy tank of that name.

The first attack alone cost Ponath's group forty casualties in dead and wounded. The exhausted men nevertheless held their bridgehead and even roused themselves to make counterattacks, without, however, managing to widen their narrow breach to any significant extent.

"Divisional orders!"

It was clear that any further advance from such a restricted bridgehead was tantamount to suicide. When the divisional adjutant arrived with a new order to attack, Ponath immediately registered his opinion to that effect.

In the book *Nur ein Bataillon . . . ,* the then Sergeant Wilhelm Assenmacher says that a discussion ensued "which at times bordered on the vehement. . . . Then the conversation came to an abrupt end. By the light of the moon, the two officers stand facing one another, their dark shadows sharply outlined on the desert sand. The Adjutant lifts his hand to his cap before our commander recapitulates the task of our battalion as briefly as possible and, when our commander counters with a question, merely repeats: 'Divisional orders . . .' "

Orders—the magic spell for the leader and the led. . . .

Rommel had just read Streich a private lecture to the effect that "it was not usual in the German army for a service order to a unit to be answered by a counterproposal from the unit concerned."

Yet the very next year he himself was to stand before his Führer and make counterproposals to rescue his army, only to hear the words: "That's an order, Field Marshal!"

But meanwhile it was he who was in the saddle: he assigned Lieutenant Schmidt to act as his divisional commander's overseer and wrote to his wife on 14 April: "The battle for Tobruk is bound to end today. The British have fought stubbornly and have masses of artillery. Despite which, we shall win. . . ."

The Afrika Korps had obtained its first maps from its allies of the defense installations.[6] It is no longer possible to guess on what Rommel's optimism was based.

[5] "Waltzing Matilda" is about a vagrant who steals a ram but prefers death by drowning to imprisonment. In 1973 the catchy tune came within an ace of becoming the national anthem.

[6] Schmidt remembers that Rommel admired the cleverness of the layout. There had been only two maps available altogether. When interviewed, Streich could not remember, but in a report on the night of 14 April, written in 1960, he mentioned a map with which he had been able to establish the place where the

Late in the night, Streich and Schmidt were on their way to the front in a general-purpose vehicle. A light Panzer II, in which Streich intended to accompany the attack, rumbled along behind.

They were driving north on the El Adem-Tobruk road. "We must branch off at Kilometer 8," the general said.

Something went wrong. Suddenly they were at Kilometer 6.2. The driver stepped on the brake. They could hear English voices, and tracer bullets were whistling around them.

In a few mighty leaps, the lieutenant and the general rushed behind the Panzer for cover. They held fast to it and pulled their legs up while machine-gun bursts kept crashing through under the hull. Of all things, the driver began to turn the Panzer around, which, as Schmidt put it, "would have exposed our rear to the enemy." They threw themselves into the ditch, where they were before long joined by the Panzer driver who, as Streich recalls, had stalled his engine and could not restart it. The starter had packed up and machine-gun bullets were striking the hull in the rear all around the crank handle as if shot from a shower.

The British artillery was also taking a hand in the affair; and when a salvo burst all around them, the driver cried out in fright.

"Are you wounded?" Streich asked.

"No, Herr General, not yet," replied the driver glumly. Streich laughed out loud.

In the east, the sky was beginning to color; soon the sun would hop above the horizon with the leap characteristic of Africa. In short rushes they removed themselves from this dangerous neighborhood and reached an artillery position safe and sound. Streich, who had sent his driver back, never saw either the driver or his car again.

Meanwhile the last act of the tragedy of the 8th Machine Gun Battalion had begun.

For General Morshead there could now no longer be any doubt about the direction of the attack, since the bridgehead had been established at such close quarters with his infantrymen and since it had been so bitterly defended. It was toward the fork where the roads from Bardia and El Adem join and then down the two jebel cliff faces to the town and harbor of Tobruk.

He therefore concentrated all his artillery and anti-tank guns, as well as all the tanks and infantry he could spare without undue risk from the perimeter. The heavy weapons formed a corridor down which the attacker had to face massed 25-pounder emplacements, in addition to being covered on both sides by more artillery, anti-tank guns, and

---

fortifications crossed the El Adem-Tobruk road. What is certain is that the 5th Panzer Regiment had no. idea that there was an anti-tank ditch. The maps must therefore have arrived later. Be that as it may, on 14 April, the 8th Machine Gun Battalion was still left in ignorance about the position of the fortifications.

Cruiser tanks which had been dug in. On one flank, a strike force of a few Matildas stood ready to close the "bag" along the anti-tank ditch —a tactic which suggested itself because of the narrowness of the causeway.[7]

In obedience to orders, the 5th Panzers and the 8th Machine Gun Battalion marched into this perfect trap. In his Potsdam Military Academy days, Instructor Rommel would certainly have dismissed as too easy the tactical question of whether or not such an advance was permissible.

It was still dark when the Panzers arrived in the bridgehead, having for a while waited in vain for Streich. As the tanks inched their way across the anti-tank ditch, the Australians stopped firing, as they had been ordered. There was no point in betraying their positions to the mighty Panzer IVs, which lobbed 13.6-pound high-explosive shells from their short barrels.

Into captivity, crying

Ponath now naturally had to divide his force: Fairly strong groups accompanied the tanks, some of them sitting on them. Some of the infantry and anti-tank gunners stayed behind to keep open the breach over the anti-tank ditch. They didn't have a chance. They were pinned down by small-arms fire from nearby strongpoints until the Matildas came. Most shells bounced off the Matilda's frontal armor without doing any damage.

As during the winter campaign against Graziani's army, the effect on morale of these monsters, rumbling on slowly but irresistibly, was shattering. Their machine guns mowed the anti-tank gunners down. It was soon over. Only a few men of the 8th Machine Gun Battalion managed to get back to their vehicles. The groups taking part in the advance were the first to lose their anti-tank guns. The guns were being brought up in the infantry column. As soon as the gun flashes lit them up, they too came under fire from the infantry weapons in the strongpoints. In that terrain, which offered no cover, they were shot up like sitting ducks.

The heaviest weapon the infantry were then left with was the small 5 cm mortar, also known as the *Bulettenschmeisster* or "meatball thrower." Since the breach at the anti-tank ditch was closed, they had no chance of getting away in any case.

Ponath and his men then hoped that the sudden silence behind them

---

[7] The Brescia Division, which at Rommel's orders "made dust" and kicked up a din with its small-arms fire in the west, had been engaged in this business for four days now and hardly even raised a weary smile.

meant that reinforcements were moving up. With their Panzers, they drove for their objective: the fork in the road where the row of telegraph poles veered away to the east.

When the Panzers reached a slight rise running across their path, they found themselves suddenly facing a line of 25-pounders. The very first salvoes had a devastating effect. One heavy Panzer lost its turret. Several others burst into flames.

Seeing that their improvised anti-tank artillery was so effective over a range of a few hundred meters[8] gave the gunners fresh heart, although the Panzers' own 75 and 50 mm high-explosive shells were inflicting heavy casualties on their open firing positions too. In Captain Armitage's battery, one of the guns sustained a direct hit. Only one of the six-man crew survived, gravely injured. Sergeant Major Batten dragged the dead to one side and went on firing by himself until the Panzers broke off the engagement.

They withdrew behind the slight rise and wheeled right to outflank the artillery position. But here too they immediately ran into massed artillery and anti-tank guns. Cleverly exploiting the cover afforded by folds in the ground and by the wadis, a few Cruiser tanks also turned up. Devastating fire struck the bewildered Panzer formation. More and more turrets jammed, struck by artillery shells or by the little two-pounder solid rounds. Seventeen of the Panzers were destroyed. Amid the black clouds of smoke from the burning vehicles and the whirling dust, Colonel Olbrich gave the order to withdraw.

Sergeant Major Wendt's Panzer was one of the few which could still turn its turret and thus defend itself. He was last to drive away, reining in his driver, whose instinct was drawing him toward the mass of other vehicles: "Easy, easy! Can't you see the gunfire they're getting? The artillery naturally fires where there are most targets."

Some Cruisers tried to creep up on the right and the left, but Wendt's gunner set several on fire and they kept their distance.

"I can't see the regiment anymore," the driver said, despairing.

"Now we'll follow their tracks, nice and slowly," Wendt reassured him.

Between the dancing spurts of the shell strikes, they rumbled back through the anti-tank ditch. There was no trace to be seen of the Machine Gun Battalion.

Ponath had tried in vain to hold the Panzer commander back, but declined the offer to retire with him by sitting on his tank: Every man

[8] The 25-pounders also carried a limited number of solid rounds, which would smash through the Panzers' armor. Their normal muzzle velocity of 365 m/sec (charge 3) could be stepped up to 425 m/sec by "supercharging" them. This made the gun recoil unpleasantly, but at 500 meters it would pierce the strongest armor.

who had done so had been picked off his steel coach. In the distance they could see Stukas diving down on the town of Tobruk. "A fat lot of use that is to us," the men grumbled. The Australians were evidently bringing up more and more reinforcements. Once again the men were lying on the ground, which offered virtually no cover, under merciless fire from all arms. Ammunition was running short.

Ponath decided to pull the battalion back. At the first rush, he was shot dead through the heart. Shortly after that it was all over. The senior surviving officer ordered his men to cease fire, signaled to the other side, and stood up. An Australian major stepped up, held out his cigarette case to him, and said in an offhand way: "Good fight. . . ."

The soldiers quickly stripped down their weapons and scattered the pieces in all directions. Many cried as they were led away into captivity.

There were tears farther in the rear as well.

Radio operator Joachim Saenger, whose Panzer, its engine at last repaired, had turned up from the desert, watched the remnants of the regiment return. Much-decorated commanders, used to victory, jumped out of their Panzers sobbing hysterically. It was a new experience that German Panzers could be so brutally stopped.

The 8th Machine Gun Battalion had lost 700 men in a fortnight. It had five officers and 92 men left altogether. Lieutenant Colonel Ponath received a posthumous Knight's Cross.

Johannes Streich, describing 14 April:

> When I drove to Corps Staff to see Colonel Olbrich, I could only find the then G1 Ops, Major Ehlert. He conveyed Rommel's order to me: The division was to make a new thrust into the belt of fortifications in the afternoon to take possession of a particular point for artillery observation. I was speechless. I then asked him to tell me with what troops I was to carry out this order. The 8th Machine Gun Battalion had been wiped out and the 5th Panzer Regiment was unfit for action at the moment. Since the forces stationed to the east were not at my disposal, there was nothing available. I pointed out that had the Australians come after us they would have been able to overrun the entire Afrika Korps and completely destroy the reputation of the German army in Africa.

Theoretically, he was right. In practice, it was out of the question because neither Wavell nor Morshead had any idea of the weakness of the Axis forces. Wavell had countless other worries; but even without them it was hardly likely to occur to him that the Germans were off balance. Psychologically, the British were in the position of a boxer, who after being battered for round after round, has hit back for the first time, and the interval before the next round is full of delighted surprise because his blow actually went home.

Rebuke from the Supreme Commander

Devastating though a breakout by the 25,000 men in the fortress would have been, especially since the arrival of the eighteen Matildas, the psychological situation, particularly in war, is often a very different thing from the objective one.

This applied to Rommel, too, who still would not believe that the British had dug their heels in at Tobruk. Although in his memoirs[9] he sought to create the impression that he had realized even before the attacks started that Wavell intended to hold Tobruk, on 16 April he was still writing to his wife: "The enemy is embarking. We shall therefore soon be able to take over the fortress."

What he said in his memoirs (dictated from notes in 1944) about 14 April is partly falsified, partly grossly unfair to Streich who, while certainly not Rommel's equal when it came to leadership, initiative, and ingenuity, was nevertheless a brave and painstaking commander—and at least as far as Tobruk was concerned had assessed the situation a great deal more clearly than his corps commander.

Talking of the predawn attack, Rommel remarks, somewhat disingenuously, that there had been no sign of the men who were supposed to cover the flanks of the breach. A soldier of his caliber knew that no troops received any such orders, because there were no troops left available. Together with his repeated references to "concentrations of German and Italian artillery," the remark was clearly intended to back up his harsh judgments: Colonel Olbrich, who, by withdrawing the remnants of his battered Panzers had saved them from annihilation, "had left the infantry in the lurch." A strange reproach, to say the least, to level at a commander who had had to leave on the field 17 of the 36 Panzers he had led into action. General Streich, Rommel went on, had not known "how to form a center of gravity by concentrating all arms, to force a breakthrough there, to roll up the flanks and, quick as lightning, before the enemy has had time to react, to penetrate into the interior."

Since in this context he never writes about a totally exhausted machine-gun battalion and a decimated Panzer regiment, but always in general terms of "the 5th Light Division," all this seemed pretty convincing. It prompted even the British military historian Liddell Hart to make approving remarks—though more about the precision with which Rommel summed up his *Blitzkrieg* theories. At Tobruk, Rommel similarly explained the catastrophe to the surviving officers of the 8th Machine Gun Battalion in terms of a failure of command at the

[9] *Krieg ohne Hass*, p. 21.

divisional level—a monumental transgression against the elementary rule of leadership which requires that on no account should the problems of higher echelons be discussed with subordinates.

But for Rommel, the scapegoats had in any case been picked: General Streich and Colonel Olbrich. Before long he suggested that they should be relieved—which left a considerable blot on their personal records. Their cases were not the only ones, merely only the most spectacular. On 9 July 1941, the mild-mannered C-in-C, Field Marshal von Brauchitsch, roused himself to issue a rebuke.

He had gained the impression, he wrote to "dear *Herr* Rommel," that measures against officers of the Afrika Korps had in a number of cases not been handled objectively. "The more awkward the circumstances, the greater the nervous strain; all the more is it therefore the duty of every superior to check most carefully whether or not intervening with threats or suggestions for the replacement of officers who have until then given the best account of themselves in battle, or sharp criticism and hasty commands are indicated; or whether a calm and instructive discussion, free of all acrimony and conducted in a spirit of comradeship, might not achieve the purpose better. I consider it my duty, not only in the interests of the Afrika Korps but also in your own personal interest, to draw your attention to these points. . . ."[10] Rommel replied on 22 July that he had had to suggest the replacement of two commanders because they had "several times failed completely and because this considerably reduced the combat effectiveness of the troops under them. . . ."

General Streich in particular had continually criticized orders and had asked them to be amended. "Having received orders that the 8th Machine Gun Battalion, surrounded by the enemy after its successful attack through the perimeter, should be relieved by elements of the 5th Panzer Regiment, or should at least have its retreat out of the fortification lines secured," Streich had refused to take any responsibility for the conduct of the operation. Moreover, the precarious situation had arisen above all through the inept conduct of the attack by the 5th Light Division.

A "successful attack" after which the attacking unit needs rescuing— now that is something really unusual.

Lieutenant General von Paulus, at that time quartermaster general at the OKW, later told Streich that he did not know of any case in military history of a hole being knocked into a planned breach in the eve-

[10] The quoted sample is a photocopy of a memorandum prepared at the OKH headquarters, copied out (illegibly) "for the sake of good order." This struggle with punctuation and syntax, horrendous to behold, does indeed appear to have been conducted by one of the foremost soldiers of Greater Germany.

ning and the operation then being successfully resumed the following morning. For him, later to be the loser at Stalingrad, the relevant experience was still to come. The military situation was quite similar; only the number of victims was to be horribly multiplied.

In 1959, the ex-generals Kirchheim and Streich exchanged their impressions of Rommel by correspondence. Kirchheim, who had of course originally come to Africa as an OKH observer, and who had returned to Germany early in the summer, wrote to his dismissed ex-colleague: "I am loath to be reminded of those times, since so much blood was shed quite uselessly. . . . Concerning Rommel, my attitude is this: Propaganda—first by Goebbels, then by Montgomery, and finally, after he had taken poison, the propaganda of all the former enemy powers—made of him the symbol of all that is best in soldiering. His qualities as a leader were glorified, as were his qualities of character—in particular his chivalry, goodness, and modesty! The idea was that any official criticism of this by now mythical character would damage the image of the German soldier."

Well, how about that?

Rommel the product of the united propaganda efforts of Goebbels and Montgomery? Tolerated on his pedestal by colleagues who know better but would rather keep quiet so that at least one of their number can represent "the German soldier" in the world's esteem?

The truth, as virtually always, lies in between.

Streich's and Kirchheim's paths crossed Rommel's at a particularly critical point of his development: He had gambled; and while he had not lost, he had not been able to pocket the great prize he had hoped for.

The lightning reconquest of Cyrenaica had certainly been spectacular enough; and the publicity-conscious Rommel noted with satisfaction in a letter to his wife, dated 22 April, that "the press of the whole world" was talking about his success. But he also knew perfectly well that the 25,000 men in Tobruk remained the symbol of a half victory unless he could subdue them. The tactic of the British not to stand and fight and thus to save their forces had—apart from the success at Mechili and the partial success at Derna—cheated him of the fruit of his daring game. As he immediately and correctly realized, desert war was rather like war at sea, in which the area held plays a very subordinate part.

Moreover, the full extent of the Tobruk defeat was revealed only gradually. At first Rommel's only worry was that the forces assembled there might slip from his grasp by sea. When they stood their ground, he went somewhat wild with rage. For it became clear that there was no way to the Nile that did not run through Tobruk. And the Nile was where he wanted to go.

BOOK TWO

The Nile Dream

1. A Reprimand for Rommel

By the pale light of the moon, the hilly stone desert at the Libyan-Egyptian border did not look quite so bleak as under the merciless sun. Lieutenant Tim Llewellyn-Palmer of the 7th Hussars leaned shivering against the side of the turret of his light Mark VI machine-gun tank and gazed westward. He had heard the sound of engines a few minutes earlier in the far distance. The Germans could not be far away now. It was the night before Easter Sunday.

The German patrol was moving with great skill. Palmer did not see it until his eye caught a fleeting shadow.

He let them come a little nearer. When the machine guns of his three tanks began to bark, Palmer again had to admire the splendid training of the "Jerries": They disappeared like greased lightning, rushing for cover now here and now there, completely confusing you, until you were just wagging your machine gun about uselessly all over the place.

But he did pick out one man: He was like a weasel, although he was a hulking great fellow, and his shoulders flashed silver.

Palmer raced along behind him with his tank, jolting and swaying over the broken ground, and fired off all the rounds in his own and his crew members' revolvers—all in vain.

In the end the tall figure disappeared into a cave. Palmer jumped from his tank and went after him, empty revolver in hand. The German officer, a second lieutenant, sensibly gave himself up but said defiantly in his school English: "You British will lose the war all the same."

Meanwhile they had arrived back at the tank. "Well, we shan't make it as easy for you as the French did, anyway," growled the patriotic Palmer as he began discarding the empty cartridge cases from the chambers of his revolver.

"My God!" said the German, utterly disgusted at having surrendered to an empty pistol; but Tim changed the subject by formally greeting him as the first German officer in Egypt and hoping that he would have a pleasant stay. To make it so, he offered him his whiskey flask.

The patrol had vanished. Palmer thought the smart lads had given him the slip. But when the sun came up, the first thing he saw was six of them lying in hollows or behind rocks. They were so fast asleep it was no trouble collecting them. The German patrol had been sent out by the motorcycle infantry of the 15th Panzer Division and had reached the frontier area after a forced drive on their red-hot motorcycles. Reinforced by anti-tank and anti-aircraft gunners, they occupied the ruined frontier villages of Capuzzo and Sollum, which consisted of heaps of stones around which flies swarmed—particularly disgusting under the burning sun and even more disgusting to men who had come straight from France.

Curt Ehle, from Uelzen, one of the company commanders, had, until shortly before, performed administrative duties with his men in Boulogne and, to their secret joy, had looked after a great supply depot left behind by the British. That was why their baggage train also contained some cases of whiskey and gin, which had been passed around during the crossing from Italy on the steamer *Alicante,* the idea being that in wartime it was as well to enjoy promptly what one has received. So it was not only because of the heavy seas that company commander Ehle fell down a stairway together with the skipper. The same applied to the much-decorated NCOs who hung groaning at the bulwarks.

They arrived safe and sound all the same, whereas one of the ships astern of them had sunk with heavy losses after being struck by a torpedo. In that incident, virtually the whole of the staff of the 15th Panzers was lost. It was to be the first link in a chain of naval tragedies which were to dot the sea bottom between Italy and North Africa with wrecks.

The German troops at the Egyptian frontier for the time being formed the farthest extremity of a precarious and overstretched supply line. No more thoughts of gin and whiskey; now they were dreaming of cool, clear water and enough of it; and without the brackish taste which was making life a misery for them here.

This scratch force, scraped together in haste and thrown forward to the frontier, was somewhat grandly called "Combat Group Knabe," after its commander. But on the British side, too, the force facing them was a somewhat improvised one. Apart from the squadron of the 7th Hussars, it consisted of elements of three infantry battalions, elements of a Royal Horse Artillery regiment with 25-pounders and some anti-tank guns, to which were added the reconnaissance cars of the 11th Hussars. In command was a man of Rommel's own caliber, as brave as he was relentless: Lieutenant Colonel "Jock" Campbell, a gunner by trade. His job was to needle the Germans as persistently as possible; since the harbor of Tobruk remained denied them, any child could figure out that they were bound to have supply difficulties. Apart from distant Tripoli, the only seaports they had were of minimal capacity—places like Benghazi or Derna, the installations of which had moreover been badly knocked about by the Germans' own Stukas.

Campbell was just the man to convince the German vanguard, which had so far seen no armor, that they were facing a strong and aggressive force. On one occasion he had even worked out a plan to take Capuzzo back from them—with an infantry battalion of the King's Royal Rifle Corps. The idea was that the 7th Hussars would provide an armored spearhead, with their tin boxes playing the part of infantry tanks—a role even the fat Matildas had found difficult in view of the Germans' anti-tank weapons. Luckily for the British, the operation never got off the ground because of organizational problems. Instead they "trailed their coats," and with their Mark VIs, the only advantage of which was their very respectable top speed of 58 kmph, raced provocatively at the enemy positions and back again, always in the hope of raising some game for the 25-pounders. But the Germans weren't having any.

No Ack-Ack against the Panzers

The terrain south of the road to Capuzzo, fairly difficult for wheeled vehicles, was suitable for reconnaissance sorties with light tanks—and the energetic Campbell usually went along.

On one of these April days he and Tim Llewellyn-Palmer observed a German column below them on the road, making for Capuzzo. A tractor was towing a powerful-looking, long-barreled gun. A solitary Blenheim bomber was droning about in the neighborhood. At a range of 2,500 meters Campbell and Palmer watched fascinated as the rig towing the gun stopped; a few men jumped down, unfolded some trails and, quick as a flash, aimed the great barrel at the aircraft.

The performance was such an impressive display of Teutonic perfection that the two Britons were glad to see that the little white bursts from the AA shells missed the ancient Blenheim. But the greatest surprise still awaited them.

They had not noticed that a small truck was struggling through the rough country behind them. It was Campbell's vehicle, the zealous driver of which had followed his boss into the stone desert. He was, of course, kicking up a great cloud of dust; and when he reached their observation point, the wretched man had to go and stop on a hill, in full sight of the German column.

Incredulously the two officers watched while the great gun barrel, like an enormous finger, swung around in a single, flowing movement and pointed at the truck. The whipcrack report of the shot came a little while after the hit, which set Campbell's vehicle on fire. In utter confusion, the driver threw himself in the dust. Campbell cursed: Among other things, his mattress and bedroll were going up in smoke before him.

Tim Llewellyn-Palmer, however, would have preferred to scream and stamp his feet. The Jerries were once again demonstrating what the younger frontline officers on the British side had been vainly urging: to employ the heavy AA gun, with its high muzzle velocity, in land warfare. The advantages of doing so were now here to see.

Simultaneously with the growing importance of the aircraft as an offensive weapon, most industrial states had soon developed specialized AA guns. These, if they were to serve their purpose, had to have as shallow a shell trajectory as possible; only thus can acceptable accuracy be combined with long range.

For this reason, long-barreled guns were developed, which would guarantee a high initial shell velocity. The German 88 mm AA gun, first produced by Krupp's as early as 1916 as the Bak or anti-balloon gun, produced a muzzle velocity of 840 m/sec with its Mark 36 and 37. With the Mark 41 and 43, this was raised to as much as 1,020 and 1,200 m/sec respectively. This high shell velocity, a feature typical of AA guns, was also the specification set by anti-tank men for their guns, to achieve accuracy, range, and particularly penetration. It was therefore the obvious thing to do to fire from the "eighty-eight" not only the delay-fused high-explosive shells normal in anti-aircraft artillery but also armor-piercing solid rounds of toughened steel. With a projectile weighing just 10 kilograms, tremendous destructive power was produced; armor plating 150 mm thick could be pierced at a range of two kilometers. Such thickness was to be found only on the heaviest tanks, such as that which was to shield the driver on the 55-ton Tiger I.[1]

---

[1] By contrast, the projectile fired by the standard British tank and anti-tank gun, the two-pounder, weighed only 0.91 kilograms, left the barrel at about the same velocity, and would penetrate 56 mm of steel at 500 meters.

Especially in the broad desert expanses of North Africa, such a gun was bound to become a kind of "wonder weapon," and the "eighty-eight" soon became a byword under just that name to both sides.

Yet the British had a heavy AA gun of the same quality, a piece of 3.7-inch (94 mm approx.) caliber. Some of the younger field officers very soon hit on the idea that this gun could be used in ground combat; and before long they had some high-ranking backers: The Commander in Chief, Wavell, personally ordered the gun to be tried out in the winter campaign against the Italians. And the man who eagerly took on the task also had gold on his cap: Brigadier McIntyre used the guns in the softening-up of Tobruk in the winter campaign of 1940/41.

Tim Llewellyn-Palmer had been standing with his little tanks on a nearby height when the "three-seven" for the first time fired at a small cube of concrete, a pillbox, using improvised sights. In time, with the typical whipcrack report characteristic of these guns, one "box" after another disintegrated into a thousand little fragments. The tankmen did not know which to praise most: the devastating destructive power of the gun or its accuracy; for the gunners, almost totally inexperienced in ground fighting, had scored a direct hit with almost every shot at a range of 2.5 kilometers.

The traditionalists in the officer corps naturally raised quite a hullaballoo about the heretics who had taken the gun away from the role ordained for it by God; and McIntyre was given the ugly nickname "Mad Mac." But Wavell declared himself delighted with the enthusiastic report and assured his young friend Palmer that at least one battery off the next convoy would be sent into the desert for ground combat. But just at this time the German Luftwaffe's activities in the Mediterranean began and every available gun had to be used in its traditional role to protect the British Fleet in Alexandria.

It was as if fate had decreed against them: Shortly afterward the action in Greece began and every available gun was needed there; and when Rommel's troops invaded Cyrenaica, there were in all sixteen 3.7-inch AA guns between Benghazi and Alexandria.

True, the supply situation improved in the course of the summer; but by that time Wavell had been dismissed as Churchill's scapegoat and "Mad Mac" fell ill and left the desert. Only now and then could you hear a conversation such as the following in the bars of Cairo between furious frontline officers and condescendingly smiling members of the military establishment:

"The Jerries are shooting us to hell with their eighty-eights. Where are those three-sevens we were to have?"

"Nonsense, old boy—they're ack-ack, don't you know. Apart from which, the carriage is quite unsuitable."

"Then bloody well build a different carriage. For God's sake, *do* something. . . ."

Nothing was ever done; in the very theater of war, where the range and penetration of guns were decisive, the standard British weapon remained the absurd two-pounder. It is virtually impossible to estimate what rivers of blood this failure of the imagination cost the British.

The omission is the more astonishing since there were men at the helm of the British forces and of the state who understood something about modern weapons: Winston Churchill, the Prime Minister and Defense Minister, from the sheer instinct of the old warrior; and the future Chief of the Imperial General Staff, General Sir Alan Brooke, by virtue of his sound professional background. Moreover, both knew that there was something amiss.

Nostalgia for cavalry

Sir Alan, at that time still in charge of the defense of the British Isles, wrote in his journal on 18 June 1941: "Drove to Larkhill to watch a demonstration of anti-tank weapons. I was disappointed with the standard achieved and will start a campaign to improve things."

Early in September he was again at Larkhill and noted: "Progress in anti-tank defense. Two-pounders, six-pounders, 75 mm, Bofors and 3.7-inch tank guns were fired. . . ."

His Britannic Majesty's most senior soldier—a first-class officer who in the course of his career had commanded the First Mobile Division, predecessor of the Armored Division, and had also headed Air Defense Command—thus saw heavy anti-aircraft artillery in an anti-tank role. Why nevertheless nothing happened has remained largely an unsolved mystery.[2]

For, the untiring Churchill too—from whom there issued an unending stream of notes, queries, and memoranda, and who had developed the relentless pursuit of detail into a carefully thought-out system with which to keep his ministers and chiefs of staff in a state of permanent

[2] General Sir John Hackett, the historian and one-time commander of the British Army of the Rhine, who was a young squadron commander in the desert, has told the author that, in 1942, yet another use was foreseen for the 3.7-inch gun: against infantry with shrapnel ammunition. In view of the continuing shortage of anti-tank guns with adequate penetration, this was a particularly silly bit of nonsense. Nor was it put into effect. It would have meant misusing a splendid high-velocity gun for something any field gun could have done equally well. (The "eighty-eight" could do something like this as a sideline, when necessary, with its delayed action anti-aircraft shells.)

tension—had very quickly identified the problem. At first, his enthusiastic nature led him astray in the search for solutions.

Thus, on 23 April, he wrote to the Secretary of State for War: "All the lessons of this war emphasize the necessity for good anti-tank weapons and plenty of them. The number of anti-tank guns that can be produced is necessarily limited; all the more need, therefore, to press forward with whatever substitutes can do the trick. I thought the bombard was distinctly hopeful. . . . Pray let me have a program."

On the same day he chased after yet another inquiry: "There are rumors that the Germans are building their tanks with very strong armor —there is talk of 100 to 150 mm. Such armor would be proof against any existing anti-tank gun. . . . Research has shown that limpet bombs have tremendous penetration. . . . In any case, we must not nod. I trust the War Office is keeping in mind the possibility of a very heavily armored tank and is busy with countermeasures. Pray keep me informed."

He felt that there must be other solutions, that he needed advice on this question, for on the very next day he was writing to the War and Supply ministers: "I propose holding regular sessions to examine the question of tank and anti-tank weapons. . . . It seems to me very important that all officers invited to these meetings should be requested to send in suggestions about the points to be discussed and that they should express their personal views freely and frankly. I have in mind a kind of tank parliament. . . ."

It is one of the many tragedies of war that the bridge between the younger, experienced, and mentally adaptable frontline officers and the aggressive and innovating man at the summit was never fully built. It was the "middle management" that failed.

The "father of British armor," Major General J. C. F. Fuller, had made a biting remark on this score back in the twenties: "There are two great conservative powers under the sun: the Catholic Church and the British Army."

What infuriated this internationally renowned expert was, of course, a general failure to develop British armored strength. The country that had developed the first serious armored fighting vehicle, and put it into action so successfully, had set course long before the Second World War for a grievous inferiority which was to have endless consequences.

Two conservative tendencies appear to have determined the equipment of the mechanized elements of the British Army: obsolete experience, drawn from the First World War; and a sneaking nostalgia for the cavalry.

Analyses of the successful tank battles of 1917–18 had led to the fallacy that the only way to use tanks was as an escort weapon for the infantry. Hardly anyone noticed that it was not battlefield experience but rather the technical shortcomings of those days which had brought about this misconception. The best you could expect to get out of the ungainly monsters of Cambrai was a smart walking pace. So "infantry tanks" were built, heavily armored and underpowered: the first Matilda, armed with a machine gun, 80 hp weak, and grinding along at a top speed of 13 kmph; then Matilda II, which would reach 24 kmph at most and was in any case inconsistently conceived: the two-pounder gun, which fired only armor-piercing rounds, wasn't a great deal of use against infantry, machine-gun nests, or anti-tank and artillery positions. For that you want high-explosive shells with impact fuses, which explode to scatter deadly shrapnel.

Nevertheless, thanks to its unusually heavy armor, the Matilda could, as in the winter campaign of 1940–41, be a surprise trump card. Which was more than you could say of the vehicles that were supposed to play a cavalry role.

First, there was an assortment of small machine-gun tanks of around five tons with a maximum armor thickness of 15 mm and speeds of up to 58 kmph. They were highly suitable for subduing insurgents in the colonies, but pity the poor soldier who had to drive them against a technically advanced European enemy.

As a first hesitant concession to the theory that large mechanized formations were not merely a substitute for the beloved cavalry but could perform independent operations in the enemy's rear rapidly and effectively, a series of Cruiser tanks was produced. The weight was kept down by their thin armor to around 15 tons in the models used in Africa in 1941–42, allowing the engine—all of 150 hp—to produce a top speed of 26 kmph.

Although the power was raised to 300 and even 340 hp in later models, so that in the end a respectable speed of 48 kmph was achieved, the inherent defects of the Cruiser were faithfully retained to the very end of the African campaign: the disastrous two-pounder gun; armor that was far too light; mechanical unreliability—for instance, the Cruiser's overlarge bogey wheels were very liable to shed the tracks during violent changes of direction, reducing the advantage of the vehicle's high speed. . . .

When Winston Churchill's War Cabinet met, somewhat disconcerted under the impact of Rommel's lightning advance, the Australian Prime Minister, Robert G. Menzies, was present. A major of the Reserve, he put his finger on the problem when he intervened in the discussion to say: "I think we still haven't fully realized that the Germans can do anything they like with their armored divisions. Just to say one has such-and-such a number of divisions says nothing about their relative power. What matters are the machines with which these forces are equipped. Wouldn't we therefore be better advised to concentrate our available manpower on tank production, even if that reduced the number of infantry divisions?"

But even a mere head count of tanks said nothing about the power balance; the alert Churchill spotted this—late enough in the day in view of the lightning victories of German forces in Poland and France based largely on tank power, but still sooner than others did. On 20 April, he wrote to the Secretary of State for War: "In Libya some German tanks are now in our possession.[3] Even if these were damaged, we should take all possible steps to get them examined by a skillful designer of British tanks or some other suitable engineering expert. If circumstances permit, a German tank, or suitable parts of one, could be sent home in due course. Meanwhile, if there is no adequate expert already in the Middle East, one should be sent out immediately, to conduct an examination on the spot."

Most instructive in several respects is a note Churchill sent to the Minister of Supply and the Chief of the Imperial General Staff. The old lion thundered:

> (1) We should really try to look to the future now and then. In Libya we have allowed ourselves to be surprised by the German six-pounder tank,[4] when in my view it was clear that they would do something to smash our infantry tank. In Bardia, etc., we could still make an impression with them on the Italians. The Germans took enough of our infantry and Cruiser tanks at Dunkirk; it was therefore easy for them to prepare weapons which would master our tanks.
>
> (2) It will now be my endeavor that we should look forward to . . . preparing a nice little tank surprise for the enemy in Libya. But immediately everyone produces a different excuse; and when in three or four months' time we shall have to do something, we shall be faced with the usual helpless incompetence. . . .

The Prime Minister's grim premonitions for the immediate future were to prove all too correct; but as for his conjectures about German tank design, he had partly overestimated Teutonic thoroughness and partly underestimated it. News of the heavily armored Matilda tank did not reach the highest quarters until 4 March 1941, despite the tanks captured at Dunkirk. On the other hand, no particular reaction was necessary, since the devastating 88 mm gun was in any case being produced by the thousand for ground combat, and since Panzers with stretched 77 mm guns, capable of firing a 6.8 kilogram projectile with

[3] They were captured six days earlier, in the abortive attack on Tobruk.
[4] Churchill is here evidently referring to the Panzer III's 50 mm tank gun which, however, fired rounds of 2.06 kilograms=4.5 pounds.

a muzzle velocity of 790 m/sec, were already rolling off the production lines in volume. This long-barreled version of the Panzer IV could annihilate even the heavy Matilda at a range of 2,000 meters.

And even uglier monsters were being conceived on the drawing boards of the designers. To the very end of the war, Britain was to limp along at least two steps behind Germany in tank design.

The German army never had to endure a handicap like the disastrous gap between the infantry and Cruiser tanks. Although light tanks armed with machine guns or a 20 mm gun (Panzer II) were produced at first, following the experience of the Polish campaign their production was canceled and no substitute was ordered to replace them. An early version of Panzer III, armed with a 37 mm gun, was also discontinued.[5]

What remained were Panzers III and IV, two reliable, robust, well-armored and powerfully armed tanks, to which only minor modifications were necessary right up to the end of the war to keep them among the leaders in international tank design.

As armaments were in 1941, they had nothing to fear from any comparable tanks in the Western world. Heavy armor of up to 80–90 mm,[6] reliable suspension, sturdy 300 hp engines, and a top speed for both Panzers III and IV in the region of 40–42 kmph so that no problems arose when they were used together in action. For in this phase of development, their weapons were complementary. Panzer IV was the "gunner" and fired only high-explosive (HE) shells from its short (L/24)[7] 75 mm gun. Despite the low muzzle velocity of 385 m/sec, its shells, because of their weight and explosive power, were just as destructive at ranges up to 1,000 meters as the British two-pounders' little steel bullets. Panzer III could likewise fire HE shells from its 50 mm gun and thus to some extent provide its own artillery support. In addition to which, its projectiles left the long barrel (L/42)[8] at a

[5] The turrets and hulls of the basic types were so built from the outset that they could, without major modifications, accept and support much heavier guns than originally envisaged.

[6] These maximum thicknesses, fitted at the fronts of turrets and hulls, are, however, not conclusive evidence. Thus Panzer III had vulnerable places of no more than 30–35 mm thickness; whereas the Matilda, with a coat of 90 mm maximum, had a minimum of 80 mm almost everywhere, apart from its somewhat vulnerable flanks. The ill-starred Cruisers, on the other hand, had nowhere more than 30 mm to show—and that was a maximum, with less in some important places.

[7] The formulae L/24 and L/42 express the so-called caliber/length, i.e., the length of the barrel relative to its caliber. In a typical case, the multiplication of the caliber by this fixed quantity (also known as the "caliber factor") gives the length of the barrel. Naturally, only the rifled part is included, without the chamber. As a rule, the longer the barrel, the higher the velocity.

[8] See footnote 7.

velocity of 685 m/sec and its solid steel rounds could pierce the armor of the British Cruiser even at 1,500 meters.

The Italian tin cans

As for the achievements of Italian tank design, suffice it to quote Rommel: "It made one's hair stand on end to think what sort of weapons the Duce had sent his forces into battle with."

The general wrote this remark in his diary when after the abortive attacks on Tobruk he saw remnants of the Italian Ariete armored division appear out of the desert: out of the one hundred brand-new fighting vehicles which had set out from Tripoli, only ten had survived the march.

But he threw even this remnant against Tobruk; as he realized how out of keeping his forces were with his high-flying plans, he fell into the same error which he later, and with justification, laid at the adversary's door: allowing units to attack unselectively, simply in the order in which they arrived, instead of waiting and assembling a force with more punch.

The tank driver Mario C., a mechanic from the Milan area, stepped on the accelerator and tried to make out the terrain through the dust cloud raised by the man in front of him. The sweat was making his eyes burn, and the overheated engine stank of boiling lubricating oil. He kept the revs high all the same. Experience had shown that she did better that way than when turning over slowly.

Somewhere in the billowing yellow mass he could see from his viewing slit, there was a bright flash. The crash of exploding shells was barely audible above the roar of the engine, only the clear tinkle of the shrapnel bouncing off. At the last moment he realized that the tank in front of him, its track shot away, had veered sharp right, into his path. Mario tore at the starboard steering lever. They trundled past the damaged vehicle, missing it by millimeters. He resumed his course. Suddenly the terrain ahead became clear and sharply visible.

They were jolting over a long ridge. Ahead to the left lay a gentle rise. Mario tried in vain to spot some enemy positions. Nothing moved in the treeless and shrubless landscape, which looked even more bleak and inhospitable than the desert with its round camel-thorn shrubs. His heart was in his throat. The enemy could not be far away. He wanted very much to come creditably out of his first action.

A confused mass of feelings and memories drove him on and overcame his fears. There was above all the picture in his mind of that German general who had traveled with them for a stretch, although artillery fire had begun. For a while he had seen him quite distinctly ahead and to the right; a shell burst and when the dust had cleared, his stance had not altered: He had stood bolt upright, facing forward. And there had been his talk with the Italian settlers, in Misurata, who had offered them bread, cheese, and wine on their way east.

One settler had come from near Naples. He had been a head shorter than Mario, but his hands had been immense and horny with hard work. All around, the orange groves had been in bloom and the well-tilled fields sprouted sappy and green.

"There was nothing here but desert when we came," the settler had said. "We pray every day that we may stay here. The Germans will stop the British, won't they?"

Mario flew into a rage. "We are here too," he had said sharply, and left. The little man had run after him and jumped up to embrace him.

There was a certain elitism about the men of the Ariete. Most of them came from northern Italy, where people look down on the *Mezzogiorno* in any case. But Mario's recollections also included two men in black uniforms[9] who had inspected his tank when it was being unloaded and had laughed themselves silly. We'll show them, thought Mario. Behind his back, he heard agitated calls. The turret was being turned to port.

When the anti-tank shell crashed into their vehicle, he felt strangely remote. A body was flung down on him; the picture of a blood-covered, shapeless head, from which an eye hung by yellowish threads, remains in his memory like a photograph.

He did not know how he got out of the tank. There was someone carrying him; then he was lying in a dark room and a face gleaming with sweat appeared above him. Someone cut open one of his sleeves; and only then did he notice his right arm was dangling about numbly. Shortly afterward he lost consciousness. The brief war of Mario C. ended in the prisoner-of-war camp.

The missing Bersaglieri

The abortive attack by the Ariete on the Ras el Madawar, a fortified hill position in the southwestern corner of the Tobruk perimeter, ended on a particularly bitter note when two retreating Italian tanks, obscured by dust, made for Rommel's command post and were not recognized as being friendly. Rommel ordered the anti-tank guns of his escort to fire and both tanks were destroyed.

"The Italian troops are most unreliable. As in 1917, they surrender

---

[9] This suggests that some members of the 5th Panzer Regiment arrived in Africa in the old Panzer uniforms.

very readily," wrote Rommel to his wife. These lines express a slight prejudice from his days as frontline commander in the First World War; on the other hand, Rommel's observation was true enough in most cases.

A sympathetic but also clear-sighted and experienced observer like General Enno von Rintelen reported the gist of the problem: All Italian officer cadets, whether regulars or reservists, were collected in schools and special units for their own kind only and did not join their men until after the completion of their training.

This system, which showed very clearly that its origins were lost in the mists of the past, was not calculated to create a body of soldiers with a common purpose. Instead, it made a clear distinction between the gentlemen giving the orders and urging the men on and a faceless mass of cannon fodder. Not merely individualists from the Mediterranean but even men from northern latitudes would have reacted to this by coming to the very sensible conclusion that in this repulsive setup one must look after one's own skin in the first place. Many externals contributed to this, such as differences in food and other supplies, which in normal circumstances were far from being only a matter of degree.[10]

The neglected Italian soldier showed himself more willing and open to encouragement when someone from the higher echelons for once paid him some attention. Rommel, who would talk to them in dreadful Italian, and was quite happy to be seen spooning tough beef out of tins marked AM (*Administrazione Militare*=Military Administration, rechristened by the German soldiers *Alter Mann*=Old Man, and by the Italians *Arabo Morte*=Dead Arab), was worshiped by the men. He was less popular in the officer corps and the following incident at Tobruk contributed to this. The Australians were far from idle after the Germans' unsuccessful attacks. The pugnacious Diggers kept the German and Italian siege troops on the hop with their raids. It was not long after the disappointing performance of the Ariete that vigorous activity was reported one night in the neighborhood of the Ras el Madawar. As usual, the next morning Rommel went out himself to see if all was well.

A battalion of Bersaglieri was supposed to be building a protective artillery screen in the area. Rommel peered carefully over the brow of a hill and found the hollow behind it covered in his allies' gaudy and befeathered tropical helmets. Not one living soul was to be seen; the

[10] When interviewing Italian war veterans, one always heard the remark: "We went thirsty, but they bathed in soda water." No one had actually seen it, but the general atmosphere and the separation into two worlds made it plausible.

artillery position was completely unprotected. The 9th Australian Division's war diary correctly reports at this time: "Brought in 370 Italian prisoners and destroyed two guns, in one night."

Rommel had the gap manned and returned to his staff, fuming. As ill luck would have it, the tall Italian liaison officer, General Calvi, a son-in-law of the king's, happened to cross his path. His Excellency spoke German and he blanched at the Supreme Commander's harsh words. Moreover, Rommel demanded, both verbally and in writing, of his nominal superior, Gariboldi, that officers showing cowardice in the face of the enemy should be shot out of hand.

Meanwhile, far away in Germany, it had not gone unnoticed that all was not running smoothly in the Afrika Korps. Thus, after the annihilation of the 8th Machine Gun Battalion, General Kirchheim had written to the head of the OKW, Keitel, that the 5th Light Division would be destroyed and the Afrika Korps beaten unless the hopeless attacks on Tobruk ceased. Amid all his other concerns, the Chief of the General Staff, Halder, noted this with satisfaction.

Operation Barbarossa, the attack on the Soviet Union, was at last to start in May. For weeks, the pages of his diary were filling more and more with entries about the strategic, tactical, technical, and logistical problems of the deployment in the east. But the inept activities of Germany's junior partner south of the Alps began to make their side effects felt: The code name Marita occurs in the entries more and more frequently. It was under this code name that the Wehrmacht intervention in Greece was being prepared.

A new Blitz campaign

In the spring and summer of 1941, the world gazed as if hynpotized at the apparently invincible German war machine, its perfection as fascinating as it was terrifying.

No one outside Germany could have suspected that Hitler had driven an unwilling corps of generals to their successes. Ironically the generals, who as professionals should have been able to assess the military opportunities, fought shy of the Blitzkrieg theory, with its modern fighting tools, the tank, and the airplane. So afraid was Halder of imminent military defeat that in the winter of 1939–40 he was even contemplating an armed *Putsch*—as indeed he had before the Sudeten crisis of 1938.

After the *Blitz* campaigns in Scandinavia and France, the atmosphere changed to the opposite extreme. A majority now had boundless confidence in themselves, in an enthusiastic Wehrmacht, and of course in "the greatest captain of armies of all time." When Hitler unfolded his Ostland plans, among the few who did utter words of warning were Göring, Ribbentrop, and Keitel, considered outsiders and vassals of Hitler.

Everyone set busily to work. As befitted a well-ordered regime, even the leaders' plans for mass murder were laid down in advance, in writing. Jodl circulated his interpretation of the Führer's directives, according to which "the Jewish-Bolshevik intelligentsia must be liquidated" and all "Bolshevik chiefs and commissars immediately rendered harmless." Whereupon the more refined gentlemen of the Wehrmacht command staff specified: "In the army's operational area, Reichsführer SS [Himmler] has had special duties assigned to him by the Führer in preparing a political administration. These duties arise from the struggle of two contending political systems, which must be carried to its ultimate conclusion." Of course after the war none of them had any idea what that meant.

In the same way, those present on 30 March 1941 at a two-hundred-strong gathering of generals, of whom Hitler openly demanded that they should be ready to annihilate the communist intelligentsia, remembered after the war only that there had been a certain amount of grumbling about this. Unlike most of his colleagues, the methodical Halder was unlucky enough to be unable to rewrite his diary after the war.[11] He wrote down the thoughts of the supreme warlord loyally and without comment, concluding with the sentence: "Commanders must demand of themselves the sacrifice of overcoming their scruples." And then, a memo in the margin: "Order of the Supreme Army Commander."

An order to this effect—a death sentence for the political cadres of the Red Army—was immediately and most eagerly drafted. (That some frontline commanders later simply did not carry it out could have been due only to their being far more hardened to danger.)

In view of the very free use of words like "honor" and "manly virtue" by this professional body, the readiness of the higher echelons to become accomplices to murder remains as astonishing as the speed with which it became commonplace.

Halder's war diary says, without any transition:

> Noon: Lunch together.
> Afternoon: Discussion at the Führer's.
> (a) Yugoslav question: Decision went my way. . . .

The Yugoslav question had again made a mess of existing plans. Operation Marita, the attack that was to get the Italians off the hook in

[11] The CGS's notes were seized by U.S. soldiers on 5 June 1945 from a lady who was keeping them for him.

Greece, had been decided on since British troops had landed there. To secure the long right flank of this operation, the route for which ran through Romania and Bulgaria, Yugoslavia had with difficulty been persuaded to join the Triple Alliance. But on 27 March, only three days after the agreement had been signed, pro-British officers overthrew the regime.

Hitler sent for Brauchitsch and Halder: "I have decided to strike Yugoslavia down. What forces do you need? How much time do you need?"

In its new awareness of its invincibility, the General Staff produced a *tour de force*. Within a week, more or less, the Marita plan was taken to pieces and put together again as a comprehensive plan of deployment. On 6 April, while Rommel's small outfit was racing through Libya, the attack on Yugoslavia and Greece was also launched. In the west, this coincidence has long been considered a superbly tuned two-pronged operation.

One more Blitzkrieg reinforced the general atmosphere of self-confidence. It was all over in three weeks. But just three years later, shortly before the end, Hitler was to curse the campaign in the Balkans in a voice choking with tears: It was because of that campaign, he said, that the attack on the U.S.S.R. had been delayed by a crucial six weeks. It was because of it that the eastern army had run into the Russian winter before the colossus had been smashed.

The postponement of Barbarossa from mid-May to the second half of June was to be frequently produced as the piece of ill fortune which had prevented the destruction of the "Slav subhumans" by autumn, according to plan. But disregarding the fact that history knows no "if onlys" and "should haves," the vast spaces of Russia would in any case have produced their own surprises, of which neither the "Foreign Armies East" Department nor the "Greatest Warlord of All Time" would have known. What is sure is that in late May and early June, 1941, unusually heavy rain fell in eastern Poland and western Russia. This in itself would have occasioned either a postponement of the attack or a corresponding slowdown of the operations of motorized and mechanized forces on roads turned into quagmires.

It is also certain that the new Blitzkrieg had a long-term consequence to which the military and political leadership gave no thought in the euphoria and arrogance of those days.

The chain of subjugated countries which had to be policed and held down ran from the North Cape to the southern tip of Greece. And then there was a Yugoslav mechanic called Josip Broz—alias Tito. His partisan army alone was to tie down twenty-eight divisions at the height of the war.

To that extent, Churchill was justified in his claim that the dispatch of a British expeditionary corps to Greece had substantially influenced the outcome of the war. Out of the 60,000 men of the corps, 50,000 got away, although once again without their heavy weapons and vehicles. Hitler, with his Ostland obsession, would certainly not otherwise have occupied the Balkans. Hungary, Romania, and Bulgaria would have sufficed to provide flank cover against the Soviet Union; and he occasionally viewed with sinister delight the embarrassment in which his fellow dictator, Mussolini, had landed himself through his Greek adventure.

However, the landing of the British expeditionary corps, which had also egged on the coup-happy military in Yugoslavia, provided the decisive impetus: It was out of the question to leave the oil wells of Ploesti in Romania within range of the RAF.

It was therefore again only half the truth when, shortly before the end, Hitler said that the Latins had always brought him nothing but bad luck and that Mussolini alone had been to blame for the Balkan campaign. It was, in fact, brought about by the appearance of the "island Germans" and occasioned not merely by the feeble advances of the Italians from Albania but at least as much by the menacing German deployment in Romania. And, of course, also by the fighting spirit of Churchill, the old lion of 10 Downing Street.[12]

The threads were tangled as Germany and Italy's "coalition war" was without any plan and marked by rivalry and mistrust. Anger at the German march into Romania had driven Mussolini to attack Greece; it was to Romania that the Greeks too were looking when, unwillingly, they allowed in the first British anti-aircraft and air force units. It seemed to them that they could cope with the Italians by themselves but against the Germans they did not stand a chance. On the other hand, might the terrible Wehrmacht perhaps spare them if they offered Berlin no provocation?

Consequently, the pilots of the RAF did not receive consent to overfly Greek territory on their way to Ploesti; nevertheless the threat to the wells which were to feed Hitler's crusade against the East remained. When the Wehrmacht threw bridges across the Danube and approached through Bulgaria, the Greeks gave in to the urgings of the British. The expeditionary corps came steaming out of Egypt, to proffer aid against the Germans, not the Italians.

[12] At another point, too, Churchill instinctively struck a nerve of Hitler's: After a British *coup de main* against the Lofoten Islands, the Führer left a much stronger garrison force in Norway than had originally been intended, further weakening Barbarossa.

The power of publicity

Toward the end of the new Blitz campaign, Rommel wrote optimistically to his wife: "Greece will soon be settled. And then it will be possible to give us more help here. . . . The battle for Egypt and the Canal is about to begin in earnest."

His ignorance of what was coming is evident; only a few days after Rommel's March visit to Germany, Hitler tricked the assembly of generals into complicity with his regime; but neither Hitler nor Rommel's immediate superiors in the OKH told him anything about the impending attack on Russia.

We can surmise that Hitler saw no reason to rob his dashing general of his impetus by telling him at an early stage that his African theater of war was about to be demoted to second-class status. Halder, on the other hand, could not stand Rommel and would in any case have told him only what was unavoidable in the course of duty. The commander of the Afrika Korps was not even told of the imminent Balkan enterprise,[18] hardly a credit mark for the Chief of the General staff, whose job it was supposed to be to co-ordinate and integrate. Thus the actions in the two Mediterranean theaters of war ran in parallel, the war in the desert mostly ignored, until the remarks which occasionally crop up in Halder's diary become more and more tetchy.

Rommel was launching his first attacks on Tobruk when Halder heard that Hitler wanted to send him a motorized infantry battalion. "In view of the great tasks ahead," he wrote, this was impossible. Next day: "Rommel wants to march on Suez. The Reichsmarschall [Göring] wants to let him have air force units for this." Halder informed the OKW that there were in any case neither the forces nor the supply capability for this—on which point he was, of course, right—and immediately made the triumphant entry: "Now he himself [Rommel] reports that his forces are not adequate to exploit the 'unprecedentedly favorable' general situation. Back here we have long had this impression."

And in a later entry, summing up the situation: "By exceeding his orders, Rommel has created a situation which has outstripped the supply capability at this time. Rommel is not up to the job."

"The job" had now gone quite a bit awry. When the wild chase was over and Rommel's troops came to a halt around Tobruk and on the Egyptian border, another characteristic of desert war became evident:

[18] Halder's deputy, Paulus, later reproached Rommel that as a result of his premature attack the British had withdrawn earlier from Greece than they would otherwise have done, and had thus escaped. That is not what happened; for, as we know, Wavell held substantial troop shipments back and ordered ships that had already sailed to return.

Everything you want to consume or use, you have to bring along with you or have it brought up behind you. Use of the port at Tobruk was being denied by the obdurate Australians. Only in distant Tripoli (and to some small extent in Benghazi and Derna) were any supplies being landed. An immense transport enterprise became necessary; lorries and coasters droned along day and night to bring forward food, ammunition, and fuel over 1,700 kilometers.

In doing so, their own engines burned millions of liters a month. Thus it was a victory that was at the same time a nuisance, since it gave rise to substantial follow-up costs and further weakened the Barbarossa adventure. At the same time, however—and this was what made Halder furious—the propaganda success was substantial and Rommel's name was in every newspaper all over the world. Even in Greater Germany, Hitler, who abhorred any personality cult—other than his own, of course—made an exception: Rommel's name was on everyone's lips, and he became a very early example of the power of publicity by the mass media: He might not be "equal to the job," but he was quite simply unassailable by the CGS.

On top of all that, Hitler, and the army commander, Brauchitsch, had committed themselves: In the early days of Rommel's successful defiance of his orders, when no one had as yet thought of the consequences, they had sent Rommel telegrams of congratulation. No matter how much ammunition might come to Halder's hand, none of it would ever strike home.

And ammunition there was in plenty. After the tragedy of the 8th Machine Gun Battalion and the frenzied assault on Tobruk, General Kirchheim, and other officers as well, sent warning signals. Halder wrote in his diary on 23 April 1941:

> For days Rommel has given none of us a clear report.[14] I feel, however, that the thing has gone bad. It appears from the reports of officers coming from down there, as well as from personal letters, that Rommel is in no way up to his command duties. All day long he races about between his widely scattered forces, ordering raids and dissipating his troops. No one at all has a general overview of the distribution of his forces and of their fighting strength. . . . Partial advances by weak Panzer forces have resulted in substantial losses. . . . Rommel's senseless demands cannot be met by air freight, if only because we lack the fuel, and aircraft sent to North Africa find no fuel there for the return journey. . . .

[14] Later there was a further row because Halder took the view that Rommel was sending the "Führer-Bureau"—the OKW—reports only on his successes, while all he sent the OKH were complaints and demands. Rommel explained that this must have been the fault of Rintelen's staff in Rome, since these reports went through it.

It was decided to send Lieutenant General Paulus to Africa to clarify the situation there. Halder remarked that Paulus was acquainted with Rommel from past service together and was perhaps the only man who could "regain control of this demented soldier by dint of his personal influence."

Attack under supervision

It must have been a bitter day for Rommel when Paulus appeared at his headquarters on 27 April 1941, asked for an account of the situation and the prospects, and then, as he somewhat pompously wrote in his report to the OKH, explained: "As the delegate of the Commander in Chief of the Army, charged with the elucidation of the situation in the African theater of war, and having been invested with the right to advise the German Afrika Korps, I reserve my attitude to the decisions of the Korps imparted to me until I have examined the situation." The decisions imparted to him simply read: "Attack Tobruk!"

His examination of the situation produced the information that the outlook for the enterprise was at least more promising than for the preceding ones: A considerable part of the 15th Panzer Division had arrived; fighters and dive bombers had been moved up to the nearby airfields of Gazala and Gambut; by way of artillery, 35 Italian and German batteries could be concentrated opposite the site of the proposed breach at Ras el Madawar, and the 5th Panzer Regiment, thanks mainly to the hectic work of the repair crews, had grown again to 74 serviceable tanks, half of them the powerful Panzer IIIs and IVs.

Paulus agreed to the attack. In distant Germany, Halder wrote in his diary: "I think it's wrong."

One point that bothered him had at least been cleared out of the way by Paulus. He told Rommel, who wanted to withdraw all German units from the Egyptian frontier and send them into the attack: "You have never ceased to stress that the Italian troops are absolutely useless. In that case, you cannot entrust the protection of your flank on the frontier to them alone. It is after all the key point for keeping up the encirclement of Tobruk." Rommel gave immediate orders that Colonel von Herff's combat group should be left in the neighborhood of Sollum-Bardia.

Last stop: minefield

The men of the 5th Panzer Regiment had not had much sleep when, before sunrise on 1 May 1941, they trundled up to their deployment positions. All night long they had heard the stuttering of small-arms fire and the thud of artillery from the direction of Tobruk. Between the flashes of exploding shells, one could occasionally see the ugly licking of the red tongues of the flamethrowers with which infantry and sappers were attacking the Australians' bunker emplacements.

"Today, it'll be okay," thought Sergeant Major Wilhelm Wendt as his Panzer III turned toward the enemy lines with the first pale light. At any rate, the battlefield looked different from those unhappy Easter days. It was more reminiscent of the days of quick victories in Poland and France. A breakthrough on a wide front into the forward fortified lines was secured on the right and left by strong infantry units with anti-tank guns, mortars, and field artillery. The adjoining area was covered by artillery. High up, from the west, the first of the Stuka formations came droning in.

On the right wing, "Sarge" Wendt surged forward. Ahead, he had seen fortified enemy field positions behind some dry-stone walls, and his instinct told him: Off we go; speed is all that matters now; getting on with it is actually safer than hesitating. But over the radio came a ticking-off: "Don't go so fast, Wendt! Stay in line!" He reined in his driver a little, but stayed a few vehicle lengths ahead of the company. They were driving between unusual-looking heaps of stones. As they were being left behind, Wendt noticed that the little heaps were daubed white on the enemy's side. Damn, he thought, that must mean something—but what? A loud bang shook the Panzer. Anti-tank gun or a mortar, thought Wendt. This is it!

"Step on it!" he called to his driver. The vehicle accelerated somewhat jerkily. And then there was a second, shattering blast. "Go on, go on!" shouted the sergeant major.

"She won't move," said his driver.

"Let's have a look," said Wendt and threw back the hatch cover. As he jumped off sideways, he was just able to give his body a small, life-saving twist. What lay there, hastily covered with sand, was unmistakably a mine. One track lay in a straight line behind the Panzer, like a caterpillar someone had run over and flattened. Cursing, Wendt jumped back on his Panzer and fished for his microphone. To think that he hadn't realized it before! Those heaps of stone of course marked a minefield. They rolled carefully back, keeping to their own ruts.

Before he had finished his radioed warning, there was a series of explosions. The whole outfit was sitting in the minefield. Only two out of twenty-two Panzers still had tracks on their bogeys. They carefully reversed along their own track marks. Wendt ran ahead of them, although the enemy artillery had now discovered the area. He saw motorcycle troops and sappers riding in trucks coming up. He stopped them just short of the markings.

"See to it that the vehicles are fixed," the company commander ordered. From the positions behind the stone dikes, there came the chatter of infantry fire. They were about 600 meters away. Wendt told two Panzer crews to give covering fire with their machine guns and guns. He set to work with the others. Mercifully, the artillery fire had stopped.

Twelve hours in a coma

It was the local Australian commander, Lieutenant Colonel Spowers of the "undisciplined" 20th Infantry Brigade, who had ordered the artillery fire to be shifted farther south: The 25-pounders couldn't do a great deal more by indirect fire than the mines had already done. In addition, the shell bursts kept setting off his own mines, which was particularly undesirable. This minefield, which was fending off a very serious threat to the fortress, had not been laid until after the April attacks. Spowers was not inclined to let his own artillery destroy the work of many a night's backbreaking work. The lieutenant colonel was at that moment tolerably relieved. For the first time in over twelve hours, his headquarters was able to get an approximate idea of what was actually going on.

That it would be something quite serious had been obvious for days. Since the Stukas had taken over the airfields around about, their attacks had become fiercer and fiercer. Although the Royal Navy had managed to bring 5,000 tons of supplies into the fortress since it had been cut off, three freighters had been sunk in the process—the last one on 29 April as it was unloading in the harbor.

The last British fighters and reconnaissance aircraft had left the wrecked airfields within the perimeter. There was no point in allowing them to be bombed to pieces on the ground.

In the afternoon of 30 April, heavy German artillery fire rained down among the positions at Ras el Madawar. As the sun sank, Stukas, their sirens howling, dived on the churned-up piece of desert. Presently the telephone lines broke.

During the night, the artillery fire became so violent that no runner could get through to the forward lines. In between the shell bursts, you could occasionally hear small-arms fire. It was clear that the German attack had begun. At break of day, the reserve company, which was stationed a mile behind the foremost line, reported that German tanks and infantry had appeared opposite them. And this time the breach was on a broader front than a fortnight ago. The German infantry had not infiltrated between the strongpoints but had overrun them, although with heavy losses.

The Panzers were now thrusting into a gap of three by three kilometers. General Morshead decided to hold his tiny tank force of twelve Matildas and nineteen Cruisers in reserve for the time being. The Germans were to be stopped by mines, anti-tank guns and, of course, the invaluable 25-pounders.

Who's the prisoner now?

A little to the west of the minefield in which Sergeant Major Wendt and his men were tugging perspiringly at their heavy tracks, the other Panzers came under light indirect fire from the 25-pounders. Signalman Joachim Saenger fired his MG-34 machine gun at Australian infantrymen whose heads would occasionally appear above the concrete reinforced dugouts. They evidently had nothing better than their ineffective anti-tank muskets.

Then an immense crash shook the Panzer, which stopped with a jolt. "Only an artillery hit. It's all right," the commander called out. "On we go!" But the engine was dead. "It won't restart," said the driver.

Dust clouds from more shells rose here and there from the stony ground. Although his common sense told him that he was relatively safe where he was, an uneasy feeling came over Saenger in his steel crate, standing there as on a platter. He hoisted himself from his hatch and put the strap of his private binoculars, his pride and joy from Poland, over his head.

Farther forward the other Panzers had now drawn the fire of the 25-pounders and appeared distinctly to be losing their drive. Here and there, you saw infantry charging, but the customary *élan* was lacking.

Far on the other side, there was a movement of vehicles, among them a few tanks. The commander let Saenger give him a few target bearings and they played artillery with high-explosive shells for a bit. They weren't doing much damage, but the bangs made them feel better.

But they had apparently attracted the notice of an artillery observer, for suddenly shells were bursting all around them again.

Without stopping to think, Saenger jumped from the Panzer and ran away at an angle into the countryside. He had a feeling he wasn't doing a great deal of good in his stranded iron box in any case. Suddenly there was a hole in the ground in front of him; an approaching shell whined; he jumped in. He landed in a much bigger space than he had expected. And the figures around him, observing him calmly, were clad in unmistakably British uniforms.

A twenty-two-year-old brain clicks rapidly, if sometimes a little irrationally. Saenger fished an egg grenade out of his trousers pocket and yelled "Hands up!" A huge man with stubble on his chin and some gold on his shoulder said good-naturedly in a broad Australian accent: "Just put that dangerous thing away, will you?"

There were up to forty men in the concrete-lined dugout and it did in fact seem quite crazy to be playing the hero with a hand grenade. He stuck the thing back in his pocket and nobody made any move to take it off him. One man, his face utterly smashed, lay on the floor, a death rattle in his throat. His nose and mouth were one bloody mess of flesh. "He was shooting at the tanks with the anti-tank rifle when he got in the way of a machine-gun burst," said the giant.

My God, thought Saenger, could it have been me? It was the first time in his life he had seen a gravely wounded man. Filled with horror and compassion he fumbled for one of the first-aid kits he had carefully stuffed into his trousers pockets. The Australians swathed the pulped face in bandages; Saenger rather doubted whether it was the best thing to do; but the man still seemed to be able to breathe.

The big Australian, a captain, spread some butter from his homeland on a biscuit. "Better get used to Australian food; that's where you'll be going now—nice and safe."

"Mm-mm," said Saenger, his mouth full. "It's you who are the prisoners." Some of the men laughed. They seemed to feel quite safe. Some of them wrote their addresses on bits of paper and stuck them in his pockets. One showed him pictures of his family, his farm, and himself shearing sheep. "Call my people when you get to Australia. You're a good chap—we'll look after you."

Outside, there was a rattle of tank tracks. The sun was getting low on the horizon. Unless I get out of here, I really will end up in Australia, thought Saenger.

He pushed nearer the edge of the hole, risked looking up, and immediately saw two legs in German trousers making off. *"Hilfe, hilfe!"* Saenger cried. The legs stood still in their tracks and a sapper with a machine pistol jumped down into the hole. Others appeared around the rim, their weapons at the ready.

For a moment, there were the makings of a bloodbath; but then the captain shrugged his shoulders and the tension vanished. Somehow their conversation had created an atmosphere which made butchery out of the question. Without a word, the Australians laid down their arms. Saenger helped them to pack up their coats, food, whiskey, and cigarettes.

Two big Australians locked arms and sat the wounded man on them. All around them, German infantrymen were withdrawing and the artillery fire was growing heavier. But the two men walked with a steady step, merely going down on one knee when the shells whined too thick and fast.

The sappers handed their prisoners over to an Italian unit and their comrades and allies grinned with flashing teeth at the thought of returning victorious with so many prisoners. For a long while, Saenger watched them milling around the group of broad khaki backs. Over them all swayed the white-swathed head of the wounded man.[15]

"Cooling water cocktail"

Meanwhile, Wendt and his men had worked themselves to the brink of total exhaustion. They suffered less from the intermittent bursts of fire than from the burning sun, for two Panzers were still standing by to give them covering fire.

Their thirst was becoming unbearable; while they were straining to drag the heavy tracks about, they sweated dreadfully and drank all their water ration for the day.

Eventually, a warrant officer reported to Wendt: "The men can't go on. They must have something to drink." The idea might also have occurred to one of their superior officers, or to a "supply warrior"; but there was not a single supply vehicle about as far as the eye could see —only the roasting-hot, shimmery air lying over the stony desert floor. To cap it all, a sandstorm blew up.

"We'll try," said Wendt. "Drain the cooling water from one of the tanks." It tasted appalling, but at least it moistened their parched throats for a few moments. But very soon one man after another had to stop working and rush off, grabbing a spade on the way. The "cooling water cocktail," it seemed, made straight for nature's exit via stomach and gut.

It was late in the afternoon by the time the last Panzer with its tracks patched up clanked back to the regiment.

Wendt stood sadly in the turret and remembered with what high hopes they had started in the morning. True, Ras el Madawar had been taken, but it was obvious that the old Blitz would not work on this blasted Tobruk. When the Panzers drove through, the Australian infantry would not give up, as the Germans had learned to expect.

At about this time, the burial detail were also finishing their work. In some armies you get an extra ration of spirits for this work. And very welcome it was, too, on the broiling Hill 209 at Tobruk. A man hacked to pieces at close range by shrapnel or machine-gun fire is poor material for a hero's memorial. But somewhere in this region a war reporter

---

[15] Saenger carried the Australian addresses about with him for a long time, until they were destroyed, together with his Panzer, at El Alamein.

remembered his obscene duty: to bring home to the youth of Germany that a hero's death is an aesthetic experience. He wrote: "The soldier nearest to me has hardly grown to boy's estate. His face is brown, its features suffused with a deep inner peace, as if suddenly overcome by sleep. His leg is pulled up; his head is slightly tilted back. The eyes are turned toward the distant sky, still hidden from us by a veil of sand. A smile plays round his lips. The picture of this death is a beautiful one. It is so touchingly impressive that I must tear myself away from contemplating this comrade."

However, at Rommel's headquarters, Paulus ordered the production of further such concoctions to be stopped for the time being.

Twelve hundred men were dead, wounded, or captured. All there was left by way of reserves that could have been thrown into battle was at most the 33rd Reconnaissance Unit. It made no sense at all. Rommel remarked that the Australian defenders were certainly crack units and superior to his soldiers in equipment. Was he really unaware how very green the Diggers were?

Around the top of the Ras el Madawar, the infantry was getting ready to defend the position. Decimated units of the 15th Panzer Division, sent into battle virtually straight off the ship, were burrowing into the stony ground and cursing the while. Where were the palms they wore on their pretty brassards? No one had expected Africa to be like this. Instead of prowling lions, they were being tormented by those far more fearful brutes of the North African coast: the flies.

Water was short but at least it did come, from the abundant sweet-water spring at Derna. The supply trucks came in the night, harassed by stray artillery fire. It would be some time yet before besiegers and besieged found a sort of *modus vivendi* up here.

Then came the British counterattack: General Morshead, who had virtually no air reconnaissance at his disposal, could spare no more than his reserve brigade and a couple of Matildas for the job, and even that involved a certain risk—a major attack might suddenly be launched by the other side.

Captain Armitage of the RHA was there as an artillery observer. After the flight from Mechili and the somewhat tremulous sea journey to the besieged fortress, he had come to terms as far as possible with the flies, the thirst, and the general hardship of siege life. And with the Stukas.

From the days of the French campaign, Armitage was familiar with the unnerving howl of their sirens, which seemed at first more effective than their bombs. But after some time in Tobruk, he began to appreciate the precise aim of the German pilots. They dived so exactly on the larger and more obvious targets that a mere 50 meters away from them one was, as a rule, quite safe.

They had built narrow slit trenches in their batteries, and in the stony ground these gave protection from almost anything short of a direct hit. So, as soon as the gun crews caught sight of one of these vulturelike birds, with their fixed cowled undercarriages, beginning to make a dive, they would rush for the trenches. In fact, during the entire siege not one soldier of Armitage's unit had been killed in a slit trench.

Three signalmen had some bad luck, though. One afternoon during one of the softening-up attacks by the Stukas prior to 1 May, they were just getting into a light truck to mend a telephone line broken by the bombardment. The lookout shouted a warning, but their worn-out old vehicle was making such a din that they could not hear it. When the first bombs fell, they were just driving past the last of the gun emplacements. The three men threw themselves into it; but the pilot had picked on this particular emplacement. Not much was ever found of the signalmen.

The Australian counterattack was to start immediately after sundown, but for some reason or other the brigade had turned up too early. It was the critical time: The daily sandstorm had abated; visibility was still good; and since the Germans held the Ras el Madawar, their artillery observers were able to see far into the country.

The result was some monstrously accurate fire. Armitage drove across the hellish plain, hoping for the best, and directed his battery by wireless. Just as the light was failing they reached the first German positions. The infantrymen in it were dead—or pretending to be; there was no time to check.

Surprisingly, the Germans' machine-gun fire had until then been far too high. But in the close combat that followed, the Australians suffered heavy losses. A bloody night brought only negligible territorial gains on the eastern flank of the breach.

When morning came, some Matildas also attacked. Quite near Armitage one of the tanks was destroyed by fire. The shell tore the turret from its circular track and the barrel hung down at an angle, like the beak of a sad, dead bird. The crew had obviously been killed outright; but the engines went on running and hummed quietly away in neutral for another twenty-four hours.

Paulus reins Rommel in

In his report, Paulus noted with marked disapproval that ammunition for the artillery had run short after only a few days, although he had earlier been told that supplies were adequate. Having verbally made it clear to Rommel that there could be no question of a glorious drive to the Suez Canal for the time being, he left behind directives for the further conduct of operations at Tobruk. No more major attacks— at most only limited operations, holding promise of "a quick success without any appreciable losses." Only after the arrival of reinforcements could a thrust to the dominating ground around Fort Pilastrino be considered.

And as if the thought had occurred to him on the way home that Rommel needed pinning down unambiguously to make sure there would be no unpleasant surprises, he radioed the Afrika Korps from Rome: "Further to No. (3) of Directive No. 35457/4 Ref. *GeKados,* 2.5.41: The directive is that before a possible continuation of an attack on Tobruk in search of a decisive result, agreement of the Supreme Commander of the Army (OKH) must be obtained, even after the arrival of the remaining elements of the 15th Panzer Division and of further reinforcements."

Paulus had interpreted very conscientiously his brief of "elucidating conditions in Africa" and had held detailed talks with everyone of whom any information could be expected: individual commanders, top air force and naval liaison staff—as well as Rommel and the Italian Commander in Chief, Gariboldi.

His conclusions were matter-of-fact, and some of them differed sharply from Rommel's views.

Concerning the precarious situation of the German and Italian units, which were stretched to the utmost, he saw no point in sending anymore reinforcements to Africa, apart from the troops which were already on the way. The reinforcements, too, would want to eat, drink, and fire off ammunition. High-flying hopes of operations aimed at the Canal belonged to the realm of fantasy. On the contrary, Paulus was by no means sure whether what had already been taken should be kept; and he ordered the Corps Commander and his G1 Ops, von dem Borne, to start thinking urgently about a disengagement which might perhaps become necessary—for instance should it prove impossible to take Tobruk or should a powerful British thrust be made from Egypt. His skepticism was later to prove very well grounded.

From the Paulus report:

> The order of priority for further shipments should be:
> (a) Supplies of all types (ammunition, fuel, food).
> (b) Vehicles to carry the supplies.
> (c) Shipment of further troops, and in this context first of all heavy artillery and replacement of armor-piercing weapons, to take place only when there are ample supplies available.

Such a set of priorities was necessary, if only because shipping across the Mediterranean had become even more problematical than overland transport in Africa.

From Rommel's letter to his wife and son, 23 April 1941: "How are you both? There must be masses of mail lying on the bottom of the Mediterranean. . . ."

And not just mail, either.

Paulus reported: "Shipping between Sicily and Tripoli is at the moment restricted to occasional convoys (in a sense blockade breakers) which arrive only at irregular intervals. Unloading in Tripoli is very hazardous by virtue of the superiority of the enemy air and naval forces, which are able to mount attacks at any time, even by day, since our own air strength and coastal defenses are totally inadequate."

In fact, the air forces of the Axis had long been overstretched, since the Balkan campaign and the preparations for Barbarossa had diverted substantial German forces. And in London, Churchill had issued one of his thunderous directives to his Chiefs of Staff: "It becomes the prime duty of the British Mediterranean Fleet . . . to stop all seaborne traffic between Italy and Africa. . . . For this all-important objective, heavy losses in battleships, cruisers, and destroyers must if necessary be accepted. . . . Every convoy which gets through must be considered a serious naval failure."

The old warrior, Cunningham, whose forces had just pulled off the costly evacuation of the expeditionary corps from Greece, and which were engaged in no less dangerous a task in keeping Tobruk provisioned, became angry when he received his orders to this effect from the Admiralty. When the Prime Minister subsequently prevailed on the Navy bosses to order him to sacrifice the battleship *Barham* which, manned by a sort of *kamikaze* crew, was to have been steered into the harbor at Tripoli and sunk to block the port, he finally blew his top and recommended his superiors bluntly to think their order over again.

Instead, in a rage, he steamed with his main force to a point 10 kilometers off Tripoli and bombarded the harbor with his guns for forty minutes. Grimly, he concluded his report on the operation with the statement: "My comments on the question of whether there was any point in the bombardment will follow at the appropriate time." So they did; and the Admiral simply stated, although in politer language, that the whole thing had been rather stupid and had gone off without loss only because the Luftwaffe happened to be otherwise engaged at the time.

The Luftwaffe was to be otherwise engaged for some time yet. The rocky redoubt of Malta, pinned down by the 10th Flying Corps during the transshipment of Rommel's first contingents, was recovering fast. Together with the forces stationed in Alexandria, its air and naval forces dominated the supply routes almost completely.

A bare few months earlier the OKW, in a statement inspired by Hitler, had written: "The war [against Britain] can no longer be lost—it need merely be finished." Yet the position now was that the Rommel corps could no longer be adequately provisioned. Malta, Cyprus, Gibraltar, the Suez Canal, even the Persian Gulf and Afghanistan—their turn would also come, once the *bagatelle* of the "Slav subhumans" was settled.

And in London, an old man bursting with energy read the German radio traffic about more and more troop movements eastward, supplied to him by the amazing Ultra service, and vacillated between hope and despair. The British Prime Minister sent Stalin a detailed warning, but received no reply.

Churchill was also reading other messages being deciphered by Winterbotham's Ultra staff: Rommel's cries for help—for reinforcements and supplies—as well as the skeptical Paulus report, which he read with particular delight.

The old warhorse could again hear bugles blowing. His signals to Wavell followed each other in quick succession. At the same time he set about the task of persuading the Chiefs of Staff and the Admiralty to undertake a daring operation.

Churchill and the generals

At this time of extreme tension, Churchill was in an absolute furious mood. A character like his merely becomes more combative with every defeat. Which meant that any associate of his who got on the wrong side of him found it a very painful experience.

The diary of Sir Alan Brooke,[16] later Lord Alanbrooke, describes a typical *contretemps* of this kind from the period around late April 1941. Over dinner at Chequers, the Prime Minister's country residence, Major General Sir John Kennedy, the Director of Military Operations, launched out on a lecture on strategy and had the misfortune to elucidate a problem for the benefit of the head of government by taking as his example the action that might be necessary after a complete evacuation of Egypt. The Prime Minister's wrath came down like an act of God upon the terrified staff officer, whose only fault was a fondness for theorizing.

Any attempt to explain merely made Churchill wilder. In the end he

[16] *The Turn of the Tide* by Arthur Bryant, based on the diaries of Field Marshal Lord Alanbrooke.

was thundering about "defeatists" and "generals who think of nothing but giving up," and of whom one must make an example. Only the united efforts of the others present around the table to divert his fury to a more distant target warded off something even worse.

Judging by eyewitness accounts, this sixty-six-year-old man must have presented an unforgettable spectacle, especially in the small hours. At these times, he would don a sort of light blue romper suit and would frighten the life out of his guests by brandishing an army rifle, complete with fixed bayonet, striding up and down before the fireplace and, between sips of whiskey, fire off brilliant aphorisms, interspersed with wild plans or maledictions. "What Wavell needs down there are a few firing squads," he said on one such occasion, enjoying the ill-concealed horror of his audience.

His treatment of the Commander in Chief in Cairo was disgraceful. In his own memoirs, he quotes from among his directives urging Wavell on in February and March 1941 the impressively unambiguous passage according to which the Greeks were to be offered "the actual frontline troops of the army mobilized to defend Egypt"; yet 150 pages later he insists indignantly that there had never been any ambiguity about giving the defense of the desert flank at El Agheila "precedence over any other operations."

Moreover, he cunningly omits a passage from one of Wavell's replies, in which the weakness of the forces on the western edge of Cyrenaica is made quite plain, so as to be able to insist angrily that he had realized only after some "bad weeks" that the famous 7th Armored Division was no longer available out there.

The custom of passing the buck downward is widely practiced, and imposing figures like Churchill and Rommel were by no means strangers to it. . . .

And, quite unperturbed, the Prime Minister went on handing Wavell fresh tasks which arose of necessity from Britain's hard-pressed position but which nevertheless overstretched the forces of the Commander in Chief, Middle East:

(1) The last piece of Greek territory the British held was Crete. A German attack was to be expected. Hitler was hardly likely to tolerate this base, since it lay within bomber range of Ploesti.[17]

---

[17] Department L (*Landesverteidigung*=Home Defense) of the OKW was at this time preparing an assessment on whether Crete or Malta should be occupied. According to Warlimont (*Im Hauptquartier der Deutschen Wehrmacht*), officers of all three arms of the Wehrmacht, considering Rommel's position, came to the unanimous conclusion that Malta should be taken. Because of the threat to Ploesti, Hitler decided otherwise. He then sent his ADC, Schmundt, to ask Department L not to make any entries about this difference of opinion in its war diary.

(2) Iraq, treaty-bound to allow British bases on its territory, was growing restive. Here, it was Britain's oil wells that were in danger.

(3) The Vichy French troops in Syria, who among other things were granting German military aircraft overflying and landing facilities on the way to Iraq, and were, under German pressure, supplying weapons to the insurgents, were to be attacked in co-operation with Free French forces.

(4) Rommel's precarious supply position, documented by his oft-repeated radio signals asking for help, which had been decoded by Ultra, should be exploited to launch an attack on him.

Wavell protested vigorously, especially against being expected to intervene against the Iraqi insurgent leader Rashid Ali as well. Churchill wrote to the Chiefs of Staff: ". . . He seems to have been taken as much by surprise on his eastern as he was on his western flank: and in spite of the enormous number of men at his disposal, and the great convoys reaching him, he seems to be hard up for battalions and companies. He gives the impression of being tired out."

As was to be expected, none of these burdens were taken off Wavell's shoulders; it seems, moreover, that Churchill's ever-bubbling pugnacity caused the clandestine Axis ally Rashid Ali to strike prematurely. At any rate, by the time Hitler wrote, in his Directive No. 30, dated 23 May 1941: "The Arab freedom movement in the Middle East is our natural ally against Britain" and ordered a military mission and a small air force unit to be sent to Baghdad, it was far too late.

From India, General Sir Claude Auchinleck, as yet threatened by no enemy and therefore more willing than Wavell, pumped troops into the Basra base. A grumbling Wavell sent a motorized brigade from Palestine. This unit quickly relieved the besieged military flying school in Habbaniya and eventually took Baghdad. Rashid Ali fled to Persia.

It was first and foremost the problems in Syria and Crete that remained in the balance. Some of the "enormous number of troops" Wavell had at his disposal, according to Churchill, were still busy inflicting a final defeat on the Italians in Eritrea and Abyssinia. Nevertheless, Wavell decided to attack on the desert flank. The Cyrenaica escarpmnt ends at Sollum, across the Egyptian frontier, in a typically North African jebel, a 200-meter step falling away steeply to the east and running 80 kilometers to the southeast. Only to the north are there two passes negotiable by vehicles which climb up this immense staircase: the Halfaya Pass and the Sollum Serpentine.

The strategic importance of these passes was evident: Anyone who wanted to operate out of Egypt to the west, perhaps to relieve Tobruk, must either hold these two passes or run his supplies far to the south through the desert, a fuel- and material-intensive operation, moreover highly vulnerable to attack by a determined adversary.

Wavell did not have a particularly impressive force to take this position with: just thirty Cruisers and twenty-five Matildas could be scratched together from the workshops of the Nile Delta for the 7th Armored Division. But the situation seemed favorable.

On 15 May the small armored force, having skirted the escarpment, advanced northward. At the same time Guards units made a frontal attack on the passes.

The tanks took Capuzzo and Sollum but were thrown back again by a counterthrust and withdrew. The Guards took the German garrisons of the passes by surprise and consolidated their position. Unlike the pillboxes on the plain, which had been shot to pieces, the positions in the rocky rim of the jebel, intersected by wadis, were not so easy to retake. It appeared that Wavell had a good jumping-off position. For great things were being prepared. They were to do with the enterprise which Churchill had embarked upon and which had cost even the Iron Prime Minister some sleepless nights.

In Egypt, Wavell had a great many good tank soldiers, but their tanks lay between El Agheila and Sollum or in the valleys of Greece.

It would therefore suffice to send him tanks without their crews. The Prime Minister had been sitting up in bed at Chequers, with a pillow behind his back, the counterpane strewn with dispatches and reports, when the idea had come to him in a flash: A convoy of fast ships loaded with tanks was to leave for Cairo via the long Cape of Good Hope route. But if one could send this shipment to Wavell the short way, via the Strait of Gibraltar and the Mediterranean, he could strike before the onset of the worst of the summer heat.

Headstrong though Churchill was and great though his power was in time of war as Prime Minister and Defense Minister, the old politician was nevertheless bound by the rules of the parliamentary game. It would never have occurred to him to take an important decision without the concurrence of his War Cabinet, the Defense Council, and the Chiefs of Staff. And no matter how much his assertive personality may have dominated these bodies, on many occasions he did growlingly defer to a consensus of his experts.[18]

[18] To what extent this difference left its imprint on the course of the war, even after the intervention of the Americans and the formation of the "Joint Chiefs of Staff," has, as far as I know, not been properly investigated: Just like Hitler, Churchill was a brilliant amateur in military matters; but unlike him, he would occasionally allow other people to persuade him. It does seem as though the much-decried principles of democracy in the long run proved their superiority in this context too.

He therefore set about convincing his panel of advisers.

The Chiefs of Staff were at first against the idea, but Admiralty and RAF representatives convinced the others in the Defense Council that "we can risk it."

"Tiger Cubs" through the Mediterranean

Churchill signaled Wavell: "I have been working hard for you in the last few days and you will I am sure be glad to know that we are sending 307 of our best tanks through the Mediterranean. . . . If this consignment gets through the hazards of the passage, which of course cannot be guaranteed, the boot will be on the other leg and no German should remain in Cyrenaica by the end of the month of June. In making your preparations . . . you should pretend that they are coming around the Cape. Secrecy is most important and very few have been told."

The tanks included 180 heavy Matildas and 99 of the fast Cruisers—Mark IVs and the newer Mark VIs, which had a somewhat improved suspension, with five instead of four bogey wheels, but were still far from being mechanically reliable and still had only the little two-pounder popgun in their turrets.

Churchill himself had thought up the code name for the operation about to be launched: Tiger for the daring cruise through the Mediterranean; it followed that the tanks were duly dubbed "Tiger Cubs." The offensive with which they were to throw Rommel and his soldiers out of the Mediterranean was code-named Battleaxe.

"During the next fortnight, my keen attention and anxieties were riveted upon the fortunes of Tiger," writes Churchill in his memoirs. In the event, only one ship, with fifty-seven tanks on board, went down when it struck a mine.

On Rommel's side too, the 15th Panzer Division was now pretty well up to strength; its 8th Panzer Regiment in particular distinctly altered the balance of power. In addition, despite his supply difficulties, Rommel never had any intention of leaving the most important positions—the passes—in the hands of the enemy.

On 27 May he ordered an attack.

Elements of the 8th Panzer Regiment skirted the escarpment to the south and attacked the rear of the troops holding the passes. Supported by assault AA guns and artillery, an infantry battalion advanced from the west. Meanwhile, the 5th Panzer Regiment made a diversionary attack in the southeast.

The commander of the infantry battalion was a Lutheran pastor who achieved some fame in the African theater of war and who was later to die in a Canadian prisoner-of-war camp: Captain Wilhelm Bach from Mannheim, almost fifty years old, with a jolly little potbelly and a Baden dialect to go with it.

Swinging his walking stick, the old gentleman would run alongside his men during a charge in temperatures of 40–50° C. (104–122° F.). The positions were being held by elite soldiers of the Coldstream Guards. The much-feared 25-pounder *Ratsch-Bums* repeatedly forced the German soldiers to take cover and caused them terrible losses. When the attack finally got bogged down, the reverend captain clambered out of his cover under infantry fire, stuck his walking stick under his arm, and established the position of the artillery with his binoculars. Then he ordered everything that could be man-hauled, and everything that could be brought up under its own power over the forbidding terrain, to take the enemy positions under fire. Shortly afterward, the passes were retaken.

The 5th Panzer Regiment, which was actually supposed to have laid on nothing more than a sort of "demonstration," nevertheless captured a battery of sixteen 25-pounders.

This battery had been firing at the company for some time; but inquiries addressed to the battle group commander, about whether it wouldn't be a good idea to attack, were dismissed in more and more irritable words. Eventually Sergeant Major Wendt heard his captain mumble audibly into the microphone: "You can all lick my arse, then."

Then, more distinctly: "Wendt, you and your troop attack immediately." Wendt immediately thundered away, urging his driver on with his customary zest, until the man yelled over the intercom: "I'm doing 43 [kmph]; she won't go any faster."

Without noticing that he had once again raced ahead of his troop, Wendt stopped 800 meters from the battery to fire, immediately moving off again. "What's that idiot doing there?" roared the unit commander over the radio.

Barely 100 meters from the first gun, Wendt saw how the loader was fetching another shell at the double. That one will get us, he thought. Then he saw the flash from the muzzle and felt a mighty crash. The Panzer rolled on—although the driver forgot to step on the accelerator —and came to rest in the middle of the battery.

"Is everybody okay?" called Wendt. They were all sitting as if struck by lightning, said not a word, but seemed uninjured. Wendt opened the turret hatch. The British gunners stared at him in amazement. Farther back, the engines of the other Panzers were roaring as they tried to catch up at top speed. The gun farthest away from them had meanwhile been hitched to its tractor; its crew was trying to escape. Wendt's gunner set fire to the tractor with a high-explosive shell.

The sergeant major jumped from the Panzer and gestured to the gunners to approach. They obeyed reluctantly; only one tried to hide behind the gun carriage. Wendt pulled him out by the seat of his trousers.

The tension was released when Wendt's East Prussian loader, whom everyone called "Grandpa" because he was all of thirty years old, remarked in the crisp dialect of his homeland: "If he had tried to do anything to you, I would have gone for him with my knife."

The shell had caught the Panzer on the spare track links carried on the front of the tank and had merely smashed the lamps to smithereens. The radio too had failed to withstand the shock.

The prisoners were being rounded up by sappers. Captain Gierga leaped from his Panzer and said: "I could already see you in heaven, Sarge."

And the battle group commander said, "Well done, well done!" and put the "idiot" down for an Iron Cross, First Class.

Sausages and pulses

Meanwhile, Crete was taken in the greatest airborne operation in the history of war up to that time. But the losses incurred were so heavy that Hitler thereafter wanted nothing more to do with parachute operations in the grand style—a fact that may have saved Malta. Only a few people know that the decoding of German radio traffic, thanks to Ultra, had a lot to do with that. General Sir Bernard Freyberg, Commander of the New Zealand Division, who was Commander in Chief on the island, had obtained all the details of the plan of attack from the code breakers.

So Cunningham's naval forces had yet another great evacuation to carry out, this time under continuous German air attacks and incurring heavy losses. Some 16,500 men were successfully brought back to Egypt. Losses came to 15,000, substantially more than the attacker's.

Once again Rommel hoped that the Luftwaffe units which became available after the operation in Crete would give air cover to his troops and supply lines; but most of them went back to the Reich: Barbarossa was imminent. Churchill thought the Germans would now build Syria up into a great base and have his Egyptian position in a pincer. He urged Wavell to advance on Damascus jointly with de Gaulle's Free French.

He signaled: "There is a storm of criticism about Crete and I am being pressed for explanations on many points. Do not worry about this at all now. Simply keep your eye on Syria, and above all Battleaxe."

The sorely tried Commander in Chief set two divisions, including the magnificent 7th Australian, into motion against Syria on 8 June. The fighting, which brought all Syria (including the present-day Lebanon) under British control, lasted until 12 July and cost 4,600 casualties.

But Churchill insisted remorselessly on Battleaxe, despite the fact that, on 28 May, Wavell had informed him that he considered the chances of success no more than doubtful, especially because of the technical inferiority of his own armored cars and tanks. The preparation of the 250 or so "Tiger Cubs," which had in the meantime arrived, was proving more difficult and time-consuming than had been supposed, since some of them were in poor shape.

Churchill's urgings were naturally due in the first place to his monitoring Rommel's reports via Ultra. When he dictated his memoirs, he was not yet at liberty to disclose this fact. He therefore gave rise to decades of guesswork when, with the lack of scruple characteristic of him, he wrote: "At this time we had a spy in close touch with Rommel's headquarters, who gave us accurate information of the fearful difficulties . . . of Rommel's . . . position."

Those difficulties were indeed gigantic. There were not enough vehicles even to provide water and fuel, and the daily water ration for the troops besieging Tobruk was generally one liter, half of which went to the field kitchen. This when the body's need for water was higher than usual, not only because of the heat but also because of the desiccating daily dust and sandstorms.

It hit the infantry particularly hard, since they had to lie motionless, baking in their holes for days on end, for the Australian marksmen on the other side were incredibly accurate. The vitamin-poor diet was causing diarrhea and liver complaints; some genius in the catering department had come to the conclusion that the best thing to send to Africa to go with the Italian shipments would be dried black bread, North German sausages, and sardines in oil (since any other fat would go rancid.)[19]

Under the broiling sun, the fat ran like water out of the smoked sausages. And no one could stand anymore the smell of sardines in oil, pleasant though they may taste when eaten occasionally in cooler climes. Joachim Saenger's crew improvised oil lamps out of the blue tins marked "King Oscar Brisling": Perforate the lid, in with the wick, and there you are.

---

[19] General Westphal, later Rommel's Army G1 Ops, told me that the 7th Bavarian Army Corps Area, which was responsible for this, could not be budged later either; it had also insisted that peas and beans were just the thing to eat in Africa of all places!

The Panzer people could, in any case, make themselves more comfortable than the infantry. Saenger's company had discovered a subterranean cave in the neighborhood, which they turned into a sort of mess. Since the company commander was called Sandrock, it was christened "Adele's Rest."[20]

An artist member of the company painted the two alternative "Homecomings of the warrior from Africa" on the wall: either victorious, riding high on a camel loaded with the treasures of the Orient; or as a skeleton.

Apart from the flies, which covered every slice of bread and butter like a black layer the moment it was prepared, and often had to be swallowed along with the food, no matter how hard you shooed them away, there was the occasional *contretemps* with snakes. On one occasion, Saenger queued up unsuspectingly for coffee. The procedure was for the orderly to stick a funnel into the mouth of one's flask and pour the hot coffee in. Suddenly, funnel and coffee both flew in his face as a plainly indignant sand viper made off.

The old military dictum that idle men become unruly and useless naturally applied at Tobruk as elsewhere. During lulls, barracks routine was immediately introduced, with kit inspection, drill, and periods set aside for cleaning and repairs. The commander of the regiment climbed into the Panzers and bawled the men out if he found any African dust.

You could be given punitive drill for such offenses. This normally consisted of carrying a stack of water canisters 50 meters, and stacking them up again. Around and around in a circle.

Some of the men, who had collected three day's CB (confinement to barracks) back at the garrison for some offense or other, were promptly rounded up to serve their stretch. A tent made a detention cell. Regulations are regulations.

Guard duty at night was most closely supervised, which made sense, since the Australians had taken more and more to amusing themselves with raids deep in the Germans' rear. True, they were looking mostly for Italian positions, where they found the guards much less alert, and where they threw hand grenades under the tanks, the Italians' favorite place for sleeping. They killed a lot of them this way. Later, the tanks of the Ariete and of the 5th Panzers were drawn up as a mixed formation and the approaches made secure with barbed wire and empty tins. But the tins were soon taken off the wire again, because there were always jerboas hopping around. This would make some nervous character bang away and wake up the neighborhood to join in the fun.

[20] Translator's note: after the German actress Adele Sandrock.

The bomber squadrons of the RAF were regular callers at this time. Unlike the Italian M-13s, the German Panzer IIIs and IVs were relatively safe: Nothing short of a direct hit was any danger to them. The sticks of bombs dropped by the Wellingtons made the parked tanks disappear in clouds of dust; but when the dust had subsided, as a rule nothing much had happened.

But anyone caught outside his Panzer was in a bad way. In Saenger's company, Corporal Heinz Schobert, a master butcher from East Berlin, was caught in an air attack. A splinter tore his belly open, he stepped into his own entrails as he ran, and he died in the most dreadful pain.

In mid-June came a decision which gave rise to considerable indignation, even among the long-suffering soldiers of the Führer in the 5th Panzer Regiment: They were to build a road.

The Derna-Sollum coastal road was blocked by Tobruk. Supply traffic gave the fortress a wide berth, through terrain which exacted a heavy toll in fuel and tires. Since it looked as though the siege might last a long time, the idea was to consolidate the badly worn track—just the job for the Panzermen who, according to the old army rule, needed keeping busy anyway.

Grumbling, they made themselves ready. But the next night, fuel and ammunition trucks suddenly arrived, a sure sign that a battle was impending. Churchill's Tiger Cubs were coming.

2. Eighty-eights Devour Tiger Cubs

Massacre at Halfaya Pass

It was the men of the famous 7th Armored Division who had now been equipped with the Tiger Cubs. Their divisional emblem was a jerboa in a circle. The soldiers of the 7th Armored had been given the nickname "Desert Rats," a nickname which was eventually adopted by the whole Eighth Army. The British and American newspaper reporters had dubbed Rommel's troops with the honorific title of "Desert Foxes."

Under pressure from Churchill, Wavell could not allow his soldiers even a few days to familiarize themselves with the new Cruiser models. This applied both to the crews and to the maintenance units, which would be equally important in the wear and tear of desert warfare.

Wavell could not throw his armor into action in a concentrated way, for two reasons: He had to detach a regiment of Matildas to retake the passes, without which the offensive could make no further progress; and his remaining mechanized units could not move together as they consisted of two slow Matilda regiments and two fast Cruiser ones, the speeds of which were very different.

This is where the whole nonsense of the gap between Cruiser and infantry tanks in the British armor program showed up. Wavell was forced to send the Matildas into action in the Cruiser role, although the Matilda, conceived for a different purpose, was liable to end up with a mechanical breakdown with alarming frequency when used for long "forced marches."

The Matildas, which were to crack Halfaya Pass open in conjunction with Indian infantry, were being used most nearly in the role for which they were intended. But they were running into an appalling trap.

After the reconquest of the passes, Rommel himself had repeatedly visited Pastor Bach's unit to satisfy himself that this key position was being turned into an impregnable fortress. The infantry was reinforced with anti-tank weapons and artillery. But Rommel's biggest trump card was a battery of eighty-eight guns. With backbreaking work, they had been dug into the hard ground in such a way that their long barrels just showed above the parapet. Huge though the guns were, they could not be seen even at fifty meters. In the hot-air layer immediately above the ground, everything is reduced in size, as if viewed through the wrong end of a telescope.

It was this murderous emplacement the Matildas of the 4th Armored Brigade were approaching at first light on 15 June—without any cover. The rule that without air or artillery support tanks are useless against well-prepared infantry positions—especially when, like the Matildas, they must advance slowly over a free field of fire and when, like this strange "infantry tank," they cannot fire high-explosive shells—was, with amazing negligence, ignored by the British command.

A battery of 25-pounders had been allocated to "soften up" the German positions, but there was no joint overall command. Thus, when the gunners got stuck in the soft sand, and when they at last dug themselves out, they turned to another task. The time they should have devoted to Halfaya according to plan had been lost shoveling.

Right at the start, four Matilda crews got their tracks around their ears—in a minefield which was supposed to have been cleared. They were part of a troop of five which was to have attacked from the plain below in conjunction with the Indian infantry. This flank was thus virtually without tank support, while the main force, up on the escarpment, was without artillery. It was a scene reminiscent of the bloody Easter days at Tobruk. . . . The jolly Captain Bach stood with his cane and cigar in the AA emplacement. There is hardly a more unnerving sound in war than the rumble and rattle of approaching tanks. But Bach said in measured tones in his Baden accent: "Lots of time yet."

British artillery was firing from the plain, but with surprising lack of accuracy. When, on a sign from Bach, the whipcrack bark of the eighty-eight smothered the duller thuds of the oncoming shells, the Italian artillery also began to fire. The effect of the AA guns' 10-kilogram armor-piercing rounds was devastating. The Matildas blew up or came

to a halt, belching smoke or with their turrets torn off. The remainder
tried desperately to make use of a few folds in the ground and to defend themselves with their toy guns. One of them did in fact manage to
blow an ammunition truck of the AA gunners sky-high with a direct
hit.

The butchery lasted four hours. The tank commander, Major Miles,
tried flanking attacks and diversionary maneuvers. The eighty-eight
crews, almost entirely undisturbed, blazed away as if they were on exercises. At ten o'clock, Miles radioed his regimental commander:
"They are shooting my tanks to pieces." An hour later he was dead.
Only one of his seventeen tanks was left. In the afternoon, the Indian
infantry tried another attack from the plain. The crews of the immobilized Matildas in the minefield supported them with their pitiful
weapons. The Indians were devastatingly raked with fire. An important
component of Wavell's plan had failed.

It did not look much better over to the west. Wavell had tried to
make the most of his handicaps: The slow Matildas made a tight sweep
around the escarpment and aimed for Capuzzo, the shell-shattered fort
behind the passes and an important point of departure for any further
thrusts toward Bardia and Tobruk.

The faster Cruisers moved in a wider arc, so as to cover the left flank
of the Matilda force, with which the bulk of the infantry—the 22nd
Guards Brigade—was also advancing.

Two fortified positions stood in the way of both these forward
thrusts: The Cruisers of the 7th Armored Brigade were faced by the
Hafid Ridge—called "Point 208" in military terminology—and farther
east, on the frontier, the Matildas of the 4th Armored Brigade had to
advance past Point 206. Once again the old-fashioned thinking of the
British about fronts and flanks showed through: Instead of scoffing at
the tiny garrisons of these places and just driving past them to reserve
their entire fighting strength for the decisive adversary—to wit the
Panzer regiments—the British attacked the two points.

There were eighty-eights dug in on Hafid Ridge. During the advance
on Capuzzo, Major R. "Jock" Holden,[1] from the neighborhood of
Dumfries, and commanding a squadron in the 4th Armored Brigade,
saw on his left the Cruisers charging away smartly like cavalry toward
the Hafid position. They had the same luck as the cavalrymen of the
First World War, whose commanders had refused to take cognizance
of the invention of the machine gun. One tank after another flew apart,
hulls shattered, turrets torn off and belching black, oily smoke. An entire squadron was rubbed out in a matter of minutes.

[1] It was a British army whim that every Scot was automatically called "Jock,"
every Miller "Dusty," and every Clarke "Nobby."

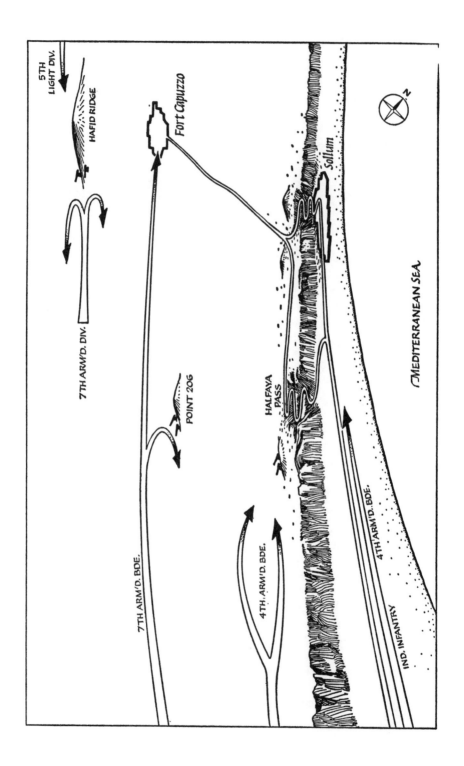

5TH LIGHT DIV.

HAFID RIDGE

Fort Capuzzo

7TH ARM'D. DIV.

POINT 206

Sollum

HALFAYA PASS

7TH ARM'D. BDE.

4TH. ARM'D. BDE.

4TH ARM'D. BDE.

IND. INFANTRY

MEDITERRANEAN SEA

N

One surviving officer landed in captivity. He insisted on being shown the gun that had done this to him. Standing before the eighty-eight, he eyed the long barrel and the great chamber and said gravely: "That's not fair—such a big gun against such small tanks."

Matildas in Capuzzo

Point 206 also cost the better part of a squadron of Matildas, although only a few heavy reconnaissance cars and 50 mm self-propelled anti-tank guns were stationed there. The German gunners defended themselves fiercely. One Matilda was struck forty-eight times before an armor-piercing (AP) round penetrated it.

The remainder of the 4th Armored Brigade, still a solid mass of some eighty thick-skinned Matildas, broke massively into the Capuzzo area.

Sergeant Jock McGinniley, in command of a Matilda and of a troop of three tanks, couldn't help laughing at his oddly assorted crew: The gunner was a Scot like himself, the driver an Irishman, and the radio operator a London Jew.

His three tanks were caught in a savage Stuka attack when the shell-shattered remnants of Capuzzo were already in sight. The driver tried to zigzag with the cumbersome thing as long as he could. Given the German pilots' confounded accuracy, it was at any rate vital not to stop. They drove through a roaring, lightning hell of dust clouds. When it was all over, they were alone. McGinniley never heard anymore of the other two crews. One of the commanders was a friend of his, "Strod" Strodwick.

They rumbled through the Capuzzo military cemetery into the German infantry and artillery positions, spraying as much lead as they could with their coaxial machine gun.[2]

A single lorry scurried in a cloud of dust among some guns. McGinniley saw the driver jump down and help hitch up a field gun, while other soldiers crowded onto the loading platform.

They were barely 50 meters away when the driver threw himself behind the wheel. "He should have one of those Knight's Crosses of theirs," he thought fleetingly. Then he called out: "Machine gun! Fire!"

Nothing happened. He looked across to the gunner, who just stood

[2] Coaxial: coupled and in line with the two-pounder gun.

On facing page. Battleaxe blunted: The infantry tanks (4th and 7th Armored Brigades) and Cruisers (7th Armored Division) ran into eighty-eight positions: Only Capuzzo was taken—temporarily.

there motionless, his eye to the optical sight, one violently shaking hand on the trigger. It was a very different thing shooting at a truck in the distance; it was quite another to fire at these clearly recognizable and terrified faces.

McGinniley reached over and pulled the trigger. His hand would not keep steady; instead of the machine gun, it was the gun that barked. The solid shot went straight through the truck and struck either the driver or the engine. The approaching vehicle stopped. The soldiers jumped off the back. The gunner recovered from his paralysis and let loose with the machine gun among the stumbling, bent figures.

In the same moment a hit shook the tank. Two 50 mm rounds struck the turret and the front where the driver sat, but without penetrating. Then a heavy artillery shell burst on the hull.

The Matilda's armor withstood even that; but the shock tore one of the two engines off its mountings. Smoke and flames filled the engine compartment. They opened the hatch and sprayed the compartment with the fire extinguisher.

One of the engines, the drive shaft of which had bent, had called it quits; but you could drive a Matilda on half power, albeit more slowly. They limped along behind the company, which was spreading out on the northern outskirts of Capuzzo. On the way, they collected more hits. The engine cut out but could be started again. In Capuzzo they saw that their tank was completely "naked" outside: bedrolls, boxes of food, lamps, spades, and replacement track links—everything was gone. That tank could really take it.

Right in the middle of a conference of commanders the Stukas came again. When McGinniley lifted his nose out of the sand, his squadron commander and two other commanders were dead. The planes came back; he ran for his tank and crawled under its hull. Just then the driver started up the engine on the quite correct assumption that he was safer on the move. Smoke from the smashed exhaust went straight into McGinniley's face; coughing, he crawled up on the stern and jumped in through the hatch. He brought the hatch cover down on his fingers. The earth shook under the Stukas' bombs. They had reached the objective of their attack, but it seemed they were not wanted there at any price. Suddenly he felt soaking wet. The temperature out there was around 50°C (122°F).

Major Holden's driver, Leslie Bowie, had steered his tank "Gamecock" plumb through the middle of the ancient Roman gate. Infantrymen of the Guards Brigade were rounding up prisoners.

Quite near them, fifteen little German mice were at play: The commander of the German combat group, with his staff and a few stragglers, had crawled into some drainage culverts a little to the north. The drains ran under the Via Balbia, the coast road. Outside, they saw Guards wandering around; the pipe shook when the great Matildas rolled over it. The lieutenant colonel had pulled the field telephone after him by its wire; now he crammed a handkerchief into the bell— against the unlikely possibility of the line being intact and someone turning the crank at the other end.

Nobody wasted any time glancing down into the drain. During the night the men crept away in small groups and reached their own lines.

A Knight's Cross for Sergeant Major Wendt

As the light faded, the first tank engagements began. Rommel's clever deployment of his fast units bore fruit: From the area south of Tobruk the 5th Light Division, with its Panzer Regiment, reached the garrison of the Hafid Ridge just in time. Although surrounded by wrecked Cruisers, the garrison was short of ammunition. With courage bordering on madness, two of the tanks had broken into the position under fire from the eighty-eights. One was destroyed at a range of a few paces; the other ran down a gun and got away.

The 5th Panzer Regiment came up against a pretty exhausted enemy. The 7th Brigade allowed itself to be forced away to the south. Joachim Saenger, promoted warrant officer and deputizing at short notice for a sick sergeant, had a brief debut as Panzer commander in this battle.

Unfortunately, he had never learned to shoot and as the arrowhead formation halted in its rumbling progress, with the massed enemy tanks before their guns, there was a bit of a debacle.

With a crew which has "played itself in," the commander gives the gunner a target and quickly adjusts his bearing. Meanwhile, the loader will have had his order: armor-piercing or high-explosive round. The commander gives the loader the range, which determines the elevation of the barrel. "Fire!" When the shot has landed, the commander corrects the range. "Fire!" To do this, you must of course be able to estimate from experience, especially in the desert, where small things look smaller and bigger ones are greatly elongated vertically.

Saenger ordered his crew to bang away as best he could. Unfortunately, the commander's vehicle stood next to his. It was damaged by a hit from a two-pounder and the commander took over Saenger's Panzer.

As he drove past, Lieutenant Colonel Mildebrath asked, laughing: "Where on earth did you learn to shoot?"

"I didn't," Saenger answered sadly.

The lieutenant colonel was still roaring with laughter when he slammed the turret hatch down on himself and his signals officer.

A little way southeast of this position, Point 206 was taken by Matildas at around this time. That's how long it was before artillery supports became available.

A fierce engagement developed in Capuzzo, too. Elements of the 8th Panzer Regiment attacked the place. Captain Johannes Kümmel broke into the fortified area with three of the heavy Panzer IVs and despite the poor muzzle velocity of his short-barreled 75 mm guns was able to put eight Matildas out of action. He was awarded the Knight's Cross.

As the sun sank swiftly below the western horizon, Rommel knew the situation pretty exactly, thanks to the liberal use of open wireless traffic by the British. Only the evening before, his monitors had been able to find out quite precisely what was coming at them, and the German-Italian troops had accordingly been alerted in good time.

At dawn on 16 June, the 15th Panzer Division set about throwing the British out of Capuzzo. But the British had not been idle during the night either.

They had dug their tanks in, exploiting every available hillock, and had heaped up rocks around them. As a result they could with relative impunity let the German Panzers come to within a range at which even the two-pounders were effective. The German losses were considerable.

Sergeant McGinniley had picked for himself a low hill, which his only tank could climb up to fire and then roll back down again. Presently an infantry sergeant major turned up with two stretcher-bearers and said: "Could you hold your fire a bit? There's a man lying down there and he's calling for help."

The men had a large Red Cross flag, and the German Panzers, too, immediately held their fire.

The three men proceeded to bring in a sergeant of McGinniley's unit, who explained that his tank had been knocked out the previous evening by one of the Panzer IVs. Since he himself had been wounded in the knee, the Germans had given him a blanket and told him: "You'll be all right; by tomorrow morning, at the latest, your bearers will be here to fetch you."

Immediately the armor-piercing ammunition began to whine again all over the place; but at around 1030 hours the 8th Panzer Regiment had to disengage. "Only thirty out of eighty Panzers are still fit for action," their commander reported to Rommel. The decisive action took place farther to the south.

There, the 5th Panzer Regiment was again attacking the 7th Armored Brigade. Young Werner Fenck was feeling fairly safe: He was loader under an older sergeant, a "twelve-pointer stag" in soldier jargon, who looked tremendously relaxed.

They began to fire. The loader is the only man who can't see anything; it's not a pleasant sensation. He shoved the shells into the barrel. Heat, sweat, and the rancid stink of cordite when the smoking shell case is ejected. Suddenly the others cried: "A hit!"

The engine roared into life. They came to a halt next to one of the newer Cruisers. All the crew except the radio operator had vanished. The poor devil was jammed behind some linkage component that had twisted, but was hardly hurt at all. Thinking of the fabulous booty at Mechili, they began to rummage. Nothing edible, drinkable, or smokable came to light, only masses of maps in their cases, marked "Major Aldridge." Disappointed, they turned back to their Panzer, only to receive an immediate chewing out; the sergeant was the troop leader, after all, and the company commander had been yelling in vain into his microphone at them for some minutes. Meanwhile Sergeant Major Wendt had again forged ahead, this time with utterly devastating success. They were racing at top speed toward a group of enemy tanks, pulling up sharply several times to fire. His gunner, Warrant Officer Thom, scored a hit on a tank with every shot. On the other side, the troop was scattering: Some drove off, others returned fire.

When they were only a few hundred meters away, Wendt saw antitank guns in position and trucks being driven, some with guns in tow, behind the tanks. "Shoot while we're driving, too," he roared at the warrant officer, who nodded. At that moment Wendt saw that the barrel was drooping at a funny angle. A hit had smashed the lower part of the barrel.

He was just able to pull the gunner away by the collar at the last moment, as he was about to fire. And then a two-pounder AP round crashed into their Panzer.

"My hands, my legs," groaned the gunner. Except for "Grandpa," all the crew reported that they were unhurt. The round lay at the bottom of the Panzer. It had penetrated the vertical plate from the front. Wendt had stood exactly behind it; it must have had quite a remarkable trajectory.

They dragged the wounded gunner out. Splinters from the disintegrating armor plate had injured him gravely. The bones of his legs had been smashed.

"Grandpa is dead," said the radio operator.

"Rubbish," said Wendt. "Grandpa can't be dead. Have you felt his pulse?"

"No," said the radio operator hesitantly.

They found the East Prussian lying in a large pool of blood. The head of a bolt had burst from its seating and cut the veins in his neck.

The medical Panzer pulled up beside them. The doctor wanted to see the gunner first. But he said: "See to Grandpa first. He's in worse shape than me."

Remarkably, both lived through the experience.

Wendt, like his company commander, was awarded the Knight's Cross. He and his radio operator had both overheard that the attack was to be broken off.

In his memoirs, Rommel wrote that the breakthrough of the 5th Light Division toward Sidi Omar and Sidi Suleiman had brought about the "decisive turning point of the battle."

It seemed it would be possible to block the way of the main British body to the south behind the escarpment. Rommel immediately ordered the 15th Panzer Division to leave only the minimum of troops north of Capuzzo and to advance likewise with every element he could move to the Sidi Suleiman area. This wide outflanking movement in their rear did not suit the British at all. Says Rommel: "One can often decide a battle merely with a broad movement to shift the center of gravity which comes as a surprise to the enemy."

And that's just what happened.

". . . everything went wrong"

The situation of the British on 17 June was distinctly precarious. In the prolonged fighting, the 7th Armored Brigade's Cruiser strength had shrunk to thirty. The Matildas, too, had suffered heavy losses between Capuzzo and Point 206, if mostly through mechanical breakdowns. Rommel's monitoring service reported that the Commander of the 7th Armored Division, General Creagh, had asked his Commander in Chief to visit his command post.

"On 17th everything went wrong," wrote Churchill in his memoirs. For meanwhile General Messervy, Commander of the Indian infantry, the 22nd Guards Brigade, and the Matilda brigade, had decided on his own initiative to evacuate Capuzzo to avoid being encircled.

It was, in fact, high time. The German Panzers were approaching from the south to close the trap. The commander put fourteen of the remaining Matildas under Major Holden to cover the retreat of the vulnerable lorried infantry.

Luckily, so it seemed to Holden and other tank officers, the German Panzermen were showing a healthy respect for the Matildas from the preceding days. "And we used every silly Boy Scout trick you could think of to give the impression that there were more of us than we really were," Holden recounts.

To the southwest, the desert was covered in nasty-looking Panzer IIIs and IVs, which mostly just sat there like fat hyenas. Behind Holden's back ran the endless line of the Guards' trucks, heading southwest. Until they were out of the way, he and his Matildas would have to hold out.

Time and time again the German Panzers would press forward to plaster the Matildas at fairly close range. They seemed to have a particular grudge against Holden's own "Gamecock," since his driver, Bowie, was complaining that his hatch cover had bent under the repeated hits and that every time another shell struck, red-hot metal splinters would fall down his neck. About now, the remaining engine of Sergeant McGinniley's tank finally gave up the ghost. They were just fiddling about with it behind a hill when a friend of the sergeant's came trundling around the corner. His gun barrel had been severed close to the turret by a shot. They decided on a symbiosis of the halt and the blind: One took the other in tow. At least one could still supply motive power and the other could defend himself with a gun.

Thus yoked together, they went on fighting for most of the day, crawling up the hill to shoot, rolling back again, and communicating with each other over the wireless. When eventually the last of the trucks had roared away, the two commanders of the coupled tractor-trailer train received the order: "You two are first off!" When darkness fell, McGinniley walked in front of the tank which had an engine, holding a glowing cigarette, to show the driver the way.

Later, in the flat country, he sat on the front of his tank, next to the driver's hatch. They were all utterly exhausted; when the driver's head nodded, and the towrope from the tank in front would run at more and more of an angle, McGinniley, half in a dream, would mechanically smack him on the head with the flat of his hand.

Major Jock Holden, too, had by now been retreating for some time. The German Panzers accompanied his battered group for a long while but, as a rule, stayed out of two-pounder range. At just outside this range, however, they could still be a nuisance in a variety of ways with their 50 and 75 mm guns, and those who were getting lifts on top frequently had to perform acrobatics, amid much cursing, to get to the lee side of hulls and turrets.

Eventually, Driver Bowie felt a jolt and a tug in the steering. He stopped and got out. An AP round had gone half through the suspension of one of his bogey wheels. The whole thing was sagging, and a leaf spring had been driven through the track.

Bowie jumped back into his seat, selected the lowest gear, got the tank moving, jumped down again with a crowbar and, walking along-

side, held the obstructing spring away to one side. After a few miles he
had to let go to correct the tank's course and soon the whole damaged
affair collapsed completely.

But by this time, the horizon on the right was again empty and wide.
The German Panzers had turned back. When they loaded their battered residue onto railcars at Mersa Matruh, some greenhorns came up
and looked on amazed. One of them said: "I thought the Germans
couldn't do a thing to these Matildas?" The tankmen managed a wan
smile.

Ninety-nine knocked out—or 220?

Rommel was furious. He was convinced that his Panzers could have
effectively barred the retreating enemy's way. It is certain that the evacuation of Capuzzo, reported in very good time by a reconnaissance
group of the 8th Machine Gun Battalion, had not been taken any notice of farther up the chain of command until much later.

Claims about the number of tanks knocked out as usual differed
widely between the two sides. Rommel thought the British were certain
to have lost 220 tanks.

To check the claims of individual units about the tanks they had sup-
posedly accounted for, special groups roamed the battlefields in the
days after the battle and painted numbers on the tanks claimed by their
own unit. The system was not all that foolproof; Joachim Saenger noticed one such group that found a number on a tank already. Shrugging
their shoulders, the lads went around to the other side and painted
their number on, too.

In fact, the British had lost 99 tanks, 64 of them Matildas. Churchill
in his turn said the Germans had lost 100 tanks.

But the German losses totaled only 12 Panzers. This was, of course,
first and foremost due to the fact that the battlefield remained in German hands, as a result of which any wreck that looked capable of
being salvaged could be towed to the workshops.

But these figures soon lost their significance. The German attack on
the Soviet Union started a few days later and the German Wehrmacht
began to get used to quite different scales of magnitude. It hardly
seemed worth bothering about the 93 dead and 235 missing in Africa.

Wavell as scapegoat

"I am sorry to have to report that Battleaxe has failed."

When General Wavell sent this signal off to his Prime Minister, he
could well imagine the effect it would have. In his memoirs, years later

and somewhat more self-possessed, Churchill wrote of Wavell: "We had ridden the willing horse to a standstill."

But at the time, he went off like a firework. He considered the whole plan to have been badly co-ordinated and, in particular, criticized the absence of a "holding attack" from Tobruk.

Such an attack had of course been arranged; but it was to have taken place only if there was a chance to join hands with the attacking force. What Rommel, with his complete freedom from frontal and flank thinking, would have done to the detested Tobruk garrison had he been given the chance is all too obvious.

For the rest, with his rapid and decisive shifting of the center of gravity to the south, Rommel had demonstrated that in desert war mechanized forces must not only be properly armored and armed, but fast as well. The dear old fat Matildas could not have reacted appropriately even if Rommel's opponent in this game had been a tactician of comparable genius. They were, in any case, immobilized—another transgression of the rules of modern war—for they were being misused as anti-tank artillery, having to protect the infantry who, with their few miserable two-pounder anti-tank guns, could not be left to fend for themselves.

But quite undisturbed, Britain's industry went on producing two-pounders, both as tank guns and as anti-tank artillery; the mighty 3.7-inch AA gun went on pointing its barrel at nothing but the sky and the duplication of the tank program went on, resulting in abortions that were either tough or fast. A painful and bloody period of instruction was yet to be gone through, despite the fact that the object lesson was running victoriously and destructively around in two continents: As in shipbuilding, the best tanks were the result of a compromise between the three elements—armament, armor, and speed, and anything that made for the neglect of one of the three factors was bad.

There are strong indications that Britain's unbroken traditions, otherwise hardly a disadvantage in military matters, acted as a handicap in this respect, especially in comparison with Germany.

It was not very long ago that it was the universally held dogma in the better London clubs that "these chaps with oily fingers" must not be allowed too much of a say in things. And the representatives of this view, looking nostalgically back over their shoulders, brave beyond measure and fabulously ignorant, still played an important part in the army.[8]

---

[8] The break with tradition essential for progress was to come with those rapid changes which are necessary in wartime; before it was all over, the British built what was to remain by far the best tank in the world for many years: the Centurion.

Churchill, on the other hand, would in the small hours of the night thunder out his suspicions that "my generals simply will not fight." A tiny skirmish on the margins of Battleaxe, quite insignificant for the outcome, made it clear to what an extent war in the desert was a matter of guns and armor: On the first day, elements of the 8th Machine Gun Battalion, now brought up to strength again, came up against the Matilda squadron of Major T. A. D. Banks on the Libyan-Egyptian border. The squadron was on its way to Point 206. The infantry had nothing more effective than the "army knocker," the 37 mm anti-tank gun. This reduced it to the role the Italians had played six months earlier. From a range of only 100 meters, the tanks shot up the anti-tank crews, whose own shots hardly even dented the tanks' thick skins. The last of these minicannon, similar in performance to the two-pounders, fired a final ineffective shot at five meters. Then the Matilda just rolled over it and its very young gunner, Black. His crushed legs were amputated on the battlefield, but he died shortly afterward.

It was not Wavell's fault that "Italian conditions" were no longer the rule with his adversary, even if, as Commander in Chief, he was bound to be held responsible for tactical errors like the pointless charge against the Hafid Ridge. In that operation, the artillery was once again left behind, unable to help, and cavalry-minded tank commanders charged ahead regardless, right into the mouth of the eighty-eights.

In any case, Wavell had to go, and with him the two commanders of Battleaxe. He cleared his desk in Cairo for General Sir Claude Auchinleck, changing places with him and becoming Commander in Chief, India.

Having got rid of their first Commander in Chief and two other very senior officers, Rommel became at last a legendary figure among British soldiers. And every now and then someone would say, "a proper Rommel" as an expression of the highest praise.

The African summer heat descended over the land, enforcing a pause in the fighting. Like Rommel, Auchinleck gathered reinforcements for the coming battle.

A chat over the fence

Meanwhile, the soldiers of both sides had a "quiet" summer. One made oneself comfortable, learned to live with sand fleas, the endless attacks of dysentery, the scorpions, and the ever-present sand. And, where there were points of contact, with the enemy too.

Warrant Officer Claus Wernicke put on his earphones, twiddled the knobs on his shortwave set and listened for a long while. Then, summoning up all his school English, he said: "We can hear you. How are things over there?"

A few seconds' pause, and a fresh young voice from the other side said: "Not too bad. How are you doing?"

The British armored reconnaissance car, which had been cruising at leisurely speed some 1,000 meters to the east through the undulating country, slowed down, turned its nose with its observation slit toward the Germans, and stopped. A chat in the desert. . . . In the coming weeks it was to become an established habit for Wernicke and his British opposite numbers on the Egyptian-Libyan frontier. However, they kept to a few noncommittal sentences—each was careful not to give the other the impression that he was trying to pump him for information. Apart from that, they both entertained the not unfounded suspicion that these unwarlike contacts had better not reach the ears of the higher echelons.

After the failure of Battleaxe, the armored cars of the 3rd Reconnaissance Unit were running patrols in this area along the barbed-wire fence on the Libyan-Egyptian border. A line of strongpoints, strung out at infrequent intervals, ran along the frontier. Here one did not as a rule exchange fire. Only occasionally would small task forces be assembled for a reconnaissance in strength. Every now and then, they would penetrate as far as Sidi Barrani, but even such operations as these for the most part went off without bloodshed. A few tanks, armored cars, a battery of artillery and motorized infantry would make a dash eastward on a broad front. Similar British units would then bar their way somewhere and set up their artillery. After the first few shots, the German vehicles would roar off with undiminished speed, but in single file. The danger of a hit remained very remote in this formation, until they approached the range of anti-tank guns and tank guns firing over open sights. Then the whole caboodle would stop in a mighty cloud of dust; sweating gunners would unlimber their guns and start banging away in their turn.

This would then make the British limber up and drive a zigzag course to change position. Provided they were quick enough about it, nothing much would happen to them either.

On occasion, however, British naval artillery would take a hand; you could hear the growling of heavy shells coming from a great distance, then the heavy 280 mm guns, or heavier ones still, would join in with their organ recital. In the German units this was mostly the signal to call off the advance, since the shrapnel effect of these heavies on the stony ground was such that even driving at top speed there would have been a risk of unnecessary casualties.

The men of the reconnaissance unit, "the last of the cavalry," would then resume their prowling up and down the fence. In the mornings, they would check on the mine-free gaps and occasionally stop off for a chat with those comrades of theirs with the different field-post numbers.

"What do you lot smoke?" was the question addressed to Warrant Officer Wernicke one morning.

"It's called R-6. It's our best brand, too," he answered. "Would you like to try one?"

Would the British just! Circumspectly, the two sides arranged a place for the swap: "Can you see that heap of stones at eight o'clock from where you are? No, the other one, with the camel-thorn bush next to it. That's the one! We'll leave you a couple of packets there."

The British car withdrew discreetly; according to the unwritten rules, one didn't approach too closely. The British would then collect the packets of R-6, replacing them with a generous quantity of Players.

This provided a noncommittal subject for discussion for the next chat, during which both sides praised the other's product.

One day a German lieutenant, arriving fresh from home at one of the small strongpoints, peered over the parapet and asked in a puzzled way: "What sort of armored car is that cruising about over there?"

"It's an Englishman, Herr Leutnant."

Whereupon a deluge of extremely warlike orders poured from the young man; and although the men grumbled, the gun had to be loaded, aimed, and fired.

The resulting uproar and the breach of the rules of the game frightened the men in the German reconnaissance car at least as much as it did the British, who, having come to no harm, drove off in a cloud of dust. They complained a little over the radio, but Wernicke, having called on the "offending" post, established the circumstances and sent them a reassuring report: It had been a new officer; they should be a bit careful for the next few days; they would soon educate the chap.

"Don't worry about it, we know the type," the British said. Relative peace was soon restored on the border, all the more so since the lieutenant soon got tired of being stared at reproachfully. It seemed as though the hostile environment—the treeless sand under the boiling, desiccating sun—consumed everyone's reserves of strength, until nothing was left for fighting.

Chivalry and the Occident

And yet, just a little farther to the north, all the remorseless horror continued as before on the Tobruk perimeter, and especially where, in the vicinity of the 1 May incursion, German and Australian infantrymen faced each other within hailing distance.

Here, where the old Italian fortification line had been penetrated, both sides had stationed strong units of élite men. Rommel did not want to lose the Ras el Madawar as a jumping-off point for a decisive attack; and for the same reason, Morshead was determined to keep a close guard on this single dent in his armor.

Roasting in their foxholes and tormented by flies and sand fleas, the men still found the strength to do each other some damage.

True, there were some tacitly observed rules. Thus, when either side displayed the Red Cross flag because the wounded had to be taken to safety, firing generally stopped. One night, when a German raiding party, in trying to jump an Australian unit who were digging a trench, themselves fell into an ambush, medical orderlies of the other side helped to take the many severely wounded men to safety. There were also times when the machine-gun crews and sharpshooters of both sides laid their weapons aside before sunset. Until by tacit agreement a machine-gun burst was fired into the air, there was a chance to stretch cramped limbs and to shake out blankets made filthy by the daily sandstorms.

But the stories that have from time to time been hawked around about peaceful games of football are pure legend; as in general the transmogrification of the war in Africa into a fair and clean "war without hate" is bound to make one uneasy. However, against the background of the horrors perpetrated in Germany's name, it almost makes one sigh with relief that this was one theater of war where at least there were no columns of refugees and no incinerated children;[4] and it is true that the rules of the Hague Convention on land war (and sometimes even more) were observed.

But it is hard not to shudder when, in praise of this well-conducted slaughter, "the culture of the Occident" is invoked—as is done in the Foreword to *Krieg ohne Hass* (*War Without Hate*).

There may have been no hate, but when the fortress of Tobruk defied all his attacks, Rommel's feelings were not altogether chivalrous. Full of hope, he wrote to his wife on 6 May 1941: "Water is running very, very short in Tobruk. The British soldiers are now getting only half a liter a day. With the help of the Stukas, I am hoping to curtail their rations further. . . ." And two days later: "We are now bombing the installation which desalinates their water."

And his celebrated war reporter—the one who found dead youths so

[4] Not altogether true, though. A witness has told me that some Arab youths would not leave a food store in Derna that had been prepared for demolition by explosive. With a shrug of the shoulder, they were blown sky-high.

enchanting—wrote about a Stuka attack: "At night the horizon is aflame with the light of exploding ammunition dumps. Even though those people over there have ammunition enough to feed to their pigs, nevertheless it is beginning to run short. Apart from which, you can't use the stuff for drinking, you can't repair your guns with it, you can't bandage your wounds with it, and you can't strike it to make water. General Wavell is no Moses—and he has no magic wand, even though he is fighting for the Jews. . . ."[5]

All right, then; no hate. Nothing but chivalry and the culture of the Occident.

Most of the common soldiery, who thought they were merely doing their duty, gave such labored tirades a miss whenever they got to lay hands on the *Berliner Illustrierte* or suchlike journals. It was much the same stuff as the newsreels shown at the Benghazi soldiers' hostel, which pictured the warriors in Africa strolling through orange groves and drinking Löwenbräu. Or frying an egg on the track cover of a Panzer under which the clever cameraman had first placed a paraffin cooker. That way, it was hot enough.

But what those people at Tobruk were enduring was unbelievable. There they were, the German army, having more or less conquered all Europe, yet the Tommies could not be driven from this tiny speck of Africa. One could virtually spit into that harbor of theirs in which the wrecks lay thickly strewn about, given a daily stir by the Stukas and heavy artillery from Bardia and Sollum. You could sometimes see what the Luftwaffe was doing to their ships—and yet they would not give up.

On the contrary: in the course of the summer, Cunningham's ships brought so many AA guns into the fortress—over and above all the other supplies—that the Luftwaffe's losses forced it to reduce its daily attacks. All the more dangerous, on the other hand, became the journey of the supply ships across the stretch in which they had no fighter cover.

The sailors of the Royal Navy could almost work out for themselves when it was their ship's turn; nevertheless they sailed. The crews of the small tankers, which set out on the dangerous trip with a few hundred tons of highly explosive fuel under their behinds, had a particularly bad time.

On 24 June, Stukas and Italian torpedo-carrying aircraft disabled the tanker *Pass of Balmaha* and two anti-aircraft launches. One was sunk,

[5] May the mantle of charity cloak the name of this poetic soul, especially since he is still alive and writing—naturally nowadays full of fairness and chivalry toward those despised Jews.

the other heavily damaged. The tanker was rendered unmaneuverable. Eventually the destroyer *Waterhen* came to its assistance. She towed the *Pass of Balmaha* and her cargo of 750 tons of precious fuel into Tobruk. A few days later the destroyer was sunk. Although the harbor area was the favorite target of the Stukas and the artillery, it was a remarkable magnet for Australian soldiers off duty. One could never know whether the arriving ship might not have a bottle or two of beer on board. Amazing exchange deals were negotiated: loot for booze. One astonished seaman was offered a Fiat Topolino in good running order for a bottle of gin. A quick snatch was also possible sometimes, although it often ended badly. The harbormaster one night caught some Australians with strangely bulging shirts and tore the booty from their bosoms: They were tins of "medicinal lemon juice." The Diggers were less upset at being caught than at being let down by their nose for serious booze in the dark.

Also slightly on the wrong side of the law, but more becoming to their rank, were the arrangements of the improvised officers' mess of Major Lindsay's C-Squadron of the KDG. Thanks to good contacts in Cairo—the other squadrons of the regiment had been sent back to the Delta—a fairly frequent supply of whiskey reached them in cases labeled "Urgent Motor Spares." But they too were badly caught out on one occasion, as one of these crates was being opened in the mess tent. The off-duty Dragoon officers were standing expectantly around with glasses at the ready, but when the packing was peeled away what emerged was a brand-new Ford radiator.

Between these two disparate types—the members of the tradition-bound regiment and the roughneck and totally unmilitary Australians —a surprisingly warm relationship developed. The first feelers took place at high level: Lindsay sent the fearless but somewhat gawky Lieutenant Williams to General Morshead's staff as liaison officer. The lieutenant reported smartly to the fortress commander: "Liaison officer from the KDG, sir!"

"KDG? What sort of a mob is that?" asked the general in his lazy Australian drawl. Williams looked at him over the top of his round schoolboy's spectacles: "King's Dragoon Guards, General—raised in 1685, before Captain Cook first sailed to Australia."

The general was man enough to take this with a straight face.

Around this time, one of the Dragoon officers had the shock of his life, as he was about to make contact with the Australian battalion commander. He asked the soldier standing guard where the officer was, whereupon the man yelled down a hole: "Oi! Bill!"

"Coming," said a deep voice from below. The next moment there appeared a head and a pair of shoulders, on which the astonished Dragoon made out a "pip" and a crown—the insignia of a lieutenant colonel.

The Diggers and the posh regiment

The KDG squadron commander of those days, Lindsay, now a retired colonel, lives in his family seat, more of a castle, near Coupar Angus in the Scottish Highlands. In the halls and corridors hang the portraits, halberds, pikes, and swords of his warlike ancestors. When I visited him, he showed me with particular delight a big antique spring trap hanging on the wall.

"What's this?" I said. "Did you ever have bears around here?"

"No. My ancestors used to set these for poachers."

Lindsay told me quite frankly: "Your Rommel was bound to become the hero of our people in the desert: You see, we had no general on our side we could look up to. Some of them were good, mind you; for instance Wavell and O'Connor. But it took three years to get rid of those who were quite useless. The real professionals only came with Montgomery. What Rommel did was mostly not really all that brilliant; you could always bet that he would come up at you from the desert with a right hook. But he did it decisively, skillfully, and with determination, just as it says in the Field Service Regulations. With our lot, in the early days, you sometimes had the feeling they hadn't even read the regulations. . . ."

A man like Lindsay was of course bound to be appalled by an outfit like the Australians; but he actually admired them: "They were as green as they were brave. . . . Incredibly plucky—and incredibly untidy. They didn't care if next to their position there was a heap of empty tins stinking the place out. But then there was the comradeship they had for one another. You could bet on it that even if they were half starved they would still share out the last crust of bread between them; and, half dead, they would still fight off anything that might bother them—whether it was the enemy or any sort of authority."

In the early days of the siege, the KDG officers noticed with amusement how doggedly the Australian soldiers shunned any kind of military mark of respect. This sprang from the suspicion that the "Pommy bastards" from the posh regiment were a toffee-nosed mob and that it would surely make them worse if you kept saluting them.

All this changed quickly, as most of the Dragoons climbed out of their Marmon-Harringtons and took up positions as plain infantry next to the Diggers. In Australia the constant confrontation with an absolutely unyielding nature has created a prevailing mentality that fits a man perfectly for life in a beleaguered desert fortress, where you are dealt blows on every side. Absolute composure in the face of catastrophe is part of everyday life on the sixth continent. What happens when a river sweeps a bridge away? When a hurricane devastates a town? Well, you just build them again. Even if that's the nth time you've had to do it. To men like these, even Tobruk was almost bearable. The men from England, as well as the Scots and Irish, who after all made up half the garrison, naturally did not want to be second to them.

The Dragoons, unused to infantry fighting, manned a post near the road to Derna under the command of Captain Tony Llewellyn-Palmer, Tim's brother. They were just about settled in when they noticed that there were sounds of trenching all night opposite them.

The night was pitch black when the little raiding party set out: Two officers and eight men, armed with a submachine gun, rifles, bayonets, and hand grenades, crept through the flat no-man's-land straight toward the men who were digging in. To their left, one officer and six men advanced westward along the Derna road. Through a wadi, which ran to the right toward the enemy positions, a sergeant and two men carried three light machine guns forward.

In the middle, the main force under Captain Llewellyn-Palmer filtered skillfully through the chain of outposts. It was to their advantage that there was something going on in the sector next to them as well, and that there was quite a rumpus taking place, complete with artillery and infantry weapons.

When they got to where the enemy troops were digging in, the noise had stopped. In the knowledge that they were in the second line only, the enemy was behaving quite carelessly. They were chatting away and some were even singing.

When they were within a stone's throw, Palmer's eight men formed themselves into a straight line, as arranged. They felt their way forward, rifles at the ready.

When the outlines of the digging men could be made out about five meters away, one of Palmer's men must have made some sort of sound. Suddenly all went quiet, the shadows disappeared into the ground, and whispered commands could be heard. The name "Karl" was called.

Palmer cocked his submachine gun. The men fired their rifles from the hip and fell on the enemy with their bayonets. From the flanks, the two machine guns began to chatter in the wadi. Actually, they had been supposed to open the action by providing diversionary fire.

On the enemy's side too, machine guns opened up to the left and the right. But their fire was inaccurate. Two KDGs threw hand grenades into their positions. The flashes from the explosions showed men running away. Palmer's submachine gun barked. Then he ordered his men to withdraw, for things were livening up all around and they still had the line to cross on their way back.

When they returned to their position, they found that one NCO was wounded. They could hear with grim satisfaction small-arms fire continuing for a long time afterward on the opposite side. The enemy must have been firing at each other. At dawn they could see trucks driving around on the enemy side, taking away the dead and wounded. The nightly sounds of digging ceased.

It was a dreadful life they led in the fortress; but in time many of them began to develop a vague feeling of affection for this forlorn place. It seemed they had never before appreciated things like the velvety African night with its enormous stars and a light breeze from the Mediterranean—until after a day under the merciless burning sun, plagued by thirst, flies, and the omnipresent sand. No sophisticated, ice-cool drink in a Cairo bar could come within miles of one mouthful of lukewarm beer if one could occasionally run one to earth.

Added to which was the pride at having in this place, for the first time in this miserable war, stood up to the Germans—and at being able to keep doing them more and more damage.

Captain Charles Armitage and his comrades of the artillery hit upon an idea from some Italian observation posts that had been left behind. These consisted of a simple post with a kind of perch on top. They got the engineers to build them overnight some splendid observation towers made of tubular scaffolding along the whole fortified salient. Every time one of these things suddenly appeared on the scene at dawn, the Germans reacted perfectly predictably. Some infantryman would exclaim: "Just take a look at that!" and would alert the artillery.

The artillery would then bang away, sometimes all day long, all over the place, without achieving anything very much, since such an airy latticework is very hard to wreck. Any damage could easily be repaired the next night, and the enemy could be relied on to get the idea after a while that this was a damned waste of ammunition.

From then on, the tower would become just part of the scenery and no longer bothered anyone.[6] One could climb up just before sunrise with almost complete impunity, look far into the enemy's rear in the clear morning light and, with some well-directed artillery fire, give them a lot of trouble. Then, in the midday heat, when the shimmering air distorted and veiled everything, one could climb down again unmolested.

Armitage had a favorite place, a tower more or less in the center of

[6] At almost the same time, Rommel himself had hit on almost the same idea, but on a different sector.

the perimeter line, from which he could see right over the high plateau all the way to El Adem. This was where the "Axis Road" was—the by-pass around the fortified area meanwhile built by the Italians. A short stretch of this road was within range of the 25-pounders.

You could see the trucks crawling down from the high ground near Belhamed; you could estimate their speed and order the guns to open fire by wireless when they reached a certain spot. However, at the extreme end of their range, the 25-pounders' fire was none too accurate, and all you achieved most of the time was to give the enemy truck drivers a good fright.

On one occasion he saw—unfortunately out of range of his guns—a huge gun being slowly driven along on a special transporter. Shortly afterward "Bardia Bill" first raised his booming voice.

For that is what the beleaguered men called one of the mighty guns —they were 210 mm howitzers—which were regularly lobbing shells into the harbor from the direction of Bardia. Another gun, stationed on the Ras el Madawar, behind the salient driven into the defenses on 1 May, was known as "Salient Sue." Somehow, once they had been dubbed with these nicknames, they were no longer quite so frightening. "Bardia Bill" and "Salient Sue" became part of the life of the fortress, like the sand, the Stukas, the flies, and the thirst.

No peace for Auchinleck

Sir Claude Auchinleck, Wavell's successor, had hardly sat down behind his new desk before somebody put before him the Prime Minister's first query. When did the new Commander in Chief think he could drive Rommel out of Africa?

Winston Churchill was determined to run the new man from the word go on a short rein. He was not very fond of Auchinleck, who in his view had been too fainthearted as commander of the British expeditionary corps in Norway, and had consented to his appointment only grudgingly.

But he would have driven hard whoever was sitting in the chair of C-in-C, Middle East. It was his view that the strategic situation demanded action at any price: Were not the Germans storming through Western Russia in what looked like another Blitz? Should the Russians manage to stand up to these devastating blows—which seemed unlikely—he did not want to give them the chance to say: "We've done it all by ourselves." And should the Russians collapse, it was all the more important to have beaten Rommel before that, since it was certain that Hitler would then turn to the Mediterranean. He and his generals were already looking to the not far distant day when the Slav subhumans would be knocked out. Hitler had even ordered studies to be made of an attack on India through Afghanistan.[7]

But Churchill, ever urging action, had to take note, to his great displeasure, that Auchinleck, now he was responsible for a whole series of theaters of war and crisis areas, was by no means a "willing horse." He too, though, saw immediately that the offensive must come as soon as possible because the enemy had engaged the bulk of his forces in Russia and no one knew how long that would last. But because of Japan's threatening posture, he had already been forced to release two splendid Australian divisions for service in the Pacific zone. He was, moreover, firmly opposed to any repetition of the Battleaxe mistake of attacking with a tank force that was not at least double the enemy's in numbers. But, at all events, by midsummer he again had 500 tanks in the Nile Delta. Half of them, however, were the slow Matildas—a wonderful weapon for knocking holes into infantry positions after a short approach drive—provided the positions were not armed with eighty-eights. The Matilda was, on the other hand, totally unsuited for the role of a tactical instrument in mobile desert warfare, as Battleaxe had shown.

To the Chiefs of Staff his arguments made sense. Grumbling, Churchill agreed to send another brigade of Cruisers around the Cape and to re-equip the two existing armored divisions out of current production as quickly as possible.

Meanwhile a new tank made its appearance in the desert: the M3 General Stuart, supplied by the Americans under the new Lend-Lease agreement. This small 13-ton tank, more or less adequately armored with a maximum 43 mm of steel, had a 220 hp Pratt & Whitney radial aeroengine, which gave it a top speed of almost 60 kmph. In its little turret sat a 3.7 cm gun with a muzzle velocity of 792 m/sec—slightly less effective even than the British two-pounder, and by no means as accurate.

When the first Stuarts were unloaded from their freighters at an Egyptian port, engineers from the U.S. suppliers were standing by, keen to have the reactions of the battle-hardened British. At the start of the first test, the crew, used to Cruisers, were skeptical when they took their places in the tiny contraption.

They went tearing through the desert, enjoyed the powerful acceleration, and dropped their speed carefully before going into a bend, as

---

[7] Warlimont (in his book about the Wehrmacht HQ) remarks that this was in no way an instruction born of megalomania, since it was to be only a "draft" directive; but in the same breath he makes use of the same document to reject the reproach that the Wehrmacht suffered from "continental narrow-mindedness"—a remarkable piece of double pleading.

they were accustomed to do with their Cruisers. The engineers said: "Don't worry about going into a bend at full throttle."

Incredulously, the British climbed back in, tried half speed at first, and then a really rip-roaring bend. The tracks stayed on the bogeys.

Shortly afterward you could see a tiny tank tear through the desert like mad, stirring up a huge cloud of dust at top speed, full of the joys of life like a foal. When the soldiers climbed out again, the tank commander's face was one huge grin as he said: "She's a honey." And the name stuck.

They certainly were not too hard to please.

The only drawback was that every Honey crew had to have one man with arms like a prizefighter. For when the radial engine had been standing still for a while, some mysterious fluid, as powerful as a hand grenade, formed in the bottom cylinder. At any rate, unless one turned the heavy engine backward twenty-seven times with the starting handle, there was a risk that the bottom cylinder head would come to rest on the desert floor in a thousand pieces.

Supplies: dream and reality

This summer, Rommel kept writing home that he wasn't feeling very well; sometimes it was his stomach that was troubling him, and sometimes his liver. By now, he must have been virtually the only man of his age in the Afrika Korps to have endured that harsh climate from the first day. And there was continual trouble too with his allies: Bastico[8] was asking for a row—very well—he could have one, he wrote to his wife on one occasion. On 31 August he seems to have had just about enough. The Italian Supreme Command was dissatisfied because it didn't have much of a say in things: They might be trying to provoke an incident to give them an excuse to send the German troops home. "I wouldn't object overmuch to a change of theater," he wrote.

Two days later he commented with pleasure on the rapid advance of the German forces in Russia, adding: "It's a pity I can't be there but must wait about here." He had meanwhile been promoted *General der Panzertruppe* or Tank General, and his German-Italian force upgraded into *Panzergruppe Afrika*. The group included the Afrika Korps—the 5th Light Division had been rechristened 21st Panzer Division—without, however, any addition to the strength of its armor. A new creation was the 90th Light Division,[9] formed mainly from additional units that had gradually been landed. Six Italian divisions were now under his command.

[8] Italian General, successor to Gariboldi as Commander in Chief, Libya.
[9] At that time still called Afrika Division.

But none of this gave him any real pleasure, proud though he had fleetingly been at first. It was now obvious that "his" theater of war, despite all the Führer's goodwill, was only a second-class one compared with Russia. Even a spectacular advance into Egypt would hardly make the headlines compared with the colossal successes on the Russian front.

And the prospects were worse than ever.

In the weeks following Paulus's visit, his G1 Ops, von dem Borne, had in proper General Staff style researched the proposition of an offensive aimed at the Suez Canal, as ordered. The result was depressing.

After examining the relative strength of the two sides, von dem Borne concluded: "If there is no sign of a threat [to the British Middle East base] by German troops from Turkey or the Caucasus, a fairly strong British offensive must be expected, with the objective of retaking Cyrenaica. An attack by the Afrika Korps with the forces hitherto foreseen will not in that case be possible.

Despite this modest appraisal, the plan—like everything out of North Africa—was not received with much favor at the OKH. Enumerating the operationl objectives, von dem Borne wrote that after the "defeat— and if possible—annihilation" of the forces in western Egypt, "Mersa Matruh must be taken, preferably by a *coup de main.*" At the OKH, someone, probably Halder, annotated: "Like Tobruk?"

In these studies a name which was to go down in history as a turning-point of the war crops up for the first time. It was a piece of terrain which from the operational point of view gave the British one more opportunity to build a defensive position. The place was "in the gap, no more than 60 kilometers wide, between the Qattara Depression and the coast, 50 kilometers east of El Daba," wrote the G1 Ops. There was a railway station there called El Alamein.

Von dem Borne, evidently driven on by the indefatigable Rommel, was, however, concerned with areas much farther ahead. But it is noticeable from his detailed work that, unlike his commander, he did not really believe he would ever get there. Under the heading "Crossing of the Nile near Cairo," he noted that a force of five divisions would need five days for the task if an undamaged bridge fell into its hands. And he added the hesitant sentence: "In case of a contested crossing, doubtful."

The remorseless critic at the OKH wrote in the margin, heavily underlined: "Bound to be."

He was surely near the mark. But the gentlemen of the General Staff also nursed plenty of illusions. Under the reference number I/0971/41 ("Secret command matter! Matter for CGS! Only by hand of

Officer!"), the Army General Staff was busy with the supply aspects of the Afrika Korps' plans. They laid down crisply (on 27 August 1941!) that from the beginning of October, motor transport and supplies must be withdrawn from the "eastern" operation and sent to Africa. "This is based on the assumption that the operations in the east will be essentially concluded and that in 1942 only campaigns requiring numerically limited bodies of troops will be taking place in the east." In that case, an attack could be launched in Africa on 15 March 1942.

Leaving aside such dreams about the future, the whole African campaign, for once examined in the light of objective numbers and dates, began to look very much like a never-never land.

So as to mount an offensive against Tobruk, immediately followed by an eastward attack, a monthly total of 43,000 tons of supplies would have to be carried across the Mediterranean for three months to meet the needs of the army alone. Such a figure was achieved only once throughout the whole African campaign: in January 1943, when the ships had to make only the short trip from Italy to Tunis.

To move the necessary supplies up to the front, a total of 11,000 tons of road transport capacity would have been necessary (even if the coastal shipping from Tripoli to Cyrenaica was substantially reinforced). This was equivalent to some 3,667 vehicles such as the Opel Mark-3 Blitz, the best-tried army truck in Africa.

At this point of their calculations the staff officers inserted a line which was doubly underscored: *"This motor transport requirement unacceptable!"*

In the course of their appreciation, they took the trouble to work out how much fuel such a fleet of trucks would consume and appended the remark: ". . . it cannot now be estimated, even *approximately,* whether the necessary supplies of motor spares, tires, and fuel can be secured over and above current requirements in the other theaters of war."

Meanwhile, a clear idea of the amounts can easily be obtained if one sticks to the theoretical assumption that the necessary transport fleet of Opel three-tonners had been sent into action. Altogether fourteen days were allowed for the 3,400-kilometer return journey between Tobruk and Tripoli. That gives stages of 242 kilometers a day. According to army specifications, the average fuel consumption of the "Blitz" was 25 liters per 100 kilometers. You could be sure that in African conditions the truck would need more than 75 liters for its daily run of 242 kilometers.

This gives a monthly requirement for the whole fleet of 3,667 trucks of 8,250,760 liters, or 5,776 tons.

This, mind you, for transport only. This amount would not have al-

lowed one single tank to move its tracks an inch; not one tractor would
have moved a single gun into position, no half-track would have moved
any infantry. In the year 1941, the monthly average tonnage of motor
fuel arriving for the army in Africa was 4,884 tons.[10]

Meanwhile, the General Staff officers trimmed their figures to make
do with the 5,400 tons of road transport capacity "to be released from
the eastern operation" and subsequently to be sent to Africa.

The navy would just have to carry a higher tonnage along the coast,
for which purpose the handling capacity of Tobruk harbor had been included in the calculation.

After the operation, the shipping capacity would have continually to
follow the movement of the troops—a marvelous idea this, when you
remember that all there was between Tobruk and Alexandria was the
miniport of Mersa Matruh. And the British sappers had explosives for
use on harbor installations.

Even the gross transport capacity of 8,000 tons (2,600 tons was
there already) was insufficient for a march to the Suez Canal, but the
missing 1,732 tons was to be made up by economies through "a system
of strongpoints, and pauses during the offensive."

This study paper was signed by General Eduard Wagner, the Quartermaster General. By contrast, the opinions of Captain (General
Staff) Schleusener, Quartermaster of the Afrika Korps, make almost
refreshing reading. As early as 9 July 1941, he had passed a cool judgment on the prospects of more audacious plans: "Given 1,000 tons of
freight capacity in round figures, which is what is available for the
Benghazi-Tobruk stretch, 200 tons of goods a day can be carried forward. This is nowhere near enough for current requirements of fuel
and food, which for the stretch east of Benghazi must be put at a minimum of 370 tons a day. Conclusion: Only one thing is sure: if these
requirements are not met, the Afrika Korps cannot even maintain itself, let alone take Tobruk or think of an offensive eastward."

On the other hand, the Führer/Supreme Commander, not in the least
"sicklied o'er with the pale cast of thought," had counted his un-
hatched chickens as early as 11 June 1941, when the campaign against
the Soviet Union had not even begun, and had thought ahead: "After
the destruction of the Soviet forces," he wrote in his Directive No. 32,
Europe would belong to Germany and Italy. The newly conquered *Os-
traum* (space in the east) would have to be organized, secured, and
economically exploited, while in North Africa, Tobruk must first of all

---

[10] Only when one understands these orders of magnitude can one appreciate the
achievements of 1942—and judge Rommel's strategic proposals, in which he saw
within his grasp the oil wells of the Persian Gulf as well as a *coup de grâce*
against the Soviet Union through the Caucasus.

be polished off so as to provide the prerequisites for the further advance to Cairo. But it was also worth considering an attack from Bulgaria through Turkey, or even an advance through Transcaucasia. Gibralter too was to be taken from the British, so as finally to close the Mediterranean to them.

Meanwhile the British still seemed to be feeling fairly at home in the Mediterranean, as can be seen from the number of German ships sunk. The soldiers grimly renamed Mussolini's *mare nostrum* the "German swimming pool."

It has hitherto been taken as an axiom in most published work that this must be put down to "the Italian betrayal." The sensible and well-informed Enno von Rintelen alone wrote that when something goes wrong in war, people always blame it on "traitors." Apart from the fact that the Ultra decoders were getting better and better at their job—how they were eventually able to give precise details of every convoy is yet to be told—it was not very difficult to keep the necessarily restricted number of routes under surveillance from high-altitude reconnaissance aircraft, particularly during the cloudless Mediterranean summer.[11]

In mid-September Hitler at last ordered the navy command to transfer at first six, and then twenty-one, U-boats to the Mediterranean. Admiral Dönitz protested in vain. The transfer naturally took some of the pressure off British shipping in the Atlantic and instead made more work for Cunningham's small fleet, which had yet another task to perform anyhow.

The Australians had to be brought out of Tobruk under Rommel's nose, and the British 70th Division and a Polish volunteer brigade had to be landed in their place.

The Aussies leave Tobruk

At the end of August, British and Soviet troops occupied Persia, which had refused to show the door to a large German military mission. The British share was borne mostly by troops from India and Iraq, now under Wavell's command, but Churchill wrote a growling letter to the Chiefs of Staff saying that since Auchinleck proposed to "remain idle for weeks" in the Libyan desert, he too must contribute some fairly strong units.

However, Churchill had tried, in vain, to spare him a further burden: When the 15,000 Australians had spent six months in the fortress

---

[11] From the beginning of June to the end of September forty-three German supply ships totaling 150,000 grt [gross tonnage], as well as some smaller vessels, were sunk. In October less than half the ships that sailed ever arrived—and November was a particularly disastrous month.

of Tobruk, the Australian Government demanded that they be relieved. Although this demand came at a time of parliamentary battles and three successive heads of government were concerned in it, the Australians remained adamant. Churchill sent off a flood of telegrams and held out the prize of the immortal glory the imminent relief of Tobruk would bring the defenders—but in the end he had to give way.

The Inspector General of the Australian Army's medical services, General R. M. Downes, judged the state of health of the Diggers in Tobruk as follows: "The men in no way feel exhausted, but hardly one of them would still be able to march 10 kilometers." Be that as it might, the similar force of almost 15,000 Britons in Tobruk, whose state of health could hardly have been any better, were not relieved, and Churchill would undoubtedly have had a fit if anyone had suggested any such thing. The first relief units to arrive were Poles. The Brigade, commanded by General Kapanski, had been raised in Syria early in 1940. It consisted of volunteers who had arrived there by adventurous routes after the fall of Poland. When France too capitulated, Kapanski led his men, complete with their French weapons and vehicles, across the border into Palestine and placed himself under British command.

British naval experts had described the relief operation as "a piece of impudence we are hardly likely to get away with." Despite this, it went off amazingly well. During the moonless nights of 17 to 27 September and 16 to 26 October, destroyers chased backward and forward between Alexandria and Tobruk. The two fast minelayers *Latona* and *Abdiel,* which were capable of 40 knots, did sterling service.

While the ships lay in harbor, British fighters and bombers attacked the German airfields around Tobruk, and artillery in the fortress plastered Bardia Bill's and Salient Sue's emplacements.

Nevertheless, on 25 October, when the exchange was almost completed, a formation of Stukas caught up with *Latona* and sank her. An escort destroyer was heavily damaged and thirty sailors lost their lives. Since the ship was on its way to the fortress, where the Poles and British had arrived safe and sound, there were no passengers on board.

On the previous trip Major Jock Holden, awarded the DSO for gallantry during Battleaxe, had been on board *Latona.* He was on his way to Tobruk to take over an independent Matilda squadron of his regiment.

He brought away a few bruises from his trip. In the hold of the ship were some small trolleys on rails, from which in normal operations the mines were launched overboard. In the hasty unloading, the crew of the ship made little distinction between pieces of freight and one unaccompanied major; a couple of sailors sat Holden on one of these trucks and slung him, only slightly damaged, into a lighter.

Sergeant Harry Dick Reid from Carlisle and his commander had an even more exciting journey to Tobruk. They were taken into the fortress on a highly explosive powder barrel. They belonged to the 4th Royal Tank Regiment, which was to take part in the forthcoming breakout during the offensive.

At Mersa Matruh they were put aboard the tank-landing craft which at Easter had put the first Matildas ashore in Tobruk. Three of the fat "infantry tanks" were now on board each craft, the spaces between them crammed full of boxes and ammunition and tins of fuel—a dangerous mixture.

The three vessels sailed from Mersa Matruh at dusk on 9 October. The sergeant was reassured to see that there were all sorts of automatic weapons mounted on board: some Swiss quadruplet 20 mm Oerlikons and the highly effective Pom-Poms.

At four in the morning, with Sidi Barrani on the beam, Sergeant Reid was awakened by wild firing. Ahead to starboard they saw in the moonlight a U-boat on the surface. Shells were screaming toward them from its gun. A stream of tracers, pretty well aimed by all appearances, was flying across from the guns of the landing craft. The two 650 hp motors roared out as the craft dashed at the enemy at full speed and some of the crew began to lower the huge forward-loading ramp which they hoped would make a good battering ram. But suddenly the effective starboard weapon, the Bofors, fell silent. Jammed! The young naval lieutenant on the bridge had to turn to starboard to bring the port Pom-Pom to bear.

Shortly after that it was all over. The U-boat dived, evidently disgusted by such vigorous resistance.

"Good thing he didn't let off any torpedoes," said the sailors; "that would have been curtains for us!"

Slowly, they limped back to Mersa Matruh. The U-boat's shells had torn away the paravane, which was fitted outboard to the bows, damaged the propeller bearings and torn a couple of holes in her side, right next to the starboard tank (containing 8,000 liters of high-octane fuel). Moreover, one of the very first shells had burst on the exhaust pipe behind the bridge. Splinters from it gravely wounded the young navigating officer in the back.

Reid looked after the lieutenant, a Scot, during the six-hour return journey. However, he needed no cheering up over his wound, which he referred to contemptuously as a "scratch." He was far more upset by the loss of his wristwatch, the glass on which had been splintered by the impact.

"I hope I can get it mended," he said, wide-eyed as a child. "My mother gave it to me when I got my commission."

The other two landing craft reached Tobruk despite heavy Stuka attacks. They sailed again on the night of 12 October. A few hours later a weak radio signal was intercepted: "Am being attacked by a U-boat. . . ." Of the thirty-seven men on board—including four Australian soldiers and two Italian prisoners of war—only one man survived. He was fished out of the water by a German U-boat after he had swum for his life for forty-eight hours.

Meanwhile Sergeant Reid was astonished by what the Navy could achieve. Hardly had their battered ship tied up at Mersa Matruh than the sailors kicked up a terrible rumpus and issued an ultimatum demanding an escort. As a result, on their next journey a dilapidated old river gunboat and an armed trawler duly accompanied them.

But once again they ran into a U-boat, possibly the same one, and this time it did fire some torpedoes. Reid and his driver "Nobby" Clarke had fetched their bedrolls from their tank and set up camp down below, next to the engine compartment; should this powderkeg of a ship get a direct hit, everything would go up anyway.

The rumbling of the heavy engines woke him: The stokers were changing over and had opened the bulkhead doors. Reid sat up and lit a cigarette. The ship was pitching more than on the first voyage. They were very handy, these craft, for landing tanks, but the need to build them especially for this purpose meant that their seaworthiness suffered.

Nobby clambered out of his blankets; he felt like a cigarette too. At the same moment there was a hard metallic impact below them. While the two tankmen were still exchanging puzzled looks, a signalman came clattering down the steel stairs, tore a lifebelt from its hook and disappeared up top again without a word. They rushed after him, not without providing themselves with lifebelts too.

The scene on deck was strongly reminiscent of the shoot-out on the previous trip except that, in addition, some furious yelling was issuing from the forward hatch. Reid's people had made themselves comfortable on its canvas cover. At the very outset of the engagement a shot from the U-boat had severed the fastenings and the men had tumbled helter-skelter onto the tanks stowed below. They got away with a few bruises.

A thin crescent moon hung, or rather lay, in the sky like an orange peel someone had thrown away, and by its light one could see the turret of the U-boat disappear below the water, tracer bullets fizzing all around it.

The coxswain, a sergeant, stood at the bulwarks and yelled furiously up at the bridge: "Ram him, Skipper, ram him!" He was a big, square-set Mancunian called Bill and in his fury he nearly dislodged the iron railings as the U-boat dived out of sight, unscathed.

When he caught sight of Reid, he relaxed a little and said: "You've never in your life been so near to being blown sky-high."

"I know," said Reid.

"You don't know anything," Bill replied. "Go up top and have a word with the skipper."

The skipper, a young Irishman, stood on the bridge, staring wildly after the U-boat. He kept shaking his head.

"Close shave, was it?" asked Reid.

"Close," the Irishman screamed. "Didn't you hear a bang down below?"

"Well, yes . . ." Reid said, hesitantly.

"That was a torpedo, you damned lucky bastard, and it slipped through a yard under your backside!"

The skipper was beside himself; Reid got the story out of him bit by bit. It started when the skipper suddenly saw a torpedo trail to starboard, far too late for any evasive action. That sonofabitch U-boat commander had obviously known quite precisely that he was firing at a boat with an almost completely flat bottom, because the thing had been set to run virtually on the surface.

The skipper closed his eyes and waited for the bang. But the craft, with her pitching motion, had just lifted her bows and when the motion was reversed, there was that metallic clang. When the Irishman opened his eyes, he saw the torpedo disappear, its course as straight as an arrow, toward Africa.

"Do you realize what's happened?" he croaked, hardly able to contain himself. "That beastly detonator had already got its nose under the craft—had even smacked her on the hull; but if the warhead doesn't run up against anything, the bloody thing won't go off."

It was some time before Nobby and Reid could go back to sleep. As they ran into Tobruk harbor at first light, a mighty waterspout rose with a roar out of the water just ahead of them.

It was Bardia Bill's usual welcome.

Attempt on Rommel's life

In late September, a complete convoy arrived for Rommel. He reported the fact with great pleasure to his wife, but added: "For the moment, we are stepchildren and must be content to remain so. Later, we shall be at the head of the queue again. . . ." The "promotion" of his force to the status of a "Panzer Group" had not brought him a great deal by way of reinforcements, but it did produce some very highly qualified officers.

He came by his Chief of Staff, Major General Alfred Gause, in a roundabout way. His old enemy Halder had woven the threads with care. . . . He wanted a German Staff in Africa that would not be subordinate to Rommel. He allowed Gause, then still a colonel, to proceed to Africa, but had first to allow him to go on leave, since a few threads of his web were still missing. He then managed to send out the newly promoted major general as "liaison officer with the Italian High Command in North Africa."

Soon afterward he was forced to remark: "Resistance to the Gause mission . . . Rommel."

Not much later, Gause became Chief of Staff to the Panzer Group. Rommel had declared categorically that *all* German troops in Africa came under his command and he brought his contacts into play. The major general made a virtue of necessity, before very long reporting to his patron, Halder, in Berlin. In the latter's diary notes this appears as: "Personal relations are disturbed by the personality of General Rommel and his ambition, which amounts to a disease. Rommel's faults of character make him a particularly unpleasant phenomenon with whom, however, no one likes to cross swords because of his brutal methods and because of the support he has in the highest quarters. . . ."

They were all complaining, as we shall see again presently—even the new general commanding the Afrika Korps, Ludwig Crüwell, and his Chief of Staff, Lieutenant Colonel (General Staff) Fritz Bayerlein. But there was at least one among the new faces who was not given to complaining, but against whose cool intelligence Rommel would only seldom wheel out his heavy guns: Lieutenant Colonel (General Staff) Siegfried Westphal who, as the G1 Ops of the group, was something like its "operational conscience."

Meanwhile, the OKH had dropped its resistance to Rommel's plan to make the decisive attack on Tobruk as soon as possible. But the difficult supply position occasioned more and more delays.

A particularly heavy blow fell on the Axis Powers in the Mediterranean on 9 November: A convoy of ten freighters, escorted by Italian destroyers and cruisers, was intercepted by "Force K," a small flotilla of surface vessels which had been stationed in Malta at Churchill's insistence. Not one of the merchant ships got away: almost 40,000 gross tonnage went to the bottom.

In a signal to the OKW, Rommel complained: "Of the 60,000 tons of material the Italians have promised, only 8,093 tons arrived in Benghazi by the end of October. Of the troops originally to be provided for the attack on Tobruk, several important signals units and a third of the artillery will not be here until 20 November. . . ."

This message was decoded for Churchill by Ultra. He urged the reluctant Auchinleck to meet the last date laid down for the offensive: 18 November. The general had thought it wiser to wait until Rommel had formed up his forces for the attack on Tobruk and then to attack him in the rear. Churchill, on the other hand, held with equal justification that the enemy might surely meanwhile receive more reinforcements. He could not have foreseen how effective the Royal Navy was to prove in the Mediterranean: Not a single ship arrived in Libya before 14 December.

Churchill pinned great hopes on the success of the offensive, which was christened Crusader. Once the Axis forces in North Africa were successfully annihilated, the neighboring Vichy French colonies might very well secede. Immediately after that, he wanted to invade Sicily.

In mid-November, Rommel flew to Rome. He had a talk with Mussolini, who promptly urged him to attack Tobruk as soon as possible. And he met his wife and celebrated his birthday with her on 15 November.

On the flight back to North Africa, one of the two engines of his He-111 failed. The machine had to make an emergency landing in Athens.

At this time, several commando operations were taking place as a curtain raiser for Crusader. The most spectacular of these was intended for Rommel. The British tried to kidnap, or else to kill, the absent Commander in Chief.

When the attempt was made, just about everything that could possibly go wrong did so. It began with an error by an outstanding agent, Lieutenant Colonel John E. Haselden, an Arabist who had complete command of the Senussi dialects. Posing as a dealer in ostrich feathers and wearing Arab clothes, he had been keeping under surveillance the former Prefecture building in Beda Littoria, near the ruins of Hannibal's city of Cyrene. The building was boarded up, but staff cars, Rommel's among them, drove up every day. Haselden came to the conclusion that this must be the headquarters of the Panzer Group.

So it had been—briefly; but since it was too far from the front for Rommel's taste, he had moved his staff to the Tobruk area. It was the staff of the supply chief, Schleusener, meanwhile promoted to major, that was working in Beda Littoria.

The operation was prepared on the basis of Haselden's reports: The idea was that the element of surprise in Crusader would be enhanced by removing the wily head of the German-Italian Army and creating chaos among his staff.

The night was stormy and the sea rough when two submarines were supposed to land fifty-three of the best men of the British commando units near Cyrene. Only twenty-nine reached the shore. Two drowned; the rest were re-embarked. The decimated force reached the Prefecture building in a heavy storm and was therefore able to enter unobserved. But the very first step—to kill the guard silently—went wrong. He struggled with his assailants and called for help. Drowsy Germans tumbled from every room. The British fired their submachine gun, and threw hand grenades.

Two German officers and two soldiers were killed.

But the commander of the commando unit also lost his life. His second-in-command was badly wounded. The British had to run for it. All but two of the survivors were captured. Although they were not wearing uniforms and their combatant status was dubious to say the least, Rommel had them treated as normal prisoners of war.

The same night another commando operation went awry even more dramatically.

Crash among the dunes

The weather was dreadful, with a cloud base less than 150 meters above ground, and the plane was dancing about in the turbulence of heavy cloudbursts as Flight Sergeant West flew around somewhere in the desert south of Gazala in his Bristol Bombay. Most of his passengers were airsick.

The majority were Australians and New Zealanders—highly trained sabotage experts who were not easily frightened. But every man jack of them would have given his right arm to get out of that reeling, heaving plane. Nor were they greatly reassured to see the flight sergeant fiddling pretty helplessly with his maps and protractors by the greenish light of the instrument panel.

The commandos were supposed to be put down between Tmimi and Gazala and blow up aircraft and fuel dumps on the German airfields there. But presently the pilot informed their commander, Captain Thompson: "I haven't a clue where we are. We'll have to land." He turned the machine into the wind and actually pulled off the feat of landing on unknown ground without wrecking it.

When the first pale light appeared in the east, Thompson and West stood on one of the wings and looked around. A solitary little figure came wandering toward them from the north. It was an Italian soldier who wanted to have a closer look at this airplane that had suddenly appeared there in the desert.

They nabbed him without any trouble, and when he had got over his initial fright, he seemed quite happy and told them that the Gazala airfield was only a few hundred meters away. Flight Sergeant West shooed everyone, including the Italian, on board and roared away with engines which had hardly had time to warm up. But as soon as he was airborne he saw two Me-109s sweep down the sand runway at Gazala.

Barely a minute later he had the fighters on his neck. Machine-gun and cannon fire tore through the plane. After the second pass it crashed among the dunes. Stunned but uninjured, Captain Thompson crawled from the wreck. His second-in-command, Lieutenant Bonnington, and the little Italian were also among the survivors. Most of the others on board were dead or gravely injured. Some people in Volkswagen jeeps arrived from the Gazala airfield and helped with the rescue work. Thompson and Bonnington were given a friendly reception and interrogation by the pilots of Luftwaffe Fighter Squadron 27. The pilots came to the conclusion that they had a couple of rare birds here. They put Thompson on board a Fieseler Storch to fly him to the German AOC, Africa.

The weather was still dreadful; the German pilot too lost his way and, his fuel gauge at zero, was forced to land in the desert.

Carelessly, he went off to fetch help, leaving the tough commando officer in the custody of his second passenger, a meteorologist of the air commander's staff. Thompson, of course, waited only until the pilot was out of sight, then knocked out the poor weatherman with a well-aimed hook to the chin and set off eastward. As ill luck would have it, because of the weather the desert seemed to be alive with airmen who had likewise made forced landings; he ran slap into the crew of a Ju-52 who were also looking for fuel and was again taken prisoner.

And so the captain arrived after all at the staff headquarters of the air commander, where he again met his victim, the meteorologist. He apologized to him and was invited to help cool the latter's aching jaw with a few drinks at the commander's well-stocked bar. Thompson shrugged his shoulders and accepted. Everything had gone wrong; his little band were dead, wounded, or taken prisoner. But that's the way it goes in lousy wartime; far worse might have happened to him than to find himself among these well-fed and good-natured airmen. There might even be another chance to run away by and by.

Drowned in the desert

Oberarzt Dr. Fähndrich was touring Libya at around this time. His brief was to report on the state of health of the German troops. But the doctor himself went down first: feverish dysentery and all the bother that went with it. He cured himself in four days with the prescription: "rest, warmth, castor oil, and starvation."

His confidential report shows his appalled discovery of the consequences this illness, in itself curable, had on many soldiers in Africa, and his alarm at the treatment they were receiving. There is a tendency in the army to send the sick away so as to concentrate on treating the wounded. But many dysentery cases were too ill to travel: "I am sorry to say that I have seen many serious cases of dysentery and a not inconsiderable number of dead from this cause, whose condition had without any doubt been aggravated by being moved. . . ." In a field hospital he found a row of dying men who had been brought to Derna in a state of deep shock. Most of them had arrived in Africa no more than four weeks earlier.

He also found conditions bleak in Derna, the finest town in Cyrenaica: Because of the never-ending air raids, most of the sick had been accommodated in tent hospitals in the numerous wadis around the area. As soon as it was reported from the airfield by phone that a plane had landed from Athens, the most serious cases were put on board helter-skelter, because the machine would have to take off again immediately from such an exposed place. Nor could the arrival of aircraft be notified in advance from Athens, since this would immediately have attracted swarms of British fighters.

The men were, in general, short of butter, eggs, and milk, as well as of easily digestible carbohydrates, Dr. Fähndrich reported. Of the 50,000 or so Germans in Africa, some 10 percent were chronically sick. After dysentery, the most widespread sickness was infectious jaundice. Time and time again, one could see men marching or traveling while pressing lower right arms over aching and swollen livers.

The army doctor went on to report on his inspection of the Luftwaffe hospital: "The equipment is by African standards fabulous. . . . Catering is excellent, in purpose-built kitchens using large cooking vessels and ranges brought over from Europe—most German medical stations use elderly paraffin stoves and steaming coppers. In the stores I saw large quantities of food such as I have never seen even approximated in any German army unit (for instance eggs, butter, milk, etc.). . . ."

When the great rains came, there was a series of tragedies in the wadi hospitals. On most stretches of the Libyan coast there had been hardly any rain for five years. Nobody, therefore, had any objections to the tents being erected in the wadis, although one could see that these great furrows on the face of the North African soil had at some time been scoured by great masses of water rushing to the sea after heavy downpours.

On this particular night of thunder and lightning, the water came again. The sick and wounded were swept away with their beds and drowned. At one wadi hospital, the staff surgeon had just arrived to do his round when a flood-wave came thundering down the wadi. The doctor managed to save himself by leaping up one side of the riverbed. His driver, who tried to save himself on the other side, was crushed by the mass of rock and swept out to sea together with his wrecked car. His body was not recovered until days later.

But even quite healthy soldiers drowned that night. Everywhere, the wadis had offered tempting sites for "settlement": they gave cover, camouflage, and protection from the sun.

Captain Curt Ehle of the Motorcycle Rifles had at this time been posted to the 15th Panzer Division: He was given a small, largely motorized unit and was to study and prepare the details of the attack on Tobruk, which was now scheduled to take place on 3 December.

They were stationed east of the fortress, in the neighborhood of Gambut. A neat sand-table model had been prepared of the southeastern corner of Tobruk, which they were to break through. Concentration areas for various arms had been reconnoitered and got ready.

Ehle slept in the same tent as his sergeant major, a great truck tire between them. When the captain woke, he saw a mighty jet of water rush through the tent, taking the tire with it. They grabbed their bags and with great difficulty reached the sloping sides of the wadi. As with almost all units along the coast, some of their vehicles could not be saved.

As yet, they had no idea what was coming at them through the desert on tracks and wheels from far away in the south. For this time, it was the British who had surprise on their side.

3. "Crusade"—with Hitches

Tanks catch planes

After the nasty experience of Battleaxe, strict radio silence had been ordered as the greatest armada the desert war had seen so far rolled into position. Tanks and vehicles stood for days, widely spaced out in the desert, camouflaged under Bedouin tents. German aerial reconnaissance noticed nothing. And on the critical day—17 November—no reconnaissance aircraft were flying because of the bad weather.

Hardly had Rommel arrived at his headquarters in Gambut on the afternoon of 18 November than it became clear that this was an offensive. A large force, with many tanks, armored cars, and motorized infantry had overrun German outposts and elements of a reconnaissance-car unit south of Sidi Omar. The force was indeed gigantic: Under General Sir Alan Cunningham, fresh from his successful campaign against the Italians in East Africa, more than 700 tanks were on the move northwestward. Another 200 or more were standing by as reserves. These units, which were swinging northward in a wide arc, were generally organized into brigades.[1] Strangely, the British were still unwilling to adopt their skillful adversary's formula of using mechan-

[1] "Armored brigade"=fast tanks. "Tank brigade"=infantry tanks. An armored brigade would consist of three regiments of 52 tanks each, as a rule, with a regiment of motorized infantry thrown in. A regiment consisted of four squadrons, one of them a headquarters squadron. A squadron was made up of four troops of three tanks apiece, plus a headquarters troop of three tanks.

ized units of all sizes clenched into one fist. The outcome was always the same.

In addition to the newly arrived American-built Honeys, Cruiser tanks of all varieties were represented: from the old A-10s through the A-13s, to the low-slung, racy-looking Crusaders. The fat, crawling Matildas made the usual shortened flanking movement northward from the desert in the south.[2] Otherwise, it was Battleaxe all over again.

The mass of the Cruisers made a rapid thrust for Sidi Rezegh, just 15 kilometers south of Tobruk on the escarpment. Neither they nor the Matildas, which were escorted by strong infantry forces, allowed themselves to be diverted on the way into first rushing blindly at strongpoints bristling with eighty-eights and thus getting themselves shot to pieces. The fearsomely fortified Halfaya and Sollum passes in particular were simply left behind on the right, handy though a direct supply line would have been.

A clear tactical concept was discernible: If the Eighth Army occupied an area vital to Rommel—i.e., the Sidi Rezegh airfield, which lay above, and close to, the Tobruk siege ring—it would compel him to give battle at this place of the Eighth Army's choosing. At the same time Matildas, supported by the New Zealand Infantry Division, cut the Via Balbia west of Bardia and took Capuzzo from the rear.

It could all have ended in a quick victory if at least the fast Cruiser brigades had stayed together. But once again the General Staffs had worked out all sorts of flank-protection schemes which divided their strength:

Although the 7th Armored Brigade went purposefully and directly for Sidi Rezegh, and although the 6th Royal Tank Regiment even captured 19 aircraft in airworthy condition (three flew off under their noses), the 22nd Armored Brigade made a wider arc, ran into the Italian Ariete Division far to the south and was held up there. Gallantly, the Italians stood to fight with their awful M-13s and lost 40 of their 154 tanks. They even managed to put 25 Cruisers out of action in the process.

Acting as a "shield for the right flank," the 4th Armored Brigade, describing a tighter arc, came up against the 21st Panzer Division. A brisk engagement ensued—an "unhappy opening chord" for the German side, as Westphal says in his *Erinnerungen*. It is clear that the division was not very well led and left the army staff utterly in the dark about the situation, despite the fact that arrangements had been made for hourly reports to be transmitted.

_____

[2] To that extent the figure of 700 attacking tanks is misleading: Only 455 Cruisers took part in the push for Sidi Rezegh.

But the 4th Armored Brigade, too, was held up and decimated. Gunner Werner Fenck had that well-known tight feeling in the stomach and midriff as he glimpsed the enemy tanks through his optical sights.

It was afternoon. They had been under way since early morning, mostly on a southerly course. Occasionally they had seen dust clouds in the distance; but it looked as if both sides were first maneuvering around each other, like warships. Then, suddenly, they were in the midst of the engagement.

As always, all at once one was unutterably alone; one did one's work mechanically: Pull the trigger, correct your aim, pull the trigger. Black smoke billowed. Change your target; right—there's one of them. Bang, stink of cordite, thick dense smoke, clouds of dust. They seemed to be advancing nevertheless.

Ahead and to the left, Fenck suddenly saw Warrant Officer Braun's Panzer pull up with a jolt. The driver, Abi Neuhäuser, known as a keen and combative type, jumped out of the hatch and collapsed after a few steps, his limbs twitching.

The warrant officer himself hung from the turret, evidently dead. A moment later, Fenck's Panzer, too, was hit. They seemed to have run up against an anti-tank line amid the billowing smoke and sand—a line through which the enemy tanks, using a Rommel tactic, had skillfully retreated. They were only the little two-pounders, but they were firing at close range.

There was a thud and a jolt as the armor-piercing shell embedded itself deeply in the frontal armor. "Let's get out," thought Fenck. Automatically, he allowed himself to roll off over the stern, as they had practiced a thousand times. That's where the food hamper was carried. There were fresh peaches in it—a rare luxury in the desert—and they were rolling about on top of the dusty Panzer.

He was seized by a weird urge to gulp down the peaches before he did anything else; and he began to chew with dribbling lips. Another AP round went through the tin food box and a tiny splinter laid his cheek open. Then he saw the wireless operator, Paulik, run from the Panzer and collapse. He crawled up to him under the hail of missiles. Paulik was dead, although he seemed to have no visible injury.

Only then did he notice how badly hurt the driver, Gustav Jansik, was. The solid shot had severed one of his legs completely. Inside, the Panzer was completely wrecked. After the first direct hit, a whole series of AP shells had struck home with devastating effect.

Together with his commander, Lieutenant Söller, Fenck lifted Gustav Jansik out of his seat. Darkness was falling rapidly; the firing stopped. At least ten Panzers had been put out of action. Söller took over another vehicle. A few days later he was dead.

Low-loaders drove up to collect the wrecks. They also took away the dead wireless operator for burial near the supply depot at Marsa Luq. Fenck was pretty dazed after the shock, but one feeling predominated: Thank God, my Panzer's bust; I'm out of circulation for the time being.

Alert at Sidi Rezegh

Despite these clashes, no great collision of great masses of tanks took place in the first three days. The British advance, which gave the impression of great energy, had made Rommel cautious. . . . "I hope we shall come through in good shape. By the time you have this letter, it will all surely have been decided. Our situation is certainly not straightforward," he wrote to his wife on 20 November.

Rommel decided to move his headquarters from the eastern to the western side of Tobruk. This did not mean that the German C-in-C had suddenly been bitten by the British sensitiveness about flanks, but it did make it clear that this would not simply be a mobile battle of limited armored units. A solid mass of troops was deployed in a wide semicircle, skirting the eastern escarpment and stretching right up to Tobruk. Their obvious aim was to join up with the fortress garrison. The need to give up the siege ring, at least in the east, could arise very rapidly.

Counting the Tobruk garrison, the Eighth Army had seven divisions, against three (partly still understrength) German and seven (mostly barely motorized and ridiculously armed) Italian. Rommel had 414 tanks, 145 of them Italian. The 200 or more powerful Panzers III and IV remained his trump card; and 50 more were expected back from the workshops.

But it was the situation in the air that was most in the balance. Air Marshal Tedder could throw over 1,000 machines into the battle. The Axis air forces had a little over 300, of which 120 were German and less than 200 Italian. The latter still had some old double-deckers flapping around.

The British commanded the air almost completely. When on the night of 22 November Rommel's staff burned a lot of papers before moving house, even the fire flickering in the chimney attracted the bombers, which killed several officers with their well-aimed bombs. Not for the first, and by no means for the last, time, the German C-in-C lay helpless in the dust. The German-Italian air force was, moreover, handicapped by the heavy rain, which had made most of their airfields so soft that it was impossible to take off from them. After the incident with the Bombay, Lieutenant Rödel was again the first to be airborne from the Gazala airfield. On 19 November he flew a reconnaissance mission and sighted the mighty column of the 7th Armored Brigade on its way to Sidi Rezegh.

His commander, "Edu" Neumann of the 27th Fighter Squadron, took Rödel's description of the mass of approaching vehicles to be an exaggeration and himself took up his Me-109 through the glutinous mud. What he then saw at first took his breath away. Then he started his stopwatch, and established that the fast bird he was flying took a full ten minutes to pass the full length of the column.

Meanwhile the roar of aircraft taking off could once more be heard in Tobruk. Four Hurricanes had been stationed in the fortress to support and cover the operations on the ground. The breakout was to take place on the morning of 21 November. But at first everything went wrong.

There was a certain amount of euphoria among the command staffs of the Eighth Army, and that is not a good frame of mind for taking decisions. In the planning stage, there had been general agreement that the objectives of the offensive could be achieved only in one particular sequence: (1) Destroy the enemy's armor; (2) mop up Cyrenaïca and relieve Tobruk; (3) take Tripolitania.

Given an enemy known for the bold and determined use of his superior Panzers, Point 2 could not come before Point 1. But now that the 7th Armored Brigade's advance to Sidi Rezegh had gone so surprisingly smoothly, the temptation was great: another 15 kilometers to go to the Tobruk siege ring, and to reach the partial objective which aroused the most emotions. . . . The code word "Pop" was radioed to the Tobruk garrison. It meant: Get ready to break out!

On the escarpment, strong elements of the 7th Armored Brigade were getting ready around the Rezegh airfield, with their support group of infantry and artillery, to advance on El Duda-Tobruk. Morale was high. Since the occupation of the airfield, all they had had to contend with on the northern rim of the escarpment had been enemy infantry units which had crept up and mounted attacks, firing their anti-tank guns.

In addition to the support group, some more infantry—the South African Division—was to follow northward in the footsteps of the 7th Armored Brigade. In view of the chronic shortage of anti-tank weapons, this move was to take place only in Stage 2.

But as it turned out, the mass of the Afrika Korps was, so aerial reconnaissance reported, engaged in the south, dealing with the two armored brigades there: the 4th, with their Honeys, and the 22nd. They

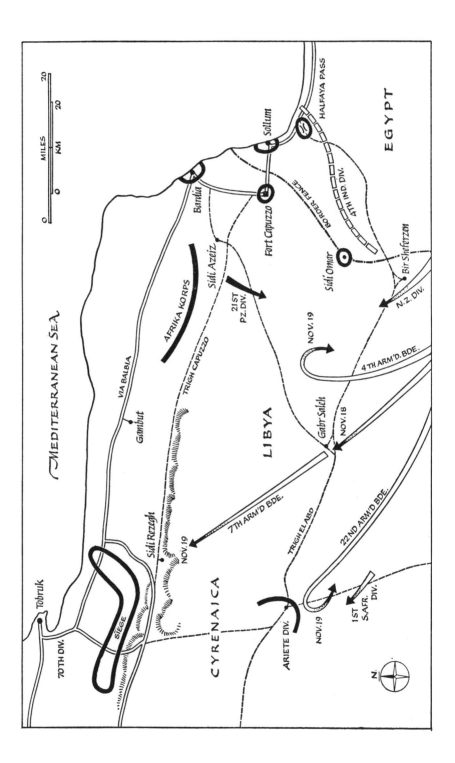

MEDITERRANEAN SEA

MILES 20 20 0

KM 0

Tobruk

70TH DIV.

SIEGE

VIA BALBIA

Gambut

Sidi Rezegh

NOV. 19

7TH ARM'D BDE.

CYRENAICA

ARIETE DIV.

NOV. 19

TRIGH EL ABD

1ST S.AFR. DIV.

22ND ARM'D BDE.

Gabr Saleh

NOV. 18

N.Z. DIV.

NOV. 19

4TH ARM'D. BDE.

LIBYA

AFRIKA KORPS

TRIGH CAPUZZO

Sidi Azeiz

21ST PZ. DIV.

Bardia

Fort Capuzzo

Solium

HALFAYA PASS

BORDER FENCE

4TH IND. DIV.

Bir Sheferzen

Sidi Omar

EGYPT

N.

had received orders in the night to attack as early as possible at first light on 21 November: "Should the enemy show signs of retreating, he is to be pursued remorselessly." The idea was to hold Rommel's Panzers down there, beating them or even destroying them already at this stage.

But that was to reckon without Rommel, master of the tactics of rapidly shifting centers of gravity.

All was ready at Sidi Rezegh for the breakout to the north when the order came: Stay where you are. Lieutenant Llewellyn-Palmer's 7th Hussars were farthest south. He was to stay in reserve and provide flank cover.

He now received the order to turn at once southeast and attack a strong Panzer force advancing northwestward.

They were again equipped with Cruisers—all types, including the brand-new Crusaders. Major Younger's B-Squadron, to which Tim Palmer belonged, had mostly the old, slow A-10s, which was why they joined battle a little later than the other squadrons.

Tim Palmer raised himself out of his turret and counted the enemy armada as it came into sight. There were 150 Panzer IIIs and IVs, as always accompanied by motorized infantry, anti-tank guns and eighty-eights.

Before the lead squadrons could do anything much with their two-pounders, the shells from the 50 mm anti-tank and Panzer guns were landing among them. It was a dreadful sight. You could see entire turrets fly into the air, tanks exploding or disabled by hits turning around on their own axes. Artillery shells screamed among them. The advance of the two German tank divisions had been conducted so rapidly that they just waded into the various British supply columns, driving them ahead of themselves in headlong flight. An unco-ordinated mass of all sorts of vehicles, milling about in front of, and between, the Panzers, was approaching the Hussars. The German anti-tank guns, exploiting their opportunity, raced forward undetected among the British vehicles. A lot of tanks were hit before their crews realized where the fire was coming from.

As soon as the range had closed enough for their two-pounders, the Hussars defended themselves desperately.

On facing page. Crusader, Phase One: The drive on Sidi Rezegh goes straight through. The 22nd Armored Brigade is stopped by the Ariete and the 4th Armored Brigade by the 21st Panzer Division. At the border fence, the New Zealanders and the Indians advance slowly with the Matilda regiments.

The Hussars wiped out

It was Warrant Officer Joachim Saenger's third attack since being promoted Panzer commander. The previous day they had stood about for a while without fuel until the tanker lorries had come. When they trundled off northward at first light, all was very quiet inside the Panzer. Everyone thought: Here we go again.

From where the commander sat up in the turret, the men looked odd: Their faces caked with yellow ocher dust, marked by runnels of sweat, their eyes appeared opened enormously wide as they glanced up at him every few moments.

During the drive, Saenger read a book. As long as the crew saw him doing that, they felt reassured—no danger. Every now and then one of them would squat over the opening in the floor through which the shell cases were supposed to be ejected in action. It was strange with dysentery: Even the man who had to go ceaselessly while off duty was much less troubled, even during deployment to starting positions. While the fighting lasted, you didn't have the urge at all—as if "everything tightened up," as one of the men put it.

Saenger was reading something about economics. The somewhat involved subject matter was best for diverting his mind. When he let the book fall down into the Panzer, the others knew what it meant. Soon they were in the thick of the fight.

The supply vehicles, transporters, and self-propelled guns, all milling about aimlessly, kicked up even more dust than usual. Even when they stopped to fire it was difficult to take aim at the target indicated in the order. Radio communication broke down completely—as it did most of the time. Fragments of words and call signs . . . The company commanders were directing their troops more with arm signals than by radio commands.

Eighty-eights drove forward between them, fired with their trails only half swung out so that the whole carriage jumped up in the air. There were fires over on the other side, and explosions lit up the black smoke in sudden flashes. "Soft-skinned" vehicles stopped and burst into flames in droves. Drivers ran for their lives, stumbled, and fell.

The Panzers rumbled forward. So far, they seemed to have had hardly any casualties. So far, so good. . . .

A fateful decision had been taken on the British side: The breakout from Tobruk was in progress. The vanguard of the troops from the garrison was expected to reach El Duda at any moment. They could not be left in the lurch. The attack northward must be continued. The Hussars would just have to deal with the Panzers as best they could.

A real Rommel chess move had come off perfectly: He had guessed (and deduced from monitored radio traffic) that the attempt to relieve Tobruk would come at this particular moment. The disengagement of his Panzers from the British in the south had paid off. The tanks of the 4th and 22nd Armored Brigades were grappling with a strong front of anti-tank guns, artillery, and eighty-eights while the concentrated Panzer force could pick off the smaller tank formations one by one—as it had always managed to do so far. Clumsy generalship had left him the 7th Hussars as first, easy victims. Brave men with inadequate weapons . . .

Major Younger's squadron joined the fighting just as a strong group of Panzers detached itself from the others and was evidently about to make a flanking move. They drove past in single file at a distance of some 1,500 meters. Some of Younger's tanks fired. It did not seem to make much of an impression on the Germans. But then they turned and came suddenly thundering on—a deadly, determined steel roller. Just outside the range of the two-pounders, they stopped to fire for the first time. Younger's tank was wrecked by a hit before he was able to fire. The tank immediately burst into flames. Somehow Younger got out, not too badly hurt. But the skin hung in ribbons from his hands. His driver was dead, his gunner and signaler had sustained severe burns.

The major took over the Cruiser of his second-in-command, Lieutenant George Murray-Smith. The young officer looked with horror at Younger's hands. It seemed days since they had last spoken to each other, but hardly an hour had actually passed since Younger had said to him: "George, we've got to go immediately. And it's going to be a nasty business." Whereupon the lieutenant, his cheeks covered in shaving foam, had answered calmly: "I'd better have a proper shave then."

There was no more need to talk now. Armor-piercing rounds were whistling all around them. Using the balls of his thumbs, Younger put on the earphones.

Just then, Tim Llewellyn-Palmer saw something he would never forget: He glimpsed a high-velocity shell coming at him. He happened to be glancing over at the Panzer they were shooting at, and there it was: the point of a pin. Then for just an instant, like the click of a fast camera shutter, a large object immediately in front of him; and then his cap was gone, complete with earphones.

He ordered his driver forward—the range was too great for the miserable two-pounder. But then, over to the left, he made out one of those huge guns he had admired on the Egyptian border. It was being towed behind a truck, which pulled up sharply. Men jumped down and busied themselves with the gun.

"Let 'em have it," said Palmer to his gunner. He hit the truck so squarely with his first shot that it blew up.

Smallish high-explosive shells were bursting all around them. They seemed to be coming from a Panzer. Something hit his machine; it caught fire, though not too badly; but the tank was finished, since immediately another shell hit the turret traversing gear, immobilizing it.

Palmer got out and ran across to one of the few tanks left intact. He sat on it, next to the driver's viewing slit, to guide the men by hand signals. A crazy idea, but it saved his life. A heavy AP round hit the tank, ricocheted about inside, and killed the entire crew. In those moments, his regiment ceased to exist as a fighting unit. You could hear the squadron and troop commanders call in vain to their seconds-in-command: "Take over! I'm hit!" Most of them got no reply.

Regimental HQ had a shoot-out at short range with three Panzer IIIs. The two tanks, containing the radios through which communications with brigade and divisional HQs were maintained, were destroyed. Brigade HQ, itself in the thick of the battle among the Hussars' tanks, tried in vain to make contact.

The commander of C-Squadron, Major Congreve, had his microphone shot from his hand by an AP round which also took the aerial with it. The regimental commander, Lieutenant Colonel Frederick Byass, was killed by a 50 mm shell in the turret of his tank. At this stage the regiment was reduced to just twelve tanks. A wedge of Panzers had thrust itself between what was left of the regiment and the airfield. The second-in-command, Major "Rhino" Fosdick, led the shattered remnants southeast through a wadi. Several of the tanks had had their guns destroyed. Others had no ammunition left; all were carrying wounded on their decks. They were pursued by artillery fire. But the Panzers trundled off northwestward: Their goal was the airfield.

Tim Palmer had been driven back there in his third tank, a Crusader. Another regiment of the brigade, the 2nd Royal Tank Regiment, was in the process of being rubbed out. The 50 mm shells were crashing into the armor of its tanks at a range of 1,500 meters while they themselves were in vain trying to get within range.

All day long, the radio operators shouted themselves hoarse. Where were the two other brigades? The Commander of the 7th Armored Division, General "Strafer" Gott, could not be found at his HQ. He was out visiting troops somewhere. Eventually someone managed to inform him of the situation and he gave orders to get the 4th and 22nd Brigades moving north immediately. But both those formations had picked this of all moments to refill their fuel tanks[3] and replenish their ammu-

---

[3] A new problem of organization, which is in any case not generally a British *forte*, had arisen with the introduction of the Honeys: They needed high-octane gasoline for their aircraft engines.

nition. They had been engaged in a running fight with the rearguards of the two Panzer divisions, which had shown immense skill. When the 4th, which was then just ten miles away, tried to come to the rescue, steering a northerly course, the fast but not very effective Honeys ran into a German anti-tank line and spent the time until dark trading shots with them.

The 22nd, on the other hand, was once actually glimpsed from Sidi Rezegh, but drove past the scene of the battle, keeping to a north-westerly course. The Corps war diary says that it was supposed to clear the enemy from some obscure "Point 4239" or other. It is possible that the Ariete were briefly there.

That was what things looked like when Tim Palmer lost his fourth tank. He was fired at from a range at which even the Panzer III's 50 mm shells arrived in a fairly spent state. But the fire from this enemy Panzer was hellishly accurate. Palmer stood in the turret with his radio operator and watched the Panzers approaching, stopping, firing, when a projectile penetrated the wall of the turret with a metallic clang and lodged there. The radio operator dropped down into the vehicle out of sheer fright. The next round pierced the portal armor and also stuck fast just in front of the poor fellow. This so horrified the driver that he jumped out and ran mindlessly into the desert.[4] A third hit jammed the gun.

At this moment, as he was getting out, Palmer saw a large staff car flying a pennant driving straight across the airfield. There was a man standing upright in the open vehicle. It was Brigadier Jock Campbell, the man with whom he had first seen the eighty-eight in action at Capuzzo and who was now commanding the brigade's support group. He was making straight for Palmer, yelling: "Tim! Catch those bloody guns there and stop them!"

A couple of 25-pounders had turned up, running from the steel roller of the Panzers. Palmer grabbed one of those small open cars the British called scout cars and the Germans "Flitzers" ("scurriers"), and chased after the howitzers. The gunners were not trying to run away; they simply lacked orders. The name Campbell, already widely known in the Eighth Army, worked wonders. They unlimbered and got out their AP rounds—at that time, and for a long time yet, the only effective defense against Panzers.

Campbell had again driven off, but he was not away long. The 25-pounders, firing over open sights, stopped the Panzers, which halted at a respectful distance and began to straddle them with high-explosive

[4] The next Palmer heard of this driver was three years later, when the man had been released from German captivity and was to be court-martialed for desertion. In his testimony, Palmer saw to it that no proceedings were taken, since it was obvious that this otherwise brave man had acted in a state of shock.

shells. That gave the survivors of the 2nd Royal Tank Regiment, six Cruisers, a little breathing space. And then up came Campbell with his last levy.

A few battered specimens of the Brigade's third regiment, the 8th Hussars, had survived the drive to the north. Campbell, with the help of a Hussar captain, the senior survivor, had quickly organized them into a small combat group. They now came trundling across the airfield, the brigadier's open staff car at their head. Under his fluttering pennant, he was holding on to a grab handle with one hand, while waving the tanks forward with the other like a cavalry officer during a charge. Which was all quite unnecessary but very brave. And which was, perhaps, precisely the sight the exhausted men on the airfield needed for a last effort.

Saenger is hit four times

Joachim Saenger squatted in the turret, his legs pulled up under him. When a shell can come crashing into the main compartment at any moment, you do feel an idiot just letting them dangle down. Apart from which, there was the chance of being able to get out like greased lightning, should the Panzer catch fire.

One did not know much about the others in this inferno of billowing black smoke and sand clouds, but it was obvious that quite a lot of Panzers had been put out of action. In Saenger's immediate vicinity, a 25-pounder AP round had gone right through Driver Herrmann Bleich in his driving seat.

The British gunners were serving their cumbersome pieces with foolhardy courage. The guns were slow to limber and unlimber; but their AP rounds, which they had at first used so seldom, were now scoring some deadly direct hits, where the earlier high-explosive (HE) shells had at best merely torn Panzer tracks off their bogeys.

Saenger was driving on the right wing, as the new lineup of the 25-pounders loomed out of the smoke and the sand clouds. The turret was turned half left at ten o'clock[5] since something that looked like a Cruiser tank was to be seen in that direction. The layer was just swiveling it to face ahead, when there were a couple of sharp reports. The Panzer gave a jolt like a stricken animal. Down below in the main compartment there was an odd sort of clattering, some shouts, and the

[5] Much used in the army to simplify indicating directions: twelve o'clock=north, six o'clock=south, nine o'clock=west, three o'clock=east. Intermediate directions correspondingly. In tank terminology, this is used not geographically but relative to the direction in which Panzer is facing: i.e., twelve o'clock=front, et cetera.

screech of tearing metal. That thing at ten o'clock had indeed been a tank.

Saenger called his men. All replied; none seemed too badly hurt. The turret would not turn anymore; but luckily, the engine still ran. He reported himself out of action and reversed out of the formation.

Inside the Panzer, there was utter devastation. They stared at each other with ashen faces as they realized how lucky they had been.

Four AP rounds had gone on the rampage inside the main compartment. Three of them had gone through ammunition compartments and had torn open the shell cases without detonating the shells. The fourth had destroyed the collecting ring for the electricity supply to the turret and the traversing gear of the gun.

Splinters had torn the gunner's trousers; the linkage to the trigger pedal of his machine gun was completely destroyed. The radio operator had the set smashed to pieces in his hands.

The holes showed where the splinters had come from: The two-pounders had made only a small hole outside, but inside they had taken a large circular piece of the flank armoring with them. And none of them had as much as a scratch. . . .

They threw the shells overboard and made off, not altogether dismayed, making for the workshop in Marsa Luq. The sun was just sinking below the western horizon. As he looked back, Saenger saw, on either side of the great glowing red ball, small points that glowed in the same color. They were burnt-out wrecks, monuments to a perfect and exceedingly hygienic method of incineration: one hell of a hero's death.

". . . not so rosy"

Two kilometers away, on the British side, two other men were also staring at the red-glowing wrecks. The victims of the latest battle were still burning under plumes of black smoke.

"I can only see Cruisers," Tim Llewellyn-Palmer said; "the Jerries don't burn as easily as we do."

Brigadier Campbell was looking at a group of tankmen who, their charred uniforms in tatters, were carrying some wounded past them. Apart from some stray artillery fire, the battle was over. They were still holding the area around the airfield, but it did not look as if they would be able to hang on to it another day. However, the corridor to the south was still open too. It was by that route that the remnants of the 7th Hussars, who had been forced away from the main body, had rejoined the brigade. Trucks with ammunition, fuel, and food were coming through almost without hindrance. They were taking the wounded back with them to the rear, while the mechanics tried to

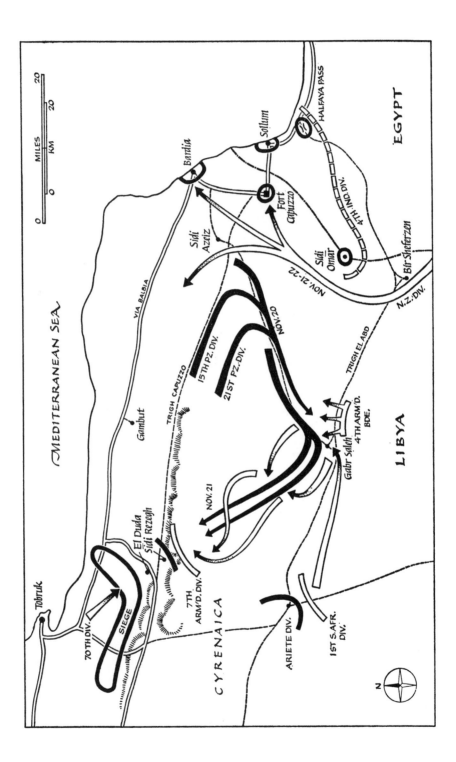

make emergency repairs to those tanks which were not completely destroyed. In the morning, the brigade boasted altogether twenty-eight battered but battle-worthy tanks.

In the evening, the brigade had radioed a report on its situation to General Gott at Divisional HQ. Since it was known that the Germans ran an excellent monitoring service, a very optimistic report was transmitted, which greatly exaggerated the brigade's remaining strength.

A little while later, there followed a message which would have been utterly incomprehensible to a stranger: "Situation not as Lloyd as reported earlier. Brink's boys would be most welcome."

Everyone in the division knew what it meant: The head of the HQ AFV section, Lloyd, was "Rosey" to his friends.

The situation was therefore not so rosy, and reinforcements by the boys of Major General G. E. Brink's South African Division would be needed.

Encounter in a wadi

The premature drive northward in the direction of Tobruk did not produce any result either except heavy losses, as was to be expected when forces are split up. The support group's infantry lost two hundred men and their escorting armored regiment, the 8th Hussars, lost all but a handful of their tanks, which Brigadier Campbell eventually led back to the airfield.

They had come up against a unit in the German defensive front in which the average age was considerably higher than in the other German units. It was the "361st Africa Regiment." This regiment had been formed, with the approval of the very highest quarters, from German ex-members of the French Foreign Legion, who were to have the chance to cleanse themselves in Africa of the stigma of having fought for the hereditary enemy. Many of these old sweats, however, would have preferred to be declared "unworthy to serve." But once collared, they made the best of it, with true German thoroughness. Moreover, Rommel and this bunch of former mercenaries hit it off immediately: kindred spirits as professionals of war.

The men of the 361st were struck by astonishment and disbelief when they were issued with their equipment. The pith helmets and the natty folding spades they threw overboard during the outward sea pas-

On facing page. Crusader, Phase Two: Rommel's combined Panzer forces have pushed away the 22nd and 4th Brigades. The 15th and 21st Panzer divisions are leading a concentrated assault against the 7th Brigade near Sidi Rezegh. The steady advance of the New Zealanders on the right wing continues. The breakthrough in Tobruk begins.

sage; but they hung on to the long nightshirts because they were useful for wrapping up one's gun in sandstorms.

They had parted with the ridiculous spades all the more willingly because they had already pinched a satisfactory number of much sturdier long-handled ones, as well as some jemmies, at the Bersaglieri barracks in Naples. They left the quartermaster's stores of the barracks empty when they went on board. There was a certain amount of guessing among them whether or not they really would find "camels and pack animals" waiting for them, as one of their orders had said.[6] But luckily they were put into perfectly ordinary trucks.

When Crusader started, they were south of Tobruk on standby to take part in the planned attack. Their supply of water worried them: There was too little of it and it was very brackish.

Lance Corporal Karl-Ludwig Heilig talked his company commander into letting him drive to Derna, in an ancient Fiat truck of dubious antecedents, to fetch a consignment of the famous Derna water. The great rains were over, and the columns of Auchinleck's armies well on their way, when he came clanking home one night, the lorry's loading platform full of 20-liter canisters each with a White Cross, the sign of drinking water, on it.

He had to turn right somewhere off "Axis Road," which made a detour around Tobruk. He had some trouble finding the spot and soon found himself back in rough country. Bucking and jolting, the ancient Fiat dived into a wadi. Heilig put his foot down on the accelerator, but the bed of the wadi had been softened by the rains and soon the rear wheels were up to their axles in mud. While he was still struggling, a reconnaissance car loomed up on the edge of the wadi. It began to pick its way down carefully to the bottom, keeping in low gear. Not until the car pulled up next to him did Heilig notice the flat steel helmets of the Tommies.

The Britishers climbed out, grinning, and assessed his situation. The good water was as welcome to them as the canisters—they called them jerrycans—which they prized highly for their sturdiness. They loaded some of the canisters onto their own car, fetching spades and sheets of perforated steel from their seemingly bottomless vehicle. The steel pieces could be slotted together and laid in front of the rear wheels. In a few minutes the Fiat was back in business. Carefully, they towed him out of the wadi.

"And now?" Heilig asked.

They were standing side by side, smoking cigarettes they had politely exchanged. Heilig had offered them some obtaining the notorious "Spe-

[6] The OKH observer, General Kirchheim, had in fact suggested to Halder on his return that the shortage of transport could be alleviated by using camels.

cial Mixture," which sometimes put even the North African flies to
flight.

"Dreadful stuff, this. You are killing yourself anyway; hardly any
need for us to do anything about it, really," said one of the Britons,
crushing the cigarette under his heel and giving Heilig a half packet of
Players.

"Look after yourself, mate," said one of the others. They clambered
back into their armored car. "We can't do anything with you," the
driver added. "We're full up to overflowing, and anyway you'll only get
stuck with that thing again. Mind how you go!"

They went grinding back up the slope. They must have belonged to
the 11th Hussars. A gray light on the horizon heralded a new day. It
was 21 November 1941. The sound of guns could be heard thundering
from the direction of Tobruk. The British had started their attempt at a
breakout.

The attack of the "Tobruk Rats"

The "Tobruk Rats," as the men called themselves after the Desert
Rats, had been bursting with impatience during the first two days of the
offensive. The newly arrived men of the British 70th Division in particular, who had not yet had the chance to discover the unique charm of
this place of daytime heat and nighttime cold, sandstorms, and dreadful
drinking water, kept on saying: "If we have to fight Jerry to get out of
here, then better today than tomorrow."

Major "Mick" Lindsay's Dragoon squadron had overhauled their
Marmon-Harringtons—which had traveled more or less 10,000 kilometers without an overhaul—at least, they had done the best one could
do in the fortress. On the day of the breakout there was an open-air
service, in which the Dragoons' own chaplain in all innocence took as
his text the business about turning the other cheek. Those who knew
the squadron commander could see the coming storm by the expression
on his face. And hardly had the padre finished his sermon than Lindsay thundered away at the men to the effect that he hoped they would
all forget the padre's words during the coming party, and behave not
meekly but as meanly as they knew how. . . . "Dismiss!" And with
that he strode, still absolutely furious, to his car, leaving behind a bewildered padre and some Dragoons choking with suppressed merri-
ment.

The operation was painstakingly planned and rehearsed, particularly
the co-operation between the Matildas, of which there were nearly
sixty, and the infantry. The spearhead of the latter was a battalion of
the Black Watch—a regiment from the Scottish Highlands with a long

and distinguished history—some of whose men had been taken prisoner by Rommel's 7th Panzer Division in the summer of the year before at St. Valéry. The battalion at Tobruk had just been brought up to strength after its heavy losses in Crete and during the evacuation of the island.

The officers memorized the positions of the enemy defenses from a sand-table model. In fact, they were to find that the reconnaissance work had not been all that good, particularly when it came to the whereabouts of some of the minefields.

In accordance with an old and somewhat dubious custom (but one which was occasionally observed in the Wehrmacht, too), the Jocks were given a stiff shot of rum immediately before the attack. Sergeant Reid was squatting in the turret of his Matilda at the start line and noticed, even in the dark, how the stuff was beginning to work on the Highlanders: They began to chat in a free and easy way. Angry commanders whispered "Psst!" from every tank turret; but then the artillery preparation began to roar from every barrel, and it didn't matter anyway. And for many a Scottish lad, that pleasant quarter hour was the last of his life.

Despite all the preparations, there was a muddle when they crossed the tank ditch. The Matildas, which were supposed to make straight for Derna with the Black Watch, were a few minutes late. It was the first link in a fatal chain reaction.

Some of Major Lindsay's men were first to come under fire: They had been trained in mine clearance and were now making for the obstacles in front of the German-Italian positions. There was hardly even a smear of gray to be seen in the east. Smoke and dust from their own infantry fire was drifting over the desert. While they cleared a lane and marked it with white tape, the defenders' fire remained inaccurate.

The battalion commander of the Black Watch, Colonel George A. Rusk, looked around in vain for the tanks. He was faced with an insoluble dilemma: At the prearranged time, to the minute, the artillery fire would move away from the proposed position of the salient. At that moment, the Jocks were supposed to close in on the enemy. Was it better to wait for the tanks and thus miss the vital moment when the hail of shells stopped?

He gave the sign to advance. Amid the crashing and whining of the shells, the pipers blew into their bagpipes and struck up their shrill, stirring clamor. Their kilts swinging, short bayonets fixed to their rifles, the Jocks disappeared in the swirling clouds. At last, the tank liaison officer's little Mark VI hove in sight. There was a sharp report and the little tank disappeared in a cloud of smoke. There seemed to be another unsuspected minefield there. With a shrug of the shoulder, Rusk turned away and nodded to his driver.

A sort of British congenital defect again became evident: There was no overall commander in the foremost line of the fighting; the various branches of the service worked side by side independently.[7]

Well, there was a plan, wasn't there?

Once visual contact between tanks and infantry was lost, the next breakdown occurred on the dead-flat plain: The tanks veered off course to the left. Captain Armitage of the artillery, who rode with the attack acting as forward observation officer, in a light Mark VI, saw the massive outline of the Matildas disappear to the east. He hesitated half a second and then made his tank scurry along behind the Jocks. It was a much more dangerous thing to do, since he could no longer hide his thin-skinned vehicle behind the fat matronly posteriors of the Matildas, as was the general practice. But the Scots would be needing the services of his 25-pounders more urgently.

How did the tanks come to mistake their course? "Mick" Lindsay, of whose positive deeds one never hears from his own mouth but only from those of witnesses, blamed himself when interviewed: "It was my fault. Ahead and to the right, I saw one of my reconnaissance cars set off a mine. The tanks stopped and did not know what to do next. I did not bother to look at the compass anymore but simply altered course a little further to the left to avoid the minefield. The tanks followed me obediently."

Every amateur pilot knows that you must work with great precision, using stopwatch and protractors, if you want to deviate from a previously set course and then resume it. It's much the same in the desert, where there are no landmarks. Except that here they also had to contend with a hail of HE and AP shells.

In addition to the usual offerings, all sorts of remarkable stuff was coming over: There were shells which either did not go off at all or went bouncing over the hard desert floor and blew up with quite a lot of noise without doing much harm. As a gunner, Armitage observed them with professional interest: The caps were oddly blunted; and in view of their poor performance, he put the projectiles down as coming from the Italian artillery, the shells of which were generally known for their poor splintering characteristics.[8]

[7] Only a little way farther west, a similar mistake had contributed to a German catastrophe: It occurred when General Streich got stuck during an attack of the 8th Machine Gun Battalion and the 5th Panzer Regiment and had failed to lay down in advance a chain of command for such an eventuality. Without Rommel's earlier interference with the 5th Light Division, however, such an oversight could hardly have happened.

[8] The ugly point about explosive-filled shells as antipersonnel weapons is that they will disintegrate into as many pieces of shrapnel as possible of similar and effective sizes. The German product counted as excellent; the Italian shells had a habit of splitting into a few large pieces, which of course seldom hit anyone.

In fact, however, they came from the German guns. Siegfried Westphal reports[9] that because of the grim supply position, artillery ammunition of various calibers very soon ran short. However, the group's artillery general told him that large quantities of hollow-charge shells were still lying around the place. . . . It had, as usual, been forbidden by the highest command echelon on pain of execution to fire off this new armor-piercing high-explosive type of shell until further orders. Westphal took it on himself to let the gunners fire away with what they had.

"The loving homeland" had also sent another useless type of ammunition all that long way. Someone or other had got wind that those "Africans" down there were laying siege to a "fortress" and immediately sent off some solid rounds for the big 210 mm mortars. They were huge things, filled with concrete, suitable perhaps for attacking the installations of the Maginot Line. But they were not much use in Tobruk. They are there, to this day, sunk deep into the desert, presumably without ever having done anyone any harm.

"A solid wall of lead"

Probably the first of the tankmen to notice that they were off course was Sergeant Reid.

They knew they were supposed to steer a compass bearing of about 200 degrees—20 degrees west of south. But, of course, nobody bothered to look at the compass, which in the Matilda sat between the driver's legs. They jolted along in a body on the left wing, until they encountered light and scattered artillery fire, which at first did not bother them much. But then, suddenly all hell broke loose.

From straight ahead, AP rounds came whizzing through their lines and machine-gun bursts rattled against the Matildas' thick flanks. Reid closed his observation slit; he saw no reason to play the hero.

He scanned the country ahead of him through his periscope, looking for a target to give his gunner, "Tug" Wilson. Instead of which, he noticed, running parallel with their course to their left, an anti-tank ditch that, according to their map, should have run much farther to the east.

Radio silence had, of course, been ordered; but this discovery seemed to him alarming enough to transmit a message.

Farther ahead, Major Lindsay saw that the tank commander, Colonel O'Carroll, had suddenly pulled up and called two of his officers to join him, despite the heavy fire they were drawing from the defenders. Colonel Rusk joined them in the nick of time, and the confusion was at

---

[9] His memoirs (*Erinnerungen*) and in conversation with the author.

last resolved. But meanwhile, the Scottish infantrymen had been badly shot up.

Behind the moving roller of fire laid down by the artillery, they had soon overrun the first German outposts, which were on their side of a slight incline. As Captain Armitage went forward in his light tank, he saw the first Germans coming back with their hands up. They were from the 90th Light Division who had been standing by for their own attack, but now had to defend themselves on two sides—Sidi Rezegh and Tobruk.

The Jocks stormed on, their bagpipes wailing. When they reached the crest of the knoll, they were struck by fire "like a solid wall of lead" (says their regimental history). The reverse side of the slope, it seemed, bristled with machine guns. Light-infantry field guns barked from time to time. Armitage directed his 25-pounders as best he could, going by the almost continuous gun flashes. Amid the howling and the bangs, the cries of the wounded, and the soft whirring sound of slowly falling mortar bombs, the shrill bagpipes were not stilled. Pipe Major Roy, who had just rejoined his unit after an adventurous flight through Turkey, having escaped from captivity in Greece, had both his legs smashed. He went on playing, sitting on the ground, and continued to play on the stretcher and at the main bandaging station, where a captured German doctor treated him.

Colonel Rusk drove his "Dingo"—a small lightly armored vehicle— over a mine. Before he could climb into his reserve vehicle, it was blown to pieces, complete with its driver, by a direct hit from an artillery shell. The artillery liaison officer, Major Birkin, came along with his driver in a tiny, battered scout car. Rusk squeezed himself in and chased off after his men.

The forward slope was now bristling with rifles with their bayonets stuck into the sand—the signal to the stretcher bearers that a wounded man lay there. Machine guns tore everything to shreds across the dead-flat, slightly inclined plain. For most of the Jocks, the medical orderlies came too late.

Armitage saw his artillery colleague's vehicle and drove across.

"Radio back that we need entrenching tools; we'll have to dig in," Rusk said. Then he drove off to find the tanks. When they saw O'Carroll and Lindsay, he got out with Birkin, who immediately fell flat on his face.

Rusk saw a hole in his leather jacket and, just below it, a small-arms bullet, clearly a ricochet, which had knocked the major out only for an instant. Birkin pocketed the projectile as a souvenir.

The tanks were brought back on course. Reid, at the far end of the left flank, moved off too. But after they had gone a short distance, there was a mighty double report and the tank stopped.

"I'll go and have a look," said his driver, Nobby Clarke.

"Stay where you are," Reid hissed. Through his periscope he saw a neat zigzag trench, over the edge of which German steel helmets showed here and there.

They were stuck in a minefield immediately in front of the German position—way outside their line of attack. To one side there were two more bangs, and two more Matildas stuck fast, their tracks gone. The commander of one of them was Eric Aines, a good friend.

The sun was climbing fast over the horizon; something must be done. Some infantrymen were coming up from behind. From the position in front of Reid, as well as from a trench a little farther away, machine-gun fire tore into the men. Reid saw a whole line of them collapse.

Until now, in their exposed position, they had not fired a single shot. Now Reid told his gunner to let them have it with the coaxial machine gun. But it did not achieve much, since after each burst the German steel helmets could be seen in front of them again.

"Use the two-pounders," Reid yelled.

After a few rounds, the position in front of them seemed well and truly to fall in on itself. Meanwhile, Eric Aines's driver had climbed out and was fumbling about with his tracks. He was fired on from the second position and turned around furiously, shaking his fist. Reid saw him fall at almost the same moment, his fist still clenched. Now the two-pounders of all three Matildas were firing into that position.

The first thing that happened was that you could not see any more movement. The infantrymen called up the medical orderlies to fetch their wounded. They were Northumberland Fusiliers who, working with Major Holden's squadron, had meanwhile taken another position at the edge of the breakout zone.

In the distance you could hear the dull thudding of artillery fire. It sounded like a deep growl; moreover, it was coming from the wrong direction. "We've run into trouble. They've called up artillery support," said Reid. The next moment, immense fountains of earth spouted from the ground. The shells came roaring at them like a London Underground train—suggesting that they were of a type that would crack even a Matilda.

Since there was, in any case, nothing he could do except go on keeping an eye on the trenches in front of him, Reid mechanically counted the strikes. They gave up after eighty-five. They must have reconciled themselves to the fact that three widely separated Matildas were too small for their caliber after all.

The tank was so full of dust and the stink of cordite after the many near misses that Reid opened the hatch. Distant sounds of fighting were now coming only from somewhere to the southwest. The sharp barks of the Panzer guns rose clearly above the rumbling of field guns and the stuttering of automatic fire.

Over there, the remnants of the Black Watch, barely 200 of the 600 young men who had advanced at first light that morning, were taking the last objectives for that day, but now with strong tank support. Driving forward, Major Holden scanned the enemy positions carefully. The heaviest anti-tank gun they had encountered so far had been the medium 50 mm gun, and their tank losses had been correspondingly light, although a few shots had pierced the Matildas' armor at close range.

"Where's my girl friend, the eighty-eight, then?" thought Holden, torn between hope and doubt. But this time he was, in fact, spared the sight of those mighty barrels.[10]

When the last position had been overrun, just 164 men of the Black Watch remained on their feet. Some 1,000 prisoners were escorted back to Tobruk; thirty machine guns and one flamethrower had been captured.

Thirteen of Major Lindsay's Marmon-Harringtons had been knocked out by shells or mines, though their crews mostly got away with injuries only. The major himself had exchanged his own car, which was destroyed, for a Dingo. That in turn was struck by a shell on the outside, but he himself got away with a punctured eardrum.[11]

When the day's work was done, Lindsay sat down and accepted a billycan of bully beef. Artillery fire was still coming at them from El Duda on the escarpment, including some of the forbidden shells; and one of the things came bouncing along the ground and knocked the can out of Lindsay's hand. He swerved away in disgust, fetched his sketch pad, and drew a picture of his two remaining reconnaissance cars, around which danced fountains of earth thrown up by striking shells.

Breakfast in a minefield

As darkness fell, Sergeant Reid was still squatting in the turret of his tank, a revolver in his lap, gazing at the German positions, in which, here and there, there was a rumbling noise. The sun went down; he

[10] The British habit of mitigating horror with humor had meanwhile resulted in a play on words: "Eighty-eight: anti-aircraft, anti-tank, anti-social."

[11] A not very capable doctor later treated the ear by syringing it. It immediately began to suppurate. Lindsay went into the hospital in Johannesburg and did not rejoin his men until a year later, just as they were entering Tripoli.

thought wistfully of a cigarette, but that was obviously out of the question.

The moon rose. All was quiet. Some time later he saw two men approach the German positions at an angle and go in through the wire.

"We'll have to do something to get away from here," he told his men.

"We want something to eat and drink first," they grumbled.

Reid pushed the turret hatch open millimeter by millimeter, for the thing had a habit of squeaking, and the slightest sound carries far in the desert night. He fetched some bully beef and biscuits from the food hamper and carefully placed a two-gallon canister of water next to the turret.

Just then, the loader/radio operator, Lance Corporal Hadley, thought he might be able to help him a bit, so he opened his own hatch. That was exactly where the canister stood, and it went, tumbling and clattering, over the side.

"They'll hear that all the way to Tripoli," thought Reid, ducking behind the turret and waiting for the first salvo. But nothing happened.

"Right," said Reid when they had eaten. "You'll take to your heels by clambering down over the stern, crawl for a stretch in single file exactly in our tracks, and wait for me."

But Hadley thought this was a case when the captain should abandon ship first. "If the Jerries get you, or you set off a mine, we'll hear it and can stay right here."

It was obvious; and when he had ordered the gunner, "Tug" Wilson, to bring the breech block with him and to give the radio a few quiet blows, Reid set out on his crawl. Not a shot was fired, and the others, too, came through unscathed by creeping along the marks of their own track. When they had left the minefield behind, they had to give a wide berth to a few vehicles which were standing around rather suspiciously. There was a faint gray light in the east again when they heard English voices ahead of them at last.

Somewhat cheekily, Nobby Clarke jumped up. There was a burst from a machine gun that very nearly parted his hair for him.

"Stop that! There are four of us here—we're a tank crew," Reid called over. They had at first to go through the correct procedure, since the others were cautious, but in the end they landed in the British trench.

They met the other two crews again at the mobile workshop. They had likewise crawled back out of the minefield along their own track marks. Only Eric Aines's driver, Billy, still lay out there next to his tank.

"He was a good lad, but he was quite crazy ever since his friend was burned to death in Battleaxe. He was dead set on fixing that track and staying in the fight."

Billy was put in a mass grave next day, along with a few hundred Germans and Scots. Most of them were later given individual graves in Tobruk; but just now it was high time to get them out of the sun.

The New Zealanders are coming

All this—from the almost complete annihilation of the 7th Armored Brigade at Sidi Rezegh; through the costly advance of their reinforced Support Group; through Brigadier Campbell's spectacular rescue operation; to the bloody breakout attempt from Tobruk—took place on 21 November, by far the most eventful day of the offensive until then. But the situation now changed distinctly in Rommel's favor.

Cunningham's spearhead at Sidi Rezegh, the 7th Armored Brigade, was smashed; farther south, the 4th and 22nd Armored Brigades stood battered but still in good order and strength, while the South African infantry advanced northward between them toward Sidi Rezegh. The right arm of the advance—New Zealand and Indian infantry with an army tank brigade of Matildas—was traveling more slowly around the back of the escarpment, which runs southwest from Sollum-Halfaya, and had already cut off the troops stationed there, including the 8,000-man Bardia garrison. The Tobruk garrison had made a 5-kilometer bulge in the siege ring, without, however, breaching it.[12]

The British forces were still separated; Rommel had kept his two German Panzer divisions together, while the Italian division was holding Bir el Gobi to the south. A number of options were open to him to pick off one of the isolated enemy units—including the Tobruk garrison, who were sitting very uncomfortably in open country.

But the German side reacted remarkably sluggishly. Its divisions even parted; the 15th Panzer Division made a 20-kilometer trip on the night of 22 November to reach the area south of Gambut, while the 21st Division skirted the Sidi Rezegh area to the north. The supply columns bringing fuel and ammunition had trouble finding them. (Meanwhile, water had run so short that washing had been officially forbidden.)

It is true that Rommel did not run things on such a tight rein as before in these first days of the battle; however, an army staff had been set up under Gause, with Westphal as a competent G1 Ops; the commander of the Afrika Korps, Crüwell, and his G1 Ops, Fritz Bayerlein,

---

[12] "Documentary" works will tell you that the 3rd Reconnaissance Unit intervened there during the breakout attempt and "fought the enemy to a standstill" or "beat him back" in brilliant fashion. It is in no way to belittle Freiherr von Wechmar's gallant men to say that their armored cars were quite unable either to "fight" Matildas "to a standstill" or to "beat them back."

were tried and tested Panzer commanders, with whom he could hardly deal in the same way as he had with "Papa" Streich—although Rommel would occasionally threaten to have them court-martialed, too, without ever being as good as his word.

Be that as it may, the C-in-C merely issued orders for "mobile combat command" methods to be used on the 22 November; and that in itself was odd.

Westphal reports an incident which cannot at this time be verified in detail, since it was not recorded but which, as he recollects, can be adduced fully to explain the events of 22 November. On Rommel's instructions, he says, he called the Commander of the Afrika Korps and his two Panzer divisional commanders and G1 Ops to the army command post. The exhausted G1 Ops of the 15th Panzer Division misunderstood him and ordered the whole outfit to move up. Says Westphal in his memoirs: "It then became necessary to find a job quickly for the two divisions which had turned up so unexpectedly."[13]

At any rate, the 15th Panzer Division did not move off southward again until noon on 22 November, eventually to stop and annihilate the 4th Brigade and its Honeys. However, it did not make any meaningful contact with the enemy in the daylight hours. Rommel himself drove over to the 21st Panzer Division in the afternoon and sent it in to attack the Sidi Rezegh airfield. He reinforced them with units from the 90th Light and some artillery. The 22nd Armored Brigade had meanwhile moved up and the advance guard of "Brink's boys"—the South Africans—had turned up.

The Cruisers of the 22nd Armored Brigade were badly shot up when the 5th Panzer Regiment moved in on them with the sun behind it. The indestructible Brigadier Campbell was once again rushing around the airfield in his open staff car to scrape reinforcements together. On the southern escarpment he found the advance guard of the 4th Armored Brigade—two Honeys of the 3rd Royal Tank Regiment. Again, he led them, his pennant streaming, until they could see the Panzers and hear them roaring toward them—which the two Honey commanders did not like at all. But they drove bravely in among the wrecks of the Cruisers, and fired away at the Panzers with their 37 mm toy guns, vainly calling their regimental commander over the radio. Only one of them, troop leader Robert Crisp, survived. After a wild chase across the airfield, he at last saw the other Honeys coming, took

[13] The fact that the army command post was moved west from the Gambut area immediately afterward makes it all the likelier that all this happened on the night of 21 November. A knowledgeable expert, Colonel von Thaysen, believes the reason was Crüwell's habit of thinking in terms of wide open spaces, dating from his time in Russia.

the mike, greatly relieved, and reported to his commander: "Seventy Jerry tanks attacking from the west." To which he received the classic reply: "I can't tell my arse from my elbow, never mind east from west!"[14]

The day ended in clouds of dust and confusion—and in the loss of the airfield for the British who, with the South Africans, retired farther south and rested. The remnants of the 7th Armored Brigade were even farther south, guarding 700 prisoners, whom "one would have been sorry to lose, since most of them were Germans" (*Regimental History of the 7th Hussars*).

When the sun vanished, the 8th Panzer Regiment, the steel tip of the 15th Panzer Division, was still chasing around the desert looking for the 4th Armored Brigade. On a pitch-dark night, the sky being overcast, the vanguard, under Major Fenski, came upon a collection of vehicles. Without being immediately able to establish what was standing around there, the major ordered the group of vehicles to be surrounded. Only a few shots were fired as one of the tanks tried to get away before the Panzermen had bagged the entire headquarters of the 4th Armored Brigade.[15]

The consequence was that on 23 November the Honey regiments, which had in any case been rather scattered in the confusion of the previous day, were driving around in scattered groups and were only slowly finding each other again to form a fighting force. Of the three brigades that had set out as the left arm of the advance with over 480 tanks, the following were, therefore, available on 23 November, German Remembrance Day: 10 Cruisers of the 7th Armored Brigade; 40 Cruisers of the 22nd Armored Brigade; 100 Honeys of the 4th Armored Brigade, of which, however, only a few were serviceable.

His general's luck had not yet abandoned Rommel. The thoroughness and completeness of his organization helped: Every Panzer that had not been blown sky-high, burned out, or totally shot to pieces was made fit for action again with the speed of lightning in mobile or stationary workshops, since the battlefield had up till then always remained in German hands. Although his two Panzer regiments were no longer up to their nominal strength of 120 tanks, thanks to steady reinforcements from the workshops there were at that time, still a pair of steel battering rams, though of no more than 75 Panzers each.[16]

[14] Robert Crisp, DSO, MC, *Brazen Chariots*.

[15] Once again, it does not detract anything from the glory of Major Fenski, who was killed the next day and was posthumously awarded the Knight's Cross, to establish that he by no means captured "the entire 4th Brigade," as most books say. Neither was Brigadier Gatehouse among those captured.

[16] The two Panzer regiments in Africa consisted of two battle groups each, one battle group containing five companies. By way of comparison, a British armored

So it was that 23 November became something a disaster for the British. Rommel gathered his mechanized forces—always accompanied by anti-tank guns, artillery, and engineers—for a strike at the remaining units south of Sidi Rezegh. Even the hundred thin-skinned things of the Ariete were summoned to the north from Bir el Gobi.

The German-Italian armored forces now enjoyed substantial superiority; but first they came up against a line of anti-tank guns, and 25-pounders in particular, all belching fire. From this line, Honeys would dash forward here and there, make rapid attacks, and then try to regain their own lines—many managed it, too, thanks to their speed and maneuverability.

The Panzer losses were substantial; and the 5th Panzer Regiment allowed itself to be driven off for the time being by heavy artillery fire.[17] Part of the 8th Regiment did, however, break through the enemy front: A bitter battle raged between the widely scattered parked vehicles of the South Africans, a battle progressively shrouded in dust and the dark smoke of burning vehicles. The gunners frequently fired the 25-pounders at ranges of only a few meters. But when darkness fell, the South Africans were forced to evacuate the area of their camp, their retreat scantily covered by a handful of Honeys and Cruisers. They lost almost 2,000 men, half of whom fell into German captivity.

Farther south, twelve light Italian tanks attempted an attack on the remnants of the 7th Armored Brigade. Every single one was knocked out.

When darkness fell the chaos was complete. Friend and foe drove through each other's lines; brief exchanges of fire kept flaring up. But there was no doubt about it: Rommel had won the day again. That night he wrote to his wife: "The battle seems to be past its climax. I'm in good heart. Two hundred enemy tanks knocked out so far." In sharp contrast to Operation Battleaxe, he was grossly underestimating the success of his troops.

But another threat had meanwhile emerged. One of the first to encounter it was Corporal Heinrich Frank, from Freiburg, a motorcycle dispatch rider with the supply section of the 8th Panzer Division. He was escorting three trucks, which were to fetch Panzer engines from Bardia, when, in the vicinity of Gambut, he saw some odd-looking

---

regiment contained three squadrons of 15 tanks apiece plus regimental HQ. Its total strength as a rule was 52 tanks. (Brigade=three regiments, with HQ, generally 163 tanks. Plus a regiment of motorized infantry.)

[17] The 5th Panzer Regiment, recruited mostly in Berlin and district, had a reputation of being a little more timid than its mostly South German sister regiment, the 8th, considered more useful in a brutal charge. It was, of course, nonsense but, like most errors and generalizations, tenaciously held.

slouch hats pop up, only to disappear again immediately among the dunes bordering the coast road.

Frank used the well-established skid technique of turning by stopping your rear wheel; and, racing back to the lorries following him, he waved them down. They stopped; and he slipped between them with his machine. They heard metallic noises, like the cocking of a machine-gun trigger. When the withering fire began, they were all lying in the ditch already.

The lorries were finished immediately; water gushed from their radiators and air escaped with a hiss from tires riddled with bullets. The motorcycle, standing between them, had come to no harm so far.

Frank crawled up to it, tickled the carburetor needle, gave the twist grip a turn, and jerked down the kick starter with his hand. The sturdy BMW sprang into life immediately. Lying alongside the tank like a cowboy, he shot away sustaining not a scratch, although the machine guns had started barking again from the dunes. The drivers and a short-service lieutenant from the workshops went into captivity. Frank's straightforward explanation of his *tour de force* with the motorbike: "Someone had to let 'em know that there were some people from the other lot there, didn't they?"

By this time the information had seeped fairly high up into the command structure that the slouch-hatted men—the New Zealanders— were there. For, on the morning of the twenty-third, they had nabbed the entire corps staff of the Afrika Korps a little farther to the south, at the Gasr el Arid escarpment. General Crüwell and his G1 Ops, Bayerlein, had left half an hour earlier. On that day (German Remembrance Day), the conduct of the battle was in no way prejudiced. Which, in view of the chaos after the loss of the 4th Armored Brigade HQ, shows what worlds separated the British and the Germans when it came to the possession of modern means of communication.

4. "That Damned Westphal"

The twenty-fourth of November was the day when Rommel seized the reins again, threw Westphal's warnings to the wind, took, as it were, his Chief of Staff Gause and the C-in-C of the Afrika Korps, Crüwell, in hand and led his entire mechanized and motorized force on one of the most frequently discussed operations of the Second World War.

What is indisputable is that the thing went thoroughly wrong, that Crüwell had until then led the Afrika Korps most successfully, and that 24 November was the turning point of the battle.

As even Westphal, for all his well-bred reticence, admits, Rommel was in a highly euphoric mood after the Remembrance Day victory. He was convinced that he could conclude the entire campaign victoriously on the spot with a surprise raid—shifting the center of gravity at lightning speed.

He had three aims in view for this far-ranging hook through the desert to the south, and subsequent wheeling maneuver to the north and east: to cut the British supply lines and at the same time, exploiting their frequently displayed fear of being outflanked, to force them to retreat; to strike in the rear and annihilate the New Zealanders, who were thrusting dangerously to the north and west along the Via Balbia with their Matilda brigade; and to break into Egypt over the passes and drive east, making for an objective that was never explicitly named but was certainly a very distant one.

There were several reasons why the plan did not succeed. The most important arises from a fact Rommel himself realized at an early stage and otherwise consistently heeded: that desert war is very much like war at sea.

At sea, the communications of a fleet are not disrupted just because an enemy cruiser squadron has sailed through between it and its home port. If there is an unavoidable route—and in fact such a route existed at the southern end of the escarpment—it must be permanently blocked. But Rommel's forces fell far short of what would have been needed for that. Not even the fact that the 21st Panzer Division had trundled past only a few kilometers to the north of two of the Eighth Army's great supply depots at Gabr Saleh[1] was as significant as it is generally made out to be. When writing history, there are good reasons for avoiding all sentences beginning with "If only" or "Had." If one looks at such a story as a curve on a graph, the paths it might have followed from any particular point begin to multiply. For instance, once you discover the existence of great supply depots, the need arises to take them, to hold them, or to destroy them. Even the latter is not so quickly done as people imagine.

Moreover, it was not in the least Rommel's intention to destroy the remnants of the brigades beaten at Sidi Rezegh, which were licking their wounds in the neighborhood of Gabr Saleh.[2] Rather, he disregarded them quite deliberately, hoping that for the third time the British would react to an outflanking movement by nervously retreating. In fact, retreat had already been considered at the highest British level—to be sure before the wild chase to the border fence. After the series of heavy reverses he had sustained, the army commander, Cunningham, radioed his C-in-C on 23 November to say that he thought it best to break off the offensive and withdraw to reorganize. Auchinleck immediately flew into the desert and ordered the battle to continue regardless of casualties. Two days later he appointed his Deputy Chief of Staff, Ritchie, to replace Cunningham, a brother of the Admiral, who had clearly lost his nerve.

At this point, Rommel's main force, consisting of the two Panzer Regiments, was already badly battered. From the time they had set out southward, they had been in action continuously, steadily fired at by

[1] At the critical moment, Tim Llewellyn-Palmer formed a mob of fleeing trucks into a strong column and made them cruise around the Panzer column to act as interesting bait, so as to draw them away from the depots, which were already in sight to the south. The trick worked, especially since Palmer's outfit was, in any case, moving more or less in the direction the Panzer Regiment had been ordered to follow: toward Sidi Omar.

[2] According to Liddell Hart, only the 22nd Armored Brigade would have been available in the area to defend the depots. He is mistaken.

tanks and artillery and, in addition, chased by RAF bombers. During the attempt to take Sidi Omar, they had run into a front of 25-pounders and heavy Matildas. Sidi Omar stayed in British hands. In the evening on 25 November, the 5th Panzer Regiment had just twelve tanks left and the 8th had fifty-three. And this time, most of the wrecks could be neither salvaged nor repaired.

Rommel was now chasing backward and forward between his units, having in his impatience driven away from his radio cars. His G1 Ops was quite unable to get in touch with him. Although in their forward thrust, the columns of the Afrika Korps were driving a bow wave of swarms of supply trucks and staff cars ahead of them, and had spread alarm and despondency among the rear services—to the secret delight of the frontline troops—it was nevertheless gradually becoming apparent that the movement of such large bodies of troops, virtually on impromptu command, was causing mounting chaos on the German side too. Infantrymen were trying to find their Panzer regiments; they in turn were looking for their fuel and ammunition supply vehicles and their C-in-C was looking for all of them.

On the night of the twenty-fifth, a patrol of the 8th Machine Gun Battalion, which was trying to make contact, accidentally found Rommel's car in the desert, was able to enlighten the solitary C-in-C on the whereabouts of some of his units, and for its pains lost one of its jeeps, which Rommel confiscated. A day later, Crüwell by chance came across Rommel and Grause shivering at the border fence: Their car had broken down. Soon afterward the three most senior German generals were driving mile after mile through an area alive with Indian troops—luckily for them in Rommel's very British-looking captured command vehicle.

Generally, everything the British so expressively called "soft-skinned" suffered in the confusion: the lorried infantry and, in particular, the supply columns of both sides, which were not even protected by anti-tank guns. Since everything was milling about all over the place, and since most of the time people were looking for their own combat units, they had a 50-50 chance of attracting the attention of some hostile, steel-splitting, hard-skinned vehicle. Countless convoys of trucks were driving around in this way or just stood about in the desert with a sentry posted on the cab, like groups of shy, grazing gazelles, always ready to race off in headlong flight.

As soon as the sun had warmed the ground and the air layer immediately above began to distort the appearance of everything, they would decamp at the sight of anything that looked vaguely like a tank. The shimmering air managed to convert a dainty little Honey into a fat

Panzer IV—and the other way around. Nor did positively identifying a tank in itself mean security, for both sides used vehicles captured from the other.

Westphal was waging war on several fronts at this time. General Bastico waited cursing at his HQ for Rommel, who had gone missing after summoning him—Rommel's senior and superior—to his headquarters, only to stand him up.

As the pressure of the New Zealanders on the Tobruk siege ring grew, so the "rumbling in the trousers" (Westphal's words) of the local Italian and German commanders intensified. In his reports to the OKH and OKW, he had to throw a veil over the fact that the Supreme Commander had disappeared—which could have earned him a monumental charge before a court-martial had Rommel failed to turn up again. He had to put aside unread all reports to, and inquiries from, his C-in-C, since no normal radio contact existed and since instead of replying, Rommel merely sent incomprehensible reports without any dateline or indication of his intentions.

Two communications aircraft had been shot down while looking for him. Reconnaissance men who managed to get back said that the armored brigades were being reorganized and resupplied at Gabr Saleh. In addition, Brigadier Jock Campbell was putting together some combat groups there, consisting of motorized infantry, anti-tank guns, and 25-pounders,[3] which, as independent columns ("Jock columns"), roamed the desert right up to the Via Balbia in the far northwest and could wipe out everything but strong Panzer units. And no Panzer units were there.

On the twenty-sixth the "Tobruk Rats" at last broke through to El Duda and occupied the height there. In the distance they saw some tanks from which three red flares went up—the prearranged signal of the Eighth Army.

It was quite a moving moment. Over on the other side, the young Lieutenant Peter Phillips, who decades later was to become the father-in-law of Princess Anne, sat at the radio set of the Regimental Commander of the Dragoons, Donald McCorquodale. He had joined the KDG shortly before the start of Crusader and the colonel had first pressed him into service as his radioman. The KDG squadrons which had been taken to Egypt from Tobruk were now advancing with the Eighth Army as reconnaissance scouts.

When, contrary to all radio practice, Phillips heard a voice call on

[3] Brigadier Campbell received the Victoria Cross for his indefatigable efforts. After Crusader, he lost his life in a motoring accident. Most British officers agree that it was he who would have been the right opponent for Rommel.

the regiment's frequency: "Hallo, Donald, Mick here!" it took him a little time before he realized that "Mick" was probably Major Lindsay of C-Squadron, which had remained in Tobruk. He called the colonel over and was amused to overhear how the two commanders, in accordance with British custom, covered their emotion with a few wisecracks.

On the Tobruk breakout party's side, Major Holden climbed out of his Matilda and talked to Bill Yeo, a young adjutant from one of the other infantry tank regiments, a friend of his. Yeo had just climbed back into his Mark VI when the vehicle was hit by a heavy armor-piercing shot and simply flew apart. The entire crew was killed.

Just then and only a few kilometers away, the father of the dead adjutant, Bill Yeo, Sr., was preparing the corresponding advance for the linkup with the Tobruk garrison. A lieutenant colonel, he was commander of the 44th Tank Regiment, one of the Matilda units with the New Zealanders.[4] The night attack commanded by Yeo, one of the first in Matilda history, became a classic of armored warfare: The heavy tanks moved off without artillery support in acute spearhead formation, at a steady walking pace, narrow rearlights showing the infantry the way. The slow, roaring, fire-spewing monsters must have made a terrifying impression in the moonlight. Resistance melted. The attackers lost one infantryman killed.

The commander of the British 13th Corps, General Godwin-Austin, radioed Cairo: "Corridor to Tobruk free and secured. Tobruk not half as relieved as I am."

But the thing was by no means as safely in the bag as Godwin-Austin had hoped. On this 26 November, Westphal, who had still not had an even halfway comprehensible report from Rommel about the situation and his intentions, at last ran out of patience. He signaled the Afrika Korps to return to Tobruk immediately, "disregarding all orders to the contrary."

He correctly surmised that the two divisions of the Korps were somewhere in the general area of Bardia in the rear of the New Zealanders. General von Ravenstein, commander of the 21st Panzer Division, was in fact just refueling in this neighborhood. Rommel had ordered him to thrust into Egypt with his utterly exhausted and almost Panzer-less unit. Ravenstein gave his staff an opportunity to write a last field postcard home, as they were about to march "straight into captivity." It gives an idea of the general mood that his communications officer

---

[4] By now some units were equipped with a new Infantry tank Mark III 1, the Valentine (A 11). This three-man vehicle (the commander was also the loader) was smaller, more maneuverable and better suited to longer journeys than the Matilda; but it was only slightly faster. Armament: still only the two-pounder. Armor: 65 mm maximum.

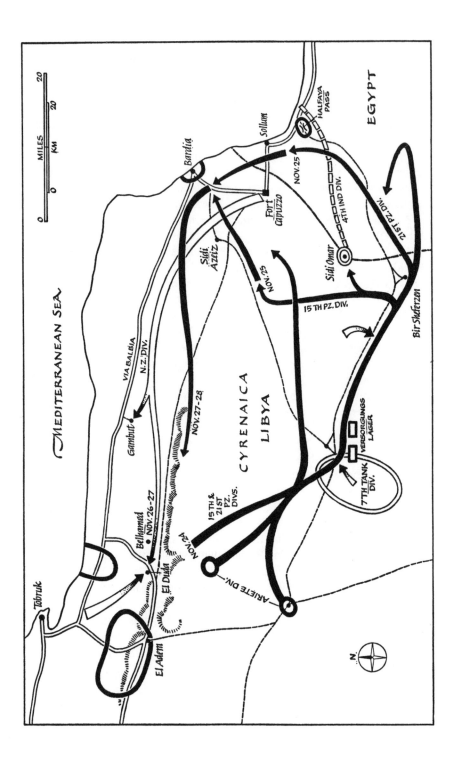

MEDITERRANEAN SEA

Tobruk

El Adem

El Duda

Belhamed
NOV. 26-27

Gambut

VIA BALBIA
N.Z. DIV.

NOV. 27-28

15TH &
21ST
PZ.
DIVS.

NOV. 24

ARIETE DIV.

7TH TANK
DIV.

VERSORGUNGS
LAGER

CYRENAICA
LIBYA

Sidi
Aziz

Bardia

Sollum

HALFAYA
PASS

Fort
Capuzzo

NOV. 25

NOV. 25

Sidi Omar

4TH IND. DIV.

21ST PZ. DIV.

15TH PZ. DIV.

Bir Sheferzen

EGYPT

N.

MILES
KM
0   20
0   20

handed him Westphal's order with the unmilitary remark: "Herr General, we're saved."[5]

The way to the west became a series of unceasing engagements for the two much-reduced divisions. The first breakthrough across the New Zealanders' barrier at Musaid cost the 8th Machine Gun Battalion, so often and so sorely tried, at least thirty dead.

When Rommel, who as usual had no radio contact, heard of the order to pull back, he raged: "It is a trap set by the British! Or that damned Westphal. I'll have him court-martialed!"

But when he got back to headquarters, he leafed through the reports sent back to Germany to see if they contained anything about a general who had gone missing, had a look at the situation map, and went to bed without a word. Which, given the boss's endearing ways, was known by everyone to amount to approval.

The great adventure was over. It had decisively weakened Rommel's mobile forces and at the same time given his adversary an opportunity to reorganize and bring in reinforcements. Three times so far, he had fought great mobile battles with the British: when he won back Cyrenaica; in Battleaxe; and now in Crusader. Twice, they had run away because—either actually or apparently—they were threatened with being outflanked. It was to grossly underestimate the British to hope that the trick would work a third time.

Occasionally Cunningham's hesitation is cited as evidence that Rommel's raid had been a heavy blow. But one must bear the date in mind: He was proposing retreat on 23 November—before the Afrika Korps' *coup*. At the time he could have had no idea that Rommel would take the pressure off him.

Sir Basil Liddell Hart, the distinguished military historian, comes to the conclusion that Auchinleck's order to continue the offensive was a gamble more daring than Rommel's wild lunge. While this may have been right for the short span of time during which it was prudent to reckon on a follow-up by the German-Italian forces south of Sidi Rezegh, it no longer applied once Rommel's new intentions were discernible. There is documentary evidence to show that this recognition occurred at a very early stage, not only through the unhindered British

[5] For the divisional commander, at any rate, the road back to Tobruk led to captivity. He was caught by the New Zealanders.

On facing page. Crusader, Phase Three: Rommel races with his combined mobile forces southeast across the border fence. The 21st Panzer Division narrowly misses the British supply camp. The shaken 7th Tanker Division has time to reorganize. The New Zealanders move unmolested toward Tobruk. The DAK must break through toward the West.

aerial reconnaissance but also thanks to the code crackers of Ultra. In any case, a signal they intercepted on 24 November is a good example of Rommel's deviousness toward his superiors. He reported that the next day he would complete the annihilation of the enemy forces beaten at Sidi Rezegh—obviously because that was what orthodox professional soldiers were bound to expect him to do—and, he added, he would advance on Sidi Omar with a part of his forces. That should do to keep them off his back.

He could be just a bit irresponsible, could the dashing Swabian. But who today can disentangle how much of that was wishful thinking and how much was due to the general grandiloquence to which hardly anyone was immune? As for the burned, mangled, holed, and maimed men who littered the way—so much the worse for them. On the other hand, the main fruits of correct and well-thought-out decisions by generals are also corpses—though perhaps mostly those of the other side.

The fanbelt trick

The survivors struggled on, rousing themselves time and time again to unbelievable efforts—exhausted, thirsty and overstretched though they were. Robert Crisp, commander of a Honey, watched a German infantry unit, which after all those days of uninterrupted fighting, had once again thrown the New Zealanders out of the blood-soaked and, by now, almost familiar airfield at Sidi Rezegh. He saw the exhausted men, staggering after the exertions of the attack, kept together only by a sort of superhuman willpower, and said to himself: "They may have won, but I think they're past knowing it."

The brigades of the virtually annihilated 7th Armored Division now had their breathing space behind them, and life in a desert crisscrossed by friend and foe was not exactly a bed of roses. At least the panic which had flared up from time to time in the highest British echelons had never percolated down to the troops at the front. And now the awareness was growing among them that even this incredible enemy might be near the end of his tether.

If there was such a thing in those crazy days as an impeccable achievement surpassing every imaginable criterion, it was that of the men who had nothing left to give but valor and defiance and strength of will, men over whose bones great men clambered into the history books.

Around this time Sergeant Major Joachim Saenger, with his Panzer III, became a sort of chauffeur to the gentry. He and his men were to realize only some time later what a winner they had thereby drawn.

They had wandered along behind their regiment, led by a lieutenant who was still pretty green. They were tired, shattered, continually nodding off, and pursued even in brief snatches of sleep by images of billowing smoke lit by flashes of fire and the terror of the battles they had just gone through. The regiment must have been in action somewhere around Sidi Rezegh. They went through a strongpoint in which Italian artillery and German anti-aircraft guns had "hedgehogged" themselves in, shooting suspiciously at anything in sight.

The air was still—even the weather was holding its breath. Every hollow in the undulating landscape was filled with shimmering air as if liquid glass had been poured into it. And all over the place, aerials stuck out of this glass surface, some with pennants, and, swinging and waving, moved about like the feelers of some curious animal.

"At last," said the lieutenant over the radio, "that must be the 8th Panzer Regiment. We are supposed to be just behind them." Saenger had hung a stereotelescope in his turret; now he was studying the aerials.

"Only the British drive with pennants," he said.

"Rubbish. Panzers forward!" ordered the lieutenant.

They started, but Saenger's driver, Konrad Müller, from Nürnberg, said over the intercom: "Don't worry. This'll only take a moment." There was a tiny jolt and almost immediately the engine began to smoke. "Fanbelt broken. Cooling system not working." Saenger reported himself out of action to the lieutenant—without many regrets. You can't fit a new fanbelt until the engine has cooled down.

"Keep it under your hat," said Driver Konrad, "but if I make a certain steering maneuver, I can break my fanbelt any time I like."

Farther forward the Panzers' guns were firing. After a few minutes, one of the tanks came clattering back, its gun barrel shot off right next to the turret. As usual, its commander had very soon lost touch during the engagement and had no idea what had happened to the others. They never did find out.

While Konrad was still lying there, fiddling with the fanbelt, a British reconnaissance car climbed the next dune. Soon more of these rectangular turrets showed up on the left and right, like ugly, curious insects. Saenger held a hand grenade ready, ready to throw it into his own Panzer if necessary; but then there was a short report behind them, spurts of dust rose from the dunes, and the armored cars disappeared like specters. From behind them came the self-propelled anti-tank gun which had fired on them. An officer clambered down and ordered them to provide cover somewhat farther back. He was Captain Dr. Eggert, Officer Commanding the Corps HQ. Evidently there were all sorts of important people at that strongpoint.

The sun sank, it became cold. Saenger pulled a blanket over his head and dozed off. It was still pitch dark when something crept around the tent next to his and called out: "Hey, soldier! Get your Panzer ready to go."

He liked that! "What do you mean, get the Panzer ready? I haven't any fuel. And for that matter have you seen a tanker lorry around here?"

The other was not easily put off. "Now look here, that's your business. See to it."

"In my outfit, the tanker always comes to us. Besides, the engine's gone. No compression," Saenger added for good measure.

"How many kilometers has it done, then?"

"Three thousand five hundred."

"Cor love you," shouted the other fellow in the darkness, "when I was in Russia the things still had compression after five thousand."

"In case you haven't noticed, mate," said Saenger in disgust, "this is Africa."

"That's a fine way to talk to your GOC." Tumult. End of the world. There was more scrabbling in the tent. A dark figure issued forth and mumbled soothing words.

"The 5th again, of course," roared Saenger's interlocutor. "What a heap of shit!"

Which was how the sergeant major made the acquaintance of Lieutenant General Crüwell from Dortmund, of whose very existence he had hitherto been unaware.

Night attack at El Duda

When the New Zealanders had again been thrown out of the Sidi Rezegh-Belhamed area, Tobruk became an isolated fortress again. But the troops of the garrison clung to the heights at El Duda.

Captain Armitage of the Royal Artillery was again there as Forward Observation Officer when some British infantry were overrun at the edge of the escarpment. The Panzers of the 15th Division rumbled unperturbed through the indirect fire of the 25-pounders. A solitary two-pounder anti-tank gun stood next to Armitage. Its gunners were firing their minibullets. Armitage had to slip away in his light Mark VI down a fold in the ground. In the failing light he glanced back once more. A heavy Panzer drove up to the anti-tank gun. A white-hot ricochet bounced off its bow armor, while its turret, with its short, thick barrel, turned. The first hit blew the gun to smithereens.

Armitage met the infantry commander, Colonel Nicholls. "Could you fetch me up here those tanks standing down there?" the officer asked. Armitage drove over to Colonel O'Carroll, who was parked farther downhill with twelve of the remaining tanks.

"Okay," said the colonel, "if you'll show me where those laddies are, I'm sure we can do something about them." He made Armitage climb up and sit on the rear edge of the turret. They drove up the hill, keeping slightly to the west, reached the escarpment, and turned left.

The moon had risen. The outlines of the Panzers were clearly visible at 800 meters. "Stop," said Armitage. "They're over there."

"So they are. I can see the fellows," answered O'Carroll.

Armitage was feeling a bit queasy. "Well, you see, sir, as a matter of fact, I think it would be a good idea if I could just sort of go away at this point. . . ."

"What's that? Oh yes, of course, run along," replied the tank colonel absently, rattling off immediately. Armitage had hardly run a few steps than all hell broke loose behind him. Tracer bullets flew around; it looked as if some solid object or other would have swept him off that Matilda in the very first second had he stayed.

This time, Sergeant Reid was commanding one of the new Valentines. His new driver, Freddy Dash, was skillful and experienced; but in the moonlight he overlooked a hole with steep sides. The tank fell in with a crash, port side down. Reid held on in the turret for dear life and heard the roar of the engines as Freddy immediately shifted gears and rammed the accelerator down hard. They would have climbed out, too—but just at that moment the shooting match broke out.

The Germans had been rather taken by surprise because a fresh breeze was blowing from the sea and the Panzer crews were dead beat. But they were soon defending themselves furiously and skillfully.

While Reid's tank was wallowing in the hole with its starboard side so unfortunately exposed, a heavy solid shot crashed into the forward, undriven sprocket and tore it right off, together with a portion of the track.

"Switch off," Reid ordered. They stayed in their places and lay low. The enemy had better things to do than to pump steel into a tank which was already knocked out. O'Carroll's tactic of creeping up to the enemy was proving effective.

At such short range even the two-pounder was a devastating weapon and the Panzers retreated, firing all the way but leaving two or three burning wrecks behind them. Reid and his men did an emergency repair on the track, by simply shortening it and running it around the bogeys, omitting the sprocket. One side of the tank looked like a half-track minus its front wheel; the thing was trying to turn right-handed

circles the whole time, but provided you steered vigorously in the opposite direction, it was drivable.

In this manner they limped back to the workshop. Although the
Panzers had driven away, the height could not be considered secure:
There was no infantry; there were no reserves available in the fortress.
Or rather, there was one battalion of Australians left, whom it had not
been possible to fetch away because of the sinking of the *Latona*.
There was an order out that these men should not be used in action.
Morshead's successor, Scobie, asked their commander, Lieutenant
Colonel "Bull" Burrows.

"Sure," said the gigantic picture-book Aussie. "We'll see to that for
you."

The Australians took the height, suffering substantial casualties.

Fate, in the ugly way it has in wartime, had again been playing dice.
And it struck Burrows. As he was talking to Colonel Nicholls in a wadi
the day after the attack, a heavy shell fell near them. A huge splinter
tore Burrows' head open. This—until then—vigorous man never recovered from the wound.

"Chauffeur" to General Crüwell

In the first days of December, the strength of the German-Italian
forces finally gave out. Rommel still tried—in vain—to hack a way to
his surrounded men at the Halfaya Pass, Sollum, and Bardia. The
Afrika Korps had just thirty-four Panzers left.

When the retreat began, Saenger and his trusted old barrel-less companion were still with the Afrika Korps staff. After his night performance, a staff officer had explained to him that he had in fact called his
general officer commanding "mate."

"I thought Rommel was our general," said Saenger. The officer
looked at him amazed.

"Rommel commands the Panzer Group—something like an army.
But the German Afrika Korps is commanded by General Crüwell—get
it?"

"Yes, sir," snapped Saenger, impressed. And since the captain
seemed so friendly, he went on, while he was at it, to ask, glancing
meaningfully at another staff officer who was approaching energetically: "Now where does he fit in?"

The captain winced only very slightly, looked reproachful, and said
quickly: "Lieutenant Colonel Fritz Bayerlein, Chief of Staff of the
Afrika Korps. He's going with you in your Panzer too."

That is how Saenger and his crew got a passenger. The general climbed into the Panzer without a gun, completely ignoring the cheeky so-and-so who had called him "mate."

But all that soon changed. Crüwell, who with his fifty years was unanimously dubbed an "old gentleman" by the young tankmen—which would never have occurred to them about Rommel, who was about the same age—revealed himself as an urbane, friendly superior. He was already a little corpulent, for which reason a chair was always placed by the Panzer for him from the escorting command bus to help him climb in. And he had a distinct predilection for good food.

To everybody's surprise, the Panzermen, who during the preceding fighting had never passed a German or enemy supply truck or food store without a quick snatch, were markedly better off for food than the general's kitchen, which as a rule only had the regulation supplies. In the outboard hamper—but also in the ammunition compartments and other holes and corners of the Panzer—there were tins and little bags of flour, sugar, et cetera, which they had quickly thrown in amid all the thunder and smoke.

The "mate" business was soon forgotten; and the general would often abandon the meager staff diet and come smiling up to Panzer 125: "Well, men, have you got something decent for your old general to eat?"

They had, of course, long ago patched up a splendid collapsible oven, complete with a griddle and baking tins, made from British gasoline cans and aluminum pots and pans. It could be fueled either with gasoline or charcoal. The general was particularly fond of Saenger's almond cake and his fruit tarts, using captured tinned fruit, served hot.

Crüwell, who during the preceding fighting had traveled around between tanks firing at each other in a Mammut vehicle he had inherited from Rommel, the armor on which was little thicker than tinplate, and who shunned no danger when there was some point to it, otherwise took the thoroughly sensible view that it wouldn't do either the Afrika Korps or the faraway Fatherland any good to let himself be shot on some casual occasion.

In view of the continuous air attacks, he made sure that the mobile radio transmitters, which had a way of being located by the RAF and saturation bombed, were set up at a respectable distance from where he was staying. He kept in touch through a runner.

Whenever they stopped for any length of time, his Panzer crew would dig him a ditch and run the Panzer over it so he could slip in there during an air raid alert. On most occasions, the business with the chair would have taken too long.

It often happened that Rommel would turn up for a talk at such a time. Then the two generals would sit with Bayerlein in Staff HQ, a touring coach brought out from Germany. On one occasion, British fighters dived on targets in the vicinity, firing their guns. Crüwell threw himself under the Panzer. Bayerlein jumped down the hatch.

Rommel leaped onto his half-track and blazed away at the departing aircraft with its machine gun.

When it was all over, he jumped lightly down again, glancing at Crüwell, who crawled out from under the Panzer covered in dust, with a smile that was not altogether fair.

"What a madman," Crüwell later said to Bayerlein. "As machine gunners, we're all surely a bit overpaid?"

Altogether, the general and his chief of staff talked very freely about their C-in-C in front of the keenly eavesdropping Panzermen—as people tend to do when the pressure occasionally grows too great and seeks an escape valve. Presumably they would have been reticent in front of junior officers, as enjoined by military convention; but the young Panzer soldiers stood so far outside their elevated staff sphere that it didn't really matter if their bile overflowed.

After his Panzer excursion to the barbed-wire fence on the Egyptian border, Rommel had again succumbed to his favorite habit of interfering on the battlefield—to turn units aside or send them into a different action because the situation had altered—without bothering about the customary command structure. Never had the consequences been so unfortunate as those of his Blitz decision on the night of 24 November; especially since they were on a smaller scale. On the other hand, it was becoming more and more obvious that he was never better than in mobile actions and in touch with the enemy, when his fighter instinct could foretell developments as if sniffing them in the wind, and fed him with fast reactions, based less on understanding than on the untutored instinct of a big cat, noble but disposed by nature to kill.[6]

The two conventional general staff officers, Crüwell and Bayerlein, did not find any of this funny, even when their C-in-Cs intervention proved successful. And they told him as much.

The three would often be seen talking most forcibly in their coach. Sometimes they would even walk a little way into the desert to conduct their discussion quite secure from eavesdroppers.

On occasion even that would not allow Crüwell to let off enough steam. Saenger would hear him hiss: "Robber baron!" or "Adven-

[6] Rommel once noted in his diary that élan and energy were more important in a commander than his intellectual faculties. Much later, his friend Ernst Jünger was to write—in the foreword to his book *Strahlungen* (*Radiances*)—that the absence of Rommel through his wounds in France had robbed the 20 July conspiracy of the only man who had "enough naïveté to match the frightening simplicity of those who were to be attacked."

turer!" It took quite a lot to trigger off his Westphalian temper. But then it was like a natural catastrophe.

Neither he nor Bayerlein could get over Rommel's ride to the fence.[7] On the night of 8 December the point was reached when the exhausted troops had to give up the siege of Tobruk. The 90th Light Division and some unmotorized Italian units had been sent along the coast toward Gazala. The mass of the Afrika Korps streamed through a new gap, only two kilometers wide, near El Duda, during the night.

When they set out, Bayerlein seemed ready for anything. He turned up in a vast driving coat, the hem of which brushed the desert ground, a briefcase with the most important secret documents in his hand. He crouched down in the Panzer, turned up the collar of his coat, and just said: "Go!"

The Tobruk Rats heard the rumbling of several hundred engines in the distance and knew what it meant.

The siege was finally over. Charles Armitage was cursing because the stream that was flowing away westward was out of range of the 25-pounders on his side, and because the tanks were not making a sortie. Sergeant Reid lay badly knocked about in the hospital. While he was sleeping with his crew under his crippled Valentine the day after the engagement, some He-111s flew past at high altitude and released their bombs. When Reid woke, he was not lying in the same position as when he had gone to sleep. Splinters had hit him in the chest and stomach and had rolled him over. He was never again fully fit for service.

In flight—through the Italian allies

During the trek through the El Duda gap the advance guard fired flares by which the drivers and tank commanders were to navigate. Nothing had been arranged with Corps HQ. Saenger asked Bayerlein: "Which star shell am I supposed to steer by?"

He was engulfed in a tidal wave of Bavarian fury: "Are you out of your mind? The fellow thinks I've nothing else to do! What the hell do I know about your blasted flares?"

They tried to stay in the stream of vehicles, keeping steadily to a westerly course. Sometimes the ungainly outlines of the Mammut

---

[7] After the war Bayerlein praised Rommel's wisdom, at least in his published work, even with reference to this controversial operation. But this seems to have been part of a sort of gentleman's agreement among generals. In conversation with the author, even the intelligent and irreproachable Westphal denied that Rommel had had further thrusts to the Canal in mind. Yet, in *Krieg ohne Hass,* Rommel's sketches show how he proposed to surmount the Caucasus and polish off the Russians—all with no trouble at all.

loomed up and Konrad Müller tried to keep it in sight, but mostly the thing was too fast for him—until the next time it got stuck.

To cap it all, Konrad started complaining over the intercom that he kept falling asleep. Saenger's head too kept lolling on his chest.

Suddenly he woke with a start. They were alone in a dead-flat plain which seemed quite vast in the moonlight, and something was banging rhythmically against the steel sides.

"Halt!" yelled Saenger.

But down below in the Panzer, hemmed in among the others, Bayerlein cried: "Keep going; get me out of here—have you all taken leave of your senses?" And he clutched his briefcase of secrets.

But outside there was suddenly even wilder shouting—Italian voices exclaiming *"Mama mia!"* and *"Madonna!"* and some figures running in front of the Panzer. Saenger jumped down. They were in the middle of El Adem airfield. Some Italian infantry had evidently dug themselves in and pulled their groundsheets over their heads in the cold night. The 20-ton Panzer had rushed right in among the poor devils. The groundsheets had got caught in the tracks and something was still hanging on to them—perhaps it was a hapless ally—and was crashing against the track guard with every revolution of the bogeys, until it sounded as if a shell was hitting the tank. Out of the Panzer came the muffled voice of the gallant colonel. Saenger leaned in over the hatch. "We're standing right in the middle of some Italians; it's an infantry position. We're churning them into a pulp!" Bayerlein roared even louder: "Drive away! Run them all down for all I care, but I've got to get out of here. I have the secret bag here, can't you see?"

With much temperamental babble, the Italians had meanwhile freed the foreign body from the track; Konrad Müller crashed into gear and they rumbled away across the airfield in a westerly direction, hoping secretly that the rest of their allies had been alerted by all the "Madonna"-ing and shouting and had run away. There was not much coming up behind them—except the British. The Italians on the airfield were evidently a lost and forgotten crowd.

America in the war

Crüwell's and Bayerlein's tactical concept brought the remaining German-Italian troops back in reasonable order through the Marsa el Brega gap. The two officers were rightly proud of their system and defended it tooth and nail against the Supreme Commander, who did not like it at all.

It was based on clear and simple considerations: the only advantage enjoyed by the much-reduced German motorized and mechanized units,[8] whose job it was to cover the slow retreat of the other formations, was the superior firepower of their weapons. At the same time the British were forced by their own tactical concept to follow up energetically and try to repeat their success of the previous year—to cut off the retreating enemy before he got to Agedabia.

It therefore seemed right to let the pursuing enemy keep running up against lines of eighty-eights, anti-tank guns, artillery, and Panzers. This rather passive and cool style of fighting was occasionally thrown into confusion by Rommel whenever, during one of his many visits to the front, he saw an opportunity and organized counterattacks with combat groups he hastily scratched together.

"He's winning a skirmish and losing the battle," Crüwell would thunder. But on one occasion he added with resignation: "What does it matter anyway? Every battle won brings the Americans into the war that much sooner."

Very soon afterward, the Americans *were* in the war. The decision about where and how he should go over from moral and material support of the British to active fighting was taken from the U. S. President Roosevelt's hands. The Far Eastern Axis partner, Japan, began hostilities on its own initiative.

It was now obvious how very dangerously this "Axis" was wobbling. In his Directive No. 24 of March 1941, Hitler had laid down the ground rules for co-operation with Japan. The key sentence ran: "The common aim to keep in mind is to subdue Britain rapidly and thus to keep the USA out of the war." For the rest, Germany had no political, military or economic interests in the Far East.[9]

In the same directive he also ordered that his Ostland plans should be kept a secret from the Japanese. The attack on the Soviet Union took them by surprise. Their moderate foreign minister, who had visited Berlin shortly before it happened, lost face—and his job. Barely six months later, Japanese warplanes wrecked Pearl Harbor, the U.S. base in the Hawaiian archipelago, likewise without any consultation with the Axis partners. On 7 December 1941, the war could well and truly be called a world war. Hitler, who until then reacted with untypical mildness to a large number of provocations by the U. S. Navy in the sea war, now tried to create the impression that he had long

[8] It was no use relying on co-operation from the Italian 20th Corps (Ariete and Trieste). Its commander, Gastone Gambara, was subordinate to the Panzer Group in this capacity, but was at the same time senior to the CGS, Bastico, and thus to Rommel. Thus, in one critical situation the CGS Gambara was able to cancel an order to Corps Commander Gambara without referring back to Group.

[9] Expressing regrets at the failure of his hopes of a Germanic complicity with Britain, Hitler once remarked that it was really a pity he should be helping to break the supremacy of the white man in Asia.

cherished the hope of declaring war on the United States. Deaf and willing, a people spoilt by victories shuffled along behind him.

Such Jewish fellow citizens who had not yet been transported were now marked out by a large yellow star as people who had been expelled from sociey.

Whispers circulated about reports brought back by soldiers from Russia, who had seen immense pits and SD[10] "Action Commandos" (*Einsatzkommandos*), who mowed people down in tiers and hurriedly covered them with earth. Many compulsively shut their eyes and ears; many more threw their chests out, proud of belonging to the *Herrenmenschen*—the master race.

But other news from Russia was gravely disturbing. Contrary to expectations, the Slav subhumans had not collapsed. The Führer's wonderful visions of victory had gone astray: the wide sweep of Russian land crisscrossed by *Autobahnen,* ruled by racially faultless heroes, defended by a network of naturally blond soldier-peasants—and naturally tilled by the subhumans, for whom, once the stratum of intellectuals was liquidated, schooling sufficient "for doing simple sums and reading place names" would be provided—more or less as for those Poles not thought "fit to be Germanized."

Instead of which, German soldiers, some of whom had actually caught a glimpse of the towers of the Kremlin glistening in the sun, were now dying in blizzards and ringing frost. Winter equipment had been declared unnecessary, had it not? Back home, Wolf Cubs (junior Hitler Youth) with sleds and handcarts went from door to door in towns and villages, collecting warm clothing. And for the first time on such an occasion, they were hearing some tart language from the Führer's most faithful followers: the petty bourgeoisie.

But Hitler dismissed Brauchitsch and took over the command of the army himself. The reassuring implication was that perhaps the Führer had once again not been told everything.

The stagnation on the Russian front gave Hitler the opportunity to withdraw an entire *Luftflotte* (air fleet) and transfer it to the Mediterranean theater. In his Directive No. 38, dated 2 December 1941, he laid down that under the command of Generalfeldmarschall Albert Kesselring, this fleet was to gain mastery of the air and sea between southern Italy and North Africa and "hold down" Malta, support the ground troops, and cut off British supplies to Malta and Tobruk (the latter was soon to become irrelevant).

Even for an entire air fleet, all that added up to quite an assignment. Nevertheless, together with the U-boats transferred to the Mediter-

[10] Translator's note: SD=*Sicherheitsdienst:* Himmler's parallel intelligence organization.

ranean, the airmen transformed the whole picture very rapidly. "Our interval of immunity and advantage came to its end," wrote Churchill in his diary, although in November he was still able to drive the Air Force and Navy on quite successfully to sink two Italian tankers making for Benghazi. But the aircraft carrier *Ark Royal* had by then been sent to the bottom by a torpedo; the battleship *Barham* followed; in Alexandria harbor, fabulously brave Italian frogmen put the battleships *Queen Elizabeth* and *Valiant* out of action for months with limpet mines; and some skillfully laid mines destroyed almost the entire cruiser flotilla off Malta just as it was putting to sea to chase a convoy.

This same convoy reached Benghazi on 19 December. It brought among other things two Panzer companies, artillery, and a considerable quantity of supplies. Rommel's troops, who had managed to improvise their way through, despite all shortages, thanks to a brilliant and versatile transport system,[11] were reinforced at a critical moment.

To stay with the comparison with a war at sea, which has again and again been so apposite, when you are being pursued by a stronger enemy, the nearer you get to the shelter of your own port the more restricted becomes your room for maneuver.

". . . it would really be a Christmas present if we should manage to escape the danger of being encircled and to bring back the bulk of our forces," Rommel wrote to his wife on 23 December. Temperamental though he could be, once he realized that the alternatives were retreat or the fairly certain annihilation of his forces, he would not allow anyone or anything to divert him from the task of saving his troops. The Italian generals Bastico and Cavallero, all of a sudden almost brave, and supported by the know-all Kesselring, urged him to hold the part of Cyrenaica which lay west of Gazala, since the loss of that area might harm the Duce.

Rommel's dealings with his Italian superiors seldom took place without some acerbity; this time Bastico lapsed into furious screaming when the German general let fall a remark about the reliability of Italian troops. But then it's always a mistake in a duel to rely on a weapon of which the other man has a better command.[12] Rommel left the arena as the victor. The retreat continued.

For the German soldiers it was a new experience to have to disengage, particularly since the exercise did not always go off in orderly fashion because of the shortage of gasoline and lack of vehicles. Thus a

[11] The performance of the supply columns, mostly in fluid fighting under continuous air attack, was recognized by Auchinleck himself as one important reason why Rommel's forces got away.

[12] Months later, by which time he had again been promoted, Rommel on one occasion remarked with a rare smile: "Isn't it great to be a field marshal and to be able to talk like a sergeant major?"

part of the 900th Motorized Engineer Battalion had to walk, although official orders had promised them motor transport.

A small group of these men marched into a food storage tent near Gazala airfield. Judging by the well-packed delicacies that lay around, it must have belonged to the Luftwaffe.

Guided by an unfailing instinct, Sapper Arthur Stenschke went straight for a box containing some gorgeously scented cigars. They filled their great African haversacks right up: Nobody minds having to groan under the weight of things like these. One man took the cigars, the next beer, tins, milk, bread. . . .

As it turned out, this was not a good idea. When, heavily laden, they tried to slip away at break of day, someone yelled "Hands up!" In the background, Stenschke saw dimly the outlines of two armored cars. With two of his comrades, he executed a smart about turn and disappeared behind a tent, which was immediately hit by a machine-gun burst.

But by then they were away, cutting a few zigzags through the lanes between the tents; their hearts heavy at the thought of having to leave it all behind for Tommy—even what their mates had in their rucksacks. In the distance, they heard someone call out, in German with an English accent: "Put your guns down!"

Stenschke, who was carrying the parcel of cigars, was cursing particularly at the loss of the other good things. The tents stood in a great wadi, which ended in a fairly steep bank on its western side. Groaning and straining, they clambered up it—it seemed the safest way—and crested the top unmolested. Beyond it lay an Italian AA battery. Stenschke swapped some of his cigars with his allies for a bottle of brandy and one of wine.

As they went along, they would take a sip now and then. The sun rose; after the cold night, it became burning hot. The mixture of spirits and wine proved rather powerful. They reached one of the airfields at Gazala and threw themselves down behind a building, where they slept right through a heavy bombing raid. Next morning they even found a vehicle belonging to their unit and continued their journey more comfortably, smoking their splendid airmen's cigars.

The ex-owners of the cigars were also traveling west in an unaccustomed manner: The fuel shortage had hit the Luftwaffe particularly hard. During the Crusader offensive, only some of the machines could take off at any one time, and in the end quite a lot of them had to be left behind. According to a British count, 458 German and Italian aircraft had fallen into the hands of the advancing Eighth Army by 20 December.

Rommel's secret plans

The Corps HQ staff also helped themselves at the Luftwaffe's expense—at any rate, Saenger and his men who, with the unerring instinct of the warrior for country you can live off, had spotted a food depot near Benina airfield. There was actually a unit quartermaster still there, who did not approve of this self-service, but he had to defer to them.[13]

They stuffed their Panzer full, including some of the ammunition boxes, which were pretty well airtight and which, wrapped in damp cloths, were at least as suitable a container for perishable food as for their customary, more destructive, contents.

This change of use was certainly in accordance with the general's intentions. He had meanwhile given his grinning approval to their adding the chimney of a field kitchen to their equipment so as to improve their oven, and to the chimney being carried outside the Panzer as a sign of their peaceable intentions.

"Only don't go and get shot up, will you?" he said in his guttural Westphalian accent. The danger of that had diminished, although it had not yet quite disappeared, for Corps HQ remained rather far in the rear during the retreat.

Crüwell was none too fond either of commanding from a distance, especially behind Benghazi, where the danger was greatest that the British tanks advancing through the desert might cut off the units which here were driving down the coast road toward Agedabia.

It was an overcast, rainy day when they drove along beside the Via Balbia there and saw to the southeast fast Cruiser and Honey tanks pounding over the rolling country. Vulnerable transport vehicles were rolling down the road: columns of trucks and motorized infantry, interspersed with artillery and AA guns.

Bayerlein jumped into Saenger's Panzer, tore down the road, and fetched from the queue everything that was usable: field howitzers, self-propelled guns, AA guns. The kitchen chimney did look rather ridiculous as they went rolling and pitching toward the tanks with this force. Bayerlein did not bang away blindly, but quickly and efficiently formed his scratch combat group into a line of concentrated firepower.

---

[13] The "warehouse Johnny" is a favorite target of pub stories ("We've finished taking stock of the depot, sir—ready to be blown up now?"), but few bother to see his point of view. It's precisely during a hectic retreat that the situation is often confused; after all, a unit in good order may still come along and demand food in accordance with regulations. If he is then found to have abandoned the depot too soon, he is bound to face an extremely unfriendly court-martial.

British cavalry tradition again overcame common sense: The Cruisers of the 22nd Armored Brigade, which had meanwhile been more or less brought up to strength but was much weakened by supply difficulties and breakdowns, attacked head on. Those in the lead were equipped with high-explosive shells. Then the armor-piercing rounds crashed in among them, before their own guns could be brought into play. Their attack collapsed; steel coffins belched black smoke. From farther south one could hear the faint barking of Panzers, drowned by the mighty voice of the eighty-eights. At Agedabia too, the British attack was running into a line that hurled steel at them and from which the Panzer Regiments sallied forth to fall upon the survivors.

Rommel's Christmas wish came true. The bulk of his force reached the Marsa el Bregr. gap intact.

But far to the east, the garrisons of Bardia and the Halfaya Pass had been left behind. Bardia surrendered on 2 January. The German-Italian force at the Halfaya Pass, under the Italian General di Giorgis, held on until 17 January.

The German units lost about 15,000 men in dead, wounded, and captured—a third of their strength. The Italians lost almost 22,000 men. The British losses were 20,000 men. Apart from 278 wrecks which were utterly destroyed, they were able to repair their disabled tanks, for this time the battlefield stayed in their hands. As against that, 220 German and 120 Italian tanks had to be completely written off.

But the "total annihilation" of the German-Italian forces, of which the British newspaper reader was several times informed in army communiqués and correspondents' reports, had not by any means come about.

Official quarters more or less demanded an advance payment of laurels. In Britain's darkest days, excessive hopes had been pinned on the Crusader offensive. Later, a British illustrated magazine somewhat maliciously collected the headlines that appeared at this time:

> 22 November: Rommel surrounded
> 23 November: A third of the Axis tanks destroyed
> 24 November: Rommel's forces smashed
> 26 November: Britain wins night battle of armor
> 28 November: First round to the Cunningham brothers[14]
> 30 November: Rommel throws his last Panzers into battle
> 2 December: Germans chased from Sidi Rezegh corridor at the point of the bayonet.

[14] General Cunningham had long before been relieved by Auchinleck and replaced by Ritchie.

At the front, in the desert at Marsa el Brega, cold, damp, and swept by howling winds, the British soldier had formed quite a different impression of the Germans.

On New Year's Eve, Rommel's troops fired tracers into the air and sang the National Anthem, extolling the "Deutschland über alles" which had sent them into the desert. "Make no mistake; this force is by no means beaten," reported an impressed 22nd Armored Brigade to Cairo. An ominous observation, which was to prove true sooner than anyone expected. Hardly anyone suspected anything; but Rommel was often seen getting out of his command car late at night with his G1 Ops, Westphal.

The distrustful C-in-C allowed neither his German nor his Italian superiors into the secret of what he was up to.

At any rate, had the British captured a ship or ditched a plane with mail on board in mid-January, their evaluators of the enemy's status would have had their store of knowledge enriched by some additional information.

That touching trait in Rommel's character—his attachment to his family, the desire to let them into his plans and hopes as soon as possible—made him violate quite brazenly all the rules designed to safeguard official secrets:

17 January 1942
"The situation is developing to our advantage and I am full of plans I dare not even discuss with my entourage. They would think me crazy. . . ."

19 January 1942
"Grause wrote [after a visit to the Führer's HQ—Author] from Rome. Clearly the Führer fully approves of my efforts. The supply situation has greatly improved, as you will find out from the Wehrmacht communiqués of the next few days. . . ."

20 January 1942
"By the time this letter arrives you will long have heard that the battle has taken place. The preparations take up all my time. . . ."

21 January 1942
"The army begins its counterattack in two hours' time. . . ."

BOOK THREE

Destination El Alamein

1. Advance into a Trap

Praise for Rommel in the Commons

Rommel certainly knew nothing about Ultra or about the worldwide antennae of the British Intelligence Service. And the fact that he was prone to gloss over or veil his intentions in his radio signals to Rome and Berlin was surely due rather to the knowledge that Halder in the OKH and his dear friends at the Comando Supremo were watching him with the greatest suspicion—with a degree of jealousy which would probably have hindered his successful operations as much as his less fortunate ones.

Yet this rattling in the machinery had a substantial advantage for the Axis operations in the North African theater never enjoyed by most protagonists on the German-Italian side: Auchinleck was taken by surprise by the German offensive in January 1942, just as Wavell had been in April 1941. Cautiously, Rommel had given nothing away and had laid on the operation in such a way that he could break it off at any time and describe it merely as an insignificant reconnaissance sortie.

There were other parallels with April 1941: Auchinleck's forces, too, were depleted by another theater of war. True, he was not forced, like Wavell, to give up "the fighting portion" of his army, since Churchill still hoped to make contact with French North Africa through Tripolitania and to prepare for the leap to the Italian mainland. Nevertheless, the C-in-C, Middle East, lost another Australian division, the 70th British, and some experienced armored units, including the Seventh Hussars, Major Younger, and Lieutenant Llewellyn-Palmer among them.

They went to the Far East, where the Japanese were beginning their triumphal progress into Burma, down the Malay Archipelago through Singapore and the islands of Indonesia to Timor and to the very doorstep of Australia. In London, Sir Alan Brooke, appointed CIGS in December, did not know what to do first. It was now his turn to be bombarded with telegrams from the Prime Minister. Churchill had sailed across the stormy Atlantic to meet Roosevelt immediately the United States entered the war, his head and briefcase full of plans for the future joint conduct of the war.

When one of his aides reminded him how cautiously he had dealt with the Americans until then, the old lion had merely smiled a wicked smile: "Oh, that was when we were courting the lady. Now we have her in the harem, we'll be talking to her very differently."

Among the detailed plans he was working on as his ship rolled and pitched was not merely the distant aim of returning to the European mainland (then known as Operation Sledgehammer) but also Operation Gymnast—a joint landing in French North Africa from the west. Under the name of Operation Torch, this enterprise was to mark the turning point of the war in the Mediterranean basin eleven months later.

But first the pendulum was again swinging in favor of the other side. Just as it had back in April. . . . What remained of the famous 7th Armored Division was in the Delta for rehabilitation. Overextended supply lines were causing a severe fuel shortage. And an utterly green 1st Armored Division, freshly arrived from Britain, was carefully picking its way between the sand dunes and the stone desert with its Cruisers.

In just three weeks, Rommel's soldiers reconquered Cyrenaica almost as far as Gazala. Nine days before this offensive began, on 12 January, Auchinleck was still informing London that "indications of weakness and disintegration" were multiplying on the enemy side. It is not clear what led him to this conclusion.

Across a Mediterranean in which no British fleet worth speaking of remained, the German-Italian forces had been rebuilt virtually without interference; the two Panzer regiments again had 111 tanks each, with 28 in reserve—and some of them were the new Panzer IIIs with stronger frontal armoring and the long-barreled 50 mm gun. Eighty-nine of the Ariete's tin tanks were also hobbling along with them.

The hapless novices of the 1st Armored Division were chased about mercilessly. This inexperienced force suffered a blow to its morale when it discovered how inferior its toy guns and its thin-skinned Cruisers were. More than a hundred of its tanks—over two thirds of its total strength—were lost. Several were captured by the Germans, some without any fuel, others just abandoned by their demoralized crews.

Rommel, accompanied by Westphal, flew about the battlefield, his G1 Ops forced to squat on the floor behind the passenger seat of the two-seater aircraft. They were often fired on. Rommel, quite unafraid, gave the unnerved pilot, who had trouble enough flying his overloaded machine anyway, orders for evasive action: "Turn left, right, down. . . ."

But Rommel's unorthodox method of flying around, doing his own reconnaissance, making rapid decisions, once again worked. Again he split his meager forces into three, this time chasing them through the back door (through the mountains from the southeast) into Benghazi, and took Mechili, Derna, and Tmimi. From time to time, heavy downpours hobbled both friend and foe. But mostly the Germans were again quicker on their feet. They overtook the British units and made them run into ambushes.

Curt Ehle, meanwhile promoted major and battalion commander, had an amusing experience while on the road from Marada to Benghazi with Colonel Geissler's Combat Group. Scattered groups of tanks from the British 1st Armored Division were still milling around here and there. Some outraged supply drivers reported that they had been fired on by a couple of British tanks from the rear. Ehle turned about with a combat group, the hard core of which consisted of three 50 mm anti-tank guns under Lieutenant Ruhf, and went looking for the intruders. But they seemed to have vanished from the face of the earth; subsequent supply convoys had seen nothing of them—until a column of medics came up.

"That's right, they banged away at us too from astern, but then they buzzed off through some shallows right in the middle of those salt lakes back there." With Ehle in his open car leading the way and the three anti-tank guns behind their tractors bringing up the rear, they splashed across the shallows. The lake narrowed and ended in a valley, which looked peaceful in the African spring, with its fig trees in bloom and its dark green coloring.

The peace was rudely shattered as the three British tanks appeared high on the hillside and came rushing at full speed at the German anti-tank guns. The gunners worked like mad to unlimber and take aim, but it was too late. All they had time to do was to scatter, splashing, before the tanks were on top of them, each running over a gun with evident enjoyment.

They drove past Ehle's car at a distance of barely 100 meters, still at top speed, bucking and swaying and throwing up a great bow wave. Ehle and his companions grabbed their rifles and fired at the tank commanders, who looked over from their turrets, didn't even bother to duck and calmly waved to the Germans as if to say they might as well give up. And in fact, there was no hitting such a wobbly target. Apart from that bit of gunplay, not one shot was fired and no one hurt, but Ruhf stood by his wrecked guns and cried. He was a dashing and tough officer; only the day before, his guns had devastatingly shot up a halted British column, but now tears were running down his face; there lay his pampered darlings, so casually slain, without any fuss or the sound of firing, and it was too much for the young man.

On 6 January, the fertile "balcony" of Cyrenaica, the northward-thrusting hill country with its harbors of Benghazi and Derna, was retaken. An American radio commentator said: "Rommel, the wayward boy among the generals, has again pulled a rabbit out of the hat."

He himself, meanwhile promoted Colonel General (his force being simultaneously "promoted" to the status of "Panzerarmee Afrika"), wrote contentedly to his wife: "World press opinion of me has greatly improved."

Churchill himself contributed to this. On his return from America, he did not have an easy job explaining to the Commons what on earth was supposed to be happening in Africa; and how it was that this Rommel, who according to all the communiqués had barely managed to get away from Cyrenaica with his life, had now been able to strike again.

Churchill's explanation was a mixture of magnanimity and cunning: "I cannot tell what the position at the present moment is on the Western front in Cyrenaica. We have a very daring and skillful opponent against us and, may I say across the havoc of war, a great general."

Presumably, it was largely necessity that had wrung these words from Churchill. It was more like him to lambast the "Hun"; but it is a likely assumption that these two kindred spirits would really have taken a liking to each other had they ever made each other's acquaintance.

For Sir Claude Auchinleck, on the other hand, the remark amounted to a distinct slight, but Churchill had most likely considered that carefully too. What he had certainly not foreseen were its consequences in the Eighth Army. For the soldiers who now saw the fruits of the prolonged and bloody battles of Crusader wiped out by one skillful blow, who were cursing their inferior weapons and clumsy leadership, Rommel became such a legendary figure that it seriously affected their capacity to fight. Auchinleck tried vainly to counter this mood.

He drafted a circular addressed to all commanders and unit leaders, warning them of the psychological consequences of the Rommel legend. They should not, he said, say "Rommel" when they meant the enemy in Cyrenaica. By personalizing the enemy in this way, there was a danger that the soldiers of the Eighth Army would ascribe supernatural powers to him. "I am therefore begging you to dispel the idea in every way you can that Rommel is anything but an ordinary German general, and a pretty unpleasant one at that, as we know from the mouths of his own officers."[1] The circular concluded with a postscript: "I am *not* jealous of Rommel—Auchinleck."

A skyscraper—with guns

The unheralded German-Italian offensive, accompanied as it was by screams of protest on the part of the Italian allies, was, for all its improvisation, much more than just a repetition of the only barely orderly forward rush of the previous April. There was a plan, which had been worked out during those long nights with Westphal, and there was an organized supply system, especially for fuel, some of which was being borrowed from Gambara, the Chief of Staff, one of the few Italian officers who was in the secret.

The British advance had been interrupted so damagingly, and supplies brought forward with so much difficulty having been captured in such quantities, that no British offensive would be possible for months, no matter how Churchill raved. Moreover, the new theater of war in the Far East was swallowing men and materials. Only very slowly would Auchinleck reconstitute some sort of a force. But he had told the Prime Minister quite frankly that because of the inferiority of the British tanks a two-to-one superiority in numbers would be necessary for any successful attack.

Such a ratio was not easy to achieve because the Axis supply system was now functioning. Malta had been bombed almost *hors de combat*. Two-engined Ju-88s were laying the first real carpet-bombing patterns of the war, smashing airfields, wharves, and docks. Churchill was assuming that the rocky island was bound to be lost.

But Hitler, fixated on the eastern theater of war, could not be persuaded to attack. His trauma about Crete was a contributory factor. Rommel, Admiral Raeder, and others tried in vain to make him change his mind. He also cheated the Duce, with whom he had agreed in April 1942 that: an offensive arranged by Rommel should go only as far as the taking of Tobruk at the end of May; a halt would be called there so

---

[1] Foolishly, almost all published work I have read omits this remark regarding the opinion of captured officers about Rommel. Even the cultivation of monuments to the dead can be overdone.

that the Luftwaffe could be withdrawn to support a combined seaborne and airborne operation against Malta.

The parachutist General Student was duly sent to Italy with some units to make the preparations, and transport aircraft and freight gliders were gotten ready. But a few days later, Hitler gave Göring a free hand to withdraw his air forces from the Mediterranean area to send to Russia. After he had spent a few days grumbling about the Italians, Greater Germany's Supreme Warlord explained bluntly to Student, who was reporting back to him, that he had no intention of letting himself in for an operation of this kind with the Italians, of all people. Even Jodl put in a feeble protest, but Hitler ordered that preparations for the operation should continue only on paper—to deceive the Italians.[2]

The ruse went so far that not even General von Rintelen in Rome was let into the secret. In accordance with an instruction from Hitler dated 21 May which had not been canceled, six days later, on 26 May, he retained a unit of engineers for the Malta operation—code-named Hercules—although the engineers were urgently needed in Africa.

On the same day, Rommel's attack began. The German troops had known at least since 14 May that there was something in the wind. On that day, Rommel had sent the divisional commanders a thunderous circular in which he pointed to the need for secrecy and stated indignantly that regrouping troop movements, then taking place to repel an impending British attack, were being interpreted by rumormongers, "especially in the rear areas," as signs of a coming German-Italian offensive. "I should like to make it quite clear that loose talk is unmanly, and above all unsoldierly. I call on all commanding officers to fight this chatter mania with severe punishments. In serious cases, sentence by court-martial must follow. —Rommel."

The pity of it was that the British were by no means informed by rumormongers in the rear areas. Thanks to Ultra, they had the most detailed knowledge of Rommel's plans—for this time he had to co-ordinate them in detail with his superiors in Rome and Berlin. But this was another thing no one could suspect, even later. For a grotesque situation, probably unique in military history, ensued: The side about to be attacked, in possession of the most detailed plans of the attacker, made virtually no use of this decisive advantage.

Auchinleck in Cairo knew the source and received full detailed information. Even the army commander, Ritchie, was not allowed to

2 See among others Warlimont and the war diary of the Wehrmacht High Command Staff. One of the most remarkable pieces of history fudging can be found in a recently published book by the one-time necrophiliac war reporter, who quite simply asserts: "Rome could not, and would not, go on."

know the source, although he had translated texts of the radio signals. But farther down the C-in-C's seizure-prone command structure, this and that detail got stuck, and all the commanders at the front got to hear was that an attack was to be expected in May. They were, moreover, told that the enemy would "probably" come up from the south with a right hook through the desert, but anyone could easily figure out that much on the basis of past experience of Rommel.

In their nostalgia for a tidy, mopped-up battlefield, with fronts and flanks, the British had tried to establish fixed points in the wide desert sea: A system of strongpoints ran south of Gazala. It consisted of "boxes," surrounded by mines and barbed wire. The southernmost of these was known as Bir Hacheim, and it was held by General Pierre Koenig's Free French Brigade.

Instead of at long last holding his tank forces ready in a mass, as Auchinleck had advised, Ritchie had as usual scattered them all over the hinterland in brigades. At the important corner behind the Bir Hacheim box, around which the expected right hook could confidently be expected to come, lay our old friend the 4th Armored Brigade. It was no longer equipped only with the fast little Honeys: Each of its three regiments now had a squadron of some heavier, old-fashioned-looking monsters straight out of their American factories: the medium-heavy General Grants.

The British had been happy to take delivery of the 29-ton monsters, although one tank officer remarked thoughtfully: "Don't the Yanks love skyscrapers?"

The Grant was indeed a very tall affair—a drawback aggravated by its design (strongly reminiscent of the old French "B" tank). Right on top in the turret sat a puny 3.7 cm gun, already familiar from the Honey; while the main armament was accommodated deep down below: a very efficient medium-length (L/31) gun of 75 mm caliber with a muzzle velocity of 564 m/sec, which could destroy a Panzer III at 1,500 meters. Moreover, for the first time the British had in this tank a weapon which could fire armor-piercing or high-explosive shells as required.

Since the heavy gun was placed so low down, all the rest of the skyscraper had to stick out way above any available cover. The worst of it was that the 75, mounted Cambrai-fashion in a sponson, could be swiveled only a few degrees—a fatal disadvantage in fast desert fighting. For the rest, the seven-man tank was well armored at 88 mm maximum, and its 340 hp engine could drive it at 40 kmph.

In his *Krieg ohne Hass*, Rommel wrote that the Grant had been "a nasty surprise." Now, there may have been generals who paid no attention to the available information about the enemy's armaments, but

Rommel was certainly not one of them. Consequently, the only remaining possibility is that we have here the phenomenon so frequently encountered in generals' memoirs: Just look in the face of what difficulties I won!

The appendixes to the 20 May orders for attack included a detailed description of the Grant; and in the "Information sheet on the enemy" (*Feindnachrichtenblatt*) No. 7/42, dated 24 May 1942, there are precise details of how many of them the British frontline troops had: 144 to be exact, distributed between the 2nd, 4th, and 22nd Armored Brigades. Further information given is that according to British tests, the 75 mm ammunition for the Grants was defective.

The first report on the new tank was given by Panzer Sergeant Joachim Saenger. During his service as "chauffeur" to the corps staff he had also been active in the following "sideline": When British prisoners were brought in, they were made to sit for a while in the sun—not so much that it amounted to actual torture, but long enough for them to be very grateful when Saenger, apparently without any orders, came strolling past with a canister of water.[8] He would say: "Drink up; the boys who want to interrogate you will be along in a minute."

This would often give rise to a conversation, in the course of which the British, otherwise so disciplined, would give away quite a lot. During the official interrogation, there was seldom more to be got out of them than name and rank. On one such occasion a tank soldier said: "Until now you have been able to shoot the daylights out of us, but soon we'll be getting the medium tanks from the Americans; then you won't have quite such an easy time of it."

Saenger, by now an experienced interrogator, smiled a superior smile: "Nonsense! They don't make any medium ones."

"You'll see. What's more, they've got four machine guns and two big guns, and one of them's a 15-pounder. They're being unloaded in Suez."

All this was immediately passed on. It confirmed reports already to hand—from a source which was almost as good as Ultra and had been merrily bubbling away since the late autumn of 1941.

The U. S. Military Attaché in Cairo, Colonel Frank B. Fellers, transmitted almost daily radio reports to Washington on the situation and prospects of the Eighth Army. He was treated as an ally and gen-

---

[8] Some overclever interrogation officer with the British 4th Armored Brigade adopted a similar idea in May, but was bureaucratic enough to issue an order (German prisoners not to be allowed to sleep, eat, or drink before interrogation), which was promptly captured and publicized. The British War Office then announced over the radio that if such an order had indeed been issued at subordinate level, it would be immediately countermanded.

erously supplied with information, even before the entry of the United States into the war. Fellers was a very active man, who visited units and assessed their armament, their fighting morale, and the ability of their commanders. He also provided information on the supply situation, the arrival of convoys and their cargoes.

For his reports, he used a code that was supposed to be absolutely safe, but it was not. The monitoring stations of the German and Italian secret services had the key to it. According to legend, it was obtained in romantic circumstances by a pretty girl agent called Bianca. But the truth is more prosaic: An Italian employee of the U. S. Embassy in Cairo, an expert at picking locks, had got it for the Italian secret service from Fellers' safe.

Thus the advantage of Ultra was canceled out, at least as far as the African theater was concerned. The Grant was very well known and the answer to it was found: The thing was to engage it from the front and then to attack it with part of your force in the flank, where its heavy gun would not traverse, and its side plates were weak. Otherwise, the principle remained, if possible, not to sacrifice any Panzers where the "long arm" of the Afrika Korps, the eighty-eight, could reach.

Saenger and the 25-pounders

On 26 May, Rommel paraded some of his Panzers before the center of the Gazala line of "boxes" to give the impression that he would be making a frontal attack there. In the afternoon, in the midst of a terrible *ghibli* which made any aerial reconnaissance impossible, the mechanized and motorized units rolled southward. At six in the morning they moved off from their deployment area south of Bir Hacheim to advance northeast.

The deployment was observed during the night by the KDG armored cars, which remained undetected. They were merely confirming what Ultra had decoded on 25 May: "General von Rintelen, Rome, to OKH: According to signal from Panzerarmee Afrika, R-Day for Theseus 1400 hours 26 May."[4]

The light was still clear; but hardly had the sun popped up over the horizon than the great mass of the phalanx, surging forward on wheels and chains, drove in a dense cloud of dust. Joachim Saenger was traveling on the left wing in his old Panzer No. 125—the only one left in

---

[4] Theseus was the code name for the May offensive. The muddle in the Eighth Army about this information was so massive that in the view of the then G1 Ops, Westphal, it was taken completely by surprise. In conversation with the author, Westphal cited Theseus as an example of one operation that "certainly was not betrayed."

the whole of the 5th Panzer Regiment of those unloaded in Tripoli in March 1941. The crew was most upset to a man because they were not allowed to drive that nice General Crüwell about anymore. But during the January advance a torsion bar had broken in the suspension. The four men had taken turns for three days and nights trying to drill through the steel rivets with a hand bit and brace; but in the end the Panzer had to go to the workshops where, as they had feared, the company had immediately commandeered it.

Saenger had time to say good-bye to the general, who was quite sad, too, and said: "Don't worry, I'll ask for you again. You are, after all, my Panzermen." But so far nothing had happened, and the serious business of life began again. Suddenly there was shooting, shells whistled about them and trucks with unfamiliar infantrymen were racing through their columns. Some keeled over in the fire; men were running and collapsing. Somewhere to one side, a small anti-tank gun was firing, but a Panzer IV straddled it and a bursting HE shell threw it on its side. The first utterly unsuspecting British unit—the 3rd Indian Motor Brigade—had been surprised while brewing up its breakfast tea and simply overrun.

No German vehicle allowed itself to be held up. Orders were: Don't get involved in fighting—gain ground!

But a few kilometers farther on, a more serious adversary appeared. Fast midgets—Honeys—popped up over the shoulder of a gentle hill, rushed at the Panzers, steering a zigzag course, stopped to fire, and the next moment were off again in wild motion, kicking up the dust, almost impossible to catch, and full of fight like furious terriers. The radios crackled with calls and orders, in characteristic confusion as the steel crates worked their way northward. On the right wing, the 8th Panzer Regiment ran into the first of the American-built Grants. Captain Johannes Kümmel, the "Lion of Capuzzo," involved them in a frontal exchange of fire with his 1st Battle Group—an unpleasant task against these colossi, which exploited their superior range and not only straddled the Panzers with AP fire but also caused havoc with HE shells among the division's artillery, which was coming up from farther back.

Meanwhile Lieutenant Teege led the 2nd Battle Group against the right flank of the Grants, which were positioned rather badly, standing as they were close together in a hollow. When the British became aware of the danger, they started firing their little steel bullets from their 37 mm guns and began clumsily to re-form. But by then the Panzer IIIs' 50 mm AP shots were already crashing into their flanks. The two Grant squadrons lost sixteen of their tanks. The rest rumbled off northward, the little Honeys swarming around them. Saenger's No.

125 clattered along in the broad arrowhead of the pursuing Panzers, filled with the familiar stink of sweat mixed with cordite.

They stopped, fired, and drove on, automatically and without thinking much about it. In the swirling dust, Saenger suddenly saw, barely 50 meters in front of him, a howitzer with a mighty barrel into which gunners wearing soup-plate helmets were just heaving a shell: a 25-pounder! At such moments the fire orders learned at exercises become superfluous. "Fire, fire, fire!" Saenger roared and waited for the bang and the usual jolt. Nothing happened. He looked quickly down and saw his gunner fiddling with the dust wiper on his optical sight, then he looked wildly around, threw open the turret hatch and jumped out of the Panzer.

Saenger looked down into the throat of the gun, pulled his head in, heard a great crash, and was amazed to be still alive. A quick glance revealed that the British gunners, as nervous as their opponents, had shot to pieces one of their own Bren carriers right next to his Panzer. "Ram them!" he roared. From the Panzer next to his, machine-gun bullets ripped into the gun emplacement. Konrad Müller drove the Panzer forward, its engines roaring, and threw the gun on its side. Over on the right, some Panzers were burning, but others, also spitting fire, were rolling over howitzers. A few men in soup-plate helmets raised their hands up in the air; others disappeared in the dust and smoke.

Saenger looked about for his gunner. There was nothing to be seen, but there were some camel-thorn bushes nearby and he tentatively fired his pistol close to one of them. The young man crawled out from behind the bushes and, hanging his head, climbed in again. He had seen the gun only indistinctly, his optical sight being covered in dust. When Saenger roared his head off, he had been so startled that he had broken the handle off the dust wiper, whereupon the wiper had stuck on the lens and he had been quite unable to see anything. They both forgot this little rush of panic until many years later they ran into each other in Hamburg and with much pleasure relived their past perils.

Trouble at strongpoint Blenheim

The first clash behind the Bir Hacheim desert fortress had caught the British 4th Armored Brigade on the wrong foot too.

This despite the fact that they had been preparing themselves for just this moment for many weeks. It was one of those pieces of good fortune so rare in war that they had been able to pick the spot that best suited them for the coming fight, since the route the enemy's units would take around Bir Hacheim was predictable. Favorable positions were therefore prepared and surveyed, gun emplacements dug, hollows in the ground marked where tanks would be positioned, and every No. 1 in the brigade's artillery, as well as every tank commander, had established with careful ranging shots at what co-ordinates certain points in the terrain ahead could be accurately hit.

Optimistically, the position was christened "Blenheim," in memory of the British victory over the French and Bavarians between Blindheim (the English name for which is Blenheim) and Höchstädt in 1704.

Naturally, the prepared position was not permanently manned, and the enemy's air reconnaissance thus not given any opportunity to come to undesirable conclusions. The three armored regiments, the infantry, and the RHA artillery attached to them were camping out much more visibly 10 kilometers to the north. For it was obvious that in view of the enemy's long approach route, there would be time enough to man Blenheim at leisure.

Major "Shan" Hackett[5] was squadron leader of the 8th Hussars' squadron of Honeys, whose role was conceived as a screen of fast, stinging wasps in front of the two squadrons of mighty Grants. In the afternoon of 26 May, a degree of alert was ordered: Movements in strength on the opposite side indicated a possible attack.

In the evening, the state of alert was raised. They prepared the tanks for action and sent all unarmored vehicles to the rear. Oddly enough, the night passed without disturbance and only just before dawn was it reported that the regiment must be ready to leave for the Blenheim strongpoint immediately. Immediately after that, at first light, came the order: "Start now!"

Hackett alerted his squadron and moved it forward a little to give the Grants room to maneuver. With engines that had barely been given time to warm up, they raced up a slight incline which, one mile farther south, formed a rounded ridge. On the way there, the regimental commander radioed: "We've had a new report. It may mean that the enemy has already advanced past Blenheim."

The only reply there was to that was a swear word, with the microphone switched off. They clanked on, and the earphones crackled again: "It could be that we'll be seeing the enemy much sooner than we expect. Report immediately you have contact."

[5] Sir John (knighted after the war for his services) commanded a parachute brigade in the Arnhem raid in 1944. Badly wounded, he avoided capture with the help of some Dutch resistance fighters, became a general, then C-in-C, BAOR, and a senior NATO commander. On retirement, he began a new, academic career as Principal of King's College, London. Nowadays he is busy writing, in his picturesque mill in Gloucestershire, on English literature and his own subject, history.

At that moment they went over the top of the hill. Ahead, in the wide, flat desert under a huge dust cloud, something was moving that looked like "all the bloody fleets of battleships in the whole world." Ahead rolled the two Panzer regiments in arrowhead formation, behind them through the haze came the lorried infantry, artillery, and anti-tank guns.

Over the radio, the major simply said: "Am engaging now." Then he hoisted on his aerial the little black pennant which, in the old naval and cavalry tradition, meant "Attack."

The drivers of the Honeys stepped on the gas. They had developed a system to exploit to the best advantage the speed and maneuverability of the Honeys by steering an irregular zigzag course: The driver would put his foot right down on the floor, pull the right lever and count five; then the left lever for three, then right again for a count of some odd number or other. The result, taken together with the power of the Pratt & Whitney engines, was such a crazy course that only a marksman could have scored a hit on them. Or, of course, such a large number of Panzers that the air developed a distinct iron content. . . .

And that is what happened to Hackett. In all the excitement, he had forgotten to haul the black pennant in again; it always attracted the attention of the Panzer gunners. While he stopped to fire, a solid round crashed through the driver's shield. They jumped out and pulled the badly wounded driver from his seat. As they were doing so, the thing burst into flames and somewhat scorched Hackett.

A Honey from his squadron came past; he jumped on the engine cover and hung on behind the turret, one hand in the hair of the tank's commander. The noise of the battle was far too great for shouting, so he turned the head of the poor man—a very brave sergeant called Joel —toward whatever target was nearest at the time. Later, the sergeant told him: "There wasn't a lot of point in it, sir. It hurt so much, the way you were tearing at my hair, that my eyes were always full of tears, and I couldn't see the target at all."

Orders came over the radio to delay the Germans at least until the Grants had a chance to warm up their engines and get into battle position. But it was too late. This concentrated Panzer force fired so much steel that even the fast Honeys were smashed up one after the other and the remainder were pushed back. Most of the Grants fell victim to Lieutenant Colonel Teege's flank attack before they had become maneuverable.

Captain Armitage of the artillery, whose unit was attached to the 4th Armored Brigade, was caught out by the order to leave immediately for Blenheim, just as he was about to take his first cup of tea. His battery was to co-operate with the Brigade's infantry; he therefore drove over to the infantry colonel. They arranged to leave in ten minutes.

On the way back, Armitage heard a shell burst somewhere. With an uneasy feeling, he told his driver: "Step on it; there's something wrong here."

Happening to glance back, he saw three or four big Panzers bearing down on his little scout car at full speed. They managed to reach the battery—just about. Armitage gave his fire orders and the Panzers made a respectful swerve when they heard the mighty voice of the 25-pounders, before imperturbably resuming their northward course. Behind them followed a great cavalcade of lorry-borne infantry, armored cars, and anti-tank guns. The infantry colonel crossed the path of this column and was promptly taken prisoner.

In the confusion of the battle, Armitage managed to keep his battery more or less together. But others were overrun. The German progress seemed irresistible. Throughout all the fury of the battle, anger at their own commanders kept gripping the officers of the 4th Armored Brigade: Why the hell had they not been inside Blenheim? Surely it was impossible that this huge force, of some 10,000 vehicles, could have driven around the Bir Hacheim corner quite unnoticed? Perhaps, thought the men bitterly, those tough Panzer boys have chucked us out of here too; but they would surely have been the worse for it when it was over.

It is today difficult to ascertain how such a failure, hardly credible in this age of modern communications, could have occurred. For the headquarters of the 7th Armored Division, to which presumably both intelligence assessments and the reports of the reconnaissance units were sent, was overrun during Rommel's initial thrust and only fragments of the documents of those days remain in the archives. General Messervy, Division Commander of the original Desert Rats, was captured, but escaped back to his own lines again. It is difficult to resist the conclusion that for all his personal courage, this was a bit of bad luck for the Eighth Army.

Hackett earns displeasure

The momentum of the first thrust chased the regiments of the 4th Armored Brigade to within sight of the heights south of Tobruk, which had been soaked in so much blood during the November fighting. By the afternoon, Major Hackett had only seven Honeys left. Like the other squadron commanders, he had willy-nilly to give up the wild zig-zag attack technique and instead try to hold up the enemy's advance as long as possible from good cover behind dunes and hills, and then race at top speed behind the next ridge. Where the transport columns had got to, God only knew. But the problem was becoming urgent, since they were running out of fuel.

Just at the right moment, Hackett saw some tents to the north—a proper depot, where there was bound to be some fuel. He drove in and, as he braked in a great cloud of dust, found himself looking into a pair of staring eyes regarding him with a mixture of boundless revulsion and suspicion.

They belonged to an officer standing in the main square of the depot in a clean and well-pressed uniform. It made Hackett realize that he was in fact looking rather repulsive: A variety of parts of his second tank had been hit and most of what was hanging outside it had either been torn off or smashed; his own uniform had been charred when he was first hit; his face was black as a devil's and covered in grime.

A short while before, the security officers of the Eighth Army had been instructed in a circular to check the identity of any strangers thoroughly as a precaution against sabotage. The well-groomed officer climbed gingerly on the tank and, ignoring Hackett's brusque demand for fuel, said: "May I see your identity papers, please?"

The other six Honeys now rushed in among the tents, looking no more confidence-inspiring, and Hackett said: "If you don't give me some fuel, chum, you'll soon have other things on your mind than identity papers. Jerry is behind that range of hills over there and he's coming this way—pretty damned fast."

"That's precisely the line of talk we have been expressly warned about."

The major was saved the trouble of a reply, for a couple of light Panzers now clambered over the top of the ridge and fired between the tents. The four-gallon tins[6] appeared with amazing speed and were emptied into the tanks. Whole piles of them were still in the tents. The sad likelihood was that they would soon belong to Jerry.

But just now the light Panzer IIs disappeared like greased lightning when the Honeys came roaring out of the depot, for with their 20 mm guns they were definitely at a disadvantage. When Hackett reached a rise farther to the south, he could do nothing but watch while the HQ of the 7th Armored Division was being "put in the bag." The camp

---

[6] Four gallons=18 liters approximately. These canisters were among the handicaps of the British army: so flimsy that they were always splitting. Fuel trucks left an explosive trail behind them in rough country. Although this was universally known, the British never did manage to introduce a more sturdy container, something like the 20-liter "jerrycans," which you could even throw off a truck without any risk. Fuel losses in transit were sometimes as high as 40 percent.

was already surrounded by the Panzers and the thing was as good as over. An open staff car came to a halt beside him.

"Where is the HQ of the 7th Armored?" asked General Willoughby-Norrie, the Corps Commander.

"Down there, General," said Hackett. Before he could say anything more, the general's driver had stepped on his accelerator. "After him," roared Hackett to his driver.

The general was at first somewhat indignant when the Honey with the singed and filthy officer blocked his way, but then he was very grateful.

At about the same time, in the captured headquarters a German interpreter was looking thoughtfully at an elderly Britisher who stood morosely among the other prisoners. "Aren't you a bit old for a private?" he asked.

"You're right," the man said. "It's a ruddy disgrace they've called me up at my age." It was General Messervy, who had stripped the insignia from his uniform. He managed to escape the next night.

First shots with the Russian anti-tank gun

As usual, all sorts of vehicles lay strewn along the Panzerarmee's line of advance.

South of Bir Hacheim, four anti-tank gunners and a warrant officer were standing somewhat cluelessly around a truck, behind which was hitched a gun new to the desert: a 762 mm anti-tank gun captured from the Russians, second only to the eighty-eight as the best anti-tank gun in the world.

One of the soldiers was the nineteen-year-old Günther Halm from Hildesheim. He had joined up in August 1941, but had already been fully trained, not only as an anti-tank gunner but also as a machine gunner.[7]

Only nobody knew what to do with the Russian gun. It had been issued to them just before the operation began.

And then their truck had to go and break down. It looked as if the fuel feed was blocked somewhere. They stripped the air filter; one of

---

[7] This arose from a special order by Rommel: Anti-tank gunners were to be able to serve machine guns and infantrymen were to know how to fire an anti-tank gun. Before the May attack, he himself supervised this training program. In Major Ehle's unit, this gave rise to an incident: A Grenadier (infantryman) produced a camera during gunnery practice and snapped the C-in-C. There was the usual army reaction: yelling and a general impression that the end of the world had come. But Rommel, himself a keen photographer, put on his best camera face and was clearly delighted.

them sat on the mudguard and dripped gasoline into the feed line, until a jet of flame shot from the carburetor. Cursing, they put out the fire in the carburetor and looked around. A little farther on stood an abandoned British scout car, a large drum of fuel next to it. Out of sheer boredom, they fired at the barrel with their pistols. After the first three shots, a tall figure emerged from behind it and approached them slowly with hands held high: It was an Indian from the 3rd Motor Brigade—a bearded and turbaned Sikh.

His small car had a flat tire. They stripped out the fuel pump, but of course it didn't fit their truck engine. While they were still struggling with it, a large British column of at least 150 vehicles drove under a cloud of dust some 500 meters away.

They threw themselves at the gun, instead of sensibly taking cover, and managed somehow to open the breech and to shove a shell into the barrel. But the brute would not fire.

At last they found the safety catch. The gun went off with a great bang, but after the third shot it was sitting under the truck: It recoiled so violently that the trail had to be dug into the stony desert ground each time it was used.

The British column drove on, but two armored cars seemed to have hostile intentions. The anti-tank gunners attached their truck to the scout car and, puffing and panting, managed to get the whole tow train into motion. The warrant officer stood on the seat to examine the enemy with his field glasses and immediately fell off into the desert. They had braked hard, and the truck naturally rammed them. Three men ran around to the back and aimed the gun, which luckily made the armored cars turn away. They need hardly have worried since the runback of the gun was so full of sand that the barrel had stuck in the recoil position.

They had some trouble joining their unit again, but they made it in the end. It had been a somewhat inauspicious start, but they had learned a lot about their gun.

A special unit put to unforeseen use

Lieutenant Hans-Günter Buchholz was as unhappy as only a twenty-one-year-old can be whose truck gets stuck fast immediately after the start of an advance. The tall Citroën—one of 1,500 trucks delivered by the French in Tunisia under a special intergovernment agreement—had had it: sump smashed by something.

His first action in Africa, his first as an officer . . . He gave his men a few orders and ran off to find something drivable that would take him where the war was.

They belonged to Special Unit 288, also known, after its commander, as Combat Group Menton. At the time of the Ostland euphoria, this unit had been set up with high hopes: As soon as the subhumans had been finished off, an advance through the Caucasus and Persia was to secure the oil wells of the Gulf for Greater Germany. From there, even India was not far distant from the phantasies of the planners; and there, they would at last join hands with Germany's Japanese brothers-in-arms.

The hardcore force for these tasks was Special Unit 288, just short of a brigade in strength. It contained crack units from all branches of the German army: anti-tank men, Alpine troops, engineers, and even three of the new "assault guns,"[8] as well as a company of the "Brandenburgers"[9]—all were there, as well as some AA guns and artillery, of course. But the most important component was a group of interpreters with their own print unit, who knew all the languages between the Caucasus and India, from Arabic and Persian dialects to Hindi, Urdu, and Sanskrit. There was also a group of highly specialized technicians and chemists attached to the unit, who were immediately to seize the oil wells and make them flow again, even should demolition work have been done to them.

When it became obvious that these plans would, to say the least, have to wait a while—which was just about when Rommel's troops had suffered some of their worst casualties—the 288th minus interpreters and technicians was sent to Africa. During loading in Piraeus, one of the assault guns fell into the harbor. Another ventured too far forward before the start of the May 1942 offensive and—to everyone's horror —was nabbed by the British.

Buchholz was an infantryman. Because there were not enough vehicles for all, the column commanders drew lots to decide who would stay with the supply group. Buchholz won and was thus allowed to ride. They overloaded their Citroën with fuel and ammunition and the men sat on top of this explosive mixture. For good measure, they were towing an anti-tank gun behind them.

During the night they drove on the right wing of the immense army column, coughing and cursing in the all-enveloping cloud of dust. There was another handicap: All lights were forbidden, as was all radio traffic. To help them navigate, the Luftwaffe bombed Bir Hacheim with incendiaries and released flares over the strongpoint. That would not attract any special notice. But only in the vanguard group and on the

[8] A short 75 mm self-propelled gun on a Panzer chassis, heavily armored. Differed from normal tank in having no turret.

[9] 800th Special Duty Brandenburg Training Regiment. Similar to Rangers or Commandos. Consisted of specialists trained for operations behind enemy lines.

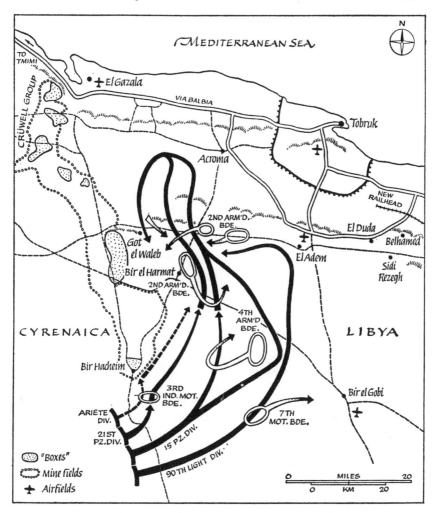

The 1942 May offensive: After rigorous thrusts to a point south of El Adem and almost to the Via Balbia, Rommel's forces must withdraw to a caldron east of Got el Waleb. The situation is awkward; but Ritchie hesitates, until the Panzerarmee manages to knock a hole to the rear through the Gazala Line and regains its freedom of movement.

left wing could one now and then catch a glimpse of these fireworks through the swirling dust. Everyone else just rolled along with the great stream. It worked surprisingly well.

And then the sump [crankcase] went kaput. Buchholz told his men: "You've got water and food enough for the time being. See what you

can do about that sump." And with that, he and Warrant Officer
Gerhard Theyson hopped on an already grossly overloaded Volkswagen jeep belonging to another unit.

The stranded men were at first quite contented to lie down in the
shade. On the third day they began to think it a bit strange that not one
other vehicle had come past them the whole time they had been there.
Eventually, Warrant Officer Moser set out to walk to the coast. He undertook the 60-kilometer march through the desert with half a canister
of water over his shoulder. Half dead with thirst, he arrived at the Via
Balbia, was lucky enough to get hold of a senior officer of the Quartermaster's Department, who said: "Not to worry, the boys won't let your
lot die of thirst out there." He laid on a Fieseler Storch and even a
Citroën sump. On the first flight Moser couldn't find the truck: Everything looks so different from the air. They took off a second time and
found that Moser's comrades had been saved from dying of thirst: Two
enemy armored cars were just nabbing them and setting the truck on
fire with their guns.

A solitary assault gun

With a lot of luck, Lieutenant Buchholz found his unit again. The VW
jeep put him down by the battalion command post, where a hyperac-
tive lieutenant was prancing about nervously. Buchholz simply followed the sound of the guns. Soon he saw the surviving assault gun
standing all by itself with nothing else in sight, shooting away at something. The light solid rounds of British anti-tank guns were bouncing
off its heavy frontal armor, ricocheting skyward. There was also a
heavy machine gun and its crew of three. They too were from the
288th.

As he went on, Buchholz collected a few engineers who had obviously
not been told by anyone what they were supposed to be doing. He
clambered on the gun, the crew of which was commanded by a jolly
and relaxed sergeant major, inspected the country around about, and
took over the fire direction.

Visibility was still good—the heat haze had not yet set in. Enemy armored cars were creeping about behind a fold in the ground just ahead.
With his binoculars, he could also make out the tops of some transporters. The assault gun's HE shells quickly set the transporters on
fire and Buchholz was able to move forward a stretch. But it had not escaped the attention of the men in the reconnaissance cars that this
strange-looking monster could shoot only forward.

"Look out, there are a couple of armored cars lurking about to the
left of that burning truck," Buchholz said. The engine roared into life;

the crew of the assault gun really did its work thoroughly: The thing turned on its own axis on screeching tracks and was immediately on target. "AP round," said the sergeant major. The first shot stopped one of the cars with a clearly visible jolt. The other one tried to run for it and was at least winged. They rumbled on after it for a while, rolled over some barbed wire, and suddenly found themselves in a strongpoint. Some infantrymen threw hand grenades out of their foxholes; they went off somewhere without doing any harm. Then the sappers came up and the men in the soup-plate helmets put their hands up.

Buchholz gathered his prisoners behind the assault gun, onto the thick hide of which small-arms fire was still pattering. But then an enemy mortar began to shoot uncomfortably accurately. The thirty or so prisoners didn't like it any more than their captors. Buchholz shepherded them into a great hole, which offered some sort of cover, and left three of the sappers to guard them. The men with the heavy machine gun came up, panting. It was time to do something about that mortar. Buchholz climbed back into the assault gun. Someone from the group of prisoners threw a Mills bomb after them, but that did no damage either.

The assault gun, with its short, fat barrel, must have been a terrifying sight head on. The mortar fire stopped. They could see people jumping up and running for their vehicles. The machine gun barked. "HE," said the relaxed sergeant and one truck after another went up in flames.

They looked around: A sizable strongpoint was taken, and they had not even been trying. The battalion command post, which was stationed in a hollow, had known nothing about it. The nervy lieutenant gave Buchholz a mighty tongue-lashing for going off on his own the way he had.

A line of eighty-eights stops the Grants

It became evident in the course of the first day that despite its initial successes, the Panzerarmee's position was not far removed from a disaster. True, the Third (Indian) Motor Brigade had been scattered to the winds, the 4th Armored Brigade badly battered, and the vanguards of both Panzer divisions and of the 90th Light were standing just south of the coastal road; but it was hard to decide just who was actually boxed in: the British troops in the Gazala line, who now found themselves between the unmotorized parts of the German-Italian army and the spearhead of Rommel's attack; or perhaps this spearhead, which had the Gazala line to the left of it and the British motorized and mechanized forces to the right of it?

What was sure was that the supply position of the well-provisioned

British in the "boxes" of the Gazala line was better than that of the attacking German troops. On the very first day British combat groups south of Bir Hacheim began to hunt down the supply columns without mercy. In any case, the Italian infantrymen who, with a stiffening of a German brigade group, were making diversionary attacks under General Crüwell[10] on the northern part of the Gazala line had the nastiest job and brought no relief: Frontal attacks on British infantry in well-built positions backed up by 25-pounders and Matildas are not exactly fun. A preparatory Army Order dated 28 May 1942 examined the likely reactions of the British. It was possible, the order said, that the enemy tank units would move sideways or southeastward during the German-Italian thrust to the north. A flanking attack might then be made by them. But this possibility was not judged very likely: "The above eventuality presupposes a great deal of keenness in response and much adaptability in execution on the part of the British command. Previous experience suggests that the enemy is not likely to take such decisions."

But that was precisely the decision he did take. True, the British still did not manage to gather their tank forces into a single concentrated thrust. Nevertheless, the brigades of the 1st and 7th Armored Divisions, which had either in fact turned east or had been alerted there, thrust into the extended flank of Rommel's Panzerarmee. All hell broke loose in the afternoon on 29 May. The heat haze distorted all contours into grotesque shapes as they came charging on, trailing a huge cloud of dust behind them: the fast Honeys and Cruisers in front, the swaying turrets of the big Grants behind.

Supply trucks, radio units, half-tracks with infantry on board, artillery tractors—all stampeded away in wild flight. Rommel himself was caught up in the stampede and, foaming with rage, was forced to flee, while his escorting force, the Kiehl battle group, put up a defense with its eighty-eights and anti-tank guns, knocking out eight of the attacking Cruisers.

But the flank of the great worm of the German army was 10,000 vehicles long. The British tanks broke into it in several places and laid about them with guns and machine guns. Panic broke out. General Nehring and the officer commanding the AA Regiment, Colonel Wolz, chased around in their open cars, picking eighty-eights out of the stream of vehicles whirling past them.

Rommel, evidently with the same idea in mind, came up in a cloud of dust, managing to find time to throw a few thunderous words at the AA gunners. "I shook myself a bit and threw myself at the guns," Wolz later reported. Soon the eighty-eights were hurling their 10-kilogram

---

[10] Lieutenant General Walther K. Nehring commanded the Afrika Korps.

solid rounds at the tanks. Lieutenant Heinrich Dammann from Eimke on the Lüneburg Heath had his battery set up in good time. His gunners knocked out a whole row of British tanks but drew the attention of those that remained.

Pouring with sweat, his men toiled away—the gunlayers ("K-2s") worked at their cranks, muscular loaders ("K-3s") pushed the heavy shot into the barrel. British tanks, black smoke billowing from them, came to a halt closer and closer to the battery; their dying crews did their comrades one last service: The oily pall from their burning vehicles provided cover for them.

A Cruiser broke into their position, firing. The men threw themselves down. The tank rammed one of the guns and rolled over the trails— none of which did the solidly built gun much harm. One gunner lay pressed close up against one of the trails. Even over the roar of battle, you could hear his screams as the squeaking track rolled over him. Bombadier Emil Berner, a girlishly handsome young lad from Stetten am Hohentwiel, jumped on the gun, cranked the barrel around and fired his solid round at the Cruiser at a range of 40 meters. The turret flew off; no one in the crew was seen to move after that.

But the man by the trail, over whom the tank had rolled, slowly and rather stiffly stood up again. The trail had protected him, and he got away with only a few superficial bruises.

Günther Halm's Russian anti-tank gun, fired personally by Rommel, also had a say in this matter. When the huge silhouettes of the tanks loomed up in the shimmering air, the C-in-C came up from the rear in an open half-track and drove a little way toward them, binoculars at his eyes. An HE shell, evidently from a Grant, burst in front of his car. It drove a little to one side and stopped again. Rommel went on looking.

Only when they were getting too close for comfort did he come tearing back; he pulled up by the anti-tank gun and said: "Watch out lads —they're right behind me. Don't let any of them get past you!"

Fifty meters farther back, Rommel stopped in a hollow. The first shots at some actual tanks—right under the eye of their C-in-C. . . . Just as well they had trained for this in the desert. They knocked out two of the British Grants; the formation turned away; Rommel drove past them and called over: "Well done, lads!" And was off after the tanks.

The desert was littered with smoking wrecks when the brigades at last turned away. An inflexible British command had once again made them run up against superior German defense gunnery without coordinating the sequence in which the different arms would go into action: The artillery had once again turned up too late.

Before the sun sank, Halm and another gunner wandered over to two burnt-out wrecks some 1,800 meters away. To their horror, they saw snow-white skeletons in one of them. But when you are nineteen, you soon forget, and the enemy helped them to: Suddenly two British armored cars appeared and chased them around the wrecks with bursts from their machine guns—until at last the rest of the German gun crew took notice and lobbed across a shell that chased the armored cars away. Rommel had long gone on ahead, driving restlessly up and down the column like a man possessed, always suspicious that someone, especially a tank crew, might be slacking.

"What will you do with that Panzer when you are ready?"

Thus questioned by their C-in-C, the crew of which Werner Fenck was the gunner sprang to attention in regulation style. On top of a long day of uninterrupted fighting, their track had been stripped. Now they were busy trying to let in some reserve links to do an emergency repair job.

"The Panzer must go to the workshop, Herr General," said the commander, a lieutenant.

"Who gave you orders to do that?"

"The mechanical engineer officer, Herr General."

Rommel inspected the barrel—it was one of the new long ones—worth at least three of those on the Cruisers stumbling around on the other side.

"My respects to the engineer officer and tell him he's a great arsehole." He drove on, possibly thinking that he could hardly insist on sending the Panzer back into action with a loose track. The story went around the regiment after Operation Crusader that he had kicked the backside of a sergeant major, who was on his way back to the rear with a Panzer that was only slightly damaged, and had chased him back to the front, brandishing a pistol.

General Lumsden's fit of rage

On the first day of Theseus, Rommel's worries were no smaller than they had been at the end of November. A third of his Panzers were out of action. The enemy's mechanized forces, however, were still intact, despite their losses. The "boxes" were being much more energetically defended than had been assumed and their minefields were more extensive than had been forecast.

The Commander of the Afrika Korps at that time, Walther Nehring, who today lives in Düsseldorf (and who gives a much younger impression than his age—eighty-four when I interviewed him—being a keen huntsman and driver), is actually mildly critical of Rommel: "In this respect Rommel was rather like Hitler, with whose methods I became familiar in Russia. He would make a plan, deploy his force, and go ahead in the firm conviction that it would go just as he had planned and that the enemy would have no choice but to react as expected. This artificial box system that the British had built there in the desert would, he thought, collapse under an energetic thrust. But they were determined and brave, those British, and they made us look a bit silly. . . . He was a hell of a lad all right, was Rommel; and the way he then brought it off after all—that was something quite wonderful." At any rate, his plans did assume an enemy who would give him respite to recover his breath and regroup. The British obliged. And that had to do with the successful escape of their divisional commander, Messervy.

When, on the afternoon of May 27, it became known that the Germans had put HQ 7th Armored in the bag, complete with General Messervy, Ritchie placed the brigades of the 7th under the commander of the 1st Armored Division, Herbert Lumsden. Together with parts of the army tank brigades in the north (Matildas and Valentines) a formidable mechanized fighting force thus came under a unified command, and Lumsden was determined at long last to use the force in concentrated form.

But Messervy escaped during the night and immediately announced that he wanted to be master in his own house again. In particular, he would not make any unit available for an attack until the whole outfit had been rehabilitated and reorganized. He was waiting for two regiments, one infantry and one fresh from the Delta and now being unloaded at the new railhead of the line which had been extended into Libya—near Belhamed, southeast of Tobruk.

General Lumsden heard the news that he must give up all the units of the 7th Armored on the radio of his tank, just as he was preparing to attack. Apart from the loss of the tanks, what hurt particularly was that all the available artillery was gone once more.

Lumsden tore his beret from his head, threw it into the desert, trampled on it, and used expressions absolutely unworthy of a British general. Then he ran the attack by himself, with his reduced formation and without artillery. Jack Ladenberg, Liaison Officer from the 8th Hussars, who despite the changed command structure did not want to leave the general by himself in such a mood, reported later, greatly impressed, that he had behaved like a man who had gone berserk, raging on top of his tank under fire, and had generally given the impression that he really wouldn't mind if his head were blown off.

Courage blind with fury is naturally quite useless against superior weapons skillfully used. The 1st Armored Division suffered further heavy losses.

Since on this May 28 there was again no concentrated attack on the widely separated German units—the 90th Division was temporarily cut off far in the north near El Adem, and the Panzer divisions were unable to help, partly because they were short of fuel and ammunition— Rommel could permit himself to heave a cautious sigh of relief. Little by little he pulled together his units east of the Gazala line along the Trigh el Abd desert track. Although they were sitting in a trap, it looked as if it would not be sprung on them. And they immediately set about drilling a hole in the back of it.

The sappers began to lay out a path to the west through the minefield. The Italians had already found a secret track from the other side of the Gazala line, but it was not suitable for supply use.

A race against time began. During a period lasting several days, had the British mounted a major attack they would have found a force that was not only short of fuel and ammunition but was uncertain of itself. Everyone understood how weird their situation was. The noise of battle could be heard from time to time from all points of the compass. Water was short, washing had long been forbidden, on top of which thirst set everyone's nerves on edge. Men who were badly wounded, had suffered burns, or had been mutilated lay moaning and screaming at the first-aid posts and could not be taken to the rear. Rumors were circulating to the effect that Rommel, Crüwell, or Nehring—first one, then another— was dead or captured.

The better of those two fates had in fact befallen one of them: General Crüwell was captured.

Saenger had heard him say: "I don't like those Fieseler Storchs. Tinny things." He was right. On the morning of 29 May he wanted to be flown to the front to lead a new attack from the west on the Gazala line. It was arranged that as the machine approached, flares would be fired. Something went wrong and the little aircraft found itself over the British lines. The cockpit was riddled by infantry fire. Luckily for Crüwell, the joystick stuck in the neutral position so that the machine flattened out and landed with relatively little damage, even though in a British "box."

A friendly British cook grilled the captive general a huge steak. Then Crüwell was taken to Cairo. Not until much later did Saenger hear of the sad loss, which affected him and his crew in particular: no more chauffeuring for Corps HQ. Faced with dark looks from the company commander when they rejoined their unit, they had long since got rid of the field-kitchen chimney.

The gloomy mood did not spare the higher ranks. The two Chiefs of Staff, Gause and Bayerlein, in all innocence, made a suggestion to Rommel: How would it be if they fought their way back to the west again and announced to the world at large that it had all been only a reconnaisance sweep which had gone absolutely according to plan?

It is fairly certain that they thus stiffened the resolution of an until then hesitant Rommel. For he would have nothing to do with resorting to such shifts, bawled the two men out, and was again quite sure what he was doing: It was bad enough to have to go on the defensive for the time being. But there was no road leading back, and decisions of this sort were still for him alone to take.

"The man grew immensely in stature in proportion with his task," Siegfried Westphal said when I interviewed him. In saying that, he touched on a point that is important in any sort of historiography, and is all too often neglected: Events chip away at every man; what remains under these influences depends on the material he is made of. Rommel's personal record, particularly after the African campaign, shows that he was by no means made of the worst stuff. In the caldron at the Trigh el Abd, he proved that he was no longer the tearaway attacker of 1941. He stood like a battered boxer, but one who is still in control of himself, both fists covering his face, peering around his glove to see what the other fellow is up to.

Ritchie has often been blamed for leaving Rommel pretty much alone, sitting holding the bag. What is certain is that the great opportunity was wasted on the morning of the second day, when Messervy escaped. Then, the Panzerarmee lay stretched out, partly already encircled, its momentum gone. Probably even in the subsequent days an energetic thrust by all British forces, especially if spearheaded by the two fresh thick-skinned brigades of infantry tanks from the north, could have concluded the African campaign. With every day the strong defensive front of heavy weapons, now being created with typical Rommel skill, improved and it was bound to have been a gruesome massacre. But one has to remember that such a massacre took place later anyway, to be sure this time with the British on the defensive. . . .

General Nehring is now not quite sure whether Rommel was not still keeping open the option in his mind of escaping through the back door, while work went ahead with great haste every night on the lane through the minefield. Astonishingly enough—either the aerial reconnaissance was no good or a navigational error was made in planning the lane—the route ended up right opposite one of the British boxes garrisoned by the 50th Brigade and a regiment of infantry tanks.

Unsuspecting, the German Afrika Korps moved off to the west on the night of 30 May. General Nehring, with Bayerlein, drove in the leading group in an armored car.

At break of day they reached a height.

They pulled up and marveled. As from a seat in a theater box, they saw at their feet an unexpected war game: Men in soup-plate helmets were running about; there were barbed-wire entanglements, tanks, and artillery, all firing away merrily at the Italians to the west of them.

Rommel came tearing up at his usual pace, allowed himself only a brief, astonished look and made his decision: "We attack." It took them seventy-two hours to clear the "box" out of their way. The Panzers stuck fast in the mine belts, 25-pounders thundered away in among them over open sights, and a new anti-tank gun, the six-pounder[11] made its appearance. The British had, in fact, managed for the first time to design something with powerful penetration, to build it, and to get it to the front, even if in only limited numbers.

Major Curt Ehle's rifle battalion bore the main burden of the infantry fighting—but without its commander.

During a briefing, Ehle stood beside General Nehring in Lieutenant Dammann's AA battery when suddenly a fighter-bomber came diving down out of the sun. Everyone threw himself flat, but one shell went through Ehle's right hand, tearing an artery. It was all over in a moment; everyone got up, Ehle cut a smart salute, and tried to report himself wounded to the general, who jumped back in horror: Ehle's blood was spurting in his face.

After first aid from the gunners, Ehle was driven to the hospital in Derna along the secret track. He ended up in the same room as General Gause and Lieutenant Colonel Westphal.

Gause had a concussion: A shell burst had knocked his head against the side of his armored car. Westphal had a great piece of shrapnel in the upper part of his thigh, for which he had his own sheer cussedness to blame. The G1 Ops had driven forward with Rommel in his reconnaissance vehicle to the Got el Waleb box to make sure that the co-ordination with the Stukas was all right: Shortly beforehand they had by mistake given some pretty rough treatment to a battery of eighty-eights.

They ran into artillery and mortar fire. Rommel withdrew under the armored part of the car and called out: "You come too, Westphal." But they had quarreled shortly beforehand and, sulking, he stayed outside. Shortly afterward he felt something strike his leg and he flew out of the vehicle. The great eight-wheeler armored car immediately drove to cover. It was Westphal's good fortune that two officers who had followed the armored car in an open jeep looked after him, dragged him out of the line of fire, and took him to Army HQ, where Rommel had meanwhile spread the news that he must be presumed dead.

[11] The six-pounder gun (57 mm caliber) had been built in prototype form at the start of the war. But after the loss of all the army's *matériel* at Dunkirk, the ill-starred decision was made not to experiment, but to mass-produce the "well-proven" two-pounder.

Westphal, too, was brought out to the western side by car along the hidden track by night. Mindful of Crüwell's fate, he absolutely refused to let himself be flown out in a Storch ambulance, saying: "What do you mean, Storch ambulance? Who on earth can see that Red Cross against this blinding sun?"

The drive along the secret track became a torture no wounded man with head or internal injuries could have survived, for the whole of the route was under artillery fire and drivers using the track went through with foot hard down on the floor. But the desert, most of which looks so flat, is no race track. Around the tough roots of the camel-thorn bushes, drifting sand gathers into hard ridges and vehicles go crashing through such country, bouncing and swaying. Westphal's batman and a medical orderly took turns to kneel on him.

He arrived in Derna in such a state that after a fleeting glance, the medics shoved him into the mortuary, from where, just as coolly, they fished him out again ("He doesn't seem to be dead after all"), when he came to and called out. They laid him next to a young soldier, whose right arm had been amputated and who kept calling out in his feverish delirium: "All this for Tobruk." "For me, that went home," writes Westphal in his memoirs.

Field Marshal Kesselring burst into the ward where Grause, Westphal, and Ehle eventually met, bustling as ever, reading the wounded men a long lecture about Rommel's habit of knocking around among the frontline troops. He attributed the ineffectiveness of his Stukas to this habit of the C-in-C's, as a result of which radio contact with him kept being lost.

But Major Ehle had been visited by some of the reserve officers posted to his battalion to replace the casualties, who had brought him some bottles of champagne. Ehle was thus in a mild trance and not in the least bothered by any of this.

2. Not a Chance for Tobruk

A massacre of Stukas over Bir Hacheim

Meanwhile back in the desert, people went on fighting and dying. The peculiar logic of war had appointed Got el Waleb, a godforsaken speck of sandy waste, to be such an important place that all of a sudden it seemed worth rivers of blood.

The German infantrymen and sappers were working themselves forward through the wire and the minefields, suffering substantial losses. But exhausted troops who had been bled white lay on the other side too. On 1 June only eight Matildas of the 1st Army Tank Brigade were still fit for action. Tank and artillery ammunition was running short.

Heinrich Dammann's battery of eighty-eights was getting its HE shells ready. When one has been fighting mostly tanks, one always has plenty of those on hand. They were to support the penetration. The lieutenant had forty shells stacked by every gun and gave orders for them to be fired off as fast as possible, without individual fire orders. With the fast eighty-eights, that sort of thing always results in a race between the gun loaders, who try to outdo each other. They thus sent a mighty heap of ironmongery over to the other side and enabled the 8th Panzer Regiment to negotiate the lane through the minefield.

Rommel himself was with the infantry, true to his principle that the men should always and everywhere have to reckon with a visit by their C-in-C. Once again the Stukas pulverized the British positions. The ar-

tillery fired air bursts, making the men in the machine-gun and anti-
tank emplacements keep their heads down. The remnants of the brigade surrendered in the afternoon. The way to the west stood open.
Ritchie had made no attempt to intervene from the east. The British
Eighth Army had wasted another chance.

Rommel no longer hesitated. The hole knocked in the Gazala line
would not be an avenue for retreat; it would serve to set the supply
trucks rolling again at last. He needed the newly delivered Panzers, as
well as those that had been repaired, and, in addition, fuel and ammunition. For now he saw his chance to eliminate altogether the static elements artificially built in by the British, and to make the desert once
more into the sort of battlefield that suited him—a wide, free-ranging
space for mobile units.

Ritchie's failure to attack and exploit the opportunities of the moment while considerable German-Italian forces were busy in the west—
standing by more or less idly while his 150th Brigade with its infantry
tanks was being destroyed—arose from a total misapprehension. Rommel was clearly making off, he informed Auchinleck; and his C-in-C
had signaled back delightedly from Cairo: "Well done, Eighth Army!
Keep it up!" The awakening was terrible.

One can safely assume that the Rommel of 1941 would have immediately rushed straight for Tobruk. Such a "shifting of the center of
gravity," so typical of him, would certainly have led to the collapse of
the rest of the Gazala line. But the shock of the last days of May had
gone deep; his next move came with true Rommel speed—but it was
strictly according to the textbook. Hardly had Got el Waleb been taken
than he and Bayerlein, who was standing in for Westphal as Army G1
Ops, jumped into a jeep and went streaking off to Bir Hacheim, the
southernmost pillar of the Gazala line, at which the Ariete and the
Italian infantry had been so far hammering away in vain.

The 4,000 Free French[1] there were holding a well-constructed
strongpoint with concrete emplacements and deep, virtually bombproof
dugouts. But now Rommel brought up heavy artillery, and Kesselring's
Stukas mashed up the whole fortified area.

The cumbersome Ju-87s, which were particularly vulnerable while
diving, were, however, falling victim to the British AA guns in alarming numbers. These pilots, much envied by the "footsloggers" because
after a sortie they could crowd around a bar, eat Hermann Göring's
grand food, and mostly sleep in proper beds,[2] were performing unbe-

---

[1] Reinforced by other units, including British heavy ack-ack, but no "Jewish
Battalion" as has been again and again reported.

[2] Favorite Wehrmacht joke: A pilot is like Joseph because he "wears a coat of
many colors and thinks himself better than his brothers."

lievable feats. Again and again, they climbed into their battered birds to provide the enemy with target practice, without any hope of the successful fighter pilot's glamour and glory, and certain of a death which might not always be quick but was always ugly.

At Bir Hacheim, the odds against them worsened by a further and decisive point: The man who lies for days on end under merciless bombardment develops an atavistic hate for the men in those thunderbirds. This applied particularly to the native levies from the French colonies.[3] Hardly one Stuka pilot who baled out landed alive. The German troops in their positions all around the strongpoint saw again and again the tracer from the machine-gun bursts aimed at those bodies dangling so helplessly from their parachutes.

On 3 June, South African fighters shot down nine Stukas out of a formation over Bir Hacheim, despite the fact that it was escorted by German fighters, one of them piloted by the renowned Jochen Marseille, the most highly decorated pilot in the German Luftwaffe. He shot down six of the South Africans in eleven minutes, although his cannon jammed after ten rounds and he could use only his machine guns.

Jochen Marseille had a unique tactic in a dogfight: As far as one can reconstruct it from eyewitness accounts, he tried to avoid aerobatics if possible, since the fast BF-109 was no better at these than the slower but more maneuverable British machines. Instead he dived under full power into the middle of the enemy formation, throttled back, and pulled up sharply, just below the enemy machine he had picked for the kill.

The trick was that his sight would drift over the engine and cockpit of the enemy machine at exactly the moment when his own machine was completely stalled and practically unable to fly for a moment— hanging virtually motionless in the air. As soon as the decisive burst of fire—which with the keen-eyed Marseille was almost always a hit—had been delivered, the machine would go into a virtual crash dive—a maneuver no enemy could follow; and which he naturally executed at a sufficient altitude to recover and return for a new attack.

A few months after Bir Hacheim, on 30 September 1942, Captain Marseille lost his life in a crash. During a sortie over enemy-held Egyptian territory, the new—and apparently insufficiently tested—engine of his ME-109 burst into flames. At this time the front line had settled into a static war at El Alamein. There was no chance for a pilot

---

[3] This remark may earn me the reproach, silly though that may be, that I am a racist. But someone from a preindustrial society who is put in uniform and then exposed to this kind of merciless war has different—if you like more "natural"— reactions from those of the average European.

who had baled out to make his way back stealthily to his own side. Marseille, his cockpit completely filled with smoke, therefore tried to fly back westward over the front. He managed it, too, but must have been semiconscious by the time he baled out. He turned the machine upside down in the correct manner, jettisoned the cockpit canopy, and let himself fall out. When following this procedure (which was necessary before ejector seats were introduced), you pushed your joystick forward during the upside-down flight, so that the nose of the machine would go up and the airspeed was reduced.

In Marseille's case, however, his comrades who were flying with him saw to their horror that his plane, still upside down, dived away steeply, gathering speed. As a result, the pilot, as he was baling out, was struck by the tail fin, knocked unconscious, and crashed to the ground, unable to pull the ripcord of his parachute. Captain Marseille was not yet twenty-two.

According to postwar research by British and German fighter pilots,[4] which drew on the war diaries of both sides, the 158 victories credited to Marseille, who was decorated with the Knight's Cross and Diamonds, were most likely an exaggeration. But this can be easily explained: Marseille as a rule no longer bothered to report his victories himself but left this to one of his "wingmen," whose job it was to follow the progress of any machine that had been shot up and had gone into a dive or was pulling away in flames. The excitement of aerial combat, and the impression of infallibility conveyed by this star among the African fighter pilots, encouraged them to report as shot down many an opponent who had managed to pull out of his dive and to reach home on a wing and a prayer. But even objective research came to the conclusion that with well over a hundred victories to his credit, Marseille was still *the* ace fighter pilot.

A dagger in the sandbag

At Bir Hacheim, Rommel once again underestimated his opponent. After bloody and vain attacks by smallish units, Kesselring, highly indignant at the losses sustained by his pilots, flew in to warn Rommel that he must "batter, not dribble."

In addition to the infantry, elements of both Panzer divisions and of the 90th Light Division, as well as of Special Unit 288, were ordered to Bir Hacheim. Lieutenant Buchholz was again commanding a platoon and was in addition driving a captured truck, a Chevrolet, which was towing the 5 cm anti-tank gun. While negotiating a lane through a

[4] Christopher Shores and Hans Ring: *Fighters Over the Desert.*

minefield north of Bir Hacheim, they were shot at simultaneously by ground attack aircraft and artillery.

On the lorry sat fifteen men, again dangerously enthroned on ammunition and fuel. One soldier had a fragment as large as a hand fly through between his legs. The man was sitting on a 200-liter gasoline drum. The precious and inflammable stuff spurted out, but luckily did not catch fire. The same fragment also went through their keg of water, which was what most bothered the whole platoon.

You could see that the Ariete's attacks had by no means been halfhearted: Masses of wrecked Italian tanks littered the ground. Some soldiers drank the cooling water from these wrecks, which gave them bad diarrhea.[5] The ground was heavily mined and any movement at night resulted in casualties. The commander of the platoon next to his, Lieutenant Eberhard Grussendorf, from Lower Saxony, was among the casualties. His car was destroyed, but he got away with a concussion and was soon back with his unit. His platoon was taken over by Warrant Officer Gerhard Theyson.

The attacks they were making against concentrated fire from infantry weapons, and even field guns shooting at individual men with pinpoint accuracy, were a nightmare. Right at the start Theyson received an abdominal wound during a charge and died the next day.

The two platoons managed to make 800 meters of progress in eight days. By that time two thirds of their soldiers were dead or wounded. At night, patrols and raiding parties from the garrison would penetrate between their positions.

Buchholz had made himself a little command post among a group of wrecked tanks, which could be exploited as cover, and surrounded it with sandbags. One night when the battalion commander happened to be in the position to present Buchholz with his Iron Cross Second Class, they heard a swooshing sound, followed by a soft thud. Next morning there was a large Arab dagger sticking out of one of the sandbags. Hans-Günter Buchholz, now Professor of Archeology at Giessen University, has it hanging over his desk.

Meanwhile, farther to the north, the two German Panzer divisions and the Ariete were holding Ritchie's mobile forces in check. On 5 June, the 22nd Armored Brigade and a regiment of Matildas mounted an attack for which co-ordination with the infantry and artillery was astonishingly bad, even by the standards then prevailing in the Eighth Army. The tanks managed to push the Ariete back a bit, then ran into a line of eighty-eights and anti-tank guns without any support from

---

[5] Owners of vehicles on both sides sensibly did the opposite, as Peter Phillips reports vividly: They drank the cooling water before it was poured into the radiator and then peed into the radiator. It seemed to work all right, but smelled a bit.

other arms. Sixty tanks were lost, and irretrievably at that, since the battlefield remained in Axis hands.

Under Lieutenant Colonel H. R. B. (Fairey) Foote, two regiments of Matildas, reinforced by a squadron of Valentines, trundled forward behind a smokescreen which had been laid down ahead of them. A line of eighty-eights, undetected by reconnaissance and unmolested by other arms, attacked them in the flank. Amid the touching mixture of bravery and ineptitude which still characterized British actions, the two regiments went under. Colonel Foote's tank was knocked out and as he was transferring to another tank he was wounded in the neck. He lost his tank, too, and wandered around the battlefield on foot—one solitary, defenseless man among the steel monsters and flying steel. He directed his rapidly diminishing force with hand signals, traveled standing on top of tanks, and then had to retreat nevertheless with the 12 tanks remaining to him of the 82 which had gone into the battle. The thundering voice of the eighty-eight put an end to the history of the Matilda infantry tank. Production ceased the same year.

At this period the German monitoring service was entertained by the growing tendency of British commanders, in their perplexity, to converse with one another in open R/T traffic.

It became evident that here was a body in a state of disintegration. The absence of discipline, and the sheer bewilderment, offered unusual opportunities: Thus the staff of the Afrika Korps succeeded, by using the much-traveled son of a shipowner from Flensburg who could imitate the drawling accents of British officers perfectly, to confuse whole units, right up to divisional level, with counterfeit movement orders.

The gunner Armitage was present when the remnants of two of the 4th Armored Brigade's tank regiments made a halfhearted attempt to relieve the hard-pressed French at Bir Hacheim. They halted within sight of the fortress and watched the Stukas dive in their last attack. This time the Ju-87s were hardly bothered by fighters at all—the latter were busy, though with but indifferent success, with the tank battles in the north.[6]

On the night of 11 June, General Koenig broke out to the south with the remnants of his garrison. Some 2,000 men got out, some after bloody hand-to-hand fighting. In the morning a heavy ground mist lay over the desert. The troops who were to lead the decisive push in the north felt their way forward—into a void. Only 500 men, wounded or

---

[6] RAF pilots were told at the beginning of the battle that they should simply "ignore" the German air superiority (which consisted less of numbers than of the fighting power and performance of their machines) and to concentrate on attacking ground targets. Naturally, in practice nobody is so feeble-minded as to take no notice of an enemy fighter sitting on the back of his neck.

just left to their fate, were left in the fortified area. They offered virtually no resistance. They included some Foreign Legionnaires of German origin.

Hitler's orders burned

The brave fight put up by the Free French (in those days known as "Gaullists," after General de Gaulle) in Bir Hacheim was given prominence by the entire world press. The reasons were not military ones alone. The status as regular troops of these units, which had defected from the Vichy regime, was in some doubt. At any rate, the 22 June 1940 German-French armistice agreement stated:

> The French Government pledges itself not to undertake hostile actions of any sort against the German Reich with any part of the forces remaining under its control. The French Government will likewise prevent members of the French forces from leaving the country. . . . The French Government will forbid French citizens to fight against the German Reich in the service of States with which the German Reich is still at war. French citizens who contravene this agreement will be treated by German troops as armed insurgents.

Insurgents—that meant being shot out of hand. In Berlin, where assiduous lackeys with fine-sounding titles tried to prove their loyalty to the Führer by outdoing each other at striking bloodthirsty attitudes, the spokesman of the *Auswärtiges Amt*—the Nazi Foreign Office—intoned that this clause of the armistice agreement surely made this matter clear, and did not need to be further elucidated. In any case, "the buffoons who lead Senagalese Negroes and who, having been stationed somewhere or other by the British, have fallen into our hands simply do not matter all that much to us."[7]

But that wasn't enough. The Supreme Warlord himself was constantly on the lookout for the chance of a few more neat little murders on the fringes of the general butchery around about. Thus he instructed Panzerarmee Afrika via the Wehrmacht Command Staff that the political fugitives reported to be fighting with the Free French must be killed. This original order was initialed by quite exalted officers, although the designation of one recipient has been inked out by an unknown hand.

Clearly another order to commit murder was also transmitted to the Panzerarmee. Westphal already lay wounded in the hospital when this order, drafted on 9 June, arrived. However, when I interviewed him, he said: "An order also arrived in May 1942, in the form of a radio sig-

[7] *Neue Zürcher Zeitung*, 15 June 1942.

nal. I recall only the gist of it. At any rate, we were to kill immediately any Jewish soldiers who fell into our hands and not treat them as prisoners of war. I immediately told Rommel I thought it best to burn this straightaway. And that's what was done."

Unlike the 9 June order, I could not find this radio signal among the documents of the Panzerarmee Afrika although there were rumors among the men that prisoners had been shot at Bir Hacheim. However, such rumors probably originated in the ravings of chairborne heroes like the spokesman of the Auswärtiges Amt.

Inquiries at French and Israeli official quarters elicited only the reply that nothing was known about any shootings. Eventually, I found a surviving French Foreign Legionnaire of German origin who had been one of the defenders of Bir Hacheim and was captured on 11 June 1942. He is Herrmann Eckstein, a much decorated warrant officer of the Legion, now a pensioner in Baden-Baden.

He reported that he and his comrades had been treated fairly and decently by the German troops. There had been no shootings, since he was bound to have known of any there might have been. (But, Eckstein reported, their treatment by the Italians, who took all prisoners over in accordance with their agreement with the Germans, had been very bad indeed.)

Westphal plays the whole thing down: "In contrast with the commanders on all other fronts, we could afford simply not to do such things—we were far enough away from Berlin, after all. Nor was it pure magnanimity—although as a soldier one is highly sensitive about this. It simply isn't done to kill a man who has fought and given up. And then there were the interests of one's own troops to consider: When you become involved in such a thing, it immediately leads to a radicalization of the methods of warfare. That's why we didn't implement that later 'commando order'[8] either."

His attitude is particularly impressive, precisely because of its pinch of super-cool common sense: One must view it against the background of the important representatives of his profession who are only too adept at firing off great broadsides of pathetic and hollow phrases. Particularly when their complicity with the dictator, whom they so unanimously condemn in their after-dinner speeches, was quite substantial.

There were four groups the gentry in Berlin would gladly have seen killed: Gaullists, political refugees, Jews, and commandos. In Africa, to some extent in defiance of orders to the contrary, they were spared.

Even at this distance from the dictator, that took courage; it would

---

[8] Also from Hitler (Directive No. 46a, dated 18 October 1942): Members of commando units who conducted operations behind the lines were to be murdered, even if they were identifiable as soldiers by wearing normal uniform.

certainly have been more comfortable to follow the example of higher echelons—put one's initials on the paper and let things take their course.

Honest historiography will write the deeds that were not done at least as large as those that are in the textbooks.

A gunner in pajamas

Lieutenant Buchholz felt his way through the wire with the last of his men. Suddenly they were in the first strongpoint. It was almost totally abandoned; just two black soldiers raised their hands anxiously. They could hear the drone of approaching Stuka formations. Buchholz fired flares up through the mist. He could see others going up from elsewhere in the fortified area. A few premature bombs went off, then the Stukas turned away.

At this time, you had to act pretty fast if you wanted to get yourself some loot. There was a Panzerarmee order out which regulated "seizure" in the best possible manner: "Booty units" followed close on the heels of the fighting troops. Using stencils, they painted "German Army Property" and, in extra large letters, "TEDESCO" (German) as a warning to their dear allies to be kind enough to keep their fingers off it.

Buchholz and his men, therefore, scurried about the shattered masonry and dragged any food they could find to one side. They soon discovered that there were four-gallon gasoline tins buried all over the fortified area and prodded about the loose sand for them with sticks and bayonets—but carefully, because these British canisters sprang a leak if you as much as looked at them. Buchholz was able quite quickly to stow away enough fuel to last his Chevrolet for 1,000 kilometers.

His new anti-tank gunner, a man with an outstandingly sure aim, unearthed an officer's bag from somewhere and considered the light blue pajamas with white stripes in it so fetching that he immediately put them on, and thus clad ran around the fortress in search of more loot. Suddenly, a great commotion: "Special Unit 288! Fall in immediately! We're moving!"

In his haste, the anti-tank gunner couldn't find his uniform again—it was lying somewhere near the bag. For the immediate future, he was to wage war in light blue pajamas with white stripes—until a new battalion commander, fresh from home, took over, had a bad turn on catching sight of him and dished him out three days' CB for wearing nonregulation clothing.

Their hasty departure had been ordered by the C-in-C personally.

With immediate effect, he was shifting all his mobile units to the north, to cut off the garrisons of the upper tier of "boxes" and then take Tobruk.

At this stage it had become clear on the British side that things were going wrong; a spirit of resignation was taking hold. The Armored Brigades had gone into battle with 650 tanks between them. At least that number of Grants, Honeys, Cruisers, and Matildas was now strewn over the desert, for on 12 June, 285 tanks were still fit for service, but in the course of the battle at least 300 more had been moved up as reinforcements.

In a cautious interim report, Auchinleck told the Prime Minister that the Eighth Army had lost 10,000 men by 7 June, of whom 8,000 were "believed captured." A worried Churchill concluded from the large number of men taken prisoner that "something must have happened of an unpleasant character."

On 12 June, Auchinleck flew to Ritchie's HQ at Gambut and ordered a line running through Acroma—El Adem—Bir el Gobi to be held in mobile defensive fighting. It is clear that he was now only half expecting to be able to keep the enemy away from Tobruk. There was no doubt that should this line be breached, Tobruk would be lost. Auchinleck knew that the fortress could not be held against another prolonged siege. The most important factor here was Admiral Cunningham's appraisal that there was not the slightest prospect of supplies by sea, as in the previous year, his fleet being now virtually nonexistent.

The ever-drifting sand had again filled up anti-tank ditches and emplacements. Barbed wire rusts quickly in that climate. Tens of thousands of mines had been lifted from the perimeter to build the Gazala position. No one knew anymore where exactly there were intact minefields still. The heavy AA batteries had been dismantled and taken to Alexandria.

Tank Sergeant Reid still lay at Tobruk hospital, tormented by unceasing pain. One morning the chief medical officer came to his bedside and looked at him critically. "Do you think you could stand a journey?"

"If you mean what I mean, I'll run to Alexandria on my own two feet," Reid answered with some difficulty.

The next day they put him on board a hospital ship. A single gun was firing at the town and harbor of Tobruk from a great distance and at infrequent intervals. Reid dangled on his stretcher from the hook of a crane between the shattered quay and the ship as a shell burst with a great roar in the harbor basin, throwing up a big jet of water.

"It would be an unworthy end for me if Jerry knocked over the bloody crane just now," thought Reid.

But he arrived on board, and in England, safely.

"The Cabinet hears with satisfaction . . ."

"Mobile defense" was what Auchinleck had ordered. Didn't he foresee that, given the old-fashioned command structure of the Eighth Army, this of all tactics was bound to get it into trouble—given moreover an opponent who quite correctly, like an admiral in naval warfare, did not stay in port, but took his decisions right in the front line, reacting rapidly to each new situation? Because of his many responsibilities as C-in-C, Middle East, in Cairo, Auchinleck thought it was indispensable for him to stay there and guided Ritchie with tactical directives. But even the Army Commander in Gambut could not be kept informed adequately and quickly enough to enable him to react to the rapidly changing situations of a war of mobile forces.

It was a vicious circle: Commanders subordinate to the Army High Command, down to divisional and brigade level, were kept on a much shorter rein than was for instance normal practice in the German Army. Again and again they were forced to conclude that orders of this kind, by the time they had filtered down to them through the unwieldy machinery of command, were no longer very relevant to realities. Consequently they became angry and impatient and began to dispute the orders that reached them with the echelons above them. Thus it was precisely the attempt to command tightly from the rear that slackened the leash. Decisive hours passed while commands were debated.

Inevitably, a feeling of perplexity and helplessness spread to the troops in the field. Hadn't even Churchill called Rommel "a great general"? Obviously, it was no use trying to do anything against him. They lost nothing of their customary courage, but there was no more fire in their bellies.

In his exchange of telegrams with Auchinleck, Churchill kept demanding binding assurance that Tobruk would be held no matter what happened. C-in-C, Middle East, answered evasively: There should be no question of Tobruk being invested in the first place. Eventually Churchill read into one of his signals what it did not say and wrote: ". . . the Cabinet heard with satisfaction that you intend to hold Tobruk at any cost." Evidently battered into complaisance, Auchinleck did not contradict him. The Prime Minister left for another meeting with President Roosevelt. The bad news from Africa was to catch up with him soon.

The Panzer divisions, as well as the 90th Light and the motorized Trieste Division, were surging north. Naturally Rommel's Panzer forces had also suffered greatly: Of the 320 German tanks which had driven around the desert corner at Bir Hacheim on 26 May, only 124—many of them reconditioned—were still available. Now that full freedom of movement was restored, salvage and repair work were pressed ahead energetically. Replacements were coming along well, too, including the new Panzer IV with the long-barreled gun.[9]

After a fortnight's uninterrupted fighting, the crews were tired and exhausted to the point of apathy. Says General Nehring: "We camped for the night in the desert, any old how, friend and foe often driving past each other. Everyone was glad if the other side didn't bother him."

Sergeant Major Saenger's company ran into a troop of Grants. The things were too dangerous just to let them sail past without a salute. The Panzers went charging up to them until they were within range; some of them made a wide arc to take the "skyscrapers" in the flank; the Panzer guns barked. Before the Germans noticed that their opponents were not defending themselves, the whole lot had been knocked out. Some were on fire, belching black smoke. Saenger went over to help any wounded, but the British had been very lucky: There were only some slight burn cases.

The tanks were brand new: The barrels still had covers on them and breeches were thickly coated in grease and wrapped in special paper, just as they had rolled off the American freighter.

Lorried infantry took the prisoners away with them. Saenger gave each man a stiff whiskey—from their own provisions, carried in one of the Grants. All the rest they carefully stowed away in the good old Panzer 125. When Konrad Müller pressed the starter to catch up with their unit, the engine suddenly began to splutter.

One glanced revealed what the matter was: The mechanics at a mobile workshop, after making some small repair to the starter pinion, had forgotten to replace the special oil filter which was mounted over the air intake for service in Africa. The cylinders must have swallowed a good deal of sand. A further stretch of driving would have written the engine off completely. They looked around. A moment ago the desert had been full of the roar of engines, the thunder of guns, and vehicles wheeling in the swirling sand. Now it stretched still and wide from horizon to horizon, with nothing but the group of Grants, silently

[9] Although even more powerful models (Tiger and Panther) were to be built, this Panzer remained superior to any tank the Western allies had. Principal data: maximum armor thickness 90 mm; 300 hp; 38 kmph; 25 t. Main armament: 75 mm tank gun, L/48, muzzle velocity 790 m/sec. The 6.8 kg round would pierce 100 mm of steel at a range of 1,500 m.

belching smoke, in between. A small distance away stood an abandoned VW jeep. Somehow they got the little thing going again and drove north to find help. In undulating dune country, a group of British suddenly stood before their car, rifles at the ready. "Hands up!"

After a few moments' irresolution, the driver stepped on the brake. "What's the point of letting ourselves be drilled full of holes . . . ?"

They put their hands up. It appeared that the Britishers had been brandishing their rifles more out of fear than for any other reason. Their unit had arrived in the desert, fresh from Alexandria, only the day before. A Stuka attack had scattered their column. Everything that could still move fled to every point of the compass. They had been left behind. They had only the haziest idea of the points of the compass, and no idea how to rejoin their unit.

"We shan't do you any harm—you can even take us prisoner—only get us out of this blasted desert!"

In the distance they could see the vehicles of their column which had been destroyed by Stukas. The twelve men also clambered aboard the VW jeep, which promptly broke down on its way to the trucks.

In the trucks they found water and food. One of the British, who had been a mechanic with Ford's in Cologne before the war, produced a drivable vehicle after twenty-four hours' work by cannibalizing the wrecks. In this they continued on their way north and duly found the 5th Panzer Regiment again. They were truly sorry to say good-bye to the Tommies.

A black giant in the dessert

Up in the north, Rommel had again managed to engage—and beat— the British brigades one by one. Both Panzer regiments, giving cover to the sixty remaining tin coffins of the Ariete behind them, fell upon the re-formed 4th Armored Brigade. When the 22nd Brigade rumbled south, its help having been requested over open radio traffic, it of course ran into a line of anti-tank guns and was horribly shot up.

By noon on 13 June, 138 more British tanks had been destroyed. The Afrika Korps enveloped one of the last "boxes"—called Knightsbridge by the British—before the coast. On the left or northern end of the Gazala line, the 50th British and South African Divisions were threatened with encirclement. The code word Freeborn was their signal from Ritchie to break out. The two British brigades stormed west through a surprised Italian infantry, then turned south and east and rejoined the main body without much trouble. The South Africans withdrew along the coast to Tobruk. It was again Colonel Foote, with the last remaining formation of infantry tanks, who was covering their drive to the east.

Using their long range, eighty-eights shot up his units from the escarpment. Major Jock Holden, now a Brigade Major (which corresponds to a G1 Ops brigade level), drove to the scene of the fighting in a fast Cruiser. Between burning wrecks, in a hail of HE and AP shells, Colonel Foote was once again running around on foot, directing his tanks.

"Oh damn," thought Holden, "if he's running around out there, I'd better get out too."

"What's going on here?"

"Hell," the colonel muttered. Presently a severe sandstorm blew up, reducing visibility to nil. The South Africans reached Tobruk. Colonel Foote became the second man in the Royal Tank Regiment to be decorated with the Victoria Cross in the Second World War. Only 120 VCs were awarded in World War II.

No matter how desperately the British were defending themselves, the barricade in front of Tobruk broke up. The last, but strongest, of the pillars of the Gazala line had been shattered in two days. What British units there were as far west as this were ordered to retreat.

The King's Dragoon Guards set out for Egypt once more. But the previous night a strong German unit of tanks and armored cars had lumbered through their camp. Everyone froze—Peter Phillips with one leg in his car and one out. In the turret of a Panzer, he saw a face turned toward him. But the Germans seemed disinclined to have a scrap and drove on northward.

Next day, Phillips, who now commanded a troop of three armored cars, saw an immense lonely figure come ambling through the desert.

He was pitch black, wore a French uniform, and stood a good bit taller than 6 foot 3 inches. He could speak no word of English but made it clear in sign language that he had escaped from captivity at Bir Hacheim by bringing some solid object crashing down on the helmet of a guard. The giant seemed to be rather hungry; they gave him a whiskey and put a seven-pound tin of jam in front of him. Using the whiskey glass as a spoon, in front of their astonished and somewhat sad eyes he shoveled in the whole lot, intended to last twelve men in the three cars a fortnight.

At this time the RAF was able to attack, virtually unhindered, strong German-Italian air units being busy with the convoys bound for Malta.[10] Some British fighters had meanwhile been modified to act as

---

[10] The attempt to reinforce the rocky island from Alexandria turned into a disaster for the British. The convoys were wiped out and a great many warships

fighter-bombers, with a bomb slung under the fuselage. Others, intended as "tank busters," were fitted with automatic 40 mm "Pom-Poms." U.S.-made Boston bombers attacked in formations of eighteen and, through their total disregard of AA fire, earned the name "Stubborn Eighteens" from the German soldiers. During the drive to the north, battery commander Dammann chased up and down his column like a sheep dog, to keep the vehicles well spread out; from his basic air force training, he knew how tempting a tight group looked from above. A formation of "Stubborn Eighteens" attacked them, and everyone ran from the vehicles into the desert. Shortly before releasing their bombs, the formation veered away in a shallow dive. An appalled Dammann noticed that in the direction they were flying another battery of eighty-eights was traveling in a close column and its *"Luki-Luki"* men (air-raid lookouts) had clearly failed to spot the Bostons. The carpet of bombs hit the column just as it was pulling up. It disappeared in a huge cloud of dust, from which wreckage, men, and whole VW jeeps flew. As a fighting unit, the battery was finished. Only forty-eight pieces of this, the most important weapon of the Panzerarmee, were still available.

Another row of graves, a few more crosses in the "burial plan" of the officer responsible for such things. And the great worm of an army went on crawling north.

The 90th Light was again creeping up to El Adem from the south. The indefatigable Rommel turned up at divisional HQ and propounded his next tactic: to advance on a wide front and to go forward only where no enemy resistance was encountered. The strength of the division lay in its defensive capability; it was to infiltrate between enemy foci of resistance and then "hedgehog" itself.

Special Unit 288, most of which was attached to the 90th, was teamed with an Italian unit:[11] Lieutenant Buchholz found this was not too bad; he had seen Italians during the storming of Bir Hacheim—some of them frightened out of their wits by the barbed wire, but attacking with great dash all the same. At any rate, their losses were frightful; and one wished they had been given German infantry training, with systematic dashes, and units taking turns to give each other reciprocal covering fire.

---

went down too. In Malta itself, rations were reduced below the bare minimum for survival.

[11] This produced an instance of Rommel's sense of direction. Colonel Menton could not find the Italians and sent out a radio signal to that effect. Rommel came immediately, nosed about in the neighborhood, drove off in one particular direction, and soon ran the Italian HQ to earth. Buchholz last saw him drive over a mine and, only slightly put out, order up a new car.

As a result of the tactics it had been ordered to follow, the division soon ran into trouble and had to retreat westward. On 13 June, its war diary read:

> Reconnaissance probe by Menton runs up against enemy with tanks and armored cars. Despite which C-in-C, in a third signal, demands immediate disengagement westward. At the same moment, report from Colonel Menton that Strongpoint Kirchner is being overrun by tanks and armored cars. At 1230, further signal from C-in-C: "Situation most favorable; disengage immediately." Order difficult to carry out, because division short of everything (ammunition, water, food).

However, it was not tanks but armored cars and fast two-man armored Bren carriers which had turned up at Strongpoint Kirchner—named after an elderly major of the Reserve. Buchholz and the pajama man whipped the anti-tank gun around. "Try not to demolish our own trucks, if you can help it," said Buchholz, for the enemy AFVs were making things awkward by driving around between them and firing.

The pajama-gunner immediately set one of the carriers on fire. Some machine guns too began to bark. That stopped the British at first. Unhappily, however, Major Kirchner found himself in cross fire and tore off southward in his staff car. Worse, the ammunition was near the trucks, and the anti-tank gun had soon run out of it. Without particularly relishing the prospect, Buchholz determined to fetch the ammunition from under the noses of the British. On his way to the trucks, he stumbled over a figure in a foxhole: his special friend, the fidgety lieutenant. He squinted over the top of his foxhole, saw the carrier burning, and bawled out the radioman who, like himself, had tried to press himself down as flat as possible. Then he sent off an open R/T signal to Rommel: "Major Kirchner has fled; I am taking command!" and was thenceforth held up to all as a war hero. The major was relegated to the baggage train.

The British retired a short way and put down a heavy artillery barrage on the strongpoint, through which the whole division in the end drove off to the west. The war diary again: "The situation is grave. There are two options: (1) Detruck and take cover; (2) Rush through this fire zone at highest possible speed. Divisional HQ and elements following behind decide on the latter. . . ."

Buchholz was driving southward, giving cover. He was driving a captured 1½-ton Morris, one track rod of which was showing signs of giving out: The nearside front wheel was fluttering like a dove. To the north, at the other end of the long column, the noise of battle suddenly flared up. AP rounds whistled about the place. It looked as if tanks were attacking too.

The column surged over an eighty-eight battery which, right in its path, was peacefully cleaning its guns. The trucks increased speed; one could really feel the nervousness mounting. The fast chase turned into flight, then panic. The shaky Morris, behind which the pajama-gunner's 50 mm anti-tank gun was bouncing along, could not keep up with the others. Trucks were bursting into flames and stopping. The wild chase led up a slight incline. The moving cloud of dust reached the crest with breathtaking speed, Buchholz's platoon on the Morris, the lone straggler, behind.

The ack-ack battery saved them: Glancing back, Buchholz saw that the gunners had got one of their pieces ready to fire again; but the British tanks fell upon the battery from all sides and shot it up dreadfully.

At the top of the slope stood a colonel with a general staff officer's red stripes down his trousers, thundering away about desertion.

"I was only following the others," said Buchholz; "they were too fast for my broken-down truck."

"You are all deserters," screamed the colonel. "Name? Unit? I'll see to it that you are made to answer for this. Now dig your gun in here and provide cover to the east." "Very good, Herr Oberst."

The pajama warrior had left the optical sight on the gun, to be immediately ready to fire. During the rickety chase it had of course fallen off. Not a pleasant thought—to have to pick a quarrel with tanks over open sights. But then another truck towing an anti-tank gun came creeping up the hill: It was Lieutenant Grussendorf, who had provided cover to the north. With one and a half guns, they felt a little safer.

Fenck loses a finger

On this day, the war came temporarily to an end for gunlayer Werner Fenck. A heavy AP round, presumably from a 25-pounder, crashed into the Panzer head on, so that its front end sank quite perceptibly.

"Get out!" yelled driver Bernhard Krause.

Heavy indirect artillery fire consisting of HE shells was plowing up the ground; but luckily they were standing in the middle of an abandoned British position with deep foxholes. The bursts threw buckets of sand over their backs, but no one was hurt.

At dusk Fenck crawled back to the Panzer to fetch the breech block of the gun. He had the heavy sharp-edged piece in his hand when a shell exploded on the tank. The breech block slipped from his hand, knocking a finger off on its way. Today, in the countinghouse of his commercial firm near the port of Hamburg, Fenck smiles at "the interesting thought that there's perhaps still a rusty wreck standing around

somewhere in the desert with my little peice of bone in it. . . ." Because he had been more than fifteen months in the desert, and because
flesh wounds in particular can heal very badly there, he was sent home.

He was in Brindisi when he heard that Tobruk had been taken. Some
Italians invited the wounded warriors to a noisy beanfeast—naturally,
only those who were up to it. There were many at that party who could
not have cared less about Tobruk.

Rommel goes for Saenger

Sergeant Major Saenger had fetched his Panzer 125 from the desert
and together with another cripple was meandering to the workshop at
walking pace on the instructions of the chief technical officer.

On the Via Balbia they encountered a staff car coming from the opposite direction. A man in a peak cap, goggles pushed up on the cap-
band, was standing behind the windscreen—Rommel.

"Halt! Where are you going?"

"The Panzers are on the way to the workshops."

"Have you gone off your head? Out of the question. At such a moment one doesn't send one's Panzers to any workshop. Back to your
unit immediately!"

An officer whispered something in his ear.

"Oh, all right then," said Rommel. "You stay here, facing east.
There's a British tank attack coming from there—your job is to stop it
here. And I'll shoot you dead with my own pistol if you withdraw by
so much as a step." They drove their Panzers into some large holes
evidently dug by the British shortly before for their tanks. There were
some British camouflage nets lying around too; they pulled them over
their tanks, surveyed the country and awaited the enemy without much
relish. Sounds of heavy fighting came rumbling from the direction of
Tobruk and there was a continual flashing of explosions. Saenger
remembered how, what seemed years ago (in fact barely seven months
had gone by), he had stood to provide cover on the other side of
Tobruk with his traversing gear wrecked by a shot. On that occasion
the Maoris of the New Zealand Division were creeping around the
area, and wondrous tales went around about the incredible speed with
which they could cut off a whole head—as we would cut a slice of
bread. So they listened anxiously—and in vain—for any sound out of
the desert night.

This time, too, the enemy never came. Next morning they were still
standing around irresolutely. Did it still apply, that business with the
C-in-C's pistol? In the end they shoved off for the workshops after all,
without encountering their grim commander.

Buchholz is chased by Bren carriers

The roaring colonel with the stripes down his trousers actually did report Buchholz. The lieutenant was summoned to the Regimental Adjutant, Captain Borchardt. He looked at Buchholz in a funny sort of way—amused rather than angry—and said: "Tell you what—you can make amends. Quite a lot of vehicles were abandoned during that wild chase. Some of them are bound to be repairable. I'll give you some fitters to take along. You run along and salvage them. Is that clear?"

What could have been clearer? He was not even allowed to take weapons of any use with him for, the captain said, "You won't be there to stand and fight but to salvage vehicles."

Off Buchholz went with a truckful of mechanics whose heaviest arms were spanners and tire levers.

At roughly the place where the furious colonel had attacked him stood an armored car commanded by a skeptical sergeant major wearing a Knight's Cross, who very much doubted whether the British farther downhill would tolerate any repair activity for any length of time. Buchholz looked down the slope and cursed: There were masses of vehicles standing around all right, but as he remembered them they had not been so widely scattered. That meant he would have to scatter his grease monkeys pretty widely too—very inconvenient for a hasty departure. They went halfway down the hill and the fitters moved off in parties, carrying their tool kits. A VW jeep from the 361st (Foreign Legionnaires') Regiment came up, with a bearded warrant officer and his driver. They too were interested in the vehicles, but only road-worthy ones or those loaded with goodies.

Buchholz and a runner accompanied them up the opposite slope. They were halfway up when a group of Bren carriers appeared on the ridge and immediately began to fire.

Coattails flying, they galloped down the slope. Buchholz threw away his scarf, as if it would be easier to run without. On the opposite side, he saw the fitters converging on the truck, abandoning their tool kits.

The warrant officer and his driver didn't follow all the way. Over his shoulder, Buchholz saw them being put in the bag by one of the carriers. That delayed them a bit and he and the runner ran a zigzag course between the wrecked vehicles, exploiting what cover they offered. But already machine-gun bursts were whistling uncomfortably close. The runner sensibly threw himself flat.

Puffing and panting, Buchholz stumbled on; the carriers were again delayed scooping up the runner. But by degrees he ran out of wind. "How can I run away from these Bren gun carriers? They are faster than a man on foot, after all. . . ." But then he remembered the date: 14 June, his mother's birthday. Was he to disgrace her by being captured on this day of all days—a footslogger in the desert? The fitters had already climbed aboard the truck and were calling to him; the engine was running. With his last remaining strength he reached for the side, strong hands grabbed him, the truck started again. He dangled for a stretch but was then pulled aboard without mishap. The driver drove a few curves to throw up the dust; and behind that cloud they got away unscathed.

Buchholz was a little depressed when he reported back to the captain: one runner, two men from another unit, and all the tools gone. But the ways of the military are wondrous indeed—his superior was now quite pleased with him and sent off a signal to Rommel: Reconnaissance patrol of Special Unit 288 had reconnoitered the venue of the previous day's fighting and confirmed lively enemy activity with Bren carriers—and so on and so on. The army was most impressed by this initiative and the captain sent Buchholz on his way with a friendly word. Only the jittery lieutenant wanted to know where the hell he had been again.

Hand grenades from their allies

Although, before leaving, Churchill had declared in an encouraging telegram to Cairo that "this" was a business not only of armor but of willpower, such consolation, as ever, merely threw defeat into even sharper light. For instance, not even the greatest willpower in the world could help Brigade Major Holden, who went around asking every Tom, Dick, and Harry in Tobruk if they had a map of the minefields. No amount of willpower would hold the tracks on the bogeys of his tanks should one of them stumble into a minefield. And no one could just hypnotize the Stukas out of the sky without some flak. On the contrary: The last of your willpower withers away when you feel that you just haven't the tools for the job, and that the whole setup is worm-eaten. Tobruk was lost before the first Panzer had even rolled over the anti-tank ditch.

Rommel was leading the two Panzer regiments west for a thrust to the Via Balbia and the sea. Herbert Lumsden's 1st Armored Division, now greatly inferior in numbers as well, tried to hold them up and was badly battered. The few remaining tanks were attached to the 4th Armored Brigade, the last remaining unit of AFVs. It now had a hodgepodge of sixty Grants, Honeys, and Cruisers of all types. The men who were supposed to go into battle in those things would need more than just willpower.

Among the last remaining obstacles before Tobruk were some "boxes" on the high ground in the El Adem-Sidi Rezegh area, manned by Indian troops.

Captain Borchardt, the Regimental Adjutant of Special Unit 288, found a hidden way through a wadi to the airfield right between two of the boxes. Amid an incredible confusion of wrecked hangars and aircraft, his little troop established itself, prevented from taking further action by withering artillery fire, which actually did little more than turn over the airplane wreckage. But the fact that the amazing Jerries were again right in there among them shattered the defenders' nerves. They were no longer in any shape to withstand an attack with Panzer support.

Rommel sent off the mass of the 90th Light toward the Egyptian border to deceive the Tobruk defenders. General Nehring's Afrika Korps gathered in the pitch-dark night on the airfield at Gambut. The confusion among the totally exhausted men was dreadful. Just as Nehring arrived, right next to him a captain of the 5th Panzer Regiment, a bearer of the Knight's Cross, stepped on a mine; and the ugly Christmas tree of glaring red remained imprinted on the general's retina for a long time to come.

Small-arms fire flickered into life again and again along the Via Balbia as British troops tried to fight their way out to the east. The Afrika Korps HQ staff pottered around, trying to identify individual units, disentangle them and get them moving. To cap it all, Rommel turned up, yelling dreadfully: "Who the hell's in command here?"

That night Buchholz and his platoon occupied one of the captured Indian strongpoints. The men were delighted with their change of diet: There was a great deal of rice about.

In the middle of the position stood a knocked-out British armored car with its dead crew. "In the morning, let's get rid of that car," Buchholz told his sergeant major.

He and his men spent the night sleeping in a dugout. He started up, cursing, when the field telephone rang outside. Of course: the jittery lieutenant again. But no matter; the call had saved him, for all of a sudden there was a rattle of machine-gun fire, the dull thud of bursting hand grenades, cries and moans. Then someone called out in Italian, and someone cursed in German.

Slowly the confusion cleared: Rommel had ordered Italian units east of Tobruk to cover the impending attack. The Italians had been told to advance along the Via Balbia, partly through enemy-held territory. When some of them saw the cigarette of a sentry glowing in the ground to the right of them, they crept up to him.

There were agreed passwords between the allies—mostly names of towns—and the Italians called out: "Bologna." The totally exhausted sentry merely thought: "What's that rubbish, then?"

They opened fire, the astonished sentry disappeared; as bad luck would have it the Italians spotted the dugout Buchholz had just left and, without any further challenge, threw a hand grenade into it.

The five sleepers were badly wounded. Buchholz and his men were still attending to them when, at break of day, a magnificent Italian staff car purred into the position. Out of it materialized a genuine general, complete with adjutant and orderly officers, come to apologize officially for the blunder made by his troops. The interpreter had just murmured his first few words when a tremendous blast-wave struck their eardrums; a mighty explosion shook the ground and fragments of metal whistled about the neighborhood. The courteous general disappeared with one leap.

The sergeant major had packed the wrecked armored car full of some of the mines that were lying around and had blown it up.

After a fairly frosty farewell, Buchholz retained a definite impression that they must somehow have made an unfavorable impression on the general.

Eighty-eights over Tobruk harbor

The storming of Tobruk began at first light on 20 June. It went according to the plan Rommel had made in the autumn of the previous year. The artillery batteries were able to move straight into the positions then dug for them, and even found again the stacks of ammunition prepared at that time.

Despite all the haste and all the frenzy to make up for the months of unsuccessful siege, the attack this time in no way resembled the improvised suicide charge of the 8th Machine Gun Battalion and 5th Panzer Regiment. Although for fear of losing the element of surprise the artillery had been brought in rather late, the "softening up" of the British positions was performed with a degree of precision unknown till then: Kesselring's "artillery of the air," the Stukas, attacked the surrounding airfields in concert with conventional bombers, twin-engined fighters, and squadrons of the Regia Aeronautica.

They only had a few minutes to fly before releasing their bombs, and could then land again, fill up, and take on more bombs.

The result was devastating. The fortifications in the southeast, together with part of the minefield, were blown sky-high. Into the resulting cleared lane stormed infantry and sappers, followed by Panzers. Improvised causeways across the tank ditches were built out of gasoline drums filled with sand. Smoke signals for the pilots were set on the flanks and spearhead of the attack. Co-operation between the Luftwaffe and the troops on the ground worked perfectly, even without direct radio contact. Flare shells fired over enemy positions signaled to the pilots: Get this one off my neck. . . .

Between the roads to Bardia and El Adem lay the 11th Indian Brigade under Brigadier Anderson, a Scot. He had warned the commander of the fortress, the South African General Klopper: Here was the logical gateway for an attack into Tobruk—from the point where the two roads joined, via the two steps of the escarpment, and down to the town and the harbor. One brigade here was far too little; here and there, the tank ditch would not even stop a lawn roller. But Klopper, supported by Ritchie, was oddly enough expecting an attack from the west.

When the Panzers, field artillery and eighty-eights reached the first step of the escarpment, the fortress was as good as lost. Puzzled British officers returning from the front remarked that at this stage Klopper still had no idea what was happening. In the afternoon Panzers appeared outside his HQ in Fort Pilastrino. His staff thereupon burned all radio codes and destroyed all communications equipment except two mobile units. But the Panzer crews had orders not to bother with trifles and drove on.

A single British 3.7-inch AA gun held them up briefly. The gunners, who had also been taken by surprise, shot their own parapet away with AP rounds, destroyed four of the Panzers and went on firing till every last one of them was dead or wounded.

Just eight of the Army Tank Brigade's Valentines were left by this time. Klopper and his staff retired to the western part of the fortress and signaled Ritchie openly, since he had no codes: "Situation not under control. Counterattack with infantry battalion this evening. All tanks lost."

Ritchie ordered him to break out toward El Adem and reminded him how important it was to destroy the fuel dump in particular. During the night, Klopper assembled as many of his commanders as he could reach. Halfheartedly, they decided to hold at least the western half of the fortress. In the early morning hours it was reported that 150 Panzers were concentrated on Height-209 in front of the Ras el Madawar. The report was as wrong as it was impressive: It convinced the general that neither a breakout nor a prolonged defense was a practical possibility. He left behind his staff car and compass for six young South Africans who were determined to break out at any price and said with a resigned smile: "I wish I could go with you."

Down in the harbor, two naval officers, Smith and Harris, had supervised to the last the unloading of ammunition under heavy indirect artillery fire. Nobody gave them any report on the situation but in the afternoon of 20 June they had seen Panzers on the escarpment. Toward evening Harris went to the enormous fuel dumps to break the pins of the ninety-minute fuses. To his horror, a huge Panzer was already standing next to the main fuel tank. Its commander gave him a friendly wave of the hand. Harris waved back, made a detour and crept up on the tank from the other side. The pins were broken already.

He went back to the harbor, where the sailors wanted to break out with every available craft by sea to Mersa Matruh. The officers went aboard a long, flat lighter, which would not do more than 15 kmph. From the edge of the jebel every sort of artillery was firing directly down on them. Several of the craft that had gone out ahead of them had already been sunk. The outlook for the slow lighter was not good.

Lieutenant Dammann's battery reached the last step of the escarpment just about then. All day long they had alternately played the role of artillery, putting down indirect HE fire, or acted as anti-tank guns during advances. Lighter pieces were already standing on the slope and firing into the harbor. It was doubtful whether one could do anything with the eighty-eight, which was as big as a barn door, particularly since the barrel could not be depressed by more than three degrees from the horizontal.

But the Commander in Chief himself put an end to any hesitation. "Erwin is coming!" called the men. Dammann stuck the spade with which he was just digging a foxhole into the ground, and went over to the C-in-C's command car to report. But Rommel waved him away and called over, as always when he was excited, slipping into his native Swabian: "Get on with it, Dammann; shoot, man, shoot! You can almost spit into that harbor!"

With their tractors, they shunted the guns onto the steeply sloping ground until the barrels were pointing downward enough. "High explosive!" called the gun commanders.

Down in the harbor, the last act of the tragedy began.

First, some eighty-eight shells exploded in the wake of the big lighter. The engine compartment was burning already. Then a shell burst on the bridge. All the officers were wounded. The vessel drifted back landward, out of control. The engine-room crew lay on deck with severe burns. One of Captain Smith's arms was smashed. He died the following night.

In the morning on 21 June, everyone in Tobruk knew what was coming. In broad daylight, seventeen officers and 183 men of the Coldstream Guards drove to the Ras el Madawar to break out. Behind their lorries they towed six of the new six-pounder anti-tank guns. Other units joined them. On the way to the fortified line, the convoy grew until it consisted of sixty vehicles. They came under withering artillery fire, but under cover of their own dust clouds they got away with only light losses.

At Army Tank Brigade HQ, the officers were setting fire to their secret papers. Brigadier Willison said: "From now on it's every man for himself."

Accompanied by the Scottish Dr. Sillar, Major Holden went down to the shore from HQ, which lay beneath the second step of the escarpment on the road to Derna. The doctor had escaped from captivity in France, making it back to England. They knew of a hidden cave down there that might offer them a chance. All was peaceful. First they had a swim. When they came back to land, there stood a tall German, holding a submachine gun and looking smart, even in his dusty uniform. He waved with his free hand and said "Komm, komm," in a friendly way.

A few hours later, after dark, Dr. Sillar and Major K. P. Harris managed to jump from the truck during a brief stop and disappear in the night. Both arrived safely in Egypt.

"Only once, Duce . . ."

Corporal Karl-Ludwig Heilig of the 361st sat dozing in a truck parked on the main road above Tobruk. Only now and then was there still a burst of small-arms fire to be heard: They had been in action almost continuously for twenty-four hours. On the first day the Stukas had caught them, despite the smoke signals, and had killed or wounded quite a few of the ex-Legionnaires.

Now it all seemed to be over. On either side of the road lay South Africans, Indians, and British by the thousand, who had not yet been taken to the improvised, fenced cages.

Suddenly a call went through the multitude and spread like wildfire in all directions. Men were running like mad for the road. Heilig came to with a start. They wouldn't . . . would they? They were storming the stationary trucks up from both sides. He leapt at the machine gun mounted on the cab and swung it around in a hurry.

"Are you out of your mind, man? Just look around!" An officer was pushing the barrel up. "All they want is to see Rommel. . . ."

Right enough, an open staff car, and Rommel holding on to the windscreen. And the thousands who had made up the beaten army thronged forward to the edge of the road to scan that taciturn face. . . .

Rommel was angry. All morning he had seen the great black cloud of smoke over the harbor: The fuel he needed for his drive to the Canal was going up in smoke there. Klopper handed over the fortress officially at 0940 hours. According to a British report, Rommel, pointing at the burning fuel tanks, hissed at him: "You'll walk, walk, walk, all the way to Tripoli for that. . . ."

It was not the style of a well-bred man face-to-face with a beaten enemy, but it meant no more than the threat of courts-martial he made to his entourage. At any rate, the 30,000 prisoners of war taken at Tobruk did not have to walk all the way to Tripoli.

The German soldiers hurried to grab some loot before the "receivers" and the "chain hounds"[12] got their hands on it.

The men of the 361st took a whole tanker lorry of water. They even washed their feet in actual fresh water—which gave them about the same feeling as if they were lighting their pipes with hundred-mark notes. The driver of a self-propelled anti-tank gun from the 8th Machine Gun Battalion turned up, puffing and wheezing under the weight of a case, and called out: "Beer, lads! Lots of it!" In one dugout he had found a stack of cases, the bottles beautifully packed in straw inside. The labels said: "Münchner Löwenbräu." Other labels showed that the noble brew had got to the British via Portugal.

The sergeant major told Dammann: "We are asked to report how long we can feed ourselves."

"What do you think?"

The sergeant major, who had just come back from the town with a truck which was sitting very low on its springs, grinned: "Four weeks. To be honest, even six."

General Nehring and his chief, Bayerlein, drove off for a swim. Hardly had they entered the water when someone called from the radio car: "It's the Supreme Commander, Herr General."

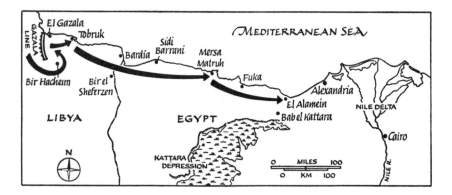

The way east: Once the Gazala line and Tobruk fell, the way to the Nile seemed free. But the end of the line was named El Alamein.

A sort of summit meeting had been called in a roadman's hut on the Via Balbia. The top men of the Italian command in Libya were there,

---

[12] German Military Police: so-called after the breastplate they wore hanging from a chain.

including Rommel's *de jure* superior, Bastico, and Generalfeldmarschall Kesselring, who was in particularly scintillating form. When
Nehring excused himself and went behind the house to see to an urgent
matter, Kesselring followed him for the same purpose and took up station next to him: "There you are, you see, the thing could be done
after all. Yet Rommel kept saying he couldn't do it. I kept having to
push him."

Nehring, astonished, muttered some platitude. So, now he wants *this*
feather in his hat as well. . . .

It was generally known that Kesselring had a way of being wise after
the event. But this was a bit steep, even for him.

Which did not alter the fact that in the ensuing, occasionally heated,
debate, the field marshal was just for once absolutely right. Rommel
explained that he would immediately make a deep thrust into Egypt.
Once more he saw not just Cairo but the Persian Gulf within his grasp.
Kesselring objected and recalled the agreement between the Führer and
the Duce: The first priority after the conquest of Tobruk would be to
take Malta; the Panzerarmee was not to advance beyond the Egyptian
border.

Rommel thought he must not give the battered Eighth Army any opportunity to establish itself somewhere and build up its strength again.
He had captured enough supplies in Tobruk; apart from which the harbor was now available.[13]

Of course with hindsight it is easy to assert that Rommel's old dream
of the Nile was just so much fantasy—let alone his dream of the Gulf.
But even then, the exact calculations prepared on Paulus' instructions
had been available for more than a year. It emerges from Rommel's ob-
servations in his *Krieg ohne Hass* that, in his view, you had only to
keep on asking the impossible of those ever-dubious logistics *wallahs* in
order to get it. Just as you did with fighting troops.

It is all very reminiscent of the convictions of the Supreme Warlord
—and for that matter of Churchill's "willpower" telegram. But for the
Nazi chief and his hangers-on irrationality was of the essence; whereas
Churchill would resort to such things from time to time, in appropriate
doses, as a means to an end.

Among the sober facts of this world was that even Alexandria, the
nearest harbor of any capacity, was 600 kilometers beyond Sollum and
the Egyptian border. But even reaching that objective was of ques-

[13] The difficulty of destroying great stocks of fuel in a hurry, already mentioned elsewhere, cropped up in Tobruk too. More fuel dumps were captured at
El Adem and Belhamed. The little harbor, with its capacity of only 500 tons a
day, was, however, not a great deal of use, especially since it was not equipped to
handle big ships.

tionable value unless not only the entire British base in the Middle East but also the long, but relatively safe, supply route around the Cape of Good Hope could be destroyed in one great thrust.

For with every kilometer you progressed eastward, you naturally got nearer to the RAF's superbly built and well-supplied bases in the Delta. And, like Malta, the island of Cyprus lay in the Eastern Mediterranean basin within range of the possible sea supply routes. Those were all problems which would have been difficult to solve, even given unimpeded communications to Tripoli and the harbors of Cyrenaica.[14] But with Malta in one's rear, such a push to the east would predictably have amounted to nothing but yet another waste of blood and sweat. Even the fact that the Axis air forces had been transferred from Sicily to Africa to support the Rommel offensive had allowed Malta "noticeably to revive again," as General von Rintelen had reported to the OKW on 5 June. In the preceding days the freighters *Allegri* and *Giuliani* had been sunk. The CGS, Cavallero, reminded Rintelen every time they spoke that the conquest of Malta was "absolutely essential."[15]

A factor which now had to be taken into all calculations in connection with an advance into Egypt went far beyond the "rubber-band effect" which both sides had several times experienced (i.e., the way forward positions had of "rebounding" because the supply lines were overstretched). Even during the battle for the Gazala line, the Axis air forces were still in a position to switch rapidly from their task of supporting the ground troops to attacking sea targets around Malta. Now this had become impossible. Now it was either/or. The result was a dissipation of forces, which were consequently insufficient for either purpose.

Kesselring knew what he was talking about: As a result of a direct request by Churchill to Roosevelt, the Americans had made their aircraft carrier *Wasp* available to resupply Malta with fighter aircraft. Immediately, the British defense was stiffened. In three days—from 10 to 12 May—more German aircraft were lost than in 11,500 sorties in the spring. Air superiority was now a thing of the past. Even at night, Beaufighters lurked over the Sicilian airfields, lying in wait for returning bombers.

During the war council in the road-mender's hut, British bombers

---

[14] The oft-voiced view that the loss of Malta would have made Britain's position in the Middle East untenable borders on an "African stab in the back" legend, but need not be further examined here.

[15] He also reminded Rintelen that in addition to its (very meager) ration of Romanian oil, the Italian Fleet would need 40,000 tons of fuel oil for the operation.

and torpedo-carrying aircraft sent the German steamship *Reichenfels* to the bottom of the Mediterranean.

Rommel broke off the discussion and took Nehring to one side. "You with your corps through the desert down under; the 90th Light down the Via Balbia. Go!" The Afrika Korps moved off immediately.

At this time General von Rintelen reported to the OKW the Duce's view, which was that the directives of 7 June required no amendment: Operations should go only as far as the Egyptian border—then it was Malta's turn. Not until 2112 hours the next day did he receive a signal from Rommel—which he immediately forwarded to the OKW and OKH—to the effect that with the capture of Tobruk the Panzerarmee's first objective had been reached. He now proposed "to open the way to the interior of Egypt." Thanks to the booty captured, the supply situation was good and the enemy weak. "Therefore please persuade the Duce to remove the existing restrictions on movement."

On his own initiative, Rintelen appended a reminder of the Duce's view reported by him the previous day.

But Hitler had already struck his lyre with a flourish, in a letter to the Duce which said: "Only once, Duce, do the laurels of victory touch a man. An opportunity once missed will not return. . . ."[16]

Mussolini could not resist such fanfares. On 24 June Rintelen reported that the Duce wholeheartedly agreed with the Führer that "the historic moment for the conquest of Egypt has come." Nevertheless, Mussolini also pointed out that because of the "revival of Malta" the Panzerarmee's supply situation had again become critical, and asked for air reinforcements.

Hitler forgot all about it. He had more important things to do. A great summer offensive was about to begin in Russia. He intended to use it to finish off the subhumans once and for all. A mighty thrust was aimed at the Caucasus, and a town on the Volga called Stalingrad.

[16] According to another draft, he wrote about the "Goddess of luck in battle," whom one must seize hold of when she approached. The Wehrmacht Command Staff/OKW which, according to its own members, was always a tower of sober good sense in contrast to the daydreaming Hitler, incidentally issued an assessment in which it likewise recommended that the Egyptian adventure should be given preference over the seizure of Malta.

3. To Cairo for Coffee

"Liberator from the British yoke"

Before their peoples and for the world public the two dictators stood arm in arm. Their heroic profiles were even joined on stamps.

But while their soldiers fought and died, covert rivalries and jealousies grew between their leaders. In the morning on 21 June, Mussolini had a special announcement published according to which the British had offered to surrender Tobruk to the GOC of the 21st Italian Army Corps. Whereupon Hitler announced with all the publicity he could command that Rommel had been promoted Generalfeldmarschall.[1] After that, an ignoble rivalry escalated virtually into the realms of burlesque: The Duce made Cavallero and Bastico field marshals as well. Count Ciano remarked in his diary that the move had "amused people in Bastico's case and made them indignant in Cavallero's."

In the expectation of an imminent triumphal entry into Cairo, Mussolini, accompanied by a numerous retinue, flew to Derna, where his private household lost a cook and a barber in a crash landing. A few weeks later he left, pale with anger and disappointment and absolutely disgusted with Rommel, who had not even paid him a formal courtesy visit.

In official documents, he continued to speak of the "Italian-German"

[1] Rommel didn't get around to having his new insignia sewn on his uniform for quite a while and later told his wife: "I would have preferred a division."

army, whereas the Germans naturally continued to refer to a "German-Italian" one.

Meanwhile, fine castles were being built in the air by all and sundry. Whereas the Duce was issuing instructions that while the Egyptian population must invariably be treated in a friendly fashion, the Egyptian authorities should be so treated only if they showed themselves worthy of it, the tightly controlled German press was ordered "to give plenty of prominence to the Axis Powers' joint declaration on the independence of Egypt and to comment on it in accordance with the points of view indicated." It was agreed that Rommel would be military governor and a former ambassador would become civil resident.

The Panzerarmee's intelligence section amassed a massive dossier which among other things contained the following appendix by a German warrant officer (who had been the branch manager of a German bank in Cairo): "The Egyptian Economy and Measures Necessary to Take it Over." Another Egyptologist reported on where, for instance, one could get hold of building material (not a lot to be had—the best would be to cut down all telephone poles).

Leaflets and radio appeals were prepared. "Rommel is coming to liberate you from the British yoke!" The intelligence section reported that one might well retain King Farouk, particularly since his sister was Empress of Persia. "A point for consideration, however, is whether one should for the time being leave in place the present Premier Nahas Pasha and his ministers, some of whom are British lackeys, or whether one should allow the king to throw them out immediately."

The experienced administrative machine must in any case be retained, the document said, since: "Disciplinary punishment arising from any steps taken against Germany will follow later!"

Ambush at Mersa Matruh

Churchill received the news of the fall of Tobruk in Washington. During a conference a telegram was handed to President Roosevelt, who passed it on to his guest without a word.

Says Churchill: "This was one of the heaviest blows I can recall during the war. . . . I did not attempt to hide from the President the shock I have received. It was a bitter moment."

Gratefully, Churchill later recorded that Roosevelt immediately asked: "What can we do to help?"

The Prime Minister replied without hesitation: "Give us as many Sherman tanks as you can spare and ship them to the Middle East as quickly as possible."

A short white later 300 Shermans and 100 self-propelled guns were on their way across the Atlantic. When a ship with a cargo of tank engines was sunk by a German U-boat on its way, the President ordered that a fast steamer should immediately be loaded with replacement engines and sent racing after the convoy. The General Sherman, a tank which was at least some sort of a match for the Panzer, was to appear in the African theater of war for the first time.[2]

But for the moment, the remnants of the British tank units were being scattered by the Panzerarmee or were shot to pieces. Auchinleck relieved Ritchie and took command of the Eighth Army himself. He decided to offer resistance to contain the advance while he built up his positions at the only place between the Halfaya Pass and the Nile Delta which could not be outflanked to the south: the gap between the Qattara Depression and the sea, barely 60 kilometers wide, where the tiny desert railway station of El Alamein is situated. But not much came of the idea at first: The Panzerarmee got there too quickly.

Meanwhile Auchinleck had an opportunity to dig his heels in at Mersa Matruh. The town had fortifications, some of them built as long ago as the time of the Italian attack and in the west there was a gappy minefield belt, which went on for another 20 kilometers to the south alongside the track to the Oasis of Siwa.

But of course the whole thing could easily be turned in the south; only strong armored forces could have prevented that in mobile combat. Rommel's Panzer regiments counted altogether eighty-six machines at this stage[3] and the *pot pourri* of the remnants of the 1st Armored Division was no match for them. The 90th Light broke through the minefield while the Panzers advanced farther to the south, sweeping the 1st Armored aside. The result was extensive chaos; strong infantry units were cut off not only inside Mersa Matruh but also farther south, around the two steps of the escarpment. Meanwhile General Freyberg's New Zealand Division was approaching from the east.

Hanz-Günter Buchholz, meanwhile promoted full lieutenant, heard in the pitch-black night a couple of trucks towing guns droning southward through his unit down the track to Siwa. "Those were Britishers," said some soldiers over whose toes the trucks had virtually rolled.

---

[2] The Sherman, henceforth the standard tank of the Western allies, also had a very high profile and none too powerful a gun (75 mm, L/40.18; muzzle velocity only 619 m/sec; AP round of 6.79 kg; would pierce 76 mm of steel at 1,500 m). But it was well-armored (maximum 85 mm on front of turret) and with a 400 hp (later 450 hp) engine, was capable of 39 kmph. Early models had insufficient protection for the gasoline tanks and could often be set on fire even by a splinter (nickname: Tommy cooker). Later Shermans were diesel-engined. Main asset: absolute reliability and availability in great numbers. . . .

[3] Two hundred more were expected from the workshops.

When the next lot came through, they began to shoot. A little way to the south one of the trucks burst into flames.

Colonel Menton drove up and said: "In such a confused situation as this, you can't just blaze away! You must first find out whom you've got there." A warrant officer volunteered to question the next unit. Four great tractors drove up slowly, each with a trailer carrying ammunition, behind which was a gun. They made a proper trailer train, with huge silhouettes, unmistakable even in the dark.

The first one stopped. The warrant officer said: "Who are you?"

"Damned Germans," said the driver in English and stepped on the accelerator. The warrant officer fired off a flare and threw himself flat on his face in the sand. The German infantrymen opened up with everything they had, but it seemed to no great avail in the dark. However, the battery came to a gruesome end all the same. The drivers left the Siwa track. After traveling a short way, all four trains crashed over the side of a steep-sided wadi and exploded. There were no survivors left to capture.

Colonel Menton came up and asked severely: "What was it this time?"

"Beg to report, Herr Oberst: this time we did ask."

Heavy 210 mm mortars were taking up position behind them, firing into Mersa Matruh. Elements of the 90th Light, under heavy bombardment by the RAF, had already reached the coastal road and the sea in the north.

Freyberg and his New Zealanders were immediately caught between the 21st and 15th Panzer divisions as they moved into the front line, which they thought was intact. The general himself, an old warrior who had been wounded any number of times in the First World War, was badly wounded once more—in the head.

The division broke out to the east during the night. The spearhead of their attack hit the 8th Machine Gun Battalion and a first-aid post. In front of the New Zealanders' trucks came, in close formation, silently and at the double, a mass of crack troops, bayonets fixed, a pouchful of hand grenades strapped to each man's chest. The soldiers of the 8th Machine Gun Battalion woke from their exhausted sleep when their sentries gave the alarm. Most never had a chance to grab their weapons. Machine guns were useless in that merciless hand-to-hand struggle. In the darkness the New Zealanders struck down anyone who stood in their way, including the medics and Dr. Tanzer, a major in the medical corps. Ammunition trucks flew in the air—but in the dark it wasn't possible to tell ambulances from other vehicles. Many wounded men were burned to death in them.

This vigorous surprise thrust threw the German units off balance over a broad front. Rommel himself had to flee with his staff. Günther Halm's anti-tank crew was stationed a little to one side to provide cover. The following morning they helped to collect the dead and wounded. A terrible smell of burning hung over the wadi. The 8th Machine Gun Battalion alone counted a hundred dead and the same number of wounded. The New Zealanders reached the El Alamein defense line with negligible losses.

The German-Italian units were too weak even to encircle Mersa Matruh. The bulk of the British troops got away, although with heavy losses.

Among the units of the 90th Light which lay to the east of Mersa Matruh on the edge of the escarpment overlooking the coastal road were the men of the 361st. They had an eighty-eight—the last survivor of a battery.

Columns of trucks, full to bursting with infantry, were trying to escape down the road, which was barely 500 meters away. A ghastly butchery ensued. The eighty-eight, field guns, and machine guns poured their fire down at the trucks. The first one skidded and turned over. Others crashed into it. Vehicles stuck fast in the jam; others tried to drive around the wrecks.

Eventually the officer commanding the AA gun said, "Cease fire!" He looked as if he might be sick. Down on the road a solid mass of vehicles was burning below a black pall. One man after another let go of his machine gun. Down below, survivors were running eastward; small scout cars picked their way through the country. Colonel Marcks came up. "Had enough?"

"Look for yourself, Herr Oberst," said Heilig. Marcks took a long look down. "See what you mean," he said, and went.

A little farther to the west, where the jebel did not rise quite so steeply and was negotiable in low gear, British columns left the road and tried to escape across country. They ran into Special Unit 288.

There had already been heavy fighting with units breaking out during the previous night. They had almost overrun the regimental HQ, where Colonel Menton fired away with his revolver in all directions. Buchholz and his platoon were stationed on top of a prominence. His position had been crossed several times already by vehicles full of wildly firing troops, and some wounded men were lying in a hollow. One of them was a lance corporal who had been hit in the cheek just as he was reporting to the lieutenant. The bullet had gone straight through, without damaging any of his teeth or his tongue. Only two harmless holes remained in the thin flesh on either side of his face.

The hillside was by now full of burning vehicles. When the next lot

came up, every gun was ready for them, including a 20 mm ack-ack
and the anti-tank gun of the pajama soldier, who had by now got properly dressed again and had heaped up a mountain of HE shells at his
side.

They heard the vehicles a long way off, whining in low gear. But
they were on top of the position in a trice because the burning trucks
and their dense clouds of smoke had unsighted the gunners.

There was a staff car in front, which accelerated and raced through
between the anti-tank gun and a machine gun, so that neither of them
dared to fire. When the anti-tank gun began to bark, the staff car was
just driving over the wounded, whom the driver evidently could not see
in their hollow. Immediately afterward one of the little HE shells of the
AA gun exploded in the vehicle. Buchholz tore open the door, and
found a driver, a captain, and a brigadier, whose right leg was badly
shattered.

They pulled him out and tried to stem the bleeding with a small first-
aid bandage pack. The elderly gentleman was very upset about the
moaning and crying wounded over whom, on top of everything else, his
car had driven. So concerned was he that he hardly paid any attention
to his own injury.

Infantrymen, in large groups and small, were breaking through from
the congested road. When it became quieter, the German units picked
out for themselves the best of the abandoned vehicles. Over Mersa Matruh hovered the black cloud of burning fuel.

Panic grips the 90th Light

Rommel knew that the enemy was preparing defenses between the
Qattara Depression and the sea. He urged his dead-tired soldiers to
hurry. In the hope of reaching the goal of their dreams, which appeared within their grasp, they drove their tortured bodies forward.
When everything threatened to come to a halt through sheer lack of
fuel, some was always found. The Mersa Matruh dump hadn't fully
burned out either, and some way to the west another 80 cubic meters
was discovered.

Rommel set up a scratch task force under Army AA Captain Briel:
"You and your outfit drive to Alexandria," he said. "The Tommies will
have pulled out anyway. Tomorrow we'll have coffee in Cairo."

But the bow had been bent too far. Briel got as far as the neighborhood of El Daba. Then his men literally collapsed—unconscious
more than asleep. Battery commander Dammann, meanwhile promoted
captain, remembers that they made a halt somewhere and his VW jeep
stopped. Then something went bang, they woke with a start and all

stared at each other: commander, driver, and warrant officer (special duties). None of them recognized the country around them. They chased off after their battery.

A train with steam up stood at El Daba station. Lieutenant Schmidt destroyed the engine with an eighty-eight shell. A Wellington tried to take off from an airstrip nearby. It fell over and blew up under their fire.

At El Alamein they came to a full stop. Intact units, including the New Zealand Division and others, offered them dogged resistance, supported by units scratched together in the Delta and made up of the retreating divisions. Auchinleck, who could no longer put a firm front together, now astonished Rommel by his mastery of Rommel's own speciality: mobile warfare.

The three "Ms" of the Light Division—Battle Groups Marcks, Menny, and Menton—were to forge ahead between the El Alamein fortifications and the line of hills called Ruweisat Ridge and then wheel north and cut some of the British off.

They drove by compass through a dust storm in which one could just about see the radiator of one's own car. Never mind—it kept the RAF away. Shortly before, its bombers and fighters had chased Rommel and his staff out of El Daba. A unit of the U.S. bombers, "Stubborn Eighteens," had caught a concentration of the battle groups and caused losses and chaos.

Corporal Heilig drove Colonel Marcks' VW jeep. After weeks of nonstop fighting and the continual shortage of water, they were all in a foul condition and Heilig saw with interest that fat lice were running about on the colonel's collar.

The dust storm ended abruptly. At the very same moment they came under withering artillery fire. They threw themselves into the dirt and halfway down Heilig felt something hit his hand. While lying flat, he was able to take a better look at it. It looked a mess. A piece of shrapnel had torn through both bone and tendon. The artillery fire was accurate and the fragments fell like heavy hail. On the left, they saw infantry with soup-plate hats making a charge.

"We've got to get out of here," said Marcks. "Can you drive?"

"I'll manage with one paw," Heilig said. Two days later he was in the hospital in Athens.

Buchholz saw the jeep with its little aerial pennant race away. He was driving on the left wing. In addition to his two German 50 mm anti-tank guns he had two British two-pounders mounted on a truck chassis from the booty taken at Mersa Matruh. They saw Marcks' radio car being captured. It had obviously got stuck in the barbed wire entanglement during the dust storm.

When Marcks' jeep returned, the trucks with their lorried infantry also turned around. In the rough country there was a certain amount of congestion when they met the troops coming up behind them. The British gunners immediately spotted this and concentrated their fire on the resulting jam, with devastating effect.

The bulk of the battle groups fell into one of those rapid flare-ups of near panic which sometimes seize exhausted troops. Buchholz and his little outfit, not for the moment of any great interest to the British, who had more worthwhile targets, dug themselves in. Some distance away he saw that the right-flank guard, who had also kept out of the mêlée, were doing the same thing.

They squatted there for two days and nights, steadily harassed by the artillery, but it was shown once again that infantry well dug in are hard to hit. Only their vehicles were smashed to pieces one by one.

Then a runner who had been sent to the rear came back with a warning of a tank attack impending from the southeast. Buchholz joined forces with the commander of the other small unit, a major wearing the Knight's Cross.

Right enough, some twenty Valentines drove up. Buchholz began by ordering one of his surviving two-pounders to fire, so as not to give away the positions of the German anti-tank guns too soon. The accurate little gun scored five hits. Each time the round bounced off and soared skyward like a flare. The tanks bore down on the gun, firing as they came. The gun crew ran to safety; and at that very moment two trucks towing Russian anti-tank guns turned up from a wadi by way of reinforcements and found themselves right in the path of the leading Valentines in the broken terrain.

Everyone held his breath as the crews unlimbered their fat guns in frenzied haste and pulled at their lanyards, obviously without stopping overmuch to aim. The two tanks were driving at a slight angle to the guns. The anti-tank projectile went through both. Both immediately burst into flames; the hatches did not open.

The other tank crews could see only the columns of smoke and turned away, clearly under the impression that they had run up against a terrific anti-tank front. In the afternoon, reinforcements arrived from the rear. The devastating artillery fire began again.

"We'll get you right"

The two Panzer regiments had advanced simultaneously with their remaining total of fifty-five tanks on either side of the Ruweisat Ridge, which lies in the middle of the gap. On the southern side, the 8th Panzer Regiment pushed back the 1st Armored Division, but then both columns came up against a front of 25-pounders and the new medium anti-tank gun.

Armitage, in command of a battery, also had a troop of these high-penetration six-pounders with him—a slight consolation, because the stuff that was coming at him had pretty nasty-looking long barrels.

In the din of battle, Armitage ran over to one of his guns. An AP round had gone through the shield and through the gunner and the gunlayer who happened to be standing one behind the other. Armitage immediately took their places, although it was an unpleasant feeling to be waiting for the next shot, which more than likely would be a direct hit too. The round had struck the hydraulic buffer, which is under the barrel, and had lodged in it. The next moment they fired—and the barrel of course stuck in the run-out position. Several Panzers were on fire; the rest turned away.

Armitage went to his car for a tot of whiskey—an unusual thing for him to do. On his way back to the battery position, he saw on his right a shell slowly coming up on the Ruweisat Ridge. "Look out!" he roared toward his guns. The very next moment an HE shell burst right at his feet. A splinter smashed his jawbone and lodged in his neck. It had the same effect as a knockout blow. From then on, everything seemed wrapped in a cotton-wool fog. He was aware only of a nice doctor looking at him and saying, "We'll get you right." However, Armitage remained speechless for several weeks because the splinter had damaged his vocal chords. It could all be put quite right, though.

Armitage said to me after a lengthy conversation: "Thirty years ago I would never have believed that I would ever talk in such a friendly way with one of you. That gives one some hope, at least, don't you think?"

Booty from the Italian allies

On 2 July, General von Rintelen was still reporting to Berlin that it was the Panzerarmee's intention to let the Italian 21st Corps isolate Alexandria, itself advancing to Cairo. Two days later, he reported that Field Marshal Rommel was temporarily going on the defensive. On 6 July he forwarded a situation report by General Gause, now back from the hospital, according to whom the average strength of the German divisions had been reduced to 1,200 men. There were only forty Panzers left altogether.

The shortage of vehicles had become so severe that the entire Italian infantry now went on foot. Moreover, there was no transport to move up the Luftwaffe's installations. It now looked as if there might perhaps be something to be said for having a look at the calculations of the logistics experts—even if their exact figures appeared to upset the high-flying plans of generals.

All plans to deal with Malta had been quietly abandoned under the pressure of events. The troops earmarked for that operation were wanted in Africa urgently: One division of Italian paratroops and the German Ramcke Brigade arrived by air in piecemeal fashion, unaccompanied by any of their transport. Churchill sighed with relief as he read the relevant orders deciphered by Ultra, and realized that with Tobruk a pawn had been lost and the queen saved: The fall of the fortress had tempted Rommel and those above him into the costly Egyptian adventure. Once more they had bitten off more than they could chew.

Rommel suddenly found himself in a ludicrous situation: He of all people had to avoid battles of movement, which guzzle fuel and wear out armored vehicles. And like the boxer who keeps hitting his opponent's damaged eyebrow, Auchinleck again and again set his crack units, like the New Zealand Division, our old friends the 9th Australian Division, now back from Syria, and the 1st Armored Division, which had been brought up to a strength of a hundred tanks again, at the ill-armed and totally immobile Italians. This forced Rommel into a role in which his adversary had so often shown himself in a poor light: He had to misuse the Panzer, a tool for attack, as a fire engine and mobile anti-tank gun.

One day, at this time when the 5th Panzer Regiment was moving forward, Sergeant Major Saenger and his crew were taking booty of a different kind for a change: They found an abandoned column of Italian trucks, which had evidently belonged to an HQ staff. Just to make sure, one always gives this sort of thing a quick looking over, and their eyes fairly popped at what they saw. The vehicles were crammed with the most fantastic food, from preserved fruit to tinned meat which underlined what dreadful rubbish the "AM" or "old man" tins really were. They packed the Panzer full of the stuff. One of the men came upon a box of lire banknotes, and another found mountains of cigarettes. As they hastily moved off again to catch up with their company, there were two bags dangling outside the tank: one full of cigarettes and the other of money; life was expensive in Cairo, so they had heard.

But their dream of the Nile was soon over: As they continued the attack, they ran into a front of anti-tank guns and 25-pounders. A hit brought the dear old Panzer 125 to her knees: The last veteran of El Agheila had met her fate.

They bailed out, perhaps a little prematurely, since nothing was burning. In the excitement Saenger forgot what they drum into you on the barrack square: Keep your heels down! He felt a knock and paid no further attention, but his gunlayer said: "You're bleeding, you know!"

There was a piece of shrapnel sticking out of his ankle. The gunlayer moaned: "What a mean trick! Now you've got your ticket home and I've got to stay here!"

While he said it, he held his head a bit too high. Then he really had something to moan about, for all of a sudden blood was trickling down his face. He kept wiping his forehead and was soon quite covered in blood. Saenger crawled up to him and saw it was only a small scratch, most likely from a stone.

"Hard luck! That's not enough for home." The crew withdrew a little way to where there were some old Italian foxholes. Suddenly the gunlayer called out again. This time he had a splinter in his calf. But he was unlucky again: The thing was only just embedded in the skin and fell out with the first movement.

"Come here," said Saenger. He bandaged the splinter nice and firmly to his leg with a first-aid bandage and poured a goodly draft of blood over the whole thing from his shoe, which was full of blood. That was enough to take the "wounded" man all the way to Athens. However, things became critical the first time he came up for treatment there, since the tiny hole under the bandage had meanwhile healed.

Luckily, one of the doctors was a countryman of his from the Nauen region, and turned a blind eye.

Saenger's war was over, too, for the time being. Today he is an editor with the West German news agency, DPA. After the war, he spent several years as a political prisoner at Bautzen in East Germany. Until that time he often suffered terrible nightmares about Panzer attacks. When he has a nightmare these days, it's always set in that prison.

"Last night's party went wrong"

In London, Churchill read Rommel's reports, decoded by Ultra, in which he complained more and more angrily about his lack of supplies and the slenderness of the reinforcements reaching him.

However, the head of Ultra, Winterbotham, had meanwhile got to know his "client" very well and realized that Rommel generally exaggerated, and never in the positive sense, unless he was trying to convince his superiors about the prospects of a proposed thrust.

He warned the Prime Minister accordingly, but at this time of worldwide disaster Churchill needed a conspicuous victory for political reasons: A conference with Stalin, who was urging the establishment of a second front to take some of the pressure off Russia, was pending In addition, he wanted to convince the American President, Roosevelt, that a joint Anglo-U.S. landing in North Africa was a promising and necessary next step. For these reasons, he was again bombarding Auchinleck with demands for an attack. The result was a pointless sacrifice, one of the most monstrously disastrous investments of sweat and blood of all time.

The slanting rays of the morning sun of 22 July 1942 filtered down through clouds of dust as more than a hundred tank engines thundered into life. A hundred and four gun barrels were trained threateningly westward as the 23rd Army Tank Brigade rumbled across the start line just south of Ruweisat Ridge.

Sergeant Mechanic Cyril Rogers watched exhausted as the fifty Valentines and two Matildas of the 40th Royal Tank Regiment moved off. With the other fitters, he had worked many hours of the day and night for this moment, listening to, tapping, and mothering engines and suspensions. Now he felt an immense pride at the healthy note from every exhaust, as every one of those steel crates swayed unerringly on its way toward the enemy, into their first action.

Lieutenant Lewis Wiard, a troop commander in C-Squadron, 40th Royal Tank Regiment, in civilian life a carefully calculating businessman, entertained only a tiny doubt in the back of his mind as he braced his six feet and one inch in the open turret against the swaying and rolling of the tank and surveyed the country around him. On his right, stretching from east to west, lay the rocky Ruweisat Ridge and on his left the rocky plain on which the tanks of their sister regiment, the 46th, were forging forward. C-Squadron was in the van, followed by the Regimental HQ, and after that B and A Squadrons. Here and there brown clouds were rising to the sky, shot through by bright flashes; and a burst right next to his tank drenched Wiard in sand and stones. He ducked and gave his signaler/gunner a reassuring grin. The gunner was an angular Scot who had his shoulder rammed up against the rubber-upholstered stock with which you set the elevation of the two-pounder.

They passed the minefield and Lewis Wiard saw with satisfaction that this at least had worked all right: Evidently the sappers had cleared a lane, as had been arranged.[4] No; the tiny uneasiness he felt stemmed from a throwaway remark by his regimental commander, Colonel Dunbar. . . .

They had only been in Egypt since 6 July. A unit of the Territorial Army, they had not been "promoted" from an infantry unit to armor

---

[4] It is still not clear whether the 40th Royal Tank Regiment found a gap accidentally: The 46th in the south and the third regiment of the Brigade, the 50th, which attacked north of the Ruweisat Ridge, suffered substantial losses, caused by mines which were supposed to have been cleared.

until 1938. Mobilized on 1 September 1939, they had been little more than anxious spectators while the beaten UK units streamed back from Dunkirk and while alarming news came in from all corners of the world. They had trained on the early waddling Matildas, remounted on the low-slung, faster Valentines, and were now engaged in their first attack, well-trained as far as firing and driving were concerned but totally without any experience of battle or of desert warfare. In fact, British experts[5] consider that this utterly green brigade was thrown, pell-mell and without time to acclimatize, into this operation with cynical premeditation; because units with long experience had meanwhile developed a healthy respect for the long-barreled Panzer and the eighty-eight.

Infantry, they had been told, would clear the Axis troops out of at least the first five kilometers of the attack zone the night before, so that they would be able to imitate the classic German Blitz tactics: Break through, fan out, annihilate.

Only—and this had been the remark which had made Wiard a little uneasy—Colonel Dunbar had tersely informed the morning briefing of squadron and troop commanders: "By the way, the party last night went wrong, but we are going ahead all the same." "The party last night" south of the Ruweisat Ridge had indeed gone completely awry: Indian infantry from the 161st Brigade, just as green as the tankmen from Liverpool, had been promptly beaten back. North of the Heights the New Zealanders had managed to make a little progress but were soon forced to withdraw when the promised support from the 22nd Armored Brigade failed to materialize. As required, the Indians had reported their failure to General Gott's 13th Corps at 0300 hours. To send the tank regiments in all the same was sheer murder: tiny little tanks they were, without any infantry support or high-explosive shells, running straight into the great jaw of anti-tank guns and eighty-eights. The outcome was predictable and is now part of the textbook of armored warfare.

Bomb hits Chianti bottle

A little way below the crest of the hill sat the anti-tank crew whose gunlayer was Günther Halm. They had hacked their way into the stony ground with pickaxes to lower a little the profile of their great 1.4 ton "growler," which was otherwise rather like a barn door. Every bone in their bodies hurt, but they had a splendid position now, with the barrel pointing to the east. When the sun went down, Italian infantry

[5] Bryan Perrett, *The Valentine in North Africa.*

from the Pavia division had still been with them; but there had been a bit of bother during the night: The anti-tank crew heard a fairly strong enemy raiding party creep past them a little way downhill, so they played possum. Later, seven or eight Indians made fairly straight for them, so they swept the area with their machine gun until all was still again. At any rate, when daylight came, the Italians had disappeared as well.

So "last night's party" had had a certain amount of success after all. A little way farther west, captain and battery commander Heinrich Dammann would occasionally frown as he heard the machine guns chattering some way off. But then Warrant Officer (Special Duties) Clemens or Driver Struntz would say "Cheers!"—for they had a bottle of Chianti wine between them and they were taking things easy in the velvety night.

When the bottle was half empty, they put what was left in the battery commander's VW jeep; Chianti was a rare luxury in the desert, so it was as well to know where to stop, hard as it was.

With a little smile, Warrant Officer Clemens asked leave to visit one of the eighty-eight crews which were scattered about the desert. Dammann thought, He wants to cadge another drink—well, let him—and crashed down in the jeep. His night's rest was rudely interrupted by the RAF. It was as bright as day when he woke, and a Christmas tree [flare] hung right above him. The engine of a low-flying plane screamed. The blasts hit him like so many boxes on the ears as he threw himself into his foxhole. Cursing, he shook the muck off his uniform. Then he heard Struntz call out, in real alarm: "Herr Hauptmann . . . Clemens. . . ."

The warrant officer's foxhole had disappeared under sand and rocks, a great crater gaping right next to where it had been. They dug like men possessed, first with spades, then with their bare hands—surely they would come upon the body sometime—no, it must be too late. . . .

Someone came whistling through the desert, which had now gone quiet again. Grinning and redolent of Chianti, he announced his return as the regulations required: "Warrant Officer Clemens reporting back, sir."

Struntz held his bleeding fingernails out at him accusingly and said: "You sod." But it sounded almost affectionate.

The three of them had a great shock when they looked at the jeep, however: The bodywork was riddled with holes, three of the tires were flat—oh well, all that could be put right—but the Chianti bottle had been smashed to smithereens. "The next time we'll slurp down the bloody lot," said Dammann as he stretched out again, grumbling, this time right in the foxhole.

Next morning the captain went from gun to gun, ears cocked to the east, where the artillery fire was growing steadily louder. A soft but deep-throated intermittent rumbling sounded suspiciously like a fairly large armored force. He ordered the guns to be limbered behind their tractors, their trails unfolded, so that they were ready at the same time both to fire and to travel, returned to his jeep at a slightly smarter pace and wondered whether he'd have time to shave.

That was when the annihilation of the 23rd Army Tank Brigade began.

The destruction of the 40th Royal Tank Regiment

Lieutenant Wiard had meanwhile closed his turret hatch. His reasons for doing so were more technical than to do with safety, for the enemy artillery fire was not too bad, while the British batteries were putting down a very reassuring rolling barrage in front of the foremost tanks.

But now that they were definitely in enemy territory, it was better to hold oneself in readiness nearer the breech mechanism of the gun, for in the tiny Valentine, with its three-man crew, the commander was also the loader; and at any moment the dreaded Panzer IIIs and IVs might emerge out of the cloud of dust being raised by the Royal Artillery.

For the moment at least, the dust cloud offered cover, but by now the lieutenant was seriously concerned.

He had heard on his radio that Colonel Dunbar's tank had been hit and the regimental commander himself put out of action. He was followed shortly afterward by John Russel, commander of A-Squadron. And Wiard thought: Who's shooting at them? They're miles behind me. Fleetingly, he thought of turning tail, but who would turn about in his first engagement? Even military caution comes only with experience. Just now, all he could think of were the evil tongues saying: Wiard ran away before he had caught a glimpse of his first German.

So he jogged on; radio contact grew weaker, but from scraps of conversation and the excited voices that filtered through, he gathered that all hell had broken loose somewhere behind him.

And it was largely Günther Halm's work.

The six men serving the Russian anti-tank gun at first sensibly kept their noses down in the sand, as the British artillery barrage rolled toward them. Then they jumped to their gun, but in the billowing clouds of dust they could make out nothing. Wiard and his troop of three tanks were thus able to drive past the position unmolested.

Heavy engines roared immediately in front of them; the clouds of

dust settled with tantalizing slowness. And then suddenly they could
survey the whole plain to the south and east of them. Never will
Günther Halm forget that sight: There were advancing British tanks
everywhere, with the mass already past their position in the south, the
nearest barely 100 meters away. They had to whip the gun around;
their lovely parapet, which had cost them so much sweat, had become
useless, and the trails were no longer firmly dug in—just too bad.
Halm's hands flew as he cranked the handwheel. "Fire!" yelled the
warrant officer.

They were all fairly nervous; and why not? Only a few anti-tank men
could ever have experienced such a moment. The loader fired before
Halm had managed to take his left leg off the huge solid rubber-tired
wheel; and because the trails were lying free, the 140 mm gun jumped
even more than usual. So the rearing steel colossus caught the layer's
leg. The bones of a nineteen-year-old are pliable. Later, the leg was
pronounced slightly bruised. Just then, he felt nothing anyway. Their
very first shot had struck home: Black smoke poured from the stricken
tank. A fleeting glance, and he was cranking the handwheel again. The
plain was full of targets; and the Russian anti-tank gun's shot, weighing
around seven kilos, could pierce the 90 mm armor of a Matilda's turret
at 2,000 meters.

However, their own situation became more awkward with every shot
they fired. Since they were firing southward, the gun was recoiling
uphill. Soon, they were standing on the slope without any cover, making a large and inviting target. Solid shot from the tanks' guns whistled
all around them. One went between Halm's legs as he stood astride;
another tore a piece as big as your fist from the loader's calf. But as yet
Grenadier Halm was able to go on firing, though he saw the gun barrels on the tanks traversing toward him; he cranked, crashing and whistling all around, sand between his teeth. "Fire!"

In the space of a few minutes the 40th Royal Tank Regiment had
lost its most senior officers. One of the very first AP rounds tore to
pieces the commander's driver, Sergeant Watts, and wounded the colonel so severely that he died next morning. Squadron commanders Russel and McBlaren were wounded. Major F. G. Pinnington, commander
of B-Squadron, was twice knocked out: His first tank was hit head-on
by an AP round and his driver severely wounded. The lanky major ran
to another Valentine which was driving past him not far away, dispos-
sessed its commander and was trying to seek out this dangerous enemy
when a shot crashed into his turret. This time, fragments smashed his
arm. The driver and radio operator were also gravely wounded.

Sergeant Harold J. Sowden, known to all and sundry as "Chesty" because of his immense thorax, was driving over on the left wing of the

squadron. As his radio buzzed with bad news, it soon became clear to him that this annihilating fire must be coming from the flank of the Ruweisat Ridge. Like all the others, he began to mark time, made his driver maneuver backward and forward so as not to present an easy target and to find a place whence to spot that blasted gun.

But black smoke drifted over the battlefield as more and more tanks were knocked out; and now the enemy artillery was clearly firing from every barrel. Amid all the dust and smoke, he made his gunner simply shoot any old where at the side of that hill, shoving the absurd little shells into the two-pounder with his left hand and calling: "Fire!"

As well shoot at pigeons with a pistol: Among the many handicaps of the inexperienced tankmen from Liverpool was the old and then still unresolved affliction of British tanks, the little cannon still had no HE shells to fire—and it was tanks like these of all things that were made to attack without any infantry on that 22 July.

Captains Phelps and Lumby had now become the senior officers. Over the radio they ordered the remaining tank commanders: "Never mind the guns! Machine-gun fire at the sides of the hill!"

It was a little better than the two-pounders' solid rounds, but all the bursts from the coaxial Besas managed to hit was one abandoned anti-tank emplacement.

Amid the howling, whining, crashing inferno, Günther Halm, the lad with the downy, girlish cheeks and the dreaming eyes, had knocked out nine tanks. After every shot the bouncing gun had to be dragged back into place and fourteen rounds were all they managed to fire off. A solid round tore away the sight assembly. For the time being, nothing much more could be done with the gun. They bandaged the loader's bleeding leg but he died on the way to hospital. The others got away with nothing worse than scratches and withdrew to regimental HQ on the northern side of the ridge. The commander of the 104th Panzergrenadier (anti-tank) Regiment, Colonel Ewerth, had seen the tank armada advancing and had alerted the 21st Panzer Regiment's HQ. The holdup and confusion wrought by that one anti-tank gun on the side of the hill had been enough, reinforcements rushed to the scene— more anti-tank guns, the mighty eighty-eight guns, and Panzers. The order to withdraw reached just eleven intact armored fighting vehicles of both British regiments. One hundred and four had gone into the battle. Among the few to return safely was Sergeant "Chesty" Sowden.

Meanwhile, Wiard drove on, full of dark forebodings but determined to sell his skin as dearly as possible. Only one tank of his troop was now following him; he had no idea where the third had got to. The first eighty-eight round went through the barrel of his gun just behind the muzzle; the tip drooped down sadly like a piece of string with a kink in it. The next shot struck the engine. From the shattered cooling system steam hissed into the fighting compartment. "This is where we get out!" yelled Wiard over the intercom. Behind them, the other tank blew up. Only the driver survived.

Wiard and his two men sought cover behind the tank. Four more 10-kilogram rounds crashed into it. "Nothing like making sure, I suppose," grumbled Wiard. Shortly afterward a German VW jeep pulled up next to them. A second lieutenant got out. The situation was so unambiguous that even putting their hands up was an empty gesture.

"I'd like to fetch my water flask from the turret," said Wiard.

"Okay," nodded the lieutenant.

The flask was gone. The AP shot had smashed everything to smithereens. They climbed into the jeep. "We are, of course, not allowed to accept any souvenirs from you," said the lieutenant politely, "but should you have a watch to spare . . . Mine's bust."

Wiard's radio operator readily handed him his pocket watch. The lieutenant was overjoyed and thanked him effusively. Wiard was amazed. The diminutive "sparks" was a Scot and his sense of ownership was as well-developed as that of the proverbial Scot in all those jokes. They were brought to the 21st Panzer Division's forward HQ, which was barely 1,000 meters away, which gave Wiard a somewhat irrational feeling of satisfaction. "I've always wanted to chuck that watch away," said the little Scot. "It's never gone yet."

Farther south a fierce shoot-out broke out. A vanguard of the 46th Royal Tank Regiment—all of six tanks—had also broken through; but they had run into Dammann's battery.

He was sitting in his jeep, having a shave, one cheek still white, when he happened to glance southeastward and saw, barely 500 meters away, some swaying tank turrets appear from a fold in the ground.

"Alert!" he roared across to the next gun.

"Couldn't we finish changing this tire?" came the somewhat surly reply.

Dammann roared with rage and, as if on cue, the tanks began to fire. Solid rounds whistled about the place with the typical whine of high-velocity projectiles; and everyone forgot all about changing tires.

Now it was a matter of movement, making dust with your vehicle, and then taking turns to fire in rapidly alternating bursts. For these old warriors it was all routine. But they would not have got away scot-free had the tanks been able to fire fragmentation shells. As it was, they got away with it once again: The first tanks were already on fire. There was also a troop of anti-tank guns, their tenor barks in counterpoint to the shattering crash of the eighty-eights. . . . Not one tank escaped. The last one was struck by an AA round where the turret joins the hull. The cupola was torn off, the steel structure weighing several hundredweight catapulted some distance from the hull—together with the upper part of the commander's body.

On the British side, the remnants of the brigade were regrouping. Lists of the dead were being drawn up. "Chesty" Sowden, back with his regiment, heard the names of old friends—Cliff Church, Albert Jenkins, Jerry Watson . . . They were not just comrades in the same regiment, these men; they had all come from the same neighborhood. He knew the mothers, wives, children of many of them.

Some of the crews had returned walking, many wounded, but at least alive and at liberty. About half the numbers making up the crews were captured, dead, or severely wounded.

A reunion in Liverpool

Halm received his Knight's Cross from Rommel himself and thus became the youngest soldier and the first Grenadier to win that high decoration. His young face smiled gently from many a front page. Here is a report in the local paper of his home town, Hildesheim: "The whole town is head over heels with joy. There is but one topic of conversation. . . . Halm's father hardly has a chance to put aside his black Sunday best." But the story has a sequel because the officers of the 40th Royal Tank Regiment discovered twenty years after the war[6] that the gallant gunner on the slopes of the Ruweisat Ridge had survived the war and was running a fuel business in Bad Münder. They invited him to their 1963 regimental dinner. The local paper wrote: "On the smoke-filled stage of the Western Desert at El Alamein there appeared an anti-tank soldier whose name is written in the Book of Fame. . . ."

Since that day, squadron commander, F. G. Pinnington, now a retired colonel, has been the owner of a signed photograph of the nineteen-year-old Halm with his Knight's Cross—a picture he often looks at in spare moments.

And when the friends of Lewis Wiard—who after regaining his liberty went back to the countinghouse of his substantial business—tease him too much by saying: "Lewis, tell us again how you ran straight off the ship and gave yourself up from a handful of spaghetti to the first Italian you met," he is liable to say at most: "You should have seen that terrible German; I simply ran off right under his gun barrel! Proper man-eater: Look!" And he shows them the picture of the shy, smiling, girlish Halm.

Only "Chesty" Sowden has never seen his former enemy; the dinner was for officers only. After nearly thirty years' service in the British

[6] From Paul Carell's book, *Die Wüstenfüchse.*

Army, he is now an inspector with the city bus company. He still has that huge chest of his and powerful arms to match. He is impeccable, loyal to his sovereign, and proud of the part the company has given him to play.

The story is told about him that he once gave a trade union official the shock of his life. The man, who was new to the neighborhood, wanted to have the "Internationale" sung at the conclusion of a meeting. "Chesty," so the story goes, got to his feet and said in level tones: "It is our custom here to sing 'God Save the Queen' to end our meetings. Anyone singing anything else will be dispatched by me through this window here." The meeting was on the third floor.

And the officers added: "Ah, yes, old 'Chesty'—pity there aren't any like him left." They warned me, moreover, before I went to interview him: "Chesty's very patriotic and—well—outspoken. . . . Not sure whether you two will hit it off."

But when I said good-bye to him after three hours' talking, he offered me an old pair of goggles as a souvenir. They had traveled a long way with him, from El Alamein to Tunis, and then via Sicily up the boot of Italy, in his little Valentine tank.

An army unsure of itself

The self-sacrifice on the Ruweisat Ridge, comparable in military fatuousness only to the sad nonsense of Langemarck[7] in the First World War, was at one and the same time the climax and the conclusion of a chain of errors which had turned the British Eighth Army into a collection of men who, though still brave and determined, were very unsure of themselves. The failure of the top echelons of command, and their utter confusion, belong to the textbooks of armored warfare as cautionary examples.

Apart from Churchill's importuning, there had been no reason for sending inexperienced troops, virtually straight off the ship, into action against bone-hard crack units. Even worse, there could in effect have been no co-ordination of any kind between the various arms. Only the artillery had been effective, as was almost always the case with the British. The RAF, although it had air superiority and was otherwise fiercely active, had achieved hardly anything more in the attack zone

[7] In October–November 1914, German troops, most of them young volunteers, charged machine-gun positions at Langemarck, singing the "Deutschlandlied"— the German national anthem. They were mowed down in rows. Although from the military point of view this action was utterly futile, the "sacrifice of Langemarck" was thereafter extolled in the most high-flown language by chauvinists and history teachers.

than the destruction of Dammann's bottle of Chianti—it had evidently
not been asked by its commanders to do anything more than that.
What had been conclusively preprogrammed was the slaughter when
the tanks were launched against anti-tank and eighty-eight AA guns,
able to shoot for all practical purposes quite unmolested by any infantry.

This sort of thing had happened too often; mutual distrust had
poisoned the army's morale. Tankmen, infantrymen, and airmen engaged in recriminations: "When you are needed, you're never there." It
was a perplexed and strife-torn army, lacking leadership, which was
asking itself: "Who the hell has been making this dreadful hash of
things?"

As before, a scapegoat for the Ruweisat Ridge tragedy was again
found at the lower echelons: The commander of the 23rd Army Tank
Brigade, Brigadier Lawrence Misa, was relieved and transferred to a
post in the rear. The Corps Commander, "Strafer" Gott, on the other
hand, was destined for higher things.

Twenty thousand two-pounders "stockpiled"

Winston Churchill had to fight on many fronts that July: On top of
all his other problems, he and his all-party coalition government had to
face a vote of no confidence in the Commons, tabled by a group of
MPs as a reaction to the recent series of military disasters. Although
the motion was thrown out by 425 votes to 25, the old lion himself
came under attack when the greatly respected Sir John Wardlaw-Milne
rose to speak about the arms production scandal.

Although it must have been clear ever since the Battle of France that
no industrialized country worth the name could send its soldiers into
battle with a weapon like the two-pounder popgun, the British war industry had diligently and imperturbably continued to build this little
cannon. In July, 1942, 20,000 of them were "stockpiled"—an instance
of waste monumental even by wartime standards. The newly appointed
Minister of Production, Oliver Lyttelton, was howled down in the
House when he sought to excuse the conduct of his predecessors by
explaining that to switch production to a more effective gun would
have temporarily reduced output.

Slowly, production was now being switched to the six-pounder—no
giant among guns in all conscience, considering the time that had been
lost and the developments in German gun design in the interval. In any
case, the Churchill tank, which carried this gun, did not go into action
in Africa until the closing stages. But an immense industrial machine

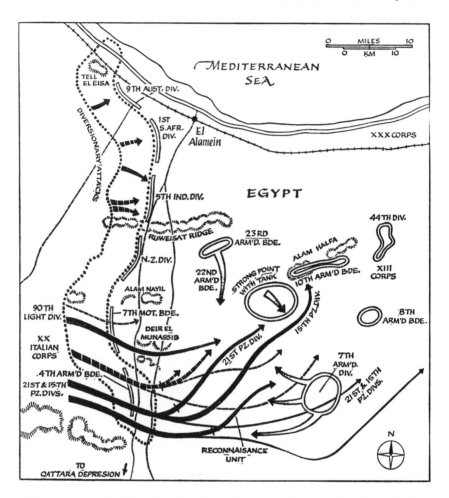

The last attack: The situation is reminiscent of the outflanking of the Gazala line; but here a minihill, bristling with arms, bars the way: the Alam Halfa Ridge. Forces are insufficient for a breakthrough. After six days, it is all over.

was going into top gear on the far side of the Atlantic. The volume production of the Sherman was on a scale European countries could only dream about. Nor was that all: There were also the mighty long-range bombers, fighters, and fighter-bombers.

Greater Germany's Air and Reich Marshal, Hermann Göring, who was prepared to concede to American industry only a certain skill at making razor blades, would have much to brood over yet.

The British desert army, too, was to regain its confidence in its commanders before the next major passage of arms. Once again Churchill took a hand.

The new man: Montgomery

Ironically, it was the well-aimed shots of a German pilot warrant officer which at last brought to the head of the Eighth Army the man who for the first time concentrated this force under one single will, who banished the nonchalant *camaraderie* among officers from the battlefield to the mess—a professional who indulgently said of his predecessors that "they knew a great deal about fighting but not much about war"—Bernard Law Montgomery.

On his way by air to see Stalin, Churchill landed in Cairo on 4 August 1942 to clear the decks. He had already decided to replace Auchinleck as Commander in Chief with General Harold Rupert Alexander—a clever, dispassionate aristocrat who had shown steadfastness, endurance, and judgment in hopeless situations in France and Burma.

But who should lead the Eighth Army under him? Churchill was unwilling to saddle his desert soldiers with yet another general from outside. Would it not be better for morale to pick an old sweat with desert experience?

He decided on General Gott, a brave man to be sure, but implicated in the recent setbacks. Nor would even his best friend have called him a tactical or strategic genius.

Two days later came the shooting down of his aircraft which, it may be assumed, altered world history.

On 7 August the British Flight Sergeant James was piloting a Bombay bomber converted for passenger service. They had taken off from the small airstrip at Burg al-Arab, some 60 kilometers east of El Alamein, and were making for Cairo. Shortly after takeoff, the oil temperature in one of the engines rose to danger point.

In the normal way, clumsy machines like the Bombay were flown close to the ground in the vicinity of the front. At that altitude, one was fairly safe from being spotted by patrolling enemy fighters. Flight Sergeant James, however, decided to climb to 150 meters, to look for a suitable spot for an emergency landing in case his engines failed.

The machine was immediately intercepted by a group of German fighters. Warrant Officer Schneider positioned himself behind the Bombay and fired. James decided to make a crash landing. Hardly had the plane come to a halt on the ground than the crew jumped out. The airmen knew what they were doing.

Although the air war in Africa was otherwise fought fairly, on one point alone no pilot on either side would give any quarter: Aircraft which had made an emergency landing more or less intact were destroyed on the ground in a further pass, to prevent them being put back into service.

Schneider's cannon shells and machine-gun bullets riddled the fuselage of the Bombay. Not one of the thirteen people left on board survived. Among them was General Gott.

When Winston Churchill heard the news, he had no option left but to accept the uncomfortable man several of his advisers had already pointed out to him: Lieutenant General Montgomery.

There is a Montgomery story that sounds so true that it is bound to be apocryphal. When Monty heard of his appointment, so the story goes, he mused aloud gloomily about the tricks his trade could play on a man: "That's the way it goes with us professional soldiers. You work your way up the ladder, make a name for yourself—but one decisive defeat is enough to lay your career in ruins."

Someone interposed: "Come, the Eighth Army's position is not all that hopeless. I wouldn't paint quite such a black picture as that."

Montgomery woke from his reverie: "What do you mean? I was talking about Rommel."

What is sure is that under the soberly calculating professional Montgomery, there were to be no more fiascoes in Africa even remotely approaching the Ruweisat tragedy. And precisely the later history of the 40th Royal Tank Regiment proved that even a poorly armed unit could consistently earn laurels if used according to its potential. The faithful "Chesty" is still proud that the first German prisoner, from the 90th Light Division they took in Tunisia, spoke most respectfully of the "little tanks." By the time the Valentines had made their way there, they had long earned the officially approved name of "Monty's Foxhounds."

An "upside-down cyclist"

The old "Desert Rats"—and Churchill was quite right to hesitate on this point—regarded with boundless suspicion anyone who came to them from Britain with "white knees." There was quite a bit of grumbling in the officers' messes about "this chap Montgomery," who would first have to be taught his ABCs. Moreover, anyone who, as is not uncommon among the military, wanted the man "to look the part" was in for a disappointment: Montgomery was rather short and slightly built, with pale blue eyes and narrow shoulders, further thrown into relief by his fondness for shapeless old pullovers.

On top of which he brought with him a whole squad of those pale-kneed chaps, fired all the corps commanders with the exception of Herbert Lumsden, shook up the army staff, and paid unannounced visits to the various headquarters so as to "push people around"—as was evidently the case, and as was widely recounted. But the word also soon went around that he left those he visited by no means cast down, but rather cheered and rather refreshed. He spoke not one unnecessary word, but both his questions and instructions were to the point.

It also appeared that the practicing Protestant, teetotaler and non-smoker Montgomery, for all his short, sharp ways, was not without a sense of humor. When he visited the HQ of the New Zealand Division, he was evidently struck by the nonchalant "down under" way in which the New Zealanders, like the Australians, reacted to the sight of top brass, for he remarked casually to General Freyberg: "Your men are not very keen on saluting, I see?"

"Oh, just give 'em a wave, sir," said the unabashed Freyberg. "You'll find they'll wave back."

When Monty drove off again, he waved. And the soldiers he passed politely returned his greeting in their informal way.

Sir John Hackett, who was something of a protégé of Montgomery's, consequently has solid grounds for his theory that Monty had a liking for "cheeky bastards." The army commander's own logical, if strongly self-confident, theory was that anyone who took him on would not hesitate to assail the most formidable enemy. In most cases he was right.

Sir John again: "His great talent for leadership was shown in the way he managed to exploit even the negative sides of his character to positive ends: His egotism, his ambition, his ruthlessness, which at times bordered on spitefulness, were all used when necessary to get people thoroughly worked up and then steer their fury and energy into the right channels."

It is equally indisputable that once he accepted a collaborator, Montgomery remained absolutely loyal to him and never tried to pass the buck downward. Sir John once more: "He would not even allow himself to think that a mistake could have been made in his circle for which he was not himself responsible." It was the unmistakable sign of a man of stature that he was an "upside-down cyclist": He kicked only upward.

The six-foot-six Scot, Dr. Douglas Wimberley, who commanded the 51st Highland Division from Alamein to Tunis, recalled: "As a superior, he was a wonderful little man, who never asked for more than you could give."

It was noticed with approval in the messes that Montgomery did not surround himself only with his cronies but, with a sure feeling for good men, also attracted into his entourage, and built up, veterans from the desert: men like Brigadier Freddy de Guingand as Army CGS and Lieutenant Bill Williams of the KDG as his Intelligence Officer.

The first official actions of the newcomer won a reluctant grunt of approval even from the last remaining skeptics.

He had all the plans for further withdrawals ostentatiously burned, sent much of the transport far to the rear, and explained: "On this line we stay—dead or alive."

He made it clear that there would be no more "messing around" with divisions, no more breaking them up into battle groups, "Jock columns," and the like: "The division is conceived as an effective fighting unit made up of various arms, and that is how it will be employed."

He made both fresh and battle-hardened units practice co-operation with other arms, especially infantry and tanks; and by degrees gave them back the feeling that you could, after all, do something with that other lot.

At this time the Ultra code breakers were producing deciphered messages from Panzerarmee Afrika, containing more and more details about a coming attack. Thus Rommel informed General von Rintelen's Rome office on 16 August that the situation was no longer so critical, since German reinforcements had arrived and his Italian units had been rehabilitated.

But enemy convoys were also arriving, so that only up to the end of August was there any certainty of the Axis forces having superior armored strength (some 500 German-Italian tanks[8] against about 400 British). The Axis had a 50 percent superiority in heavy artillery, Rommel reported; in other arms the two forces were equal.

Rommel, therefore, proposed to attack during the period of the full moon at the end of August. A condition was that the fuel he needed would turn up by then. The unsuspecting field marshal proceeded to spell out his tactical concept: Since the British had built up strong defensive positions only in the north, he would once again lead with a right hook from the south and then turn north for the coast at night, between 0100 and 0300 hours, and trap the enemy's forces. His own concentration in the south before the attack would be camouflaged; diversionary attacks by infantry, with heavy artillery fire in the north, were to trick the enemy into bringing his armor nearer to the front up there.

Four days later, the Duce put his oar in: "The earlier guidelines for the advance to the Delta remain valid. . . . The Italian-German army's

---

[8] Rommel was itching to attack, so he exaggerated a bit—apart from which more than half the tanks were of Italian manufacture—and of the familiar quality. At least the newly introduced Littorio Division had a new self-propelled gun: the 75 mm Semovente.

present positions between the Qattara Depression and the Arabian Gulf will be held in any case."

Montgomery, who in his new job was for the first time shown the Ultra reports, was not by any means overjoyed. He reacted rather like the First World War U.S. general whose view of such intelligence activity was that a gentleman did not read other people's mail. Or like a virtuoso of the fine art of fly-fishing when told that the beasts can surely be killed much more efficiently by using hand grenades.

In fact, he had made a careful study of his man and would, even without Ultra, have been prepared to swear that Rommel would swing his usual right hook in the south.

But Montgomery more than anyone did not fail to recognize that in war you can save blood by resorting to cunning and trickery. An entire department on the Eighth Army Staff did everything possible to confirm Rommel in the belief that his units would easily break through in the south. A map was put in his way on which the main minefields were omitted and bottomless quicksands were marked as negotiable by vehicles.

Just at this time all occasions conspired against Rommel in the intelligence field. British direction finders had spotted that his brilliantly efficient monitoring service was sited on a hill in the Tel al-Aysa area, behind a sector of the front in the north held by Bersaglieri. During an attack by Morshead's tough 9th Australian Division, a special raiding party was detailed to deal with the unit. The Australians jumped the Italians and took the listening post, with all its secret papers, despite the fact that its personnel put up such a fierce resistance that out of over a hundred men only a few badly wounded casualties were left in the end.

The material that was captured contained some considerable surprises. The neatly compiled notes showed that thanks to the careless way in which British radio traffic was run, Rommel was exhaustively informed about the plans of his adversary during the whole of the campaign up to that time. Security procedures were immediately tightened and a monitoring unit set up to ensure that they were adhered to.

Even worse for Rommel, the captured documents showed that the code used by the U. S. Military Attaché in Cairo had been broken and that his reports were being read by the Germans.[9] The code was immediately changed. The source ceased to flow. On top of which, the British caught, in Cairo, two German agents who had been planted there with great difficulty but who up to their arrest had to all appearances

[9] In pursuance of the theory that the Italians were to blame for everything, this too has been blamed on "excessively careless circles in Rome" who were supposed to have, as it were, betrayed the treachery.

conducted their espionage operations mostly in bars and in the beds of dancing girls. The British secret service was now using their frequency to transmit "play material."

Three marshals and no fuel

Immediately after the war, Brigadier Desmond Young wrote one of the earliest biographies of Rommel. He had briefly encountered the German army leader in Africa: When Young was captured, a German captain wanted to force him to order a British battery which was making a terrible nuisance of itself to cease fire. Young refused, and at the height of the ensuing altercation Rommel happened along and immediately made it clear to the captain that he could not force the captured enemy officer to do any such thing. For a moment they stood looking at one another, the British brigadier and the German general, and Young thought he could see just a flicker of a smile on Rommel's face.

When he was writing his book about Rommel a few years later, Young fell victim to the temptation of many biographers: He extensively identified with his subject. It was a most creditable thing to do, particularly since this was a time when it took that typically British mixture of stubbornness and fairness actually to find anything good to say about a German general. But on some points it did not go well with the writing of history.

Moreover, at that time the archives had not been thrown open, so that for many things, especially relations between the Germans and Italians, he relied on Rommel's papers and remarks by him relayed to Young.

Thus he reports that before the start of the last offensive Cavallero had said to Rommel verbatim: "You can go on with the battle. Fuel is on its way." No such remark was ever made. Nevertheless, it still haunts most published work about the war in Africa, even now, when one can look up in the archives just how far the "promises" of the Comando Supremo really went.

The documents of the Wehrmacht command staff, for instance, include a signal from General von Rintelen, who gives an account of this "conference of marshals" (Cavallero, Kesselring, Rommel): "Field Marshal Rommel judges the tactical and operative, but not the supply, situation, to be particularly favorable. . . . Fuel stocks in the frontline are not adequate either for the German or for the Italian side. Marshal Cavallero gave an assurance that every measure has been taken to bring fuel over to Africa; but in view of the present shipping situation he could not guarantee that it would be delivered on time, or in adequate quantity, to meet the indicated deadline."

The minutes of this conference are also among the documents of the Panzerarmee. This paper, drawn up either by Rommel or by one of his closest collaborators, reads:

> His Excellency Cavallero promised that he would seek in every possible way to ensure that by X-Day
>
> (a) The fuel asked for [6,000 tons] is shipped across;
>
> (b) ships with the two required categories of ammunition (especially ammunition in short supply) are immediately loaded and shipped on a priority basis,[10]
>
> (c) that 750 tons of fuel is taken up to the front in Italian vehicles to provide supplies for the German forces;
>
> (d) that the rate at which the lorries bring up the fuel and ammunition is to be increased. . . .
>
> His Excellency Cavallero stresses that he will do all he can above all to bring the necessary marine transport over on time. Naturally, given the difficult position in the Mediterranean, this would also be subject to any intervention by the enemy. . . .

It is the purpose of such minutes, in the army as in business, to provide oneself with an alibi. Anyone familiar with this practice will have surmised that Cavallero must have spoken very emphatically about possible "interventions by the enemy." Who it was who did in effect say, "You can go on with the battle," is reported by Westphal in his book *Erinnerungen*. Rommel, he says, hesitated for a long time, until Kesselring promised "on his honor" to fly across up to 400 tons of fuel in his Junker air freighters if necessary. When he, Westphal, asked the others to consider that this amount would require nearly 250 of the Ju-52s, and that these machines would have to use a part of the fuel thus ferried over for their return flights, Kesselring had sent him away with a flea in his ear. The two marshals had presently shaken hands firmly, with Rommel saying: "Agreed!"

Presumably Kesselring at that time knew more than Rommel about the Italians' shipping difficulties. On 20 August 1942 he had taken part in a conference at the Comando Supremo with Cavallero and the German Admiral Weichold[11] at which it was stated (again according to the report by Rintelen to the Wehrmacht Command Staff/OKW): "Italy has so little fuel oil that either shipping or convoy escort work must be reduced." Since the tankers, with their low speeds, were in any case especially at risk, things looked bad. As a precaution, Cavallero again reminded Rommel that: "As you well know, shipments are coming through with great difficulty, since the means available are less than

---

[10] The language is somewhat confused, which is understandable in the circumstances.

[11] Chief of the liaison staff attached to the Italian Navy Admiralty Staff.

what is required. Latterly the situation has further deteriorated. . . ."
(Signal dated 21 August.)

While one may impute nothing but the best intentions to Desmond
Young, who was handicapped by the incompleteness of available information, it is clear from more recently published German work, in view
of the data now available or easily obtainable, that we are in the presence of an eager and unscrupulous attempt to construct an "African
stab in the back" legend. In such books, the oilfields on the Persian
Gulf, and even more remote objectives, are portrayed as having been
"already within Germany's grasp" had not the wicked Italians, either
through treachery or ineptitude, constantly undermined her.

Our friend the ex-war reporter in particular explains four times on
four pages, with true occidental fairness and chivalry, that the El
Alamein offensive failed because the motor fuel guaranteed by the
Comando Supremo did not arrive. Just for good measure, he throws
in the remark that an Italian officer betrayed the plan of attack.

In fact, the tankers which were to bring the 6,000 tons of fuel were
sunk nearly without exception—one right in the mouth of Tobruk harbor. Italian seamen, who have weighed anchor in the knowledge that
they were virtually doomed men, died in the horrible manner reserved
for those who sit on an immense barrel of gasoline. The chivalrous oc-
cidentals we have spoken of do not think that worth mentioning. Naturally, Kesselring could not even remotely keep his promises either. But
it is in any case highly doubtful whether Rommel's last offensive could
have been driven home—even if he had received those 6,000 tons of
promised fuel.

"I am about to die, Herr General"

On 19 August 1942, Winston Churchill visited the front at El
Alamein for the second time in the space of a few weeks. General
Montgomery invited the head of the government into his map caravan.
"There he gave us a masterly exposition of the situation," Churchill
later wrote. "He accurately predicted Rommel's next attack and explained his plans to meet it. All of which proved true and sound." The
Prime Minister, who was the No. 1 recipient of the Ultra reports, of
course knew exactly where Montgomery had obtained his "predic-
tions." What he had come to see were Montgomery's preparations.

And they greatly reassured him: "I was taken to the key point southeast of the Ruweisat Ridge. Here, amid the hard, rolling curves and
creases of the desert lay the mass of our armor, concealed and
dispersed yet tactically concentrated. . . . Every crevice of the desert
was packed with camouflaged concealed batteries. Three or four hun-

dred guns would fire at the German armor before we hurled in our own."

And not guns alone.

As the Panzerarmee moved off shortly after nightfall on 30 August 1942—the 90th Light on the left wing, the two German Panzer and the Italian Ariete and Littorio divisions in the center, cover on the right flank provided by the reconnaissance units—it soon ran into minefields it knew nothing about. Almost simultaneously with the first mine explosions, heavy artillery fire began. Machine guns swept the entire area and it cost the sappers heavy casualties to clear a lane.

And the RAF made its appearance with dreadful precision. Its Christmas trees turned the moonlit night into day. Carpets of bombs crashed down between the German formations, and fighter-bombers swooped over their columns, cannon hammering. Considering the vast quantities of explosive used, the German losses were, relatively speaking, not all that great. Even on that stony and mostly dead-flat ground, the old rule held: Scatter and flatten yourself. The worst part of it was the feeling of utter helplessness and the resulting slowdown of all operations.

Three out of four German generals were lost in the first hours. General Georg von Bismarck, commander of the 21st Panzer Division, was killed in the minefield. At almost the same, Major General Kleemann of the 90th Light was wounded.

General Walther Nehring expected the worst when a Christmas-tree flare blossomed out right over his half-track. A bomb went off with a deafening crash close to the left front wheel. The general was hit by fragments in the head and upper arm. The other passengers—Colonel Bayerlein and the radio operators—had, between them and the impact, the big radio sets which completely shielded them from the shrapnel.

When the general picked himself up, streaming with blood and dazed, he saw his supply officer, Lieutenant Colonel Walter Schmitt from Würzburg and a friend of Bayerlein, standing by his car. He said: "Herr General, I am mortally wounded; I am about to die."

"I've been hit too," the general replied. The lieutenant colonel collapsed and died.

Another officer who had been outside the car succumbed to his shrapnel wounds. As the advance faltered, Sergeant Major Wendt lay down near his Panzer and tried to sleep. He was awakened by a huge explosion. A parachute flare stood right over his head. Splinters struck sparks off the flanks of the Panzer and tore holes into his jacket, which he had hung on the turret.

Warrant Officer Lohbrügge stood behind his Panzer a little farther down the row when a bomb struck. A great fragment flew under the floor pan and struck off both his legs. Lohbrügge had worked for Wendt in the orderly room and kept asking him to take him into his crew as gunlayer. This had been his first taste of action. His Panzer commander, himself utterly worn out by amoebic dysentery, dragged him to the rear.

It was dawn before lanes had been cleared through the minefields and the British troops had slowly withdrawn. By that time it was clear that the attack could no longer proceed according to plan; the little height of Alam Halfa, bristling with guns and earlier inspected by Churchill with such satisfaction, was to have been bypassed before daylight. Rommel considered breaking off the attack, but then he ordered that the enemy positions should be attacked head on and broken through.

He thus allowed himself to be lured into an operation which he had always tried to avoid—apart, that is, from the unhappy decisions he took when his judgment was clouded by too much emotion during the first attacks on Tobruk: a bullheaded frontal charge against better-armed and fortified positions.

For with their six-pounder the British now had a high-penetration anti-tank weapon—true, with nothing like the performance of the eighty-eight, but nevertheless enabling Montgomery to copy a typical Rommel tactic: Instead of risking his precious tanks in a fight with the enemy's massed armor, to lure him and his tanks on to his own powerful anti-tank line. And the tactic worked against Rommel, too.

Luckily, a great sandstorm raged that 31 August and hampered RAF activity. When at last they moved forward again, riflemen were sitting on the track guards of Wendt's Panzer.

"Why don't you sit behind the turret?" asked the sergeant major.

"Why bother? Whatever could happen to us, right in the middle of a Panzer pack?"

They came up against a Bofors Pom-Pom firing HE shells, which swept the poor fellows off the Panzer with a couple of shots.

Another series of eight shots "welded" the turret's turntable track to the hull so that the turret seized up and could not be turned. They had to retire to safety.

The 15th Panzer Division's 8th Panzer Regiment penetrated farthest, but could not break through the Alam Halfa position either. True, it consisted mostly of the new Panzer types, unmatched by anything the Anglo-Americans could build either by way of armoring or guns,[12] but the whole situation now no longer resembled in any way the fast mobile battles of which Rommel was such a master.

---

[12] At the start of the battle: 27 of the long-barreled Panzer IVs and 73 of the long-barreled version of the Panzer III.

Cleverly exploiting the available cover and mostly firing from "hull down" positions (i.e., with only the turret showing above the cover), two brigades of the 10th Armored Division were fighting a battle of attrition. In the south, the 7th Armored Division, which during the night had considerably slowed the crossing of the minefield, had withdrawn a short way in face of the Panzerarmee's advance and now stood facing the latter's flank, from which position it not only inflicted heavy losses on the lightly armored vehicles of the reconnaissance units but also, and more particularly, shot the supply columns to pieces. This was the main cause of the supply difficulties of the fighting troops, for while there was as yet enough fuel, no more was coming forward.

The following night the bombers came again. Sitting at ease in our armchairs today, none of us can conjure up with hindsight the sheer nervous stamina needed by men who lay hour after hour under the blows of the RAF. And when day came, it all went on without a pause: This time there was no obliging sandstorm to rescue the attackers.

On 2 September, Rommel decided to withdraw his troops step by step. They left behind 49 destroyed Panzers, 55 guns, and 400 vehicles.

Montgomery resisted another temptation—that of following up with a counterattack by his armored divisions. There was no doubt that the battle was won; but the army that was retreating before him was not a beaten and demoralized mob, but an intact force which could still deal heavy blows.

So he reined back his tanks and allowed only the fast Honeys of the 7th Armored Division to make limited thrusts on the southern flank. In his book *Operation Victory,* the then Chief of Staff, Freddy de Guingand, says that the dashing cavalryman, and later parachutist, "Shan" Hackett, had the time of his life down there. He was referring to the attacks by the Honeys, steering their unpredictable zigzag course at high speed—a speciality of Hackett's, who at this time was second-in-command of the 4th/8th Hussars.[13]

But units consisting of the larger tanks were held on the leash. Sergeant McGinniley, who now commanded one of the squat Crusader tanks, early in the morning on 6 September watched the last German units moving back through the minefield. His unit "escorted" the retreat, occasionally slipping behind a hill and venturing a quick shot.

[13] The 4th, badly mauled in Greece, had again lost one of its three tank squadrons in the desert. The 8th had lost two. The two regiments, both once members of the famous Light Brigade at Balaclava, were temporarily put together as the 4th/8th Hussars. They have since the war been permanently amalgamated into The Queen's Royal Irish Hussars, of which regiment General Hackett was lately regimental colonel.

But they had been ordered not to get involved in anything that might reduce their combat capacity for the greater tasks yet to come.

Just before the minefield, a last opportunity offered to cause a bit more aggravation, and somewhat hastily McGinniley drove up a small eminence. While he was still focusing his binoculars, he saw the muzzle flashes of three guns simultaneously, felt a crash and an impact, and fell down into the fighting compartment. Blood ran down his face and uniform and his gunner bent over him. "You've been wounded."

"You don't say," said McGinniley, angrily; but while the gunner bandaged his head, he relaxed and thought: "Hooray! Hospital!" But his relaxation was premature, for despite the profuse bleeding, his injury proved nothing more than a superficial scratch. The tank, however, was a write-off and had to be towed away.

4. An Object Lesson, Clausewitz-Style

An army of invalids

There was a certain amount of grumbling in the armored regiments of the Eighth Army: "At last Jerry's on the run for a change, and here we are, sitting on our backsides!" But in general, the ranks of British desert soldiers heaved a great sigh of relief: Jerry was evidently not all that irresistible after all, nor were their own weapons all that inferior anymore either. The new six-pounder anti-tank gun was thoroughly serviceable and the basic evil of tank warfare had been done away with: No longer were their own tanks misused as self-propelled anti-tank guns which had to be driven right up to the enemy to compensate for the difference between their range and his, and to be shot to pieces in the process.

For the first time, a coolly calculating commander had suppressed the "cavalry mentality" and had allowed the enemy to run into massively concentrated formations.[1] And for the first time, the German troops had had to experience the fate of their adversaries in Poland, France, and in Russia in the early stages: the fatal effect of enemy air superiority, not only on the fighting troops but also, and above all, on their vitally needed supplies.

[1] To do Montgomery's predecessors justice, it should, however, be said that he had the benefit not only of new weapons but also of the Alamein position, with its protected flanks.

Omens of what the coming battle in the west would be like were now visible: Already not only the twin-engined "Stubborn Eighteens" drew their trails virtually unmolested through the sky; already the air resounded with the deep-throated rumble of the four-engined jugger-nauts from America's factories—the Fortresses and Liberators—which flew to Benghazi and Tripoli in broad daylight and rained down their carpets of destruction. And already swarms of fighters were buzzing around the streams of heavy bombers, forming a virtually impenetrable screen against the German fighters, superior though the Focke-Wulfs and Messerschmitts still were.

On 3 September 1942, Rommel sent a long signal via General von Rintelen to the Wehrmacht Command Staff and the Comando Supremo, in which he gave the nonarrival of the required motor fuel as the primary reason for the failure of the attack.

He was, however, forced to admit that at this time he still had three "consumption units" available. (One consumption unit=enough for 100 kilometers of travel in normal, not too difficult, country.) Moreover in recent days 2,610 tons (4.2 consumption units) had reached him. There is no doubt that even with this limited amount of fuel Rommel would have continued the attack, given some hope of success (and thus of some captured fuel).

By this time Rommel had long been the only German of his age to have endured the African campaign from the beginning. He had been ill for a long while: as early as 21 August he had teleprinted to Berlin a diagnostic report by the consultant physician of the Panzerarmee Afrika: "Generalfeldmarschall Rommel suffers from the consequential symptoms of low blood pressure, with a tendency to fainting fits. His present condition can be traced back to stomach and intestinal complaints of fairly long standing, aggravated by the excessive physical and psychological strains of recent weeks, particularly in view of the un-favorable climatic conditions." Only after prolonged treatment at home would he be fully fit again, the physician wrote. Rommel himself added: "In view of the above diagnosis, I request the dispatch at the earliest possible moment of a Supreme Commander capable of standing in for me; and I would suggest Colonel General Guderian as suitable. In view of the difficult circumstances and the planning work which must be done, early arrival desirable."

But Guderian, too, was ill just then—and out of favor to boot. Rommel therefore decided that he would lead the attack himself. He wrote to his wife on 30 August: "Healthwise, I feel in top form. Such great things lie before us! If our stroke is successful, it may have a decisive effect on the outcome of the war." With a man of Rommel's ambition it is, however, quite conceivable that the hope of a decisive victory, of the fulfillment of his dream of the Nile, had once more completely suppressed the symptoms of his illness. But after the failure of his attempt, his health broke down completely. Several times he suddenly collapsed in a faint. Although he once more wrote to his wife that he was really quite well, in the end he could not escape the doctor's entreaties any longer. He allowed himself to be talked into taking a cure in Europe.

But not until he had conducted an extensive teleprinter war with the Comando Supremo—via Rintelen and with the inclusion of the Wehrmacht Command Staff/OKW—a war Churchill and Montgomery must have followed with absolute delight. It was, of course, about supplies. It must have made both remarkable and hopeful reading for the leaders of the enemy side to see how cordially the Axis allies dealt with one another over this.

Officially, shipping tonnage was supposed to be shared fifty/fifty between Germans and Italians. There were just under 100,000 German soldiers, and according to their allies' figures, just under 140,000 Italians to be supplied. These figures, however, were energetically contested by the Panzerarmee: There were only 48,000 Italians under Rommel's command, they said; where then were the missing 90,000? The figures were correct, the Comando Supremo insisted. Rintelen meanwhile was constantly being requested by an ineffectual OKW to find out the actual number of Italians in Africa ("German general in Rome is still instructed . . . is again ordered . . . to obtain clarification . . ."). What was he supposed to do? He could go to the Comando Supremo and ask to be shown the figures.

In the end he sent off a signal with the cold numbers:

> Between 1 August and 12 September the following supplies destined for the Panzerarmee were sunk:
>
> | | |
> |---|---|
> | Fuel | 6,126 tons |
> | Ammunition | 1,246 tons |
> | Food | 1,141 tons |
> | Sundries | 651 tons |
>
> Landed:
> | | |
> |---|---|
> | Fuel | 9,403 tons |
> | Ammunition | 2,586 tons |
> | Food | 1,338 tons |
> | Sundries | 1,492 tons |

Conclusion: "The Panzerarmee was warned orally of the expected supply crisis." Little wonder that Rommel was not all that fond of General Rintelen.

The bitter and tragic background to the story was that the simple

Italian soldier was, in any case, permanently hungry and that now, because of the deficient and unsuitable diet, hardly a man was left in the German units who could be described as being really well. Virtually all of them had swollen livers, accompanied by the usual permanent desire to vomit. And as for the state of affairs at the other end, Heinrich Dammann describes it graphically: "You always had the feeling that you had to go at any moment and produce a great heap, but all that came out was a teaspoonful of blood and mucus. . . ."

Moreover, it hit the novices almost harder than the old Africa hands; Rommel declared that in one regiment of the 164th Light Division, which had only recently been airlifted in, there was a sick list of one thousand, and they were men who did not simply have a slight case of diarrhea; they could actually no longer even crawl.[2]

The pressure on casualty clearing stations and hospitals, which would occasionally escalate by leaps and bounds, often led to dreadful conditions: How often in wartime do you get conditions in which medical orderlies have the time to help weakened diarrhea patients with their business, and then wipe their bottoms for them . . . ?

At this time Lieutenant Buchholz was in a defensive position built by the British, with proper concrete emplacements and covered dugouts. The defensive installations of the position naturally faced west, but the reverse side could also be made quite effective with some barbed wire and mines.

The New Zealand Division also lay in this area, a bit farther to the east, of course. The New Zealanders were always sending their men out on reconnaissance patrols and raiding parties. It was sundown and Buchholz was just gulping down something by way of supper when all of a sudden there was a great tall blighter standing there by the barbed wire, snipping away with a pair of long-handled wire cutters as cool as you please. It was a truly peaceful evening. In their emplacement right next to the man who was snipping away at the wire sat some gunners with their 20 mm ack-ack, having a peaceful smoke.

"Hey, what do you think you are doing with that wire?" said one of them.

The man went on cutting away calmly.

"Stop that nonsense and come into the emplacement!"

When there was still no reaction, one of the anti-aircraft men fired a shot. It was much less than a warning shot—more of a shot in jest, really, for they were all amused by the silent sniper, who couldn't have been anything but an individual infantryman—a bit of a straggler.

---

[2] In August 1942 alone, 30,000 hospital cases, most of them sick not wounded, were flown out of Africa. In the same period 45,000 men were flown in.

The next moment a terrific shooting match with infantry weapons broke out from the east. The man by the wire threw himself flat. Two of the AA gunners fell dead. The others leaped into the deep dugout.

In less than a minute it was all over. The man at the wire, a New Zealand lieutenant, who was in a hopeless spot, raised his hands. Two others had got stuck in the wire a little way along and were rather relieved to be fetched out of it in the gathering darkness. They had, it seemed, been covering the retreat of a largish raiding party, for forty cartridge cases lay on the ground around them.

They were big fellows, the three of them, with chests like double wardrobes, who looked around the dugout with a grin and said: "Proper Children's Crusade you are running here, aren't you?"

Buchholz looked around too and felt a slight pang; the man was right: The young soldiers looked like a confirmation class, drained by unceasing dysentery, pale and bloodless like children brought up in a cellar.

He himself was racked by a curious fever, which could rise to 40° C. (104° F.) in a trice and then fall just as quickly, leaving him trembling, limp, and off his food.

A doctor farther back in the fortifications was treating him with quinine. Luckily it was not malaria, which in this area had also made its appearance in many cases. On one occasion when Buchholz, feeling a bit tremulous after an attack of the fever, was at the doctor's, a casualty was brought in—a very young and drained-looking lad from his own company, who had fallen victim to one of those sudden artillery bursts which even a single soldier going a little too conspicuously for a pee was liable to provoke in an enemy who was all too well supplied with ammunition.

This lad had evidently been caught in his bunker by a virtually direct hit. The medical orderly who was supposed to hold the candle for the doctor was a hard-boiled old legionary, who had fought in Indo-China and Syria. Yet when he saw this casualty, he crashed to the concrete floor in a dead faint. "For God's sake," said the doctor to Buchholz, "there goes the toughest cookie I've got. Would you be so kind as to hold the candle for me?"

Trembling, and luckily still somewhat dazed, the lieutenant held the candle. The eighteen-year-old boy was conscious. "Lucky thing for me you're here to help me, Doctor," he whispered.

"Well now, where's it hurting you, young man?" asked the doctor.

"Oh, everywhere, actually. I really can't tell anymore."

He had three severe skull injuries, through which the brain was visible; one eye had been torn from its socket; there was an enormous hole under one shoulder blade, which went deep into the lung; one elbow joint was shot to pieces; and barely a finger was left on one of his hands.

The doctor removed the hairs and pieces of clothing from the wounds and bandaged him. There was nothing more he could do for the time being.

"Surely this is one of those rare cases where he should have a Storch ambulance here," Buchholz said. "He is not fit to be moved over these broken tracks." "That's true," the doctor replied. But when still no Storch had come the next day, he let him be taken away all the same in an ordinary army ambulance over the stony desert: "He'll probably die on the way, but here he'll certainly die on my hands."

Later at the main bandaging station in Mersa Matruh, Buchholz discovered by chance that this tattered bundle of humanity had arrived alive and had been dispatched to Italy, still alive.

Adventure in a cargo glider

You could tell the dimensions of the supply catastrophe which ensued after Rommel's last attack from the vehicles pressed into service at least to mitigate the bottlenecks. The airfields of Libya were invaded by unwieldy artifacts of wood and canvas: cargo gliders.

Machines of this sort—the lighter DF-S-230 and the Goliath-242, with a payload of 5.5 tons—had been used to take supplies to units which had been cut off in Russia. Thoughtful people could hardly suppress a slight shudder at the parallel.

The engineless air freighters, which had to be towed by costly He-111, Ju-52 or He-177 aircraft, were extremely inefficient. Their use was in fact justifiable only in temporary emergency situations, such as the rapidly developing "caldrons" which had to be equally rapidly broken up in the war of movement in Russia.

There must have been something amiss if things of this sort had to be pressed into service to supply an entire army—an army to which only so recently such high hopes had been pinned. . . . Yet now they had to send these "Elastoplast bombers," which had originally been designed to put down airborne troops and their equipment—tools of the last desperate heave, intended for short-term efforts and quite unsuited to the sober world of the logistician's calculations and long-term planning.

"This war is getting more and more irresponsible," muttered gray-haired staff officers among themselves, needless to say finding no contradiction in their words. Their view was that wars, of all things, must be run in a serious and well-considered manner. All this improvisation looked to them like the behavior of the incompetent, or even dishonest, businessman, who keeps raising more and more money to stop more and more holes, but who after all is one's employer and to whom one is, alas, unable to give notice. For even those who thought in rational numbers were enmeshed in the irrationalities of loyalty and honor, with their apparently boundless obligations based on the soldier's oath of loyalty.

One tiny cipher in the logisticians' game of numbers sat over the Mediterranean on 12 October 1942 and felt great, if a little anxious. He was the nineteen-year-old Corporal Siegfried Kurre, from Nienburg on the Weser, and he was piloting his Go-242 cargo glider behind the He-111 that was towing it on a southerly course at a speed of 240 kmph. The sun was shining through the Perspex canopy, the airstream whistled past the fuselage and the wide and blue Mediterranean, flecked with tiny white crests, stretched below.

"Now we're really on our way to Africa," said flight mechanic Paul Hapke in his thick Berlin accent, as if he still couldn't quite believe it.

"Shut up," said Kurre. This business of being towed virtually at sea level still struck him as a bit uncanny. They were flying in the "high tow" configuration—in other words, the glider flew a little higher than the tug; and from where he was sitting it looked as if the He-111 below and in front of him was likely to hit the next little wave at any moment. Sergeant Major Wald, the towing pilot, held his machine at a steady two meters above the water—like running on rails. "Only low-level flight is safe," he had said in Athens before they took off; "the British are prowling about everywhere with their damned Spitfires, and lately also the Americans with these twin-boom things—Lightnings they call them. And just remember, if you pull, we'll do a belly flop in the ditch."

It was that which made the flight a bit ticklish—the drag on the towrope must stay nice and steady—no slacks and jerks! If the glider lifts the tail of the tug by even a little, so that her nose goes down, she'll be in the drink before you know what's happened. At this speed it's bang-crash immediately.

Luckily, there are no vertical air movements over an evenly cool water surface and the two aircraft stayed marvelously steady. A few days ago, things had been different on an unlucky flight to Athens.

In Lecce, in the heel of the Italian boot, they had taken off in the broiling midday sun. They had gone lumbering down the whole length of the grass runway, and still they had not worked up enough speed—and thus enough lift—when the tug pilot pulled the nose of his Heinkel sharply up, just managing to miss the olive groves and vineyards. All went quite well over the Adriatic but then, as they were coming in to land in Athens, they were shaken by a series of savage turbulences.

Now the hawser would hang alarmingly slack, now it would suddenly go taut with a jerk so that the teeth rattled in your head and the He-111, its tail jerked high, would go into a dead stall, the pilot cursing and pulling at the joystick with all his might. In the end he managed to climb to 3,000 meters, where things were a bit quieter. And there was Athens. They cast off.

In his forty hours on freight gliders, Siegfried Kurre had done one flight to the front, when he had put his machine down in the Kholm caldron and earned himself an Iron Cross Second Class. So he thought of himself as an old hand at the game, but the landing in Athens went all wrong.

First of all they seemed to be coming in too high. "Paul, flaps out," Kurre yelled.

Paul Hapke unfastened his belt and jumped behind the seat so as to turn the clumsy handwheel for the landing flaps more easily.

And all of a sudden they were too low. "Retract flaps." Hapke cranked like a world champion, but there were a couple of knee-high stone dykes at the near end of the runway. The glider, heavily loaded with spares for the Me-109 squadrons in North Africa, plowed right into them in a stall.

There was a frightful crashing and banging, and Siegfried Kurre didn't need to open the cockpit canopy to climb out of the heap of wreckage. Looking a bit bewildered, Hapke managed to clamber out as well, a steadily rising bump in the middle of his forehead. A sympathetic weatherman, the insignia of the glider pilot embroidered on his chest, assured the crash pilot that there had been unusual down draft. The Go was a write-off. The only usable thing was the dashboard clock, and that only because Kurre had pocketed it as a precaution. They also managed to salvage the gasoline stove and their homemade frying pan on which Paul Hapke cooked such fantastic potato pancakes.

It was ten days before a replacement machine was towed in from Lecce. That was the one in which they were now careering over the Mediterranean, again with Me-109-G spares in the cargo hold behind them.

Some of their comrades from No. 2 Go Squadron had already been shot down on this trip or had ditched for other reasons. But they came through without any trouble; and after barely three hours' flight, the coast of Africa hove into sight. Only it was looking rather odd. A yellow seething mass, like boiling pea soup, lay over the land.

"They're having a sandstorm down there," said Sergeant Major Wald over the intercom.

He knew his Africa well and took no further notice, while they made another sweep over the Tobruk airfield. "We're in luck; the windsock's sticking out of it," Wald said.

True enough, Kurre could see the billowing red-white sausage just above the yellow swirl.

"Now pay attention like a good boy," the sergeant major said. "I'll tow you exactly into the right direction for landing. When we cast off, you go into the soup on your own; you steer by the windsock, and you land."

"Doesn't he make it sound simple?" thought Kurre.

As he dived, it became almost completely dark. Sand rustled against the Perspex canopy; and then great black shadows rushed past on his right at regular intervals. Kurre held the machine rock-steady on a level course. Slowly they lost height until he felt that the wheels were running on terra firma.

They got out, and the next moment were covered in sand— everywhere, even down their underpants. His eyes watering, Kurre stumbled back a few steps; he wanted to know what those black shadows had been. When he saw them, he began to sweat even harder: Grim and brooding, there sat several Ju-52s on their tails. And he had whizzed past them only a few meters away at 100 kmph!

Somewhere behind the yellow wall, the roar of many hundred horsepowers' worth of engine died. The desert-wise sergeant major had, it seemed, also managed to get down on the sand strip.

"Of course we'll take off again in the sandstorm," said Wald cheerfully once Kurre had found him again in the traffic-control room, after wandering about aimlessly for quite a while.

"For you two back there in the glider, it won't make any difference anyhow. Once I really begin to put my foot down, you won't see a thing anyway."

That proved only too true. When they lined up for takeoff, Kurre could at least see the fuselage of the He-111 at the end of the 40-meter rope. But when Sergeant Major Wald opened the throttle, the whispering of the sand on the Perspex canopy became the rattle of a mighty sandblaster whipped up by the propellers of the Heinkel.

They began to bump along. After a few feet of progress at most, the rope vanished in the yellow brew. Kurre crammed his feet against the rudder controls, grasped the joystick, and felt the sweat streaming down in rivulets between his shoulder blades.

Using the electrical turn indicator, he held the machine straight, keeping an eye on the rope. When they reached 120 kmph, its angle gently changed and began to rise. He pulled the stick back, too, and they were airborne. A little while later they were again soaring in glorious sunshine.

"Just wait," said Paul Hapke somberly.

They were flying eastward, toward the front. Their destination was the frontline airstrip of Qu'taifiyah. The sun, which stood low behind them, threw into sharp relief the bizarre forms of the wadis and the edges of the escarpment. To their left, the coastal road snaked along by the sea.

Sergeant Major Wald first climbed to 150 meters, the minimum safe height for civilian traffic. But the farther east they went, the lower Wald took the tug and glider. The idea was to avoid not only the British fighters but also the beams of the radar stations on the far side of the Alamein line.

When they cast off before landing on the airstrip, they were already flying at such a low altitude that Kurre could swoop down directly, without making a landing turn. Wald banked steeply and disappeared like greased lightning, making for Tobruk. Unless it was absolutely necessary, one did not leave expensive aircraft standing about on airfields near the front.

Kurre and Hapke discovered why—soon and forcibly. They were still gathering up their personal belongings in the machine, when they heard the throaty roar of many aircraft engines approaching fast.

Sharp commands from a battery of 88 mm ack-ack by the side of the runway; then the whiplash crack as the guns fired. The two glider airmen threw themselves out of their machine in such indecent haste that Kurre grazed his eyebrows on a transom.

In neat formation, eighteen two-engined Bostons approached, AA bursts dancing around them. Just beside the runway there were a few one-man foxholes. Kurre saw the bombs glistening in the evening sun as they tumbled from the bellies of the planes.

The bomb carpet, a thundering tidal wave of smoke and dust and blinding flashes, rolled with precision from one end of the airstrip to the other.

A little weak at the knees, the two men clambered out of their holes. Their glider was a sad sight. Splinters had plowed zigzag trails into the leading edges of the wings.

"She won't fly awfully well like that," said Hapke philosophically. There were bomb fragments even in the crates of spare parts that they had gone to so much trouble to tow across that pond. The runway was pockmarked with craters—not very big, but all the more numerous. No tug aircraft would land here for some time. They gathered up their most prized possessions—parachutes, gasoline cooker, frying pan, and potatoes—and wandered over to the AA emplacement from which the gunners were looking across at them with grins on their faces.

An orderly put a plaster on Kurre's eyebrow and insisted on trying to talk him into accepting a certificate for a war-wound badge. "Forget it," said Kurre. "It would only be a standing reminder to me of my own stupidity."

Hapke had meanwhile wasted no time striking up a friendship with the cook. He was grating potatoes; the cooker was hissing; life would go on somehow.

Dream of a Greater Germanic Reich

Between his two visits to Cairo in August, Winston Churchill had another important mission, and one he found a little awkward. He flew to Stalin in Moscow to make him swallow a bitter pill (by agreement with President Roosevelt): There would be no second front in Europe in the immediate future. Ever since the wartime coalition had come into being, Stalin had urged such a front, and he had grounds for his assumption that his Western allies would create one by September 1942. The German summer offensive was in progress in Russia; it was clear that Stalin was waiting impatiently and with concern for some relief for his hard-pressed Red Army.

The discussion was accordingly stormy; in the end, Stalin withdrew into a bitter silence. He only started paying attention when Churchill told him of a substitute operation, known under the code name Torch: an Anglo-American landing in French North Africa, aimed at striking at the rear of Rommel's army. And more: "When we are in possession of North Africa at the turn of the year," said Churchill, "we shall be able to threaten the belly of Hitler's Europe."

Carried away by his own idea, he compared the mainland of Europe to a crocodile. "In this way," he said, "we shall simultaneously attack the soft belly of the crocodile as we attacked his hard snout."

That kind of talk went straight to Stalin's heart, and he became downright religious: "May God prosper this undertaking."

The diaries of Lord Alanbrooke, the CIGS, show the trouble he had holding back his restless sixty-eight-year-old head of government from overdoing the pressure he was putting on the joint planning of Torch with the Americans, who were having considerable doubts about venturing too far into the Mediterranean with a vulnerable landing fleet; and also restraining him from his favorite pastime of sending off furious telegrams urging the generals of Middle East Command to premature offensive adventures.

In these few weeks between August and November, 1942, lay the cli-

max and turning point of the Second World War. The military theorist
Karl von Clausewitz, possibly the most intelligent German general of
all time, with the fundamental thinker's knack of articulating what is
obvious (and is therefore so often overlooked), postulated the doctrine
of the "diminishing strength of the attack." According to this, every attack that does not lead immediately to peace is bound to grow weaker
as it proceeds and at a certain point end up by turning into defense.
Clausewitz called this moment the "culminating point."

It is clear that the time and place of this culminating point is determined by the relative strength of one's own and the enemy's reserves.
In this autumn of 1942 the crooked Berlin-Rome-Tokyo Axis had
reached its culminating point. What followed after November was at
best "offensive defense."

The two sides concerned did not of course know this yet, Hitler least
of all. In mid-August, when the spearheads of the German attack were
pointed at Baku and Astrakhan, he was visited by his Armaments
Minister, Speer,[3] and some German industrialists at his headquarters in
Vinnitsa in the Ukraine. The Führer already saw himself on the far
side of the Caucasus, allied with the Persian and Iraqi insurgents
against the British and on the road to India: "Twenty or thirty German
crack divisions are enough!" Then there would arise a Greater Germanic world empire—naturally including the Dutch, Scandinavians,
and Flemings.[4] All these—and of course the Germans most of all—
would then breed children most prodigiously: "The few hundred thousand fallen of this war hardly matter at all in this context. . . ."

Sure, sure. One feels sure it would all have been a consolation to
them.

Nothing would have come of the Greater Germanic Reich even if
Clausewitz's culminating point had come a little later; but for the impatient and pugnacious Churchill it came very late as it was. When he
heard that Rommel's offensive had foundered, the CIGS noted in his
diary: "My next trouble will now be to stop Winston from fussing at
Alex and Monty and egging them on to attack before they are ready."

At least in Alexander and Montgomery the Middle East now had
two commanders who did not allow themselves to be so easily bothered
and needled. They understood and complemented one another; Alexander's back was broad enough to shield Montgomery, who was once

[3] Albert Speer: *Spandau: The Secret Diaries,* London, 1976.
[4] Reacting to the tough resistance of the French at Bir Hacheim, Hitler had
earlier enthusiastically agreed to a suggestion of Himmler's, intended to tidy up
his Master Race ideology, by nominating most Frenchmen as belonging to the
Germanic race: "We must take everything off France that she has by way of
provinces with Germanic populations: Flanders, the Champagne . . ."

again in an impregnable position after the defensive success he had achieved with such superior aplomb—a success which was never in any jeopardy.

Sir John Hackett believes that Churchill would nevertheless have gladly fired him when he allowed the September full moon period to elapse without making an attack, preferring instead stubbornly and patiently to forge his steadily growing army into a first-class offensive instrument.

Little wonder that in these decisive weeks the views of the soldiers and politicians diverged. After his painful admission in Moscow, made eye to eye to his hard-pressed ally, Churchill wanted a victory he could show off—wanted a second front as soon as possible—even if it was not in France but in "the soft belly of the crocodile."

Furthermore, the German summer offensive was at first very successful—at the cost of an entire German army, as was to be seen later; but just then the Soviet Union seemed to be tottering. Stalin reported that since their last conversation, the situation had greatly deteriorated. He demanded more American aircraft and tanks. And the Allies had to pick just that moment to decide to abandon the October Murmansk convoy in favor of Torch. . . .

The brakes were beginning to grip, but the utmost efforts were being made world-wide. In the Pacific, as in Burma, the Japanese were again on the offensive; German U-boats were combing the Atlantic in bigger "Wolfpacks" than ever—the location devices which were to prove their undoing had already been invented, but meanwhile the submarines remained virulent. And such was the shortage of warships that important convoys had to sail for Africa without escort.

After three dark years, a silver streak was clearly visible on the horizon; one could make plans again—even for a return to the European mainland, which Churchill had never lost sight of—only the last thirsty stretch had still to be endured; and the U.S.S.R. especially had to hold out. That was why Churchill was beside himself with impatience and demanding the impossible.

A convoy to Murmansk was badly mauled in September; the Prime Minister conjured out of his hat a plan he had agreed on with Stalin, in a euphoric moment in Moscow: Why not establish a foothold in Norway and set up a base from which one could provide cover for shipping in the North Sea?

The universal headshaking of his military advisers merely made him think all the harder of ways around the problem. In secret, he had called in the Canadian C-in-C, McNaughton, in an attempt to soften him up during the whole of one long night so that the wretched man sat in Alanbrooke's chair the next morning utterly shattered, no longer knowing whether he had agreed or not. Luckily, the Canadian Prime Minister intervened. Churchill was close to tears of anger.

A few weeks more, and he would be nearer to tears of joy.

A conjuror on the Army Staff

"In war truth is so precious that she should never be allowed to appear without a bodyguard of lies." This was one of the many pithy sayings of Winston Churchill which people like to misinterpret to imply that he was trying to justify the use of lies in propaganda.

True, he did not disdain those either, but in this instance he had another meaning in mind: deceiving the enemy to save blood and effort.

Rommel had long held the monopoly of foxy tricks in Africa, with "dust driving"—Panzers made of plywood and lightning-quick evasive movements. In the first Battle of Alamein, Monty's people had already resorted successfully to misleading the enemy; but in preparing the second one, they raised deception to the status of professional perfection. The expression is not in any way out of place, for a genuine professional was a member of the unit in charge of these things: the conjuror and illusionist Jasper Maskelyn.

What this unit did under the cover name Operation Bertram was the exact equivalent of what conjurors do on the music-hall stage. They know how to show the audience one thing convincingly, and then, quickly and unobserved, do another thing.

Therefore the Axis audience on the other side of the Alamein line was, in the course of September and October, treated to everything that suggested an attack on the southern sector of the front—moreover an attack for which the preparations seemed by no means complete in the second half of October.

German-Italian air reconnaissance brought back pictures showing mounting stocks of supplies, particularly of ammunition. A long pipeline was clearly approaching this area and by the progress it was making one could work out that it would be November before it was ready.

In the north, on the other hand, there were no great changes. True, a tremendous number of trucks were standing about behind the front, and it was striking how many of them were heavy lorries. But the tanks were still stationed in the south. It was impossible to tell from the aerial photographs that night after night more and more tanks were being concealed under the bulky outlines of those transport vehicles in the north; for proper tire tracks led to the dummy lorries; whereas broad track marks could be made out behind the dummy tanks which remained in the south.

At the same time, heavy radio traffic was steadily mounting in the south—traffic quite obviously coming from an armored formation, and from which one could conjecture the symptoms of slowly escalating preparations for a major operation. All this activity was provided by the staff of the 8th Armored Division (which was not yet ready for action), while the units slowly concentrating in the north observed complete radio silence.

Thus the growing concentration of forces in the north was concealed from the Panzerarmee's reconnaissance eyes. The change in the British behavior was so extreme that not even the most experienced intelligence evaluation officer could have suspected it. With the one exception of Crusader, in preceding years, largely because of their open-voice radio traffic, they had not even been able to keep secret either their preparations or the movements of their units—and this despite the enormous distances usually available in desert warfare. This time, by contrast, their deployment was taking place with painful slowness, you might say on the doorstep of the Axis forces. No one could have suspected that they had succeeded in pulling off a perfect piece of deception in the process.

It was a particularly remarkable rule of Montgomery's—and a very unusual one in war—to initiate the whole army by degrees, down to the last common soldier, into the rough outlines of the overall plan. He began on 19 and 20 October by gathering all his senior officers, down to the rank of lieutenant colonel, at the Amriyah Cinema in Alexandria, where he himself addressed them about his plans. Not even the oldest hands could remember ever leaving a cinema so impressed. Montgomery's style of never saying an unnecessary word and convincing only with cold facts was the only way left to make an impression on the skeptical and so often disappointed Desert Rats.

According to a carefully laid plan, he then had the details, and with them his confidence in victory spread through the army. The more senior officers informed their immediate subordinates; and finally, two days before the attack, the subalterns gathered their units around themselves and drew sketches in the sand with sticks to show what would be happening. At the same time absolutely all leave was canceled. For the first time since Wavell's day, an entire army, guided by one undivided will and convinced of its superiority, waited only for the starting pistol.

In a book brought out in 1967,[5] Field Marshal Viscount Montgomery of Alamein published his manuscript notes, which were evidently the basis of his address to the senior officers of his army. Under Point 6, "The enemy," he says: "Fairly small strength, only small stocks of petrol and ammunition." And the key sentence under Point 8,

[5] *Alamein and the Desert War,* edited by Derek Jewell.

"General conduct of battle," runs: *"He* cannot endure a prolonged battle of attrition; we can."

Montgomery explained to the officers that he had modified his ideas in recent weeks. In September, he had still intended to start by destroying the enemy's mechanized force, in accordance with the desert-war dogmas which had been valid until then. Then he had come to the conclusion that the training of his people (especially with the new Sherman, the only serious opponent of the German Panzers III and IV) was not good enough for that. He had therefore decided to begin by wearing down the Axis infantry forces "in a methodical advance, unit by unit, slowly and safely." In this battle of attrition, the Axis armor was also bound to shrink if one had the skill to let them run up against defense lines and tanks in hull-down positions.[6]

No one was to expect spectacular successes in the first days. But if everyone stuck to the plan, victory was assured.

One note runs: "The whole affair about 10 days (12)." Exactly twelve days after the start of the offensive, the decisive breakthrough was achieved. "Monty" added the explanation that this exact forecast had not been "a lucky shot in the dark" but the result of long days and nights of reflection and discussion. It is today difficult to verify whether he really did speak of twelve days in the cinema at the time; what is certain, however, is that Montgomery was no less concerned with his posthumous fame than his opponent. It is also known that to Churchill and Alanbrooke, he had spoken of seven days. On the eighth day, the Prime Minister rang the CIGS and gave him a scolding: "What's that Monty of yours doing out there? I think he's letting the battle go to sleep. . . ."

Moreover, not everything went according to plan, impressively and precisely though it had all begun. The superiority of the Eighth Army in most arms exceeded Napoleon's classic requirement that attackers should outnumber defenders by at least 2 to 1. On the Axis side there were again 530 tanks, but 300 of them were the Italian models.[7] Montgomery was able to send 1,200 tanks into action—470 of them heavy Shermans and Grants. When it comes to artillery and anti-tank guns, comparing figures is even more problematic than with other weapons;

---

[6] This was probably the most important point: It was born not so much out of borrowing Rommel's tactics as out of a painstaking and shrewd analysis. Only at the Alamein position was it possible to make the Desert Fox expend his precious Panzers on such an offensive-defense task as holding the only defile between Alexandria and El Agheila. Rommel's substitute, Stumme, immediately rose to the bait, and Rommel continued on the course that had been set. Not that he had any other choice.

[7] A detachment of the mighty Tigers armed with eighty-eight guns, which Hitler had promised, did not materialize.

the 78 eighty-eights, well dug in on the German side, are hard to weigh against British guns when it comes to assessing their effectiveness in combat.

But the other figures indicate how times had changed: The Eighth Army still had 500 of the old two-pounder anti-tank guns, but it also had 753 of the new six-pounders as well as no fewer than 832 of the proven 25-pounder field howitzers. And behind these guns were piled mountains of ammunition.

Twenty thousand tons of ammunition had arrived in recent weeks in Africa for the Panzerarmee, too. But it lay in the harbors of Cyrenaica. Transport and fuel were both in short supply; it was barely eighteen months earlier that the logisticians had made their quickly forgotten calculations about the fleets of trucks that would be required. . . .

The most important factor was that the Luftwaffe had nothing serious to put up against the RAF's 500 fighters and 200 bombers.

The outcome was never in doubt.

As Monty went to bed

The turning point of the war in Africa came on 23 October 1942, at 2140 hours. On the dot, 882 field and medium artillery pieces began to bombard the German-Italian artillery positions. There was some concentration in the north, but since the deception had to be maintained and a diversionary attack mounted in the south, the batteries had perforce to be distributed over the whole width of the Alamein line. After twenty minutes, the drumfire was broken off. The gunners aimed their 882 pieces at new targets. Then their steel muzzles roared into life again. This time, the shells exploded immediately in front of the infantry's own deployment positions, behind which the squat silhouettes of the Valentine support tanks were ranged.

Slowly, and according to a precise timetable, the barrage began to creep westward. The leading companies of the attacking infantry had the task of "keeping in touch" with this moving hell of lightning flashes, dust, and jagged fragments and to be on top of the positions of any surviving defenders the moment the fire had passed over them.

Immediately in front of the first-line positions, the explosions multiplied: Rommel's "devil's gardens"—most meticulously thought-out combinations of mines of all types, aircraft bombs, and barbed wire—were going up in the air. The ground shook; behind the boom of the explosions one could just make out the drone of heavy aircraft engines. A first wave of 125 two-engined aircraft flew in to unload their bombs by the glaring light of Christmas trees over the artillery positions.

Unerringly, and keeping in well-drilled step, the assault troops marched westward. The 51st Scottish Highland Division's bagpipes wailed out their stirring cries. Navigation officers led the way with their pedometers and compasses; beside them, sappers with electric mine detectors. Commandos marked out the cleared lanes and laid out a broad white tape to indicate the center line of the attack. In some places, Bofors Pom-Poms with fixed barrels were firing colored tracers in an uninterrupted stream to indicate the boundaries between sectors. It was hell—strictly based on a well-considered system. When the artillery's creeping barrage abruptly stopped, it was an indication that a specific intermediate point had been reached, where according to predetermined plans strongpoints were to be established. Each gun fired an average of 600 shells apiece for five and a half hours, with staggered pauses of ten minutes an hour (for the sake of the tired barrel, not the tired gunners).

The objectives of the first night—to knock two "corridors" through the mine fields and the main defense line—were reached with relatively insignificant losses. The first prisoners, exhausted and confused, were coming stumbling to the rear. At this time the German divisions averaged fewer than 4,000 men each.

All this while Montgomery lay peacefully in his caravan and slept. Punctually at 2200 hours, he had gone to bed: "There was nothing I could do at this time. The battle was in the hands of my generals. I knew there would be a crisis—and perhaps even several—before the twelve days were over and I was determined meanwhile to rest whenever possible. I was soon fast asleep."[8]

The German-Italian artillery hardly fired a shot that night. Rommel's stand-in, General Georg Stumme, an experienced commander of armor, had not at first given the order to fire, in view of the shortage of ammunition. He wanted first to see where he was. Following Rommel's example, he drove to the front himself at dawn on 24 October. He ran into an unexpected artillery attack and died of heart failure.

A few hours later Rommel received the following signal at Semmering, near Vienna:

SECRET HIGH COMMAND MATTER—MOST URGENT

(1) ENEMY ATTACKING SINCE 23 OCT AT FIRST NORTHERN SECTOR AND SINCE MORNING OF 24 OCT ALSO SOUTHERN SECTOR. INTENSIFICATION AND EXTENSION OF ATTACK TO ENTIRE FRONT AS FROM 25 OCT MUST BE ANTICIPATED.

(2) GENERAL STUMME RAN INTO AMBUSH WHILE DRIVING TO FRONT ON 24 OCT AND MISSING SINCE 0930 HOURS DESPITE EXHAUSTIVE SEARCH. IT MUST BE ACCEPTED THAT HE HAS BEEN WOUNDED AND CAPTURED. . . .

8 *Alamein and the Desert War.*

PANZERARMEE AFRIKA ROMAN ONE-A SECRET HIGH COMMAND MATTER
NO 2794++
POSTSCRIPT FROM RADIO CENTER ROME:
PLEASE NOTIFY RADIO STATION HRFX IMMEDIATELY OF TIME OF DE-
LIVERY OF THIS SIGNAL TO GENERAL FIELD MARSHAL ROMMEL++

Rommel was back in Africa on the evening of 25 October. He was still unwell, but he knew that during these days the fate of "his" theater of war—and more—was being decided.

Probably he hoped to be able still to rescue something from the wreckage. He had stopped over briefly in Rome. After a talk with General von Rintelen, he knew what supply arrangements had been made. Submarines and destroyers would try to take fuel to Mersa Matruh. More last resort devices, like the poor cargo gliders. . . .

When he arrived, the 15th Panzer Division had been reduced to 38 Panzers in fruitless counterattacks—exactly as Montgomery had planned. Rommel immediately brought the 21st Panzer Division, which was stationed behind the front in the south, up to the north as well.[9] It, too, was soon badly mauled; and Montgomery informed the Imperial General Staff with satisfaction that Rommel was, so far, dancing to his tune. Rommel for his part received a remarkable signal from Rome: "I have been instructed by the Duce to express his profound appreciation of the successful counterattack personally led by you. The Duce wants you to know that he is fully confident that the battle now in progress will end victoriously under your command. Ugo Cavallero." Rommel simply could not spare the time to ask himself whether he was being mocked. The last act was beginning.

Montgomery calculated that his opponent must meanwhile be convinced that he was trying to force a breakthrough up by the coast. It was indeed what he had intended, but now it was time to shift the center of gravity. During the night of 27/28 October, he quietly withdrew the New Zealand and 1st Armored Divisions from the front line. When Churchill heard of this in London, he very nearly blew his top, and sent his Minister of State for the Middle East to Monty to ask him whether he was perhaps trying to lose the battle.

With the terse reply: "On the contrary, but we are busy now," de Guingand showed the hapless man the door.

The northern half of the front now had a pronounced westward bulge; and Monty had decided to make the decisive penetration from

[9] Not all of it, however; necessity forced him to "dribble"—the very thing he most hated to do. He could not totally denude the southern front, the shortage of fuel being now so acute that it was doubtful whether he could have shifted his tanks back south in case of need.

the bottom corner of this bulge, in a southwesterly direction, where he hoped to strike the "seam" between the Germans and the Italians.

He struck it exactly, but even here the penetration became an appalling massacre all the same. When the infantry reached its objectives, the 9th Armored Brigade was sent through the gap with 132 tanks to overcome the last resistance and to destroy gun emplacements. Only 19 survived; but the operation smashed the way open for the 170 tanks of the 1st Armored Division as a second wave. And two more armored divisions stood in reserve, including the renowned 7th, the original Desert Rats.

The unrelenting resistance of the German-Italian forces—the Italians, too, for the Ariete, like the Littorio and the Folgore paratroop divisions, were completely wiped out—had made Montgomery even more cautious. He still thought it better not to let himself be drawn into the kind of combat of which the Desert Fox was such a complete master: the rapid mobile battle of mechanized and motorized units. He could not have known how catastrophic the supply situation had meanwhile become on his opponents' side. So he kept his force together and resisted the temptation to imitate the Blitz tactics of breaking through and fanning out. It is easy to say today that had he done so, he would most probably have ended the war in Africa there and then. There is all the difference in the world between wrong decisions taken in the full knowledge of all the facts—such as a thrust aimed at Egypt without secure supply routes—and those which arise out of the careful appraisal of unconfirmed information and assumptions.

The knight who had enough

In these critical days, communications between Rommel and the Führer's HQ became the sort of comedy of errors one would find entertaining if it had not been played out against a backdrop of blood, death, and suffering.

On 2 November, Hitler and his entire staff returned from Vinnitsa to his East Prussian Headquarters, the "Wolf's Lair." That the situation at Alamein was critical was, of course, clear from Rommel's dispatches. The Führer therefore decided to give him a morale booster, the key sentences of which are inevitably reminiscent of Churchill's "willpower" telegram from the bygone days of the fighting between Gazala and Tobruk. "It would not be for the first time in history that a stronger will has triumphed over stronger enemy battalions. But you cannot show your troops any other way than that to victory or death. Adolf Hitler."

For some reason or other—the Ultra expert Winterbotham's guess is that sand must have got into the deciphering machinery—the signal had to be rerun either between Berlin and Rome or between Rome and Africa. Rommel thus was not able to see it until noon the following day, 3 November. He must have taken it to be the reply to a long teleprint he had sent off the evening before. In that signal, Colonel Westphal had given a detailed assessment of the situation agreed by the Generalfeldmarschall, and had bluntly stated that the retreat which had now become inevitable was about to begin.

To get such a piece of sheer propaganda twaddle by way of a reply to his factual analysis was a bit too much, even by Hitler's standards. While Rommel with gnashing teeth countermanded his orders for a withdrawal and himself saw that his army HQ was prepared for defense from all directions, the most frightful *brouhaha* broke out in the faraway Wolf's Lair.

Rommel's dispatch, with its announcement of the retreat, which had arrived at Rintelen's office in Rome at 0200 hours, was received in the East Prussian HQ at around 0300 hours. The duty officer in General Warlimont's "Security Zone II" had come on duty in the evening and therefore knew nothing about Hitler's "Last man, last round" telegram.

The elderly major of the Reserve took the signal to be the continuation of an earlier telecommunication and put it aside to be attended to next day, since it was about Hitler's bedtime and the signal, which bore the imprint of Westphal's African self-confidence, did not even ask permission for a retreat, but simply reported it in the most matter-of-fact way.

When Hitler saw the dispatch at noon next day, the uproar was terrible. The hapless major was threatened with being shot immediately and was told to make a deposition admitting his guilt. Had the delay in submitting the matter been a carefully prearranged ploy between Rommel and "Security Zone II"[10] to enable the Field Marshal to make off from Alamein, undisturbed by orders to hold out to the last?[11]

The major was demoted and Warlimont fired on the spot—a measure which Hitler's evidently well-intentioned Adjutant, Schmundt, was later able to countermand. Meanwhile Rommel's propaganda and orderly officer Berndt, a Nazi of high repute from Goebbels' Propaganda Ministry, had arrived in East Prussia and explained the situation.

Kesselring, too, who only two days earlier had tried to make himself

[10] Hitler's HQ was divided up into several "Security Zones." No one could go from one to the other without a special pass. "Security Zone II," which contained Hitler's private quarters, had the highest security rating.

[11] Hitler apparently never did find out that his earlier signal had looked like a reply and had, in fact, stopped the retreat; for according to Warlimont, much later he would still whine that he had never been given a chance to make Rommel "stay put up forward."

important by sending reports about the situation having become "less tense," and had thereby helped to bring about the "last man, last round" telegram, now sent word from Africa that he supported Rommel in his demand for "a free hand." With bad grace, Hitler gave in. The official retreat began with a twenty-four-hour delay which settled many a man's fate. The coast road was already choked with a disorderly mob that was scrambling back among burning wrecks and abandoned vehicles and British fighters pouring down fire.

Immediately he heard of Hitler's last-man last-round order, Nehring's successor as commander of the Afrika Korps, Lieutenant General Ritter[12] von Thoma (an old warrior from the First World War, who had been wounded twenty times) grabbed a canvas bag with his toilet things, had himself driven to the front, and disappeared into a foxhole, from which not even the yells of the driver could fetch him out when the vanguard of the British tanks turned up. Bayerlein would have us believe that he last saw him "standing bolt upright in a hail of fire." Well . . . one does read of such things occasionally, although the laws of physics seem rather to militate against the likelihood that anyone would stay bolt upright for long in a real "hail of fire." Be that as it may, von Thoma was soon afterward entertained to a light meal by Montgomery. An irreproachable officer had taken a decision on his own initiative—a decision on which one can only congratulate him. The pity of it was that lack of information and innumerable sanctions deprived the ordinary soldier of the opportunity for such self-determination. . . .

Bayerlein took temporary command of the Afrika Korps. These were the hours of vacillation; Hitler had not yet revoked his standfast order; Ritter von Thoma had shown in no uncertain manner what he thought of it; the level-headed Westphal was arguing that an order given from so great a distance could not be obeyed—for reasons which could not be appreciated except by those on the spot; and the eager and ambitious Bayerlein was asking what he was supposed to do with the Afrika Korps now.

When Brigadier Young questioned him shortly after the war, Bayerlein said Rommel's answer had been: "I cannot authorize you not to obey this order."

That would have been quite a dirty bit of work: No commander worth the name can shrug off a decision of that order and pass the buck to a man so very much his junior, in view of the risk of the latter being court-martialed, at a moment when his corps, now barely of division strength, was bleeding to death and summoning up its last ounce of strength in defensive fighting.

[12] Translator's note: i.e., Knight.

And just see how Bayerlein's own recollection of Rommel has altered with the years and the growing Rommel cult! For in Paul Carell's book, *Die Wüstenfüchse,* he quotes Rommel as saying: "The Führer's order has become meaningless. . . . If we are court-martialed for disobeying it now, we must stand by our decision. Do your duty well. All your orders are given in my name. Say as much to your senior commanders should you have any difficulty."

That version presumably originated in the same way as the story about the "erect knight." Westphal reports (in his *Erinnerungen*) that at the time Bayerlein had asked him earnestly not to tell anyone that von Thoma had gone to the forward line intending to let himself be taken prisoner.

A dying man plays the mouth organ

Fate plays dirty tricks with people in wartime, especially during retreats of this kind. One man walks away, unscathed, the other stops a bullet—it can be one thing, or the other. . . .

One of the few formations left intact was Special Unit 288, complete with vehicles, fuel, serviceable weapons, and ammunition. Lieutenant Buchholz and his men were traveling in a wide detour deep in the desert, providing flank cover. They were being harassed from the air—on one occasion actually by the Luftwaffe; they kept patching up their worn tires, they kept at bay the reconnaissance units continually rising up to them, and they kept burying the dead. At the dangerous Marsa el Brega defile, they were ordered to hold up a strong body of Shermans until the mass of the beaten and fleeing army had gone down the coastal road.

Sergeant Major Wendt, the upper part of his thigh mangled by shrapnel, lay in the hospital at Mersa Matruh. There were over a thousand men there who could neither walk nor be moved. Anyone who could even crawl had already begged a lift from units that had gone through.

The number of orderlies was diminishing steadily; a surgeon was walking through the ward between the long rows of two-tiered bunks. Wendt sat up in bed with difficulty and asked: "What's actually happening? Shall we be taken prisoner?"

"Yes," said the doctor. "It is only a matter of hours now."

The great ward went very quiet. Opposite Wendt lay a boy, very young and very emaciated, who began quietly to play songs of home on his mouth organ. It was quite a while after he had stopped that an orderly looked at him, then made a sign to another to help take him away. He was dead.

All of a sudden, Englishmen were walking through the ward, friendly and solicitous. The worst cases were immediately flown out to Cairo and Alexandria. It was two years before Wendt could walk again.

Günther Halm, the lad with the Knight's Cross, was also in the hospital. Wasted after weeks of dysentery, he had simply keeled over, so thin you could almost see through him. When the withdrawal began, the field hospital was dissolved. "It's every man for himself now," they said. Luck had been on his side: A truck had taken him as far as Derna. When everything fell to pieces there, too, he went down to the little harbor and sat forlorn among hundreds of soldiers on the beach, all of them nursing a tiny hope that someone might come in a boat and take them off.

A navy chief quartermaster came past, looking thickset and well-fed. He stopped short and examined the emaciated youth with the Knight's Cross glinting at his neck.

"You come along with me, lad," he said, clearly moved. Halm lay in his cabin all the way to Athens, shaking with fever. It was months before he was fit again.

Near Fuka, British units bombarded the road down which the Germans were retreating. Fires broke out in the tightly packed columns of vehicles; in the livid light of the Christmas trees, demoralized men were running for their lives—away from their vehicles and from the road.

A fair-haired youth in the uniform of an air force lance corporal was scraping stones together with his bare hands and building himself a protective wall to take cover behind. It was Siegfried Kurre, the cargo glider pilot, who had got stuck at the bomb-cratered airfield at Qu'taifiyah.

Kurre and his flight engineer Paul Hapke had at first still hoped that they might manage to patch up their riddled crate and that a tug plane might come to fetch them.

A few days after the attack, the airfield was put back into operation on an emergency basis, the craters having been filled up. A few Me-109s flew in and occasionally took off to engage the bomber formations and their escorting fighters—whenever there was any fuel.

Dogfights were taking place above their heads; shattered and crash-landed machines of both friend and foe lay all around them in the dessert. Kurre, an enthusiastic flyer, dismantled the main instruments from an Me-109 in good condition, to which no one was paying any attention. Remarkably enough, he was to hang on to them through all the viscissitudes of war and even take them home and thirteen years later build them into the first glider of the newly founded Nienburg Flying Club.

On the airfield at Qu'taifiyah the days slipped by; the two airmen made friends with the AA gunners, not least thanks to Paul Hapke's potato-pancake wizardry. Another formation of bombers appeared and once more devastated the field; the remaining Me-109s vanished.

It was some consolation to them that at least the undamaged spares from their cargo glider had been unloaded and used. Kurre and Hapke made their quarters in the empty cargo space, where they were safe from sandfleas and scorpions. They were put down on the AA gunners' mess list, made themselves useful humping ammunition, and marveled at the wonders of the radar installation, which they were seeing for the first time. When Montgomery's offensive began on 23 October, they heard the thunder of the concentrated artillery fire in Qu'taifiyah.

"Don't worry, we'll take you with us if we have to cut and run," said the sergeant major of the radar section. In next few days the noise of battle became louder and louder. Eventually Italian soldiers, ragged and without their weapons, came streaming past the airfield, going west. Kurre, who had experience of the Russian campaign, could occasionally make out the bark of tank guns.

On the evening of 4 November, the AA battery was ordered to withdraw. Kurre provided himself with ten stick hand grenades from the sergeant major, built himself a concentrated charge, and blew up the cockpit of his glider. The AA sergeant major turned up with a captured British jeep. The two airmen's most important possessions could just be accommodated on board; parachutes, instruments from the fighter, and naturally the stove and potato-pancake pan.

They kept their eyes for a long while on their poor hard-done-by glider. They should really have set fire to it, but they hadn't the heart.

For the nineteen-year-old Kurre, who had grown up and been brought up in faith in the Führer and in the superiority of the German master race, the first sight of the coastal road was a great shock. Exhausted and demoralized soldiers, many with blood-soaked bandages, were hurrying west.

There was no heavy weapon to be seen far and wide in the tightly packed column of vehicles. Everyone was simply saving his own skin. Kurre had only seen such a sight before in newsreels showing the end of foreign armies.

When in the pitch-dark night near Fuka, the Christmas trees of the enemy bombers' blossomed out in the sky above them and sticks of bombs plowed through the column, panic broke out. The dead-flat plain on either side of the road offered no cover. The hard, rocky soil enhanced the effect of the fragmentation bombs. Running soldiers cast grotesque shadows in the lurid light of the flares. After every burst they would jump up again and plunge on—anywhere—away from the road, where the dark-red fires were spreading.

"Keep down, idiots!" a voice eventually bawled. "Don't you realize they can see us?"

Kurre fought back his anger and pressed himself to the ground. Amid the shrill whining of the bombs, he imagined he could feel the place on the back of his neck where they would get him. All around him voices were crying; you could smell the stench of cordite. He murmured the Lord's Prayer, which ever since his Hitler Youth Wolf Cub days he had thought was a sissy thing to do, and was strangely reassured by it.

When the bomber formation wheeled away, Kurre hurried back to his jeep, which stood undamaged among the burning trucks. The AA gunners were there already. "Paul!" shouted Kurre.

"Yes?" A figure crept out from beneath the jeep.

"You must have a screw loose," said Kurre, startled. "What on earth were you doing under the car?"

"Didn't feel like running," said Hapke coolly.

The column moved off. On the second day it began to rain, which must have saved a large part of the army.

The RAF could not fly that day. Otherwise it would have been able to inflict appalling slaughter on the mass of troops which had gathered at the foot of the serpentine road through the Halfaya Pass.

The military police would pick out one vehicle at a time from the throng and pilot it up the pass road. Whenever there was a break in the cloud cover, everyone would look anxiously eastward.

"Low-level raid!" someone suddenly shouted. Everyone scattered and ran panting into the desert. But nothing happened. Someone's overwrought nerves had given way. At least two men slept in the jeep every night, laying their heads on the precious cans of gasoline. As long as one had fuel, at least one didn't have to walk, like the wretched Italians who trudged, hollow-cheeked, along the side of the road or just lay around exhausted.

One of them staggered up to the jeep on the Halfaya Pass. *"Sete—ho sete,"* he croaked from between cracked lips. The man was dying of thirst. Kurre gave him what was left in his water bottle.

On 8 November they reached Tobruk.

One of the last He-111s took them out. As it happened, the pilot had to go to Lecce, in Southern Italy, where Kurre's squadron of Go's was stationed.

The beaten army in Africa seemed like a distant nightmare when they sat that evening in their quarters over a good meal and an extra billycan of red wine.

As every year, the Führer made a speech to commemorate the anniversary of the unsuccessful Nazi Putsch in Munich. The airmen at

Lecce listened to him on the radio. After a few minutes, Kurre once again believed firmly in a final victory. Thirty years later he still recalls with astonishment at himself how on that day in Lecce he had goose pimples out of sheer enthusiasm and excitement.

"That old gangster Roosevelt . . ."

Generalfeldmarschall Erwin Rommel also heard the Führer's speech on the radio. However, because of the difference between the information available to a general and that obtainable by a private soldier, it had a diametrically opposite effect on him.

He was sitting in the command coach of General C. H. Lungershausen, commander of the 164th Division, which was drawn up amid the ruins of Fort Capuzzo, listening to the Führer's speech to his old comrades—that insinuating mixture of apparently factual information and pseudological conclusions; that variable voice—now deep, rolling the R in *Ausrottung* (extermination), now teetering on the edge of hysteria—the voice which had after all inebriated an entire people.

". . . and therefore when they are now saying that they are advancing somewhere or other in the desert—they have advanced a few times already, only to go back again—the decisive thing in this war is—who deals the final blow. And that will be us—rest assured of it!"

Around the coach lay the remnants of a beaten army which would never advance again. When Lungershausen asked his Supreme Commander how many troops fit for action he had left, Rommel's depressed answer was: "Perhaps an augmented brigade."

The deep voice played on like an organ and an entire people listened, in factories, living rooms, and in the emergency reception centers of cities falling apart under the blows of the bombers. Were they listening attentively—was the Field Marshal listening attentively?

"You will remember that Reichstag session at which I explained that if Jewry imagined it could bring about an international world war to exterminate the European races, then the result would be not the extermination of the European races but the extermination of Jewry in Europe. They always laughed at me, calling me a prophet. Many, many of those who laughed then are no longer laughing today; and many of those who are still laughing will perhaps not be doing so in a little while. . . ."

A rare case of confession to mass murder before an audience of millions.

But that morning Torch—the landing of Anglo-American assault forces in Morocco and Algeria—had begun. Hitler skated over it in a sentence: "Roosevelt is now attacking North Africa on the pretext that he must protect it against Germany and Italy; there is no need to waste words on such lying claptrap by this old gangster. . . ."

He preferred instead to brag about the conquest of Stalingrad. Eleven days later began the Soviet offensive which spelt the end of the entire Paulus army.

Had Hitler, nevertheless, begun to suspect that General von Clausewitz's "culmination point" had been reached? Using a piece of pseudologic that was to be continually repeated from then on, he "proved" that only Germany could win the war: "One or the other must fall—either they or us. We shall not fall—it follows that they will." At least as far as the African theater of war was concerned, Rommel was unable to follow this logic all the way: "We must get the remnants of our army back to the mainland. In Africa, we have lost," he told Lungershausen.

Even the staff of the Panzerarmee heard of the Anglo-America landing only on the radio. "The official reason given was that they did not want to confuse us," Westphal reports. In fact, the majority of those at the Führer's HQ, staring hypnotized at the western front, were now treating the Mediterranean theater of operations even more cursorily than hitherto.

As early as 10 October, Rintelen had reported to Berlin that the Comando Supremo was expecting a landing in French North or West Africa: "From time to time recently, senior officers have shown their astonishment that the question of countermeasures to be taken against an enemy landing in North/West Africa has not been more closely gone into by the OKW. . . ."

Seven days later the OKW replied: "The Wehrmacht High Command considers the defense of French colonies to be a matter for the French themselves and takes the view that the French will defend their colonial empire—if only in their own interests. . . ." The move into Tunisia envisaged by the Comando Supremo would merely drive the French into the arms of the British and Americans, it added.

As might have been expected, the French resistance was none too vigorous.

On the other hand, Churchill's wish to go east as far as possible, and to take the key Mediterranean positions of Tunis and Bizerta as soon as possible, had not prevailed. This omission was to prolong the war in the Mediterranean substantially. General Nehring, on his way back to Rommel after his convalescence, was sent to Tunisia and improvised a German-Italian bridgehead out of nothing. In the first days, he caught up with his intelligence reporting on the position of the enemy by ringing up the French girls in the various telephone exchanges and chatting them up: "Have the Americans got to you yet? Are there many of them? Have they got any tanks?"

But the place was to become a proper Greater German theater of war all the same. Immediately after Nehring, a unit of the infamous Sicherheitsdienst (SD) also arrived in Tunis, led by the SS Obersturm-bannführer Rauff, whose letters and teleprinted signals to his "Dear Walter" [Schellenberg][18] report proud deeds against the local Jews; under the eyes of French and Italian officials no proper "Final Solution" was, of course, possible; but at least one could always make arrests, round people up for forced labor, extort "contributions" from them, and generally play at being the master race. In one of his letters, Rauff was beside himself with joy at having managed to obtain a death sentence and having it carried out quite quickly, before the French Resident-General, Esteva, could intervene. Always obliging and co-operative, Kesselring, as Supreme Commander, South, ordered that "Jews must be mobilized for fortification work." He was presently to become Supreme Commander, Land Forces, Africa. In view of his high opinion of his own strategic abilities, this was a post he had always greatly fancied. And when in the later phases Nehring expressed realistic opinions about the military situation, he told him cunningly: "You must submit that to me in writing." Nehring soon had to go.

[18] Translator's note: Close associate of Himmler, the Gestapo and SD chief.

Epilogue

"Rommel's War in Africa" came to an end in these November days after the defeat at El Alamein. It was no longer his war, since he now had nowhere to go but back, and since the promise of the Nile and of more distant, more exotic, and more glorious objectives had vanished forever.

At the end of November he flew unannounced to see Hitler. On the Führer's express orders, the minutes of their conversation were destroyed. But it is certain that Rommel wanted to persuade the Supreme Warlord to evacuate Africa completely, even at the cost of abandoning their heavy weapons, and to bring the troops home to Europe to defend the Continent.

But Hitler had by now arrived at the dogma of "every inch of ground"—the dogma of the loser. Much of what has transpired about their conversation orally is doubtful. Thus it is difficult to imagine that Hitler of all people, who knew more about weapons and their effectiveness than many of his generals,[1] would really have offered "6,000 rifles" as the solution to the Africa problem. It is more likely that Hitler put an end to all further discussion with the words: "North

[1] For instance as early as 1940 he had ordered that the Panzer III should be built thenceforth only with the long-barreled 50 mm tank gun; and there was the most frightful row when, to keep up production figures, the order was not implemented.

Africa will be defended and not evacuated. That is an order, Herr Feldmarschall!"

He was reported to have thereupon shown him the door and then to have run after Rommel again with tears in his eyes and words of apology. That, too, may be credible, for Hitler was no fool and by this time he probably saw that it was not at Stalingrad alone that things were going wrong.

Rommel went back to Africa once more and stayed there until early March 1943. He led his force back to the Tunisian bridgehead, soon to be cynically rechristened "Tunisgrad." But before 252,000 men went into captivity there, they offered the Allies some fierce fighting and as many men again lost their lives as in the entire campaign outside the frontiers of Tunisia.

To what end? When Nehring left that theater of war and reported to Zeitzler, Halder's successor on the General Staff, he offered to recount his experiences. But Zeitzler cut him short impatiently: "Africa?—I've written all that nonsense off long ago!"

Sir John Hackett takes the view that although Montgomery's failure to surround and annihilate Rommel's retreating force between El Alamein and Tunisia, as he had intended to do, may have been something of a tactical setback, it led to a great strategic success: Since Hitler could never resist the temptation to invest as heavily as possible in an obvious failure, the Tunisian bridgehead swallowed up another substantial slice of Axis power.

In fact, a flood of the best men and materials poured into Tunisia—a process made easier by the short sea route to Africa's projecting rocky nose. And when the sky above the shrinking bridgehead was swarming with Anglo-U.S. fighters, Hitler was still having personnel flown over in troop transporters—with appalling consequences.

The ungainly transporters—many of them were Me-323s, giant plywood machines conceived as enormous gliders, with six engines added on as an afterthought—were knocked down like ninepins by the fighters, a massacre involving no danger for the combat pilots, who were themselves sickened by it.

By the time the Axis forces surrendered on 13 May 1943, Rommel had been in Germany for two months receiving treatment, but not—as the U. S. General Eisenhower contemptuously said—"to save his skin": The treatment had been ordered by Hitler and the relevant signal is on record and available.

"The turn of the tide" had arrived in the November days, as already mentioned, but many people still hadn't noticed. In July the Allies landed in Sicily—six months later than Churchill had hoped; but the operation was all the more successful after the African bloodletting the Axis had suffered. Four days later, the last German offensive in the east—Citadel—collapsed. Preparations for Operation Overlord, the final return to the European continent, began in Britain.

At this time Rommel was the only German field marshal who could judge from his own experience how, given the Allies' obvious air superiority, the battle for Western Europe would end.

He was in command of Army Group B in France, and he was loosely in touch with a group of dissident officers and politicians who were planning a Putsch against Hitler and the Nazis.

It was quite obvious that it was less moral revulsion against a murderous regime than the realization that the war was lost which drove him to maintain this connection. He stipulated that Hitler was not to be killed and offered to persuade the Führer to face the political consequences of the hopeless military situation and make peace.

At their conference in Casablanca, the Allies had long ago demanded unconditional surrender. They had made it clear that, for them, Hitler was no negotiating partner and that their coalition, despite all its internal contradictions, was an indissoluble bond for the purpose of achieving this aim.

But this idea was built on air in two senses: For one thing, Hitler could not be persuaded to sue for peace; for another, it would have been no use. Allied forces, under Rommel's old adversary Montgomery, had obtained a foothold in Normandy; their bomber squadrons flew through the European sky in broad daylight without leave or hindrance. The end was already in sight when Rommel, with others of like mind, developed another illusion: to conclude a separate peace with the Western Powers, bypassing Hitler. This dish was served up by the writer Ernst Jünger with a garnish of "Occident" in cream sauce: a common "Christian Front" against the Communists.

Similar ideas had already been discussed, and considered particularly promising in case there should be an unsuccessful Allied invasion.

As always, there remained the fantasy that one could rape half the world and then, when they have got you by the throat, call out to one half of the enemy coalition: "Just look at those frightful Bolshevik types on your side there. . . ."

And then to offer yourself as a far superior partner—guaranteed Christian and Western. . . . Shortly beforehand, one would have put out the fires in the incinerators—only the naughty boys had done that: We had nothing to do with it. . . .

Vice Admiral Ruge, certainly no enemy of Rommel, has reported that Rommel told him: "If we had the atom bomb, I think we should fight on." How does this go with the picture of a man with a calling, the man who went into opposition on moral grounds, the man who wanted to make an end of it out of indignation at the Nazis' crimes, of which he had only just heard from the resisters and their circle?

Three days before the unsuccessful attempt on Hitler's life—on 17 July 1944, Rommel was critically wounded in Normandy in a low-level strafing attack. With the vitality characteristic of him, he recovered quickly and had himself taken to his family at Herrlingen near Stuttgart. There, he worked on his memoirs, fought the battles of Africa over again, and bemoaned the vast strategic opportunities which in his opinion had been missed in that theater of war.

With nothing but the armored and motorized units which were "standing around idly in France and on Reich territory," he could have polished off not only the British base in the Middle East but the whole Soviet colossus as well, he daydreamed. We read with astonishment (in *Krieg ohne Hass*) that the Nile Delta and the Persian Gulf with its oil wells were not enough for him by far: He would have pressed on— across Iraq and Persia, easily surmounting the obstacle of the Caucasus, into the Russian plain, and very fast, at that; "The Russians would certainly not have been able to conjure out of the ground at a moment's notice a motorized force which would have been any sort of a match for ours, either in organization or in tactics on the open plains. . . ."

And yet it was the late summer or autumn of 1944, by which time not only were the Russians proving themselves "any sort" of a match for a still mighty war machine which could be kept supplied by the straight, short route from Germany; they were also energetically attacking "Fortress Europe." And Rommel was still annoyed that back in 1942 people had called his plan "castles in the air."

On 14 October 1944, he was visited by Hitler's accessories to murder. It seemed that before the 10 July Putsch the conspirators had, with German thoroughness, drawn up a list on which Rommel without his knowledge appeared as Reich President. It is also possible that the arrested men had implicated him under torture.

Through two of his generals, Hitler presented Rommel with the choice of either taking a quick-acting poison in front of them—or appearing before a "People's Tribunal." The Field Marshal chose the poison, took leave calmly of his wife and son and of his trusted Captain Aldinger, who implored him not to give up: "We have arms; we've been in worse situations, haven't we . . . ?"

It was not actually all that far-fetched: His men still idolized him; they could have fought their way out. . . . But the murderers knew the Achilles heel of this otherwise so fearless man. They were to tell him that nothing would happen to his family: a pension for his wife, a State funeral with full honors, no obstacles to the boy's career. . . . Thus it

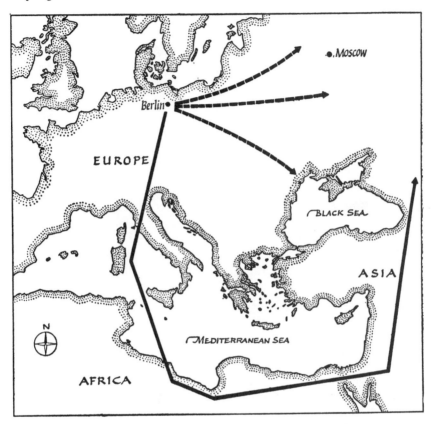

What did not succeed by the shortest route (dotted lines, rough illustration) was supposed to succeed "through the back door": Rommel's strategic concepts, showing length of supply lines.

was not a question of his giving up; it was a sacrifice for his family. That tipped the scale.

So he went with the two generals and climbed into their car for this last journey. Whatever the legends may say, no daring chess move in the field, no deed amid the mortal dangers of battle was greater than this last one, which was motivated not by ambition or pugnacity, but by love and concern.

Bibliography

Aberger, Heinz-Dietrich and Taysen, Adalbert von Ziemer, Kurt, *Nur ein Bataillon . . .* (The 8th Machine Gun Battalion), Essen, 1972

Alman, Karl, *Ritterkreuzträger des Afrikakorps*, Rastatt, 1968

Barnett, Corelli, *The Desert Generals*, London, 1961

Bauer, Eddy, *Der Panzerkrieg*, Bonn, 1965

Bayerlein, Fritz, Nehring, Walther, et al., *Marsch und Kampf des DAK*, Munich, 1945

Bayerlein, Fritz, "El Alamein" *Fatal Decisions*, London, 1956

Bekker, Cajus, *Verdammte See*, Oldenburg and Hamburg, 1971

Bender, Roger James, and Law, Richard D., *Afrikakorps: Uniform, Organization and History*, Mountain View, Calif., 1973

Brown, Anthony Cave, *Die unsichtbare Front*, Munich, 1976 (*Bodyguard of Lies*, London, 1976)

Bryant, Arthur, *The Turn of the Tide* (based on Field Marshal Lord Alanbrooke's diaries, 1939–1943), New York, 1957

Bullock, Alan, *Hitler*, Düsseldorf, 1961 (London, rev. ed., 1965)

Burdick, Charles B., *Unternehmen Sonnenblume*, Neckargemünd, 1972

Caidin, Martin, *Flying Forts: The B-17 in World War II*, New York, 1968

Carell, Paul, *Die Wüstenfüchse*, rev. ed., Stuttgart, 1974

Churchill, Winston S., *Der zweite Weltkrieg*, vols. 1–5, Berne–Munich–Vienna, 1953 (*The Second World War*, vols. 1–3, London, 1948–49; vols. 4–6 1951–54)

Ciano, Count Galeazzo, *The Ciano Diaries 1939–1943*, New York, 1973

Crisp, Robert, *Brazen Chariots*, London, 1959

Davy, George, *The Seventh and Three Enemies*, Cambridge, 1952

Esebeck, Hanns-Gert von, *Helden der Wüste,* Bielefeld, 1943
────── *Afrikanische Schicksalsjahre,* Wiesbaden, 1949
────── *Das Deutsche Afrika-Korps,* Wiesbaden and Munich, 1975
Engel, Gerhard, *Heeresadjutant bei Hitler,* Stuttgart, 1974
Eppler, John W., *Rommel ruft Kairo,* Gütersloh, 1959
Fergusson, Bernard, *The Black Watch and the King's Enemies,* London, 1950
Greiner, Helmuth, and Schramm, Percy Ernst, *Kriegstagebuch des Oberkommandos der Wehrmacht (The War Diary of the Wehrmacht High Command),* vols. 1–4, Frankfurt am Main, 1963
Greiner, Helmuth, *Die Oberste Wehrmachtführung, 1939–1943,* Wiesbaden, 1951
Hagemann, Walter, *Publizistik im Dritten Reich,* Hamburg, 1948
Halder, Col. Gen. Franz, *Kriegstagebuch,* Stuttgart, 1962
Hart, B. H. Liddell, *The Rommel Papers,* London, 1953
────── ed., *The Other Side of the Hill: Germany's generals with their own account of military events, 1939–45,* London, 1948
Haupt, Werner, and Bingham, J. K. W., *Der Afrika-Feldzug,* Dorheim, 1968
Heckstall-Smith, Anthony, *Tobruk,* London rev. ed., 1961
Hillgruber, Andreas, *Hitler, König Carol und Marschall Antonescu, 1938–1944,* Wiesbaden, 1954
Hissmann, Joseph, *Insh'Allah,* Bochum, 1968
Horrocks, Lieut. Gen. Sir Brian, *The 7th Queen's Own Hussars,* London, 1975
Hubatsch, Walther, *Hitlers Weisungen für die Kriegsführung,* Frankfurt am Main, 1962
Irving, David, *Hitler und seine Feldherren,* Berlin, 1975
Jacobsen, Hans-Adolf/Rohwer, Jürgen, *Entscheidungsschlachten des Zweiten Weltkrieges,* Frankfurt am Main, 1960
Jacobsen, Hans-Adolf/Dollinger, Hans, *Der Zweite Weltkrieg in Bildern und Dokumenten,* Munich, 1963
Jolly, Cyril, *Take These Men,* London, 1955
Kesselring, Albert, *Soldat bis zum letzten Tag,* Bonn, 1953 (*Memoirs,* London, 1953)
Kühn, Volkmar, *Mit Rommel in der Wüste,* Stuttgart, 1975
Lewin, Ronald, *Rommel as a Military Commander,* London, 1968
Long, Gavin, *To Benghazi,* Canberra, 1966
Luftwaffe War Reporting Company, *Balkenkreuz über Wüstensand,* Oldenburg, 1943
McCorquodale, Col. D., OBE, *History of the King's Dragoon Guards,* Glasgow, n.d.
Macksey, Maj. K. J., *Afrika-Korps,* London, 1972
Maughan, Barton, *Tobruk and El Alamein,* Canberra, 1966
Mellenthin, F. W. von, *Panzer Battles,* Oklahoma, 1958
Montgomery, Field Marshal Bernard Law, *Von El Alamein zum Sangro,* Hamburg, 1949 (*El Alamein to the River Sangro,* London, 1948)

—— *Weltgeschichte der Schlachten und Kriegszüge*, vols. 1 and 2, Munich, 1975

—— *Alamein and the Desert War*, London, 1967

Moorehead, Alan, *Afrikanische Trilogie*, Brunswick–Berlin–Hamburg, 1947

Perrett, Bryan, *The Valentine in North Africa*, London, 1972

—— *The Matilda*, London, 1973

—— *Through Mud and Blood*, London, 1975

Phillips, C. E. Lucas, *Alamein*, London, 1962

Picker, Henry, *Hitlers Tischgespräche im Führerhauptquartier 1941–1942*, Stuttgart, 1963

Platt, Brig. J. R. I., *The Royal Wiltshire Yeomanry* (Prince of Wales's Own), London, 1972

Playfair, I., *The Mediterranean and Middle East*, vols. 1–4, London 1954–66

Rintelen, Enno von, *Mussolini als Bundesgenosse*, Tübingen und Stuttgart, 1951

Rommel, Field Marshal Erwin, *Kreig ohne Hass*, Heidenheim, 1950

Schmidt, Heinz Werner, *With Rommel in the Desert*, London, 1951

Shores, Christopher F., *Pictorial History of the Mediterranean Air War*, London, 1973

Speer, Albert, *Spandauer Tagebucher*, Frankfurt–Berlin–Vienna, 1975 (*Spandau: The Secret Diaries*, London, 1976)

Staffens, Hans von, *"Salaam," Geheimkommando zum Nil*, Neckargemünd, 1960

Sündermann, Helmut, *Tagesparolen, 1939–1945*, Leoni, 1973

Warlimont, Walter, *Im Hauptquartier der deutschen Wehrmacht 1939–1945*, Frankfurt am Main, 1964

Westphal, Siegfried, ed., *Schicksal Nordafrika*, Döffingen, 1954

Westphal, Siegfried, *Erinnerungen* (Memoirs), Mainz, 1975

Winterbotham, Grp. Capt. Frederick, *The Ultra Secret*, London, 1974

Young, Desmond, *Rommel*, with foreword by Field Marshal Sir Claude Auchinleck, London, 1950

Note on the Bibliography

The temptation was great to separate in the preceding list the run-of-the-mill "Whoops, there goes Tommy, up in flames" kind of literature from those works about which one could be sure that they contained nothing but verified information. I have resisted that temptation because most published books do deserve respect in one way or another, even if in them one comes across again and again—almost like welcome friends—the mistakes of the earliest authors who could least help making them; because there are borderline cases and mixed cases, which indeed predominate; and because no one is proof against error, and to establish a differentiated pecking order may be a presumption. Thus, the eminently respectable editors of Halder's

War Diary remarked as a footnote to some figures about British Cruiser tanks: "i.e., heaviest tank"; the no-less reputable publishers of the OKW *War Diary* absolutely insisted that fighting had taken place in Mersa Matruh as early as April 1941; and the otherwise well-informed General of Cavalry (Retd) Siegfried Westphal makes the slip of saying that in the autumn of 1941 the British had 75 mm tank guns (how happy they would have been to be so fortunate!).

There remains only to make acknowledgments and to explain that one is responsible for one's own mistakes, no matter how hard one has pestered the patient gentlemen in the archives. Here I must record my most grateful thanks to the gentlemen of the Military Archives, Freiburg; the Imperial War Museum, London; the Black Watch Museum, Perth; the Bundesarchiv (German Federal Archives), Koblenz; and the Public Records Office, London. And my thanks, too, to soldiers of every rank from Singem am Hohentwiel to Coupar Angus in the Scottish Highlands, who racked their memories for me—and my apologies to those whom I pestered for hours and then, because of the wealth of material, did not even mention.

Although, as regards named witnesses, I limited myself to selecting a circle from both sides small enough to keep in sight, no testimony was wasted: The mosaic image of the whole was, in the end, made up of many snapshots of memory.

Index